The Origins of Antisocial Behavior

The Origins of Antisocial Behavior

A Developmental Perspective

EDITED BY

CHRISTOPHER R. THOMAS

AND

KAYLA POPE

OXFORD
UNIVERSITY PRESS

OXFORD
UNIVERSITY PRESS

Oxford University Press is a department of the University of Oxford. It furthers the
University's objective of excellence in research, scholarship, and education by publishing
worldwide.

Oxford   New York
Auckland   Cape Town   Dar es Salaam   Hong Kong   Karachi
Kuala Lumpur   Madrid   Melbourne   Mexico City   Nairobi
New Delhi   Shanghai   Taipei   Toronto

With offices in
Argentina   Austria   Brazil   Chile   Czech Republic   France   Greece
Guatemala   Hungary   Italy   Japan   Poland   Portugal   Singapore
South Korea   Switzerland   Thailand   Turkey   Ukraine   Vietnam

Oxford is a registered trademark of Oxford University Press in the UK and certain other
countries.

Published in the United States of America by
Oxford University Press
198 Madison Avenue, New York, NY 10016

Library of Congress Cataloging-in-Publication Data
   The origins of antisocial behavior: a developmental perspective/
   edited by Christopher R. Thomas, Kayla Pope.
     p. cm.
   ISBN 978-0-19-975347-5
   1. Antisocial personality disorders.   I. Thomas, Christopher R.   II. Pope, Kayla.
   RC555.O75 2012
   616.85'82—dc23
   2011048017

9 8 7 6 5 4 3 2 1
Printed in the United States of America
on acid-free paper

CONTENTS

PREFACE: OVERVIEW OF RESEARCH AND IMPORTANCE OF CONVERGING LINES OF INQUIRY

Antisocial behavior is one of the most intensely studied areas of human pathology. Countless research studies, journal articles, conferences, and scholarly volumes have focused on the origins and development of aggressive and antisocial behavior. Antisocial behavior was seen as an inherent moral defect in the early 19th century. Benjamin Rush described the criminal character as "innate, preternatural moral depravity, there is probably an original defective organization in those parts of the body which are occupied by the moral faculties of the mind" (Rush, 1812). The concept of antisocial behavior as a result of biological determinism was increasingly challenged at the beginning of the 20th century by research that focused on environmental causation. W. Douglas Morrison stated "juvenile crime arises out of the adverse individual or social conditions of the juvenile offender, or out of both sets of conditions acting in combinations" (Morrison, 1895). Diverse definitions, along with the heterogeneous factors associated with antisocial behavior, have only complicated the debate over its origins. Although most descriptions of the development of antisocial behavior have acknowledged the importance of both "nature and nurture," it is only recently that the interactions between the different factors have begun to become clear (Pope & Thomas, 2007). The advances in technology, with new means of investigating brain activity, genomics, and behavior, have been astounding.

This volume provides a concise review of the most important advances in understanding the origins of antisocial behavior. It originated with an Institute on Recent Research in Antisocial Behavior at the annual meeting of the American Academy of Child and Adolescent Psychiatry. The theme for the institute was a developmental perspective, and this provided a common framework for the research presentations. One of the more striking aspects of the Institute was the growing convergence in findings from different areas of research. This volume covers the research presented at the Institute. Many of the chapter authors were panelists at that Institute; other leaders in the field have contributed chapters to more fully describe the full scope of current research and its implications for intervention, policy, and future study.

ADVANCES IN NEUROSCIENCE

The first section is devoted to the discoveries made with genetic and neuroimaging techniques that have had the most dramatic impact on research in the past decade. The identification of potential genetic risk is only part of the story of understanding how those risks contribute to unfolding neurodevelopment through gene and environment interaction. Advances in neuroimaging have provided additional and complimentary insights into associated brain development with respect to both normal and pathologic aggression.

ADVANCES IN BEHAVIORAL AND CLINICAL RESEARCH

Advances in research on antisocial behavior have not been confined to new laboratory techniques, as behavioral research has seen similar changes. The second section provides an overview of new assessment tools, as well as of the role of parenting, peers, and neighborhood in antisocial behavior. Foremost have been improvements in screening and assessment coupled with longitudinal study. These techniques have provided a more detailed view, with recent studies investigating early relationships and social environment. Another key aspect has been recognition of the pathology associated with antisocial behavior and the impact that has on planning effective interventions.

LEGAL AND POLICY IMPLICATIONS

The final section addresses the impact of new findings in antisocial behavior and aggression on public policy and the judicial system. Scientific evidence can offer guidance and be useful in public debate and judicial inquiry, but it also raises new questions about how best to apply new insights. Questions as to culpability and competency demand careful consideration in light of new information.

CONCLUSION

The heterogeneous nature of antisocial behavior has long been evident, with no one explanation, no single critical factor nor solitary pathway of origin. Recent advances in research with new tools have better defined not only the risks but also how they interact to result in antisocial behavior. Prior academic debate over the causes of aggression and antisocial behavior resembled the ancient parable of the five blind men trying to describe an elephant. Each argued vehemently for a different interpretation based on what part of the elephant they grabbed. Although there is much yet to be done, research on antisocial behavior is beginning to see the whole rather than the parts.

REFERENCES

Morrison, W. D. (1895). The juvenile offender, and the conditions which produce him. *International Journal of Ethics, 5*(2), 162–181.

Pope, K., & Thomas, C. (2007). The etiology of antisocial behavior: Biopsychosocial risk factors across development. In C. Kessler & L. Kraus (Eds.), *The mental health needs of young offenders* (pp. 122–145). Cambridge, UK: Cambridge University Press.

Rush, B. (1812). *Medical inquiries and observations upon the diseases of the mind.* Philadelphia: Grigg.

CONTRIBUTORS

Elizabeth Adeyemi, BS
Intramural Research Award Trainee
Child Psychiatry Branch, NIMH

Aaron Alexander-Block
Child Psychiatry Branch,
National Institute of Mental Health

Lindsay Anderson, MA
Department of Psychology
Queens College and Graduate School
    and University Center
City University of New York

Laura A. Baker, PhD
Professor of Psychology
University of Southern California

Christopher T. Barry
Associate Professor
Department of Psychology
University of Southern Mississippi

Michael C. Bazaco, MS
Graduate School of Public Health
University of Pittsburgh

William Bernet, MD
Professor
Department of Psychiatry
Vanderbilt University School of
    Medicine

James Blair, PhD
Chief, Unit on Affective Cognitive
    Neuroscience
National Institute of Mental Health

Benjamin Bregman, MD
Department of Psychiatry and
    Behavioral Sciences
The George Washington University
    Medical Center

Anil Chacko, PhD
Assistant Professor
Department of Psychology
Queens College and Graduate School
    and University Center
City University of New York

Chung-Yu Chen, MS
Graduate School of Public Health
Epidemiology Data Coordinating
    Center
University of Pittsburgh

Anthony Fabio, PhD, MPH
Assistant Professor
Graduate School of Public Health
Epidemiology Data Coordinating
    Center
University of Pittsburgh

Jay N. Giedd, MD
Chief, Brain Imaging Section
Child Psychiatry Branch
National Institute of Mental Health

James J. Hudziak, MD
Thomas M. Achenbach Chair of
   Developmental Psychopathology
Professor
Departments of Psychiatry, Medicine,
   and Pediatrics
Director of the Vermont Center for
   Children, Youth, and Families
Director of Child and Adolescent
   Psychiatry
Fletcher Allen Healthcare
University of Vermont

Julia Huemer, MD
University Lecturer
Department of Child and Adolescent
   Psychiatry
Medical University of Vienna

Soonjo Hwang, MD
Department of Psychiatry
Massachusetts General Hospital

**Riittakerttu Kaltiala-Heino, MD,
   PhD, MSc**
Professor of Adolescent Psychiatry,
   School of Medicine
Director, Department of Adolescent
   Psychiatry
University of Tampere, Finland

Niranjan Karnik, MD, PhD
Assistant Professor of Psychiatry and
   Behavioral Neuroscience
University of Chicago

Ellen Kjelsberg, MD, PhD
Centre for Research and Education in
   Forensic Psychiatry
Oslo University Hospital
Oslo, Norway

Suzanne E. U. Kerns, Ph.D.
Assistant Professor
Department of Psychiatry and
   Behavioral Sciences
Division of Public Behavioral Health
   and Justice Policy
University of Washington

**Young Shin Kim, MD, MS, MPH,
   PhD**
Associate Professor
Child Study Center
Yale University School of Medicine
Department of Psychiatry
Yonsei University College of Medicine

Louis Kraus, MD
Woman's Board Professor and Chief
   of Child and Adolescent Psychiatry
Rush University Medical Center

Markus J. P. Kruesi, MD
Professor and Director, Youth
   Psychiatry Division
Department of Psychiatry and
   Behavioral Sciences
Medical University of South Carolina

Ana V. Kuny-Slock
Vermont Center for Children, Youth,
   and Families
Department of Psychology
University of Vermont

Nancy Raitano Lee, PhD
Research Fellow, Brain Imaging Section
Child Psychiatry Branch
National Institute of Mental Health

Terry G. Lee, MD
Assistant Professor
Department of Psychiatry and
   Behavioral Sciences Division of
   Public Behavioral Health and
   Justice Policy
University of Washington

Rhoshel K. Lenroot, MD
Professor of Infant, Child and
    Adolescent Psychiatry
University of New South Wales
Neuroscience Research Australia

Bennett Leventhal, MD
Deputy Director, Nathan S. Kline
    Institute for Psychiatric Research
Professor
Department of Child and Adolescent
    Psychiatry
New York University Langone
    Medical Center

Mallory L. Malkin
Department of Psychology
University of Southern Mississippi

Sharon Niv, MA
University of Southern California

Kayla Pope, MD, JD
Director of Neurobehavioral
    Research,
Boys Town National Research
    Hospital

Armin Raznahan
Child Psychiatry Branch,
National Institute of Mental Health

Estrella Rajwan
Department of Psychology
Queens College and Graduate School
    and University Center
City University of New York

Hans Steiner, MD
Professor Emeritus of Psychiatry and
    Behavioral Sciences
Stanford University School of
    Medicine

Michael Stockman
Predoctoral IRTA
Child Psychiatry Branch
National Institute of Mental Health

Christopher R. Thomas, MD
Robert L. Stubblefield Professor of
    Child Psychiatry
University of Texas Medical Branch

Jean Thomas, MD
Clinical Professor
Department of Psychiatry and
    Behavioral Sciences
The George Washington University
    School of Medicine

Panos Vostanis, MD
Professor of Child Psychiatry
Greenwood Institute
    of Child Health
University of Leicester

James S. Walker, PhD
Clinical Neuropsychologist
Neuropsychology Consultants, PLLC
Nashville, TN

PART ONE

Advances in Neuroscience

Genetic Markers for Antisocial Behavior

SHARON NIV AND LAURA A. BAKER ■

The interest in identifying specific genes associated with criminal, aggressive, and antisocial behavior drives a considerable amount of psychology and criminology research. As more discoveries point to unforeseen complexities in the pathways between genes and behavior, the genetic underpinnings of antisocial behavior (ASB) become even more intriguing. In this chapter, we review the evidence for specific genetic markers for antisocial behavior and aggression and how these markers have begun to shed light on biological mechanisms involved in such deviant behaviors.

Early behavioral genetic research focused primarily on heritability estimation, with an emphasis on additive genetic influences on behavior. Since the field's understanding of these systems has advanced and molecular genetic techniques have become more accessible and affordable, greater attention is being paid to mechanistic details. Studies using both quantitative and molecular genetic approaches suggest that the genetic contribution to antisocial, criminal, and aggressive behavior is substantial but nuanced. Gene-by-gene (GxG) and gene-by-environment (GxE) interactions each play a significant role in determining individual differences in antisocial behavior. Furthermore, emerging understanding of epigenetics and transcriptional/translational systems help explain the pathways that lead from DNA to behavior. Although considerably more research is necessary to understand fully the genetic influences on ASB, several candidate genes related to antisocial and aggressive behavior have emerged and have been supported in numerous studies.

This chapter reviews research on genetic markers for ASB and aggression and suggests directions for future studies stemming from current knowledge. Following a brief description of the definition and scope of ASB in studies considered, we summarize the quantitative genetic literature showing heritability of ASB and then provide a detailed review of various candidate genes and their effects on ASB. The extent to which these candidate genes may suggest mechanisms involved in the gene-behavior pathways is also discussed.

SCOPE OF ASB IN GENETIC RESEARCH

ASB comprises a wide range of behaviors, syndromes, and tendencies that are useful to consider when examining its genetic underpinnings. Criminal behavior, delinquency, and aggression immediately spring to mind in defining ASB, but within each broader category there exist important subcategories. Criminal behavior, for example, may be broken down into violent and property offending, each of which exhibits different patterns of genetic influence (Mednick et al., 1984). Aggressive behavior is also well studied in genetic research, with consideration of different types of aggression including (1) a reactive form, which involves more defensive responses to external triggers; (2) a proactive form, which is more planned and generally considered to be instrumental (Dodge, 1991; Dodge & Coie, 1987); and (3) a relational form of aggression, which involves social manipulation such as gossip and peer exclusion and is often more indirect compared with other forms (Crick & Grotpeter, 1996). Reactive and proactive aggression have been found to exhibit different patterns of genetic and environmental influences (Baker, Raine, Liu, & Jacobson, 2008), as well as different patterns of change in those influences from childhood to adolescence (Tuvblad, Raine, Zheng, & Baker, 2009), providing support for the idea that they may be at least somewhat distinct.

In contrast to studies of criminal offending and aggression, some studies focus on symptoms of DSM-IV disorders that involve ASB. Conduct disorder (CD) and oppositional defiant disorder (ODD) in youths, for example, are often considered preludes to adult antisocial personality disorder (ASPD; Kim-Cohen et al., 2003; Robins, 1966). Additionally important are disorders that show high comorbidity with ASB, such as substance use disorders (SUD) and attention-deficit/hyperactivity disorder (ADHD). The comorbidity of ADHD alone with ODD and CD may be as high as 42.7–93% (Jensen, Martin, & Cantwell, 1997), and the overlap among these disorders in childhood stems primarily from common genetic etiologies (Tuvblad et al., 2009).

Other behavioral or psychological correlates of ASB—often called risk factors—are also pertinent phenotypes for genetic research. To the extent that these risk factors share genetic etiologies with ASB, they may serve as endophenotypes, that is, heritable intermediate traits that could signal a genetic propensity for ASB. Understanding these risk factors and their genetic relationships to ASB could lead to understanding of the underlying mechanisms involved in the gene-behavior pathway. Such risk factors for ASB include impulsive behavior and disinhibition, both of which have been targeted for genetic research. Because callousness and lack of empathy constitute a significant portion of psychopathy, they may also be important endophenotypes for ASB.

HERITABILITY OF ASB

Behavioral genetics research concerning aggression and ASB has examined both clinical and normative populations. The selection of clinical or criminal populations ensures a higher proportion of the trait of interest and thus a straight-forward ascertainment of genetic and environmental influences. On the other hand, selection of normative populations allows examination of trait variance in the general population.

Early adoption studies suggested considerable genetic influence on criminal behavior (Cadoret, Yates, Troughton, Woodworth, & Stewart, 1995; Mednick et al., 1984; Torgersen et al., 1993). More recently, a meta-analysis of twin and adoption studies estimated that 41% of the variance in ASB—including criminal behavior, aggression, psychopathy, and psychiatric disorders in which ASB plays a key role—could be explained by genetic factors, with the remaining 59% of variance being explained by environmental factors (Rhee & Waldman, 2002). However, there has been more evidence for genetic influence in property offend-ing than in violent offending, with some studies showing little or no genetic basis to violence.

The meta-analysis of twin and adoption studies by Rhee and Waldman (2002) also demonstrated that genetic influences significantly decrease across develop-ment, such that child and adolescent ASB is more genetically influenced than adult ASB. Phenotypically, violent criminal offending has appeared more stable than nonviolent criminal offending, although a common genetic component has been found for both (and unique genetic contribution to each, additionally). Together, these findings strongly support the notion that there are genetic factors underlying criminal and aggressive behavior.

Gene-by-environment interactions (GxE)

Importantly, it has been repeatedly demonstrated that the influence of genetic factors on ASB varies across different environmental conditions. The depen-dence of genetic risk on environmental factors, and vice versa, is referred to as a gene-by-environment (GxE) interaction and is most clearly demonstrated in adoption studies. Adopted children with greater genetic risk for criminal offend-ing (by virtue of having a convicted biological parent) display far greater convic-tion rates when raised by adoptive parents who also have convictions (Cadoret, Cain, & Crowe, 1983; Cloninger, Sigvardsson, Bohman, & von Knorring, 1982; Mednick et al., 1984).

GxE interactions for ASB have also been suggested in candidate gene stud-ies, as is discussed further in the review of specific genes here. For example, one allele found to confer risk for ASB in a Dutch pedigree (Brunner et al., 1993) was later found to be benign in the absence of aversive environmental conditions, such as physical discipline or abusive parenting (Caspi et al., 2002). In other words, whereas some environmental conditions may constitute exacerbating factors to genetic predispositions, other environmental conditions may instead be protective. Given the importance of GxE found in heritability studies of crim-inal behavior, it is important to consider the moderating effects of environment on genetic risk in candidate gene studies and to identify specific environmental conditions that exacerbate or ameliorate the effects of candidate genes on the risk for ASB.

Gene-by-gene interactions (GxG)

In the meta-analysis of twin and adoption studies (Rhee & Waldman, 2002), one aspect of ASB—namely, criminal offending—was found to have genetic effects that were nonadditive, meaning that dominant and epistatic genetic influences contributed to the risk of engaging in criminal behavior. Evidence for such non-additive genetic effects also emerged when twin studies demonstrated genetic influences on violent offending whereas family and adoption studies did not (Cloninger & Gottesman, 1987). Such nonadditive genetic effects can arise when alleles within a given locus operate in a dominant or recessive manner (*genetic dominance*) or when genes at one locus affect gene expression at another locus (*epistasis*). Additionally, when the twin correlation of monozygotic (MZ) twins is more than twice that of dizygotic (DZ) twins, it also provides evidence for non-additive genetic effects, such that a specific combination of genes contributes to greater risk for a trait beyond what would be expected by the sum of individual contributions from specific alleles across loci. Both genetic dominance and epistatic effects are referred to as *gene-by-gene interactions* (GxG), meaning that expression of a given allele depends on the presence or absence of one or more other alleles, either at the same locus (dominance) or at different loci (epistasis).

Based on the heritability estimates from these twin and adoption studies, it is clear that genetic factors influence aggression, criminality, and other ASB. Identification of the specific genes involved in ASB is the next important step, and we thus turn to the review of various candidate genes associated with ASB phenotypes. Given the importance of both GxE and GxG interactions in twin and adoption studies in this domain of behavior, these are also important effects that must be taken into consideration in candidate gene approaches. Although identification of specific alleles that confer greater risk of engaging in ASB is useful, of equal or perhaps even greater importance will be the identification of specific environmental risk factors that may enhance or ameliorate these genetic effects.

CANDIDATE GENES FOR ASB

The search for candidate genes often involves examination of neurotransmitter systems known to be involved in ASB. For example, aggressive behavior in both animals and humans has been linked to varying levels of norepinephrine, dopamine, and serotonin (Arce & Santisteban, 2006), rendering all three of these neurotransmitter systems targets for candidate genes. Several studies have been instrumental in specifying candidate genes. For example, a study of one particularly violent Dutch family led to the finding of a sex-specific *MAOA* mutation as a candidate gene for aggression in males (Brunner, et al., 1993). Through studies of probands with specific behavioral patterns, scientists have found clues for alleles involved in the etiology of criminality, aggression, and ASB.

In this chapter, we provide a detailed review of several candidate genes involved in the production and regulation of these neurotransmitters, including the monoamine oxidase genes (*MAOA* and *MAOB*), several markers related to dopamine (*DRD1-DRD5; DAT; COMT*), serotonin (*5HTTLPR; TPH; 5HT1* and *5HT2*), norepinephrine and epinephrine (*DBH; NET1; PNMT*), and another marker involved in neuronal transmission (*NOS1*). We also summarize studies of genes involved in oxytocin and vasopressin (*OXTR; AVPR1a*), which have appeared to be important contributors to empathy and social behavior, as well as two genes for hormonal factors involved in sexual development (*ESR1; AR*), which in turn have shown relationships to aggression in males. Studies investigating the associations of these candidate genes to aggression and other ASB are reviewed in detail in the following sections, and these results are summarized in Tables 1.1, 1.2, and 1.3. Wherever possible, we consider moderating factors for gene expression, either by environmental factors (GxE interactions) or by other genes (GxG interactions). A general discussion of epigenetic influences, implications for treatment, and future research directions is also provided.

Monoamine Oxidase A (*MAOA*) and B (*MAOB*)

The most highly studied candidate gene associated with aggressive behavior is the monoamine oxidase A gene (*MAOA*), a gene on the X chromosome (Xp11.4-p11.3) that codes for the *MAOA* enzyme. *MAOA* breaks down catecholamines such as dopamine, norepinephrine, epinephrine, and serotonin. *MAOA* first came to the attention of ASB researchers through the Brunner et al. (1993) study, which followed a Dutch family with several male members who exhibited violent, aggressive, impulsive, and other socially inappropriate behaviors.

In addition to the Brunner findings, *MAOA*'s involvement in the catalysis of a number of neurotransmitters involved in behavior also rendered it an attractive choice as a candidate gene for ASB. Dopamine and serotonin are two of the neurotransmitters most strongly associated with mood regulation and psychopathology, whereas epinephrine and norepinephrine regulate sympathetic autonomic nervous system responses and the fight-or-flight response, and both serotonin and dopamine have been implicated in mental disorders such as depression and ADHD. *MAOA* actions include decreasing levels of catecholamines, regulating monoamine transporters and receptors, and regulating embryonic levels of serotonin (Shih, Chen, & Ridd, 1999; Shih & Thompson, 1999). Because *MAOA*'s influence on behavior is so substantial, its high-activity and low-activity allele variants differently affect a broad range of behaviors, from executive function to reward response, mood regulation, and arousal. The effects of *MAOB*, a homologous enzyme found only in blood platelets, have been examined less frequently,

Table 1.1. Dopaminergic Candidate Genes for ASB

Candidate gene	Location	High-risk alleles	Biological substrate or function	Behavioral outcome	Brain areas or manifestation	Potential moderators
MAOA	Xp11.3	2- and 5-repeat VNTR	Breakdown and regulation of catecholamines including dopamine, norepinephrine, epinephrine, and serotonin	Aggression Violence Lower sustained attention	Increased reactivity in the left amygdala	Child abuse; testosterone
DRD4	11p15.5	7-repeat VNTR	Reward and punishment response, movement modulation, mood, attention, learning	Novelty-seeking; ADHD symptoms	Cortex Limbic system	IQ
DRD2	11q23	A1 variant of the Taq SNP	Learning and attention in prefrontal cortex, motor control in basal ganglia	Transient psychosis Alcoholism Cocaine use Opiate use Impulsivity	Substantia nigra Prefrontal cortex Basal ganglia	Risky family environment; DRD4 7-repeat VNTR
DRD3	3q13.3	BalI variant of SNP	Motor control in basal ganglia, nucleus accumbens, and ventral tegmental area for behavioral control and reward	Impulsivity Novelty-seeking	Nucleus accumbens	Impulsivity moderated by violence

Gene	Location	Variant	Function	Associated behaviors	Expression	Other associations
DRD1	5q35.1	B2 variant of SNP	Most prevalent dopamine receptor in brain with functions of cognition, behavior and motivation, homeostasis and motor control	Aggression in patients with Alzheimer's disease	Widely expressed throughout brain	Alzheimers disease; Caucasian race
DAT	5p15.3	10-repeat VNTR	Removes dopamine from extracellular space	ADHD symptoms, violence, delinquency	Dopaminergic pathways: mesolimbic, mesocortical, nigrostriatal	
COMT	22q11.21	Val variant of resulting protein at 158th codon (SNP rs4680)	Enzyme involved in production of dopamine	Aggression, criminal offense convictions, conduct disorder	Frontal lobes	ADHD; birth weight

Table 1.2. Serotonergic Candidate Genes for ASB

Candidate gene	Location	High-risk alleles	Biological substrate or function	Behavioral outcome	Brain areas or manifestation	Potential moderators
5HTTLPR	17q11.2	Short variant of promoter VNTR	Serotonin transporter for reuptake into pre-synaptic cell	Aggression, violence, externalizing behavior	Serotonergic pathways: midbrain, anterior cingulate cortex	Childhood adversity; low socioeconomic status; level of impulsivity; DRD4 long-repeat allele
TPH1	11p15.3-p14	A218 L SNP; A779C SNP	Enzyme involved in synthesis of serotonin	Violence, aggression, anger, but not nonviolent ASB	Serotonergic pathways	
TPH2	12q21.1	A1473C SNP	Enzyme involved in synthesis of serotonin	Aggression, cognitive impulsivity	Serotonergic pathways	ADHD
5HT1	5q11.2-q13	A allele of rs1406946 SNP; A161T SNP	Serotonin receptor; cognition, memory, mood, sleep	Aggression, addiction, impulsive aggression	Serotonergic pathways	
5HT2	13q14-q21	G1438A SNP; His452Tyr SNP	Serotonin receptor; cognition, memory, mood, sleep	High impulsivity; nonaggressive delinquency	Serotonergic pathways	Alcohol dependence

Table 1.3. OTHER CANDIDATE GENES FOR ASB

Candidate gene	Location	High-risk alleles	Biological substrate or function	Behavioral outcome	Brain areas or manifestation	Potential moderators
DBH	9q34	C1021T SNP	Conversion of dopamine into norepinephrine	Impulsivity, aggression	Monoamine pathways: global	ADHD; personality disorders; MAOA, MAOB, COMT risk alleles
PNMT	17q	G148A SNP	Converts norepinephrine to epinephrine	Cognitive and aggressive impulsivity, ADHD	Adrenergic pathways: somatic	
OXTR	3p25	Several SNPs	Oxytocin receptor	Altruism and prosocial behavior	Amygdala, brainstem, hypothalamus, septum, nucleus accumbens	
AVPR1a	12q14-q15	Low-risk allele: 2-repeat microsatellite in promoter region	Vassopressin receptor	Increased lifetime aggression	Hypothalamus, forebrain	
ESR1	6q25.1	Longer variant of TG repeat	Estrogen receptor	Aggression		
AR	Xq12	Shorter variant of CAG repeat	Androgen (testosterone) receptor	Aggression		Race

Table 1.3. (CONTINUED)

Candidate gene	Location	High-risk alleles	Biological substrate or function	Behavioral outcome	Brain areas or manifestation	Potential moderators
NOS1	12q24.2-q24.31	Short variant of Ex1f VNTR	Facilitates neuronal transmission globally in brain; disrupted functions of reward-response and outcome monitoring	Impulsivity, hyperactivity, aggression, lower conscientiousness	Reduced function in anterior cingulated cortex, prefrontal cortex	Female sex
BDNF	11p13	T allele of rs10767664 SNP; A allele of rs13306221 SNP	Nerve and synapse growth and maintenance	Aggression; ADHD; impulsive aggression	Serotonergic pathways	
NR4A2	2q22-q23	Long-repeat allele of AC sequence	Transcription factor in dopaminergic circuit development	Antisocial behavior in females	Dopaminergic pathways	
TFAP2B	6p12	Medium-repeat allele of TC sequence	Transcription factor with role in development of monoamine pathways and brain structures	Antisocial behavior in females	Monoamine pathways	
CHRM2	7q31-q35	5 SNPs	Muscarinic acetylcholine receptor involved in arousal, reward, and attention	Alcohol abuse, externalizing behaviors	Acetylcholine pathways: pons, thalamus, cortex, hippocampus	

although some evidence has emerged that *MAOB* alleles also have some relations to conduct problems (Oreland, Nilsson, Damberg, & Hallman, 2007).

MAOA's role in aggression was first demonstrated in nonhuman studies involving mice; knockout strains for the *Maoa* gene showed increased aggressive behavior (Kim et al., 1997). Specific disruptions of *Maoa* activity were also found to increase brain levels of dopamine, serotonin, and norepinephrine and resulted in higher aggression in mice (Cases et al., 1995; Shih & Thompson, 1999). An association of aggression with *MAOA* has also been demonstrated in rhesus monkeys (Newman et al., 2005), interestingly opposite to that found in humans: the low activity *rhMAOA* allele was found to be associated with social dominance and increased aggression in males, but species differences in the social benefit of aggression must be considered in interpreting these results.

The most studied region of the *MAOA* gene is a 30-base variable nucleotide tandem repeat (*VNTR*) in the promoter region of the gene. Polymerase chain reaction (PCR) analysis of *MAOA* yields fragment sizes of 2, 3, 3.5, 4, or 5 copies of the repeat sequence, with the 3 and 4 repeats as the most common. The 3.5- and 4-repeat alleles have been found to produce more mRNA activity and therefore more *MAOA* enzyme than the 3- or 5-repeat alleles (Sabol, Hu, & Hamer, 1998) and much higher than the 2-repeat allele (Guo, Ou, Roettger, & Shih, 2008). The low-activity alleles have been consistently associated with higher levels of aggression and ASB, plausibly because of a dysregulation of neurotransmitters involved in behavior. The highest activity allele (2-repeat) has also been associated with serious and violent self-reported delinquency (Guo et al., 2008). Significantly, these effects show much clearer patterns in males than in females due to the X-linkage of the gene. That is, because males only have one X chromosome and therefore a single copy of the *MAOA* gene, deleterious effects of the low-activity variant may be more pronounced due to the absence of a more prevalent high-activity allele. In imaging studies, the low-activity alleles of *MAOA* have been associated with increased reactivity in the left amygdala, a region that produces fearful and aggressive responses. The 5-repeat allele was also found to be associated with lower levels of sustained attention in individuals with ADHD (Manor et al., 2002). In a second imaging study, high-activity alleles were associated with more inhibitory control, as measured through increased right ventrolateral prefrontal cortex (VLPFC) activation (Passamonti et al., 2006).

MAOA's influence on aggressive behavior has been found to interact significantly with adverse environment; that is, gene expression depends heavily upon environmental conditions. A significant GxE interaction was found between *MAOA* and childhood adversity, in that the low-activity allele of *MAOA* in combination with childhood adversity predicted ASB but that neither childhood adversity alone nor the presence of the low-activity allele alone were sufficient to predict ASB (Caspi et al., 2002). At least five additional studies have replicated these findings (Edwards et al., 2010; Foley et al., 2004; Kim-Cohen et al., 2006; Nilsson et al., 2006; Nilsson et al., 2007), but at least two known studies have failed to replicate them (Haberstick et al., 2006; Young et al., 2006). *MAOA* genotype was found to interact significantly with parental physical discipline to predict aggression, delinquency, and externalizing behavior (Edwards et al., 2010). However, at least one study found that the interaction was significant in Caucasian but not in non-Caucasian juveniles (Widom & Brzustowicz, 2006), an intriguing albeit tentative and as yet unreplicated finding that could aid in elucidating racial differences in the development of ASB.

In females, findings have been less consistent regarding *MAOA*'s interaction with environmental conditions. Some studies suggest that in females, a combination of the low-activity allele with childhood abuse predicts juvenile (but not lifetime) violent and other antisocial behavior (Widom & Brzustowicz, 2006), as well as CD (Prom-Wormley et al., 2009). In a potential GxG interaction, the low-activity *MAOA* alleles in combination with high cerebrospinal fluid (CSF) levels of testosterone were found to predict ASB (Sjoberg et al., 2008), suggesting that serotonin genes may be involved as moderators of *MAOA* gene expression. Additional *MAOA* interactions were suggested with testosterone and gluticocorticoids through transcription factors Sp1 and R1 (Craig, 2007).

There is intriguing evidence that humans show positive selection for high-activity alleles of *MAOA*. High levels of linkage disequilibrium have been found for *MAOA*, and its allelic diversity is lower than would be expected for its mutation rate, supporting the idea of positive selection (Gilad, Rosenberg, Przeworski, Lancet, & Skorecki, 2002). Together, these findings suggest classical Darwinian natural selection for an allele that conveyed reproductive benefit in the form of prosocial behavior. Notably, such positive selection was not demonstrated in nonhuman primates (Andrés et al., 2004).

In summary, numerous studies have suggested that the low-activity alleles of *MAOA* (3-, 5-, or 2-repeat *VNTR* alleles) predict aggression, violence, and externalizing behavior, primarily in males due to its X-linkage. There is strong evidence for a GxE with childhood adversity or abuse and some evidence for GxG interactions involving combinations of *MAOA* and serotonergic genes as well.

Dopamine Receptors (*DRD1-DRD5*)

Dopaminergic systems in the human brain are vast, versatile, and complex; dopamine acts in reward-response, mood regulation, motor control, learning, attention, and arousal, among many other functions. The five known receptors that bind dopamine when it is released and relay its effects (*DRD1-DRD5*) are located in different areas of the brain ranging from the midbrain to the prefrontal cortex.

The dopamine receptor 4 gene (*DRD4*) codes for receptor expressed in portions of the cortex and limbic system. Like *MAOA*, this gene's promoter region carries a *VNTR* (a 48-base-pair sequence in its third exon), with repeat variants ranging from 2 to 10. Several studies have found associations between novelty seeking (a positive correlate of ASB) and both the 7-repeat allele and other long alleles (Benjamin et al., 1996; Savitz & Ramesar, 2004). However, one meta-analysis of similar studies did not find a significant effect size for the association (Schinka,

Letsch, & Crawford, 2002), although a separate meta-analysis confirmed an association between the 7-repeat allele and ADHD symptoms (Faraone, Doyle, Mick, & Biederman, 2001). An interaction was found for *DRD4*, in which individuals without the 7-repeat allele showed an inverse relationship between IQ and externalizing behavior, whereas individuals with at least one copy of the 7-R allele showed no correlation (DeYoung et al., 2006). Given that IQ is influenced by both genetic and environmental factors, it is not clear whether its moderating role on the *DRD4*–externalizing behavior relationship represents a GxG or GxE interaction, or possibly both.

DRD2 receptors, expressed primarily in the substantia nigra, prefrontal cortex, and basal ganglia, are most strongly associated with psychotic symptoms and are the target of antipsychotic medication. The *DRD2* gene carries one of the most studied single nucleotide polymorphisms (SNP) in behavioral research—the *Taq* polymorphism. There are two alleles for this gene, *A1* and *A2*, of which *A1* codes for a reduced receptor binding strength. Findings regarding allele variants and antisocial behavior have been mixed. A significant association was found between the *DRD2 A1* allele and alcoholism (Blum et al., 1990), as well as cocaine use (Noble et al., 1993), and opiate use (Xu et al., 2004), although some studies did not find an association with alcoholism (Blomqvist, Gelernter, & Kranzler, 2000; Edenberg et al., 1998). The *DRD2 A1* allele was associated with poorer performance on a stop-signal task and continuous-performance tasks designed to gauge ability for impulse inhibition (Rodriguez-Jimenez et al., 2006), but it was not associated with self-report measures of impulsivity (see review by Verdejo-Garcia, Lawrence, & Clark, 2008).

There is some evidence that both environmental adversities and other genes may serve as moderators of the associations between *DRD2* alleles and ASB. In particular, a GxE interaction between the *DRD2 A1* allele and risk level in family environments has been suggested in a sample of adolescents with criminal offenses, in which later onset of first police contact was predicted by *A1* allele only in individuals from more favorable home environments (DeLisi, Beaver, Wright, & Vaughn, 2008). Two other studies have suggested the importance of considering combinations of risk alleles, based on findings that (1) neither *DRD2* nor *DRD4* high-risk allele presence alone predicted adult criminal offending but their joint presence did (Beaver et al., 2007); and (2) the *A1/A2* heterozygous genotype of *DRD2* has demonstrated a protective effect against the development of alcoholism in comparison with the *A1/A1* genotype in Han Chinese men, after stratifying for the 4-repeat allele of *MAOA* (Wang et al., 2007). However, although the *A1* allele is considered the riskier for ASB, a heterosis effect has been reported in males, in that the *A1/A2* genotype predicted the highest level of serious delinquency in the United States (Guo, Roettger, & Shih, 2007). Unexpectedly, in the Guo et al. (2007) study, the risk for ASB (i.e., delinquency) was highest for *A1/A2*, followed by *A2/A2*, and finally *A1/A1*, findings that contradict prior ones showing greater risks associated with the *A1* allele. Clearly there is a need for further investigation of the *DRD2* alleles and their associations with ASB, substance use, and impulse control.

DRD3 receptors, primarily in the nucleus accumbens, have also been impli-cated in impulsivity, as individuals with SNP *DRD3 BalI* polymorphisms scored higher on the Barratt Impulsiveness Scale questionnaire (Limosin et al., 2005) and on novelty-seeking measures (Thome et al., 1999). In addition, the *DRD3* polymorphism was found to predict impulsivity levels in violent, but not nonvio-lent, individuals (Retz, Rosler, Supprian, Retz-Junginger, & Thome, 2003).

In canines, the *DRD1* gene was found to carry an SNP associated with aggres-sion (Vage et al., 2010); human studies with patients who have Alzheimer's dis-ease demonstrated that Caucasians with the *B2/B2 DRD1* homozygous genotype exhibit higher aggression levels (Sweet et al., 1998). However, limited literature exists beyond this study to support *DRD1*'s role in human aggression.

In summary, the dopamine receptor genes show some associations with ASB. Long-repeat *VNTR* alleles of *DRD4* are associated with externalizing behavior and sensation seeking, and the *Taq1* allele of *DRD2* is associated with alcohol-ism, impulse control, and disinhibition; their joint presence, but neither alone, is found to predict criminal behavior. There is limited evidence that either *DRD3* or *DRD1* is associated with impulsivity or aggression, respectively.

Dopamine Transporter (*DAT*)

An additional dopaminergic candidate gene codes for the dopamine trans-porter (*DAT*), a plasma membrane protein responsible for dopamine trans-mission and for removing dopamine from the extracellular space. This gene carries the *DAT1* (or *SLC6A3*) *VNTR* polymorphism in the 3' untranslated region (*3'UTR*), which can have between 3 and 13 repeats. Although this region is not translated into protein, it is transcribed into mRNA and affects translation rates and therefore protein levels. *DAT1*, specifically even one copy of a common 10-repeat allele, has been associated with ADHD (Waldman et al., 1998), as well as with violent behavior and delinquency in adolescents and young adults (Guo et al., 2007). One study found that the 10-repeat allele predicted externalizing behavior in children as young as 4 and 7 years old (Young et al., 2002). *DAT1* additionally contributes to ADHD etiology, with some studies finding association with hyperactivity-impulsivity (Faraone et al., 2005; Roman et al., 2001). A GxG interaction was also reported for *DRD4* and *DAT1* high-risk alleles in predicting ADHD, with no main effect find-ings for either allele on its own (Carrasco et al., 2006).

In summary, several studies have found that the 10-repeat *VNTR* allele of *DAT1* is associated with ASB. Moreover, these associations span several develop-mental periods from childhood to adulthood, as well as several manifestations of ASB, including ADHD and violent delinquency in adults and adolescents, and externalizing behavior in children. There is some evidence for at least one GxG interaction (between *DRD4* and *DAT1*), although no study has yet revealed any moderating environmental factors, which may be one of several potential areas for future research.

Catecholamine-O-methyltransferase (COMT)

Catecholamine-O-methyltransferase (COMT) codes for an enzyme responsible for the production of dopamine, and has been implicated in behavioral tendencies related to ASB. Comt knockout strain rodents were found to exhibit violent and aggressive behavior (Gogos et al., 1998), which prompted research into the gene's effects in humans. The COMT gene, located on chromosome 22q, carries an SNP (CGTG or CATG) that codes for a single amino acid change in the translated protein; the polymorphism results in either a valine (val) or a methionine (met) amino acid at the 158th codon. The val variety of this protein is the more prevalent one and is known to have a higher stability and a higher level of activity than the met variety (Lotta et al., 1995). Across several studies of children with ADHD, those who were homozygotic for val/val were found to be more aggressive, to have more symptoms of CD, and to have more criminal convictions than met carriers (Caspi et al., 2008). However, these studies did not find the val variant of COMT to behave as a susceptibility gene for ASB across the board, as children without ADHD exhibited no increase in ASB; this suggests possible GxG interactions with other genes involved in ADHD. An interaction has also been found between birth weight and the val protein in predicting ADHD itself (Thapar et al., 2005), whereby children of lower birth weight were more susceptible to developing ADHD symptoms if they carried the val/val genotype. COMT has also been shown to be associated with overt and aggressive CD symptoms but not with covert CD symptoms in one study of children and adults with ADHD (Monuteaux, Biederman, Doyle, Mick, & Faraone, 2009), but one study failed to predict CD from COMT genotype and ADHD (Sengupta et al., 2006).

Overall, COMT has been examined primarily in children and adults with ADHD, and there is mixed evidence for its association with CD and aggression. The relationship between COMT genotype and ASB has not yet been confirmed in individuals without ADHD.

Serotonin Transporter Linked Promoter Region (5HTTLPR)

A second neurotransmitter system often studied in relation to ASB is the serotonin system. Serotonin (5HT) is involved in functions ranging broadly from mood to memory, learning, sleep, and appetite. It is also considered influential in the inhibition of impulses, the regulation of emotions, and social functioning, each of which is related to aggression and ASB (Krakowski, 2003). Serotonin's role in ASB was first suggested by findings of 5HT metabolites 5-hydroxyindoleacetic acid (5HIAA) in CSF. 5HIAA, which is used to estimate neural 5HT activity and concentration, was found in lower levels in violent, impulsive men and in impulsive offenders (Linnoila et al., 1983; Roy, Adinoff, & Linnoila, 1988), in boys with CD (Kruesi et al., 1992), in adult offenders with recidivistic patterns (Virkkunen, De Jong, Bartko, Goodwin, & Linnoila, 1989), and in individuals with ASPD (Moss, Yao, & Panzak, 1990). One studied protein is the serotonin transporter

(5HTT), involved in serotonin reuptake from the synapse into the presynaptic terminal, and its gene, *5HTT* (or *SLC6A4*). This gene carries a *VNTR* in its promoter region (*5HTTLPR*) that codes for a long or short number of repeats (L, S), or for a long repeat with one SNP (Lg). The S allele and the Lg allele have been associated with reduced promoter activity, binding, and reuptake (Lesch et al., 1996).

The S allele has been associated with higher rates of aggression and violent offending in incarcerated adults (Liao, Hong, Shih, & Tsai, 2004; Retz, Retz-Junginger, Supprian, Thome, & Rosler, 2004), as well as in adolescents (Gerra et al., 2005). Using both case-control and within-family analyses, the S allele has shown associations with aggressive tendencies, whereby the likelihood of S allele transmission was higher in individuals with CD and with at least one aggressive symptom, but not in those with CD without aggressive symptoms (Sakai et al., 2006). Childhood aggression and externalizing behavior have also shown associations with the low-activity alleles, highlighting the relevance of this gene throughout the course of development (Beitchman et al., 2006; Haberstick et al., 2006). However, at least one study failed to find an association between alleles of *5HTTLPR* and self-reported impulsivity as measured by the Barratt Impulsiveness Scale (Baca-Garcia et al., 2004), suggesting that 5HTT is involved specifically in impulsive aggression and not in all aspects of impulsivity.

There is some evidence for a GxE interaction in the *5HTTLPR* association with adult violence, whereby home violence, familial financial difficulties, and educational or home life disruptions during childhood were found to predict violent behavior later in life only in individuals with the S allele (Reif et al., 2007). A similar GxE interaction between the S allele of *5HTTLPR* and childhood adversity was reported for ADHD (Retz et al., 2008). Another *5HTTLPR* GxE interaction has been suggested in primates, such that a correlation exists between genotype and stressful rearing conditions, as 5HT CSF metabolite concentrations appeared in rhesus monkeys reared in stressful conditions but not in the monkeys reared in favorable conditions (Bennett et al., 2002). These findings are mirrored in a recent human study that examined attachment and autonomy style of adolescents and found that carriers of the *5HTTLPR* S allele displayed more autonomous behavior, but that in cases of secure attachment the autonomy was agreeable and in cases of insecure attachment the autonomy was hostile (Zimmermann, Mohr, & Spangler, 2009). Thus it appears that stressful rearing conditions enhance the effect of *5HTTLPR* on aggression, hostility, and violence.

At least four recent studies have examined potential GxG interactions between *5HTTLPR* and *DRD4* in predicting externalizing behavior. The joint presence of the long-repeat allele of *DRD4* with the S allele of *5HTTLPR* has been shown to predict greater levels of both externalizing and internalizing behavior in adolescents (Schmidt, Fox, & Hamer, 2007), whereas the *DRD4* 7R allele, together with the S *5HTTLPR* allele, predicted aggressive and delinquent behavior in another study (Hohmann et al., 2009). In contrast, the L allele of *5HTTLPR* with the 7R *DRD4* predicted increased consumption of alcohol in a study of adolescents

(Skowronek, Laucht, Hohm, Becker, & Schmidt, 2006). Finally, a fourth study found that the L allele of *5HTTLPR* with long-repeat alleles of *DRD4* predicted externalizing behavior in individuals of low socioeconomic status, suggesting a GxGxE interaction (Nobile et al. 2007).

In summary, several studies have provided evidence that the low-activity *VNTR* alleles of *5HTTLPR* (S, Lg) show associations with aggression, violence, aggressive symptoms of conduct disorder, and other forms of externalizing behavior. At least one study found that adverse childhood environment predicted adult violence only in the presence of the S allele, indicating the importance of GxE interactions. There is also mixed evidence for GxG interaction with *DRD4* in predicting externalizing behavior and aggressive delinquency, and further studies are needed to clarify the nature of these interactions.

Trypthophan hydroxylase (TPH)

Trypthophan hydroxylase (TPH) is a rate-limiting enzyme involved in the synthesis of 5HT. Two forms of TPH are known: TPH1, which operates outside of the brain and the gene for which is located on chromosome 11p, and TPH2, which acts both inside and outside of the brain and the gene for which is located on chromosome 12q. The *TPH1* and *TPH2* genes have been examined for potential links to aggression. Two polymorphisms in the seventh intron (untranslated region) of the *TPH1* gene, the *A218C* and *A779C* polymorphisms, have been examined for associations with violence and anger. The less frequent *TPH1 A218C U* allele has shown stronger association with aggression and anger than the *TPH1 A218C L* allele (Manuck et al., 1999). A later study of adolescents failed to confirm any association between *TPH1 A218C* and nonaggressive adolescent ASB or delinquency, again suggesting the possibility of different developmental pathways to aggressive and nonaggressive ASB (Burt & Mikolajewski, 2008). The *779A* allele has been associated with lower CSF 5HIAA levels in impulsive alcoholics (Nielsen et al., 1994). Interestingly, another study found the *A779C* allele to be associated with aggressive hostility but not neurotic hostility (Hennig, Reuter, Netter, & Burk, 2005), a finding that has been interpreted by some as support for the distinction between reactive and proactive aggression (Craig & Halton, 2009). Associations have also been found between the *TPH1* variants and violent suicidal behavior (Abbar et al., 1995; Zaboli et al., 2006).

TPH2 was initially found to predict aggressive behavior in mice (Kulikov, Osipova, Naumenko, & Popova, 2005). In humans, a *TPH2* SNP, *A1473C*, has been found to similarly predict aggression (Popova, 2006). This SNP has also been associated with aggression and cognitive impulsivity in a sample of boys with ADHD (Oades et al., 2008).

In summary, there is evidence for associations between SNPs of *TPH1* (*A218C*, *A779C*) and violence, anger, and aggression. Neither of these SNPs was associated with nonaggressive delinquency, suggesting the associations may be specific to aggression and may not extend to other forms of ASB. The *TPH2* SNP *A1473C* has also been linked to aggression and hostility. In all, there have been few studies of these genes in relation to ASB, and replications would help in confirming these associations.

5HT receptors (5HT1 and 5HT2)

In addition to the genes involved in the synthesis (TPH2) and reuptake (5HTT) of serotonin, two families of serotonin receptors, 5HT1 and 5HT2, have been targeted in studies of aggressive behavior, as both are known to be involved in regulation of mood, aggression, addiction, and other behavioral facets relevant to ASB. Knockout studies of mice first revealed the roles of specific 5HT receptors in aggression. For example, mice knockout in 5HT1B (gene *Htr1b*) were found to display increased aggression and increased consumption of alcohol and cocaine (Brunner & Hen, 1997; Crabbe et al., 1996; Rocha et al., 1998; Saudou et al., 1994). Canine studies have also shown associations of *HTR2C* and *HTR1D* with aggressive behavior (Vage et al., 2010). Similar associations have been found in human studies between alleles in the 5HT1 and 5HT2 families, including a family-based association between an *HTR1E* SNP and tendencies toward impulsive aggression (Oades et al., 2008), between the *HTR1B* promoter SNP *A-161T* and impulsive-aggression in suicide completers (Zouk et al., 2007), and between *HT2A G-1438A* promoter region SNP and high impulsivity in individuals with alcohol dependence (Preuss, Koller, Bondy, Bahlmann, & Sokya, 2001). At least one candidate gene association in the 5HT2 family has also been found for nonaggressive forms of ASB, such that higher levels of nonaggressive delinquency and ASB were associated with the *5HT2A His452Tyr* polymorphism in adolescents (Burt & Mikolajewski, 2008).

In summary, SNPs in genes from the 5HT1 and 5HT2 families of serotonin receptors have been associated with aggressive behavior in rodents and canines, as well as impulsive aggression in humans. There have also been links of these same genes with nonaggressive ASB in humans, as well as substance use and abuse in both mice and humans. Interestingly, in humans, associations between these genes and ASB have been found both for adolescents and for adults, suggesting there may be some developmental continuity in these associations.

Norepinephrine- and Epinephrine-Related Genes (*DBH, NET1, PNMT*)

Animal studies first suggested that epinephrine (adrenaline) and norepinephrine (noradrenaline) are involved in aggression (Haller, 1993; Haller, Rusu, Giurgea, & Puica Dat, 1990; Saha, Manchanda, Bhatia, & Nayar, 1993; Summers & Greenberg, 1994). Dopamine-β-hydroxylase (DBH) is the enzyme that converts dopamine into norepinephrine, and it has been targeted in studies of aggression. Early evidence suggested that children with CD who came from risky home environments showed low levels of serum DBH (Galvin et al., 1991; Rogeness,

Hernandez, Macedo, & Mitchell, 1982). *Dbh* knockout strain mice were found to display significantly reduced aggression patterns (Marino, Bourdelat-Parks, Cameron Liles, & Weinshenker, 2005), but unfortunately there have been few *DBH* human studies. Two human *DBH* studies found that SNP *C-1021T* predicted impulsive and aggressive behavior in adults with ADHD or personality disorders (Hess et al., 2009; Zhang, Wang, Li, Wang, & Yang, 2005). A recent GxG study found *DBH* to predict conduct problems to varying degrees in combination with the presence of risk alleles of *COMT*, of *COMT* and *MAOB*, or of *COMT, MAOB,* and *MAOA* in boys (Grigorenko et al., 2010). An additional gene, the noradrenaline (norepinephrine) transporter (*NET1*), has an SNP, *3081T*, that was associated with ADHD in Caucasian American children and adolescents (Kim et al., 2006), but little research has been conducted on this gene in other populations. At least one study additionally found that a specific SNP, *G148A,* of the gene phenylethanolamine methyl transferase (*PNMT*), which codes for an enzyme that converts norepinephrine to epinephrine, predicted ADHD symptoms in children, adolescents, and adults (Comings et al., 2000). A more recent study linked two additional SNPs of *PNMT* to cognitive and aggressive impulsivity in children and adolescents (Oades et al., 2008).

Several forms of ASB have shown associations with SNPs of epinephrine and norepinephrine genes in various age groups. ADHD has been linked to SNPs in *DBH, PNMT,* and *NET1* in children, adolescents, and adults, and *PNMT* and *DBH* have both additionally been linked to aggression and impulsivity in children, adolescents, and adults. There is also some evidence for GxG interactions for *DBH* with other genes, including *COMT, MAOA,* and *MAOB,* although no research to date has investigated GxE interactions involving these norepinephrine and epinephrine systems.

Oxytocin and Vasopressin (OXTR, AVPR1a)

Oxytocin and vasopressin play important roles in empathy, trust, and socialization (Kosfeld, Heinrichs, Zak, Fischbacher, & Fehr, 2005; Zak, Stanton, & Ahmadi, 2007). Deficits in oxytocin have been shown to increase activity in the amygdala, a region involved in hostility and aggression (Kirsch et al., 2005). It has been suggested that oxytocin inhibits aggressive tendencies in mammalian females, thus potentially accounting for sex differences in aggression (see review by Campbell, 2007). Additionally, human studies have found a positive correlation between CSF levels of vasopressin and lifetime aggression in individuals with impulsive-aggressive tendencies (Coccaro, Kavoussi, Hauger, Cooper, & Ferris, 1998). The vasopressin selective V1a and V1b receptors have been suggested as antagonism targets for development of neuropeptide pharmaceutical agents to treat disorders of interpersonal violence such as ASPD (see Heinrichs & Domes, 2008).

Mice from knockout strains for the oxytocin gene show exaggerated aggressive behavior (Ragnauth et al., 2005). However, human genetic studies of oxytocin and vasopressin have been sparse. At least one study found no association between ASB and either the human oxytocin gene (*OXTR*) or the human vasopressin gene (*AVPR1a*; Prichard, Jorm, Mackinnon, & Easteal, 2007). However, both the length of the promoter region repeats of *AVPR1a* and several SNPs in *OXTR* have been linked to altruism and prosocial behavior (see Knafo & Israel, 2008).

To date, therefore, only animal studies have shown elevated aggression as a result of knocking out the *OXTR* gene, with no replication found yet in humans. Although no human studies clearly link *OXTR* or *AVPR1a* to ASB, some researchers still suggest that these genes are appropriate targets for future research on ASB due to their role in prosocial behavior.

Hormonal Factors (*ESR1, AR*)

Given the role of hormones in both animal and human aggression (Dixson, 1980; Haller, Makara, & Kruk, 1998), it seems appropriate to consider various receptors for both androgen and estrogen as possible candidate genes for ASB. One human study examined 15 different repeat-sequence polymorphisms for associations with antisocial traits (measured as substance use, unemployment history, police contact, and adolescent misconduct) and identified two positive associations for males: estrogen receptor alpha (*ESR1(TG)*, long-repeat allele) and androgen receptor (*AR(GCA)*, short-repeat allele; Prichard et al., 2007). *ESR1* and *AR* are hormone-binding transcription factors involved in sexual development. Additionally, it was found that female mice from knockout strains for the estrogen receptor gene behaved in an aggressive, masculine manner (Ogawa, Lubahn, Korach, & Pfaff, 1997). These findings suggest that sexual development may have an important role in antisocial tendencies in humans and animals. Two additional human studies have linked the higher expression, shorter *GCA* repeat alleles of the *AR* gene to higher levels of aggression in males (Jonsson et al., 2001; Rajender et al., 2008). Several studies of allele frequencies in various human ethnic groups supported the finding that African Americans have the highest proportion of short *AR* alleles and Asians have the lowest proportion (Edwards, Hammond, Jin, Caskey, & Chakraborty, 1992; Ingles et al., 1997; Irvine, Yu, Ross, & Coetzee, 1995). It is therefore possible that further research into the *AR* and *ESR1* genes could potentially inform investigations of interracial differences in aggression.

Specific variants of repeat sequences in both the androgen receptor gene (*AR(GCA)*, short-repeat allele) and estrogen receptor gene (*ESR1(TG)*, long-repeat allele) have been identified as predictive of antisocial traits in adult human males. The nature of these associations has yet to be verified in children and adolescents. Additionally, there are known racial differences in the frequencies of the *AR* alleles, but few studies have examined racial differences in aggression, so interpretation of these results may be premature.

Neuronal Nitric Oxide Synthase (NOS1)

Neuronal nitric oxide synthase (*NOS1*) facilitates transmission between neurons. Rodent studies have linked *Nos1* to aggression, impulsivity, and anxiety reduction (a feature of human psychopathy; Nelson et al., 1995), as well as to higher testosterone levels (Kriegsfeld, Dawson, Dawson, Nelson, & Snyder, 1997). However, until recently the human gene variant had not been examined in relation to ASB. The human *NOS1* gene, located on chromosome 12q, has a *VNTR* in the promoter region with either a high- or low-repeat sequence (Reif et al., 2006). The transcription of exon *Ex1f* has generated interest, as it codes for regions that bind several important neural proteins, including the estrogen receptor. A recent adult human study examined *NOS1 Ex1f* alleles in the general population and in a psychiatric population and found that the *NOS1* short allele was more prevalent in the psychiatric population and that it correlated with adult ADHD and with cluster B personality disorders (narcissistic, antisocial, borderline, and histrionic personality disorders; Reif et al., 2009). This study also found a gene-by-sex interaction, as females with the short *Ex1f* allele exhibited lower levels of conscientiousness (a prosocial and empathetic trait) as measured by the NEO Personality Inventory—Revised (Costa & McCrae, 1992). Additionally, the *NOS1 Ex1f* short allele correlated with reduced activity in the anterior cingulate cortex (ACC), a prefrontal area involved in reward-response and outcome monitoring (Reif et al., 2006). In combining these results, the authors posit that the short *NOS1 Ex1f* allele may confer risk for disorders of dysfunctional impulsivity.

Although *NOS1* has been linked with aggression in animal studies for many years, human studies of *NOS1* only began recently. An *NOS1* variant has been linked to impulsivity-based personality disorders and ADHD. Additionally, an imaging study linked this variant to reduced outcome monitoring activity. This gene shows a potential interaction with sex, but further studies are needed to verify the relationship of this interaction, as well as *NOS1*'s role in child or adolescent ASB.

Additional Candidates

Apart from the more well-studied candidate genes for ASB or those candidates that are well justified based on phenotypic evidence for investigating certain systems involved in aggression, impulse control, and reward pathways, a handful of other candidate genes for aggression and ASB have been identified. For example, some polymorphisms in genes involved in brain-derived neurotrophic factor (BDNF) have been suggested as possible human candidate genes. BDNF is involved in nerve and synapse growth and maintenance, and, using knockout mice, this growth factor's gene has been linked to increased aggression (Lyons et al., 1999) and reduced 5HT levels (Ren-Patterson et al., 2005). Two SNP polymorphisms in the human *BDNF* gene have been associated with ADHD

(Schimmelmann et al., 2007) and with impulsive aggression in children and adolescents in a recent family-based association study (Oades et al., 2008).

Two additional polymorphisms have shown associations with early conduct problems and adult externalizing behavior, specifically in human adult females (Prichard et al., 2007): transcription factor activating enhancer-binding protein 2 beta (*TFAP2B(TC)*, medium-repeat allele) and nuclear-related receptor 1 protein (*NR4A2(AC)*, long-repeat allele). *NR4A2*, a member of the steroid-thyroid hormone-retinoid receptor superfamily, is a transcription factor involved in development of dopamine circuits (Sacchetti, Mitchell, Granneman, & Bannon, 2001). *TFAP2B* has a crucial role in the development of certain brain structures in the midbrain, including monoamine pathway regions (Takeuchi et al., 1999).

CHRM2, a gene on human chromosome 7q, has shown an association with alcohol abuse and externalizing behavior in adults, using lifetime symptom measures of adult ASPD, childhood CD, and alcohol and drug dependence (Dick et al., 2008; Wang et al., 2004). *CHRM2* codes for a muscarinic acetylcholine receptor, present both in the central and peripheral nervous systems, which is involved in arousal, reward, and attention.

These additional polymorphisms are interesting candidate genes for future research using other measures of ASB across various age groups. It is not yet clear what sex differences may exist in *CHRM2* and *BDNF* associations, if any, and how environmental factors and other genes may moderate their associations with ASB. It is also unclear whether *TFAP2B* or *NR4A2* play a role in child or adolescent female ASB.

LINKAGE STUDIES

Although this review is primarily focused on studies attempting to identify specific polymorphisms that increase risk for ASB, it is important also to consider a few genome-wide association studies that have provided some information about regions of interest in ASB. Genome-wide screening studies approach genetic markers from a different perspective than do candidate gene association studies. Whereas candidate gene studies target alleles of interest based on hypotheses, genome-wide studies employ linkage methods to identify quantitative trait loci (QTL) of chromosomal regions that associate with specific phenotypic outcomes. Although no major studies have been conducted to exclusively seek regions related to ASB, there are several linkage studies of substance use that also included measures of ASB, including CD. In these studies, several important findings have emerged.

A genome-wide screening for genes associated with childhood CD and CD symptoms found regions on chromosomes 2 and 19 that exhibited high LOD scores (a statistical test used to gauge association strength) to CD, as well as evidence for association with regions in chromosomes 1, 3, 19, and 12 (Dick et al., 2004). A second large-scale screening study found associations in chromosomes 3 and 9 as potential risk markers for CD and SUD and 17 for CD alone (Stallings et al., 2003; Stallings et al., 2005). A later study found evidence for linkage with CD traits on chromosomes 1 and 2, lending some support to the findings of Dick and colleagues but not to those of Stallings and colleagues (Kendler et al., 2006). An additional linkage study conducted with American Indians found significant LOD scores for ASPD on chromosome 13 and for ASPD/CD on chromosomes 1, 3, 4, 14, 17, and 20 (Ehlers, Gilder, Slutske, Lind, & Wilhelmsen, 2008). These findings provide suggestions for future research.

SUMMARY AND CONCLUSIONS

Nearly two dozen candidate genes associated with ASB in humans have been identified, many of which are supported by replicated human and animal studies. A majority of these candidates were identified through examination of neurotransmitter, hormonal, or other systems involved in ASB or its known risk factors. One of these is the dopamine system, involved in mood, motivation and reward, arousal, and other behaviors. Another is the serotonin system, involved in impulse control, affect regulation, sleep, and appetite. A third involves epinephrine and norepinephrine, which facilitate fight-or-flight reactions and autonomic nervous system activity. All three of these systems are affected by *MAOA* function, a fact that perhaps contributed to its appeal to researchers. The low-activity alleles of *MAOA* interact with maladaptive childhood environment and have been associated with aggression, violent delinquency, externalizing behavior, and lower inhibitory control. There is even evidence for positive Darwinian selection for the high-activity *MAOA* alleles.

Additional dopaminergic candidates include dopamine receptors *DRD4*, involved in ADHD and externalizing behavior, and *DRD2*, involved in substance abuse and disinhibition. Limited support exists for associations between ASB and *DRD1* or *DRD3*. Dopamine transporter gene *DAT1* has also been linked to ADHD and violence. Dopamine synthesizing enzyme COMT's genotype has shown mixed results for association with ADHD, CD, and overtly violent behavior. Dopaminergic candidate genes appear to predict disinhibited, aggressive behavior.

In serotonergic genes, the S or Lg repeat alleles of serotonin transporter gene *5HTTLPR* has been associated with violent, but not nonviolent, CD and externalizing behavior; this gene also shows an interaction with maladaptive childhood environment. *TPH1*, coding for a synthesizing enzyme, has similarly been associated with violent but not nonviolent aggression. *TPH2* was associated with impulsivity, both aggressive and cognitive. Serotonin receptor families 5HT1 and 5HT2 have candidate genes associated with aggressive behavior and substance use. With the exception of one *5HT2A* SNP, serotonergic genes appear to predict more violent than nonviolent ASB.

Adrenergic genes were primarily found to predict aggression and ADHD symptoms. Synthesizing enzyme *DBH* variants predicted aggression and impulsivity, potentially in combination with risk alleles of *COMT, MAOA,* and *MAOB*.

Variants of synthesizing enzyme *PNMT* and serotonin transporter *NET1* also predicted ADHD and aggressive impulsivity.

Additional candidates include hormonal factors estrogen receptor *ESR1* and androgen receptor *AR*, both linked to ASB in males. In females, two neuronal transcription factors, *TFAP2B* and *NR4A2*, were linked to ASB. The gene for NOS1, which facilitates neural transmission, was linked to ADHD and impulsivity-based disorders in both sexes and to lower conscientiousness in females. The neurotrophic factor *BDNF* was linked to ADHD and impulsive aggression, as well. *CHRM2*, which codes for an acetylcholine receptor, was linked to externalizing behavior and alcohol abuse. Lastly, though no studies specifically link either *OXTR* or *AVPR1a* to ASB, oxytocin and vasopressin are involved in prosocial behavior and thus might be appropriate targets for future research.

Epigenetics and Future Directions

Although there is much interest in candidate genes, molecular biologists now understand that DNA sequences of various polymorphisms do not tell the whole story. Especially when considering the profound influence of environment on ASB, it is important to consider how environment interacts with DNA on a molecular level. A new field of genetics has emerged that examines an additional level of complexity in genes—cellular level modifications to DNA that do not affect DNA sequence but that determine frequency of translation, as well as protein shape. This field is called *epigenetics*. One commonly studied epigenetic phenomenon is methylation, which refers to methyl groups attached to nucleotides in the DNA by an intracellular enzyme that can alter the DNA's attractiveness for transcription. One striking finding is that monozygotic twins begin life with a similar methylation profile, or methylome, but diverge with age (Fraga et al., 2005). This finding helps explain phenotypic differences in MZ twins for genetically influenced traits. To illustrate the powerful influence of the methylome, an examination of methylation in *DRD2* sites between MZ twins discordant for schizophrenia revealed that the twin with schizophrenia showed a methylation profile more similar to other individuals with schizophrenia than to his or her own identical twin (Petronis et al., 2003). Some researchers have posited that postpartum environmental conditions may be responsible for frequency of methylation, a potential mechanism of GxE (Weaver et al., 2004).

A few ASB-specific epigenetic effects have already been found, such as MZ discordance in *COMT* methylation. A study that examined cytosine methylation at a CgP site of the gene found discordance among twins as young as 5 years of age (Mill et al., 2006). As *COMT* is associated with CD and aggression, this finding might explain how unique environment influences genetic tendencies in children.

Epigenetic effects have also been demonstrated in rats, when maternal licking and grooming were found to contribute to differences in methylation levels of gluticocorticoid receptor (GR; Weaver et al., 2005). The GR transcription levels modified response rates of the hypothalamic-pituitary-adrenal axis (HPA), involved in stress response (Liu et al., 1997). This provides a potential explanation of how different parental influences lead to different coping mechanisms in offspring.

Cocaine use also demonstrates epigenetic effects. Cocaine use induces acetylation of histone groups (proteins that shape chromosomes) at the *FosB* gene, rendering it more attractive for transcription, which explains increased FosB expression after cocaine use (Kumar et al., 2005). This finding highlights the potential of drugs to influence DNA expression.

Other levels of complexity besides methylome and histone modification have been examined by geneticists, including transcription profiles, protein profiles, and glycoselation profiles of cells. Transcription and protein profiles of a cell can give "snapshot" views of what actually occurs in the cell regardless of what exists in the genome. A cell's glycoselation profile represents the sugars on the surface of the cell, which influence cellular communication central to neural development. These are only some examples of the vast complexity of the biology that underlies human behavior and are meant to draw the reader's attention to potentially revolutionary future developments. Although research of this nature has been minimally applied to the fields of psychology and criminology, it will likely become common in these areas as next-generation sequencing technologies become more prevalent. Such detailed study will provide a fuller picture of the mechanisms behind GxE phenomena in ASB.

Research developments of this sort could inspire approaches to predicting and treating ASB. Heightened understanding may even result in new personalized pharmaceutical agents targeted at calming aggressive tendencies and enhancing prosocial behavior. For example, the vasopressin receptors V1a and V1b have already been suggested as antagonism targets for neuropeptide pharmaceuticals.

Although candidate genes provide a solid foundation for future research, rapidly advancing sequencing technologies will soon allow for more sophistication. Future genome-wide association studies should identify further chromosomal regions associated with ASB and may inspire future research on mechanisms involved in behavioral development. Epigenetic studies should concentrate on mechanisms of the pathways from genes to behavior. Together, these new approaches should help psychologists and criminologists understand how ASB develops and hopefully suggest targets for intervention.

REFERENCES

Abbar, M., Courtet, P., Amadéo, S., Caer, Y., Mallet, J., Baldy-Moulinier, M., et al. (1995). Suicidal behaviors and the tryptophan hydroxylase gene. *Archives of General Psychiatry, 52,* 846–849.

Andrés, A. M., Soldevila, M., Navarro, A., Kidd, K. K., Oliva, B., & Bertranpetit, J. (2004). Positive selection in MAOA gene is human exclusive: Determination of the putative amino acid change selected in the human lineage. *Human Genetics, 115,* 377–386.

Arce, E., & Santisteban, C. (2006). Impulsivity: A review. *Psicothema, 18,* 213–220.

Baca-Garcia, E., Vaquero, C., Diaz-Sastre, C., García-Resa, E., Saiz-Ruiz, J., Fernández-Piqueras, J., et al. (2004). Lack of association between the serotonin transporter promoter gene polymorphism and impulsivity or aggressive behavior among suicide attempters and healthy volunteers. *Psychiatry Research, 126,* 99–106.

Baker, L. A., Raine, A., Liu, J., & Jacobson, K. C. (2008). Differential genetic and environmental influences on reactive and proactive aggression in children. *Journal of Abnormal Child Psychology, 36,* 1265–1278.

Beaver, K. M., Wright, J. P., DeLisi, M., Walsh, A., Vaughn, M. G., Boisvert, D., et al. (2007). A gene x gene interaction between DRD2 and DRD4 is associated with conduct disorder and antisocial behavior in males. *Behavioral and Brain Functions, 3,* 1–8.

Beitchman, J. H., Baldassarra, L., Mik, H., De Luca, V., King, N., Bender, D., et al. (2006). Serotonin transporter polymorphisms and persistent, pervasive childhood aggression. *American Journal of Psychiatry, 163,* 1103–1105.

Benjamin, J., Li, L., Patterson, C., Greenberg, B. D., Murphy, D. L., & Hamer, D. H. (1996). Population and familial association between the D4 dopamine receptor gene and measures of novelty seeking. *Nature Genetics, 12,* 81–84.

Bennett, A. J., Lesch, K. P., Long, J. C., Lorenz, J. G., Shoaf, S. E., Champoux, M., et al. (2002). Early experience and serotonin transporter gene variation interact to influence primate CNS function. *Molecular Psychiatry, 7,* 118–122.

Blomqvist, O., Gelernter, J., & Kranzler, H. R. (2000). Family-based study of DRD2 alleles in alcohol and drug dependence. *American Journal of Medical Genetics, 96,* 659–664.

Blum, K., Noble, E. P., Sheridan, P. J., Montgomery, A., Ritchie, T., Jagadeeswaran, P., et al. (1990). Allelic association of human dopamine D2 receptor gene in alcoholism. *Journal of the American Medical Association, 263,* 2055–2060.

Brunner, D., & Hen, R. (1997). Insights into the neurobiology of impulsive behavior from serotonin receptor knockout mice. *Annals of the New York Academy of Sciences, 105,* 836–881.

Brunner, H. G., Nelen, M., Breakefield, X. O., Ropers, H. H., & van Oost, B. A. (1993). Abnormal behavior associated with a point mutation in the structural gene for monoamine oxidase A. *Science, 262,* 578–580.

Burt, S. A., & Mikolajewski, A. J. (2008). Preliminary evidence that specific candidate genes are associated with adolescent-onset antisocial behavior. *Aggressive Behavior, 34,* 437–445.

Cadoret, R. J., Cain, C. A., & Crowe, R. R. (1983). Evidence for gene-environment interaction in the development of adolescent antisocial behavior. *Behavior Genetics, 13,* 301–310.

Cadoret, R. J., Yates, W. R., Troughton, E., Woodworth, G., & Stewart, M. A. (1995). Genetic-environmental interaction in the genesis of aggressivity and conduct disorders. *Archives of General Psychiatry, 52,* 916–924.

Campbell, A. (2007). Attachment, aggression and affiliation: The role of oxytocin in female social behavior. *Biological Psychology, 77,* 1–10.

Carrasco, X., Rothhammer, P., Moraga, M., Henríquez, H., Chakraborty, R., Aboitiz, F., et al. (2006). Genotypic interaction between DRD4 and DAT1 loci is a high risk factor for attention-deficit/hyperactivity disorder in Chilean families. *American Journal of Medical Genetics: Part B. Neuropsychiatric Genetics, 141,* 51–54.

Cases, O., Seif, I., Grimsby, J., Gaspar, P., Chen, K., Pournin, S., et al. (1995). Aggressive behavior and altered amounts of brain serotonin and norepinephrine in mice lacking MAO-A. *Science, 268,* 1763–1766.

Caspi, A., Langley, K., Milne, B., Moffitt, T. E., O'Conovan, M., Owen, M. J., et al. (2008). A replicated molecular basis of subtyping antisocial behavior in children with attention-deficit/hyperactivity disorder. *Archives of General Psychiatry, 65,* 203–210.

Caspi, A., McClary, J., Moffitt, T. E., Mill, J., Martin, J., Craig, I. W., et al. (2002). Role of genotype in the cycle of violence in maltreated children. *Science, 297,* 851–854.

Cloninger, C. R., & Gottesman, I. I. (1987). Genetic and environmental factors in antisocial behavior disorders. In S. A. Mednick, T. E. Moffitt, & S. A. Stack (Eds.), *The causes of crime: New biological approaches* (pp. 96–100). New York, NY: Cambridge University Press.

Cloninger, C. R., Sigvardsson, S., Bohman, M., & von Knorring, A. I. (1982). Predisposition to petty criminality in Swedish adoptees: II. Cross-fostering analysis of gene-environment interaction. *Archives of General Psychiatry, 39,* 1242–1247.

Coccaro, E. F., Kavoussi, R. J., Hauger, R. L., Cooper, T. B., & Ferris, C. F. (1998). Cerebrospinal fluid vasopressin levels: Correlates with aggression and serotonin function in personality-disordered subjects. *Archives of Genetic Psychiatry, 55,* 708–714.

Comings, D. E., Gade-Andavolu, R., Gonzalez, N., Wu, S., Muhleman, D., Blake, H., et al. (2000). Comparison of the role of dopamine, serotonin, and noradrenaline genes in ADHD, ODD, and conduct disorder: Multivariate regression analysis of 20 genes. *Clinical Genetics, 57,* 178–196.

Costa, P. T., Jr., & McCrae, R. R. (1992). *Revised NEO Personality Inventory manual.* Odessa, FL: Psychological Assessment Resources.

Crabbe, J. C., Phillips, T. J., Feller, D. J., Hen, R., Wenger, C. D., Lessov, C. N., et al. (1996). Elevated alcohol consumption in null mutant mice lacking 5-HT1B serotonin receptors. *Nature Genetics, 14,* 98–101.

Craig, I. W. (2007). The importance of stress and genetic variation in human aggression. *Bioessays, 29,* 227–236.

Craig, I. W., & Halton, K. E. (2009). Genetics of human aggressive behavior. *Human Genetics, 126,* 101–113.

Crick, N. R., & Grotpeter, J. K. (1996). Children's treatment by peers: Victims of relational and overt aggression. *Developmental Psychopathology, 8,* 267–280.

DeLisi, M., Beaver, K. M., Wright, J. P., & Vaughn, M. G. (2008). The etiology of criminal onset: The enduring salience of nature and nurture. *Journal of Criminal Justice, 36,* 217–223.

DeYoung, C. G., Peterson, J. B., Seguin, J. R., Metja, J. M., Pilo, R. O., Beitchman, J. H., et al. (2006). The dopamine D4 receptor gene and moderation of the association between externalizing behavior and IQ. *Archives of General Psychiatry, 63,* 1410–1416.

Dick, D. M., Aliev, F., Wang, J. C., Grucza, R. A., Schuckit, M., Kuperman, S., et al. (2008). Using dimensional models of externalizing psychopathology to aid in gene identification. *Archives of General Psychiatry, 65*(3), 310–318.

Dick, D. M., Li, T.-K., Edenberg, H. J., Hesselbrock, V., Kramer, J., Kuperman, S., et al. (2004). A genome-wide screen for genes influencing conduct disorder. *Molecular Psychiatry, 9*(1), 81–86.

Dixson, A. F. (1980). Androgens and aggressive behavior in primates: A review. *Aggressive Behavior, 6,* 36–37.

Dodge, K. A. (1991). The structure and function of reactive and proactive aggression. In D. Pepler & K. Rubin (Eds.), *The development and treatment of childhood aggression* (pp. 201–218). Hillsdale, NJ: Erlbaum.

Dodge, K. A., & Coie, J. D. (1987). Social-information-processing factors in reactive and proactive aggression in children's peer groups. *Journal of Personality and Social Psychology, 53,* 1146–1158.

Edenberg, H. J., Reynolds, J., Koller, D. L., Begleiter, H., Bucholz, K. K., Conneally, P. M., et al. (1998). A family-based analysis of whether the functional promoter alleles of the serotonin transporter gene HTT affect the risk for alcohol dependence. *Alcoholism: Clinical and Experimental Research, 22,* 1080–1085.

Edwards, A., Hammond, H. A., Jin, L., Caskey, C. T., & Chakraborty, R. (1992). Genetic variation at five trimeric and tetrameric tandem repeat loci in four human population groups. *Genomics, 12*(2), 241–253.

Edwards, A. C., Dodge, K. A., Latendresse, S. J., Lansford, J. E., Bates, J. E., Pettit, G. S., et al. (2010). MAO-A-uVNTR and early physical discipline interact to influence delinquent behavior. *Journal of Child Psychology and Psychiatry, 51,* 679–687.

Ehlers, C. L., Gilder, D. A., Slutske, W. S., Lind, P. A., & Wilhelmsen, K. C. (2008). Externalizing disorders in American Indians: Comorbidity and a genome-wide linkage analysis. *American Journal of Medical Genetics: Part B. Neuropsychiatric Genetics, 147B,* 690–698.

Faraone, S. V., Doyle, A. E., Mick, E., & Biederman, J. (2001). Meta-analysis of the association between the 7-repeat allele of the dopamine D(4) receptor gene and attention deficit hyperactivity disorder. *American Journal of Psychiatry, 158,* 1052–1057.

Faraone, S. V., Perlis, R. H., Doyle, A. E., Smoller, J. W., Goralnick, J. J., Holmgren, M. A., et al. (2005). Molecular genetics of attention deficit/hyperactivity disorder. *Biological Psychiatry, 57,* 1313–1323.

Foley, D. L., Eaves, J. L., Wormley, B., Silberg, J. L., Maes, H. H., Kuhn, J., et al. (2004). Childhood adversity, monoamine oxidase A genotype, and risk for conduct disorder. *Archives of General Psychiatry, 61,* 738–744.

Fraga, M. F., Ballestar, E., Paz, M. F., Ropero, S., Setien, F., Ballestar, M. L., et al. (2005). Epigenetic differences arise during the lifetime of monozygotic twins. *Proceedings of the National Academy of Sciences of the USA, 109,* 10604–10609.

Galvin, M., Shekhar, A., Simon, J., Stilwell, B., Ten, E. R., & Laite, G. (1991). Low dopamine-beta-hydroxylase: A biological sequela of abuse and neglect? *Psychiatry Research, 39,* 1–11.

Gerra, G., Garofano, L., Rovetto, F., Zaimovic, A., Moi, G., Bussandri, M., et al. (2005). Serotonin transporter promoter polymorphism genotype is associated with temperament, personality traits and illegal drug use among adolescents. *Journal of Neural Transmission, 112,* 1397–1410.

Gilad, Y., Rosenberg, G., Przeworski, M., Lancet, D., & Skorecki, K. (2002). Evidence for positive selection and population structure at the human MAO-A gene. *Proceedings of the National Academy of Sciences of the USA, 99,* 862–867.

Gogos, J. A., Morgan, M., Luine, V., Santha, M., Ogawa, S., Pfaff, D., et al. (1998). Catechol-O-methyltransferase-deficient mice exhibit sexually dimorphic changes in catecholamine levels and behavior. *Proceedings of the National Academy of Sciences of the USA, 95*(17), 9991–9996.

Grigorenko, E. L., DeYoung, C. G., Eastman, M., Getchell, M., Haeffel, G. J., Klinteberg, B., et al. (2010). Aggressive behavior, related conduct problems, and variation in genes affecting dopamine turnover. *Aggressive Behavior, 36,* 158–176.

Guo, G., Ou, X., Roettger, M., & Shih, J. C. (2008). The VNTR repeat in *MAO-A* and delinquent behavior in adolescence and young adulthood: Associations and *MAO-A* promoter activity. *European Journal of Human Genetics, 16,* 626–634.

Guo, G., Roettger, M. E., & Shih, J. C. (2007). Contributions of the *DAT1* and *DRD2* genes to serious and violent delinquency among adolescents and young adults. *Human Genetics, 121,* 125–136.

Haberstick, B. C., Smolen, A., & Hewitt, J. K. (2006). Family-based association test of the 5HTTLPR and aggressive behavior in a general population sample of children. *Biological Psychiatry, 59,* 836–843.

Haller, J. (1993). Adrenomedullar catecholamine liberation and carbohydrate metabolism during the first thirty minutes of an aggressive encounter in rats. *Physiology and Behavior, 54,* 195–197.

Haller, J., Makara, G. B., & Kruk, M. R. (1998). Catecholaminergic involvement in the control of aggression: Hormones, the peripheral sympathetic, and central noradrenergic systems. *Neuroscience and Biobehavioral Reviews, 22,* 85–97.

Haller, J., Rusu, V. M., Giurgea, R., & Puica Dat, C. (1990). Energetical cost of aggression in rats: Resident–intruder conflicts. *Revue Roumaine de Biochimie, 27,* 217–228.

Heinrichs, M., & Domes, G. (2008). Neuropeptides and social behavior: Effects of oxytocin and vasopressin in humans. *Progress of Brain Research, 170,* 337–350.

Hennig, J., Reuter, M., Netter, P., & Burk, C. (2005). Two types of aggression are differentially related to serotonergic activity and the A779C *TPH* polymorphism. *Behavioral Neuroscience, 119,* 16–25.

Hess, C., Reif, A., Strobel, A., Boreatti-Hummer, A., Heine, M., Lesch, K. P., et al. (2009). A functional dopamine-β-hydroxylase gene promoter polymorphism is associated with impulsive personality styles, but not with affective disorders. *Journal of Neuronal Transmission, 116,* 121–130.

Hohmann, S., Becker, K., Fellinger, J., Banaschewski, T., Schmidt, M. H., Esser, G., et al. (2009). Evidence for epistasis between the 5-HTTLPR and the dopamine D4 receptor polymorphisms in externalizing behavior among 15-year-olds. *Journal of Neural Transmission, 116,* 1621–1629.

Ingles, S. A., Ross, R. K., Yu, M. C., Irvine, R. A., La Pera, G., Haile, R. W., et al. (1997). Association of prostate cancer risk with genetic polymorphisms in vitamin D receptor and androgen receptor. *Journal of the National Cancer Institute, 89,* 166–170.

Irvine, R. A., Yu, M. C., Ross, R. K., & Coetzee, G. A. (1995). The CAG and GGC microsatellites of the androgen receptor gene are in linkage disequilibrium in men with prostate cancer. *Cancer Research, 55,* 1937–1940.

Jensen, P. S., Martin, D., & Cantwell, D. P. (1997). Comorbidity in ADHD: Implications for research, practice, and DSM-V. *Journal of the Academy of Child and Adolescent Psychiatry, 36,* 1065–1079.

Jonsson, E. G., von Gertten, C., Gustavsson, J. P., Yuan, Q. P., Lindblad-Toh, K., Forslund, K., et al. (2001). Androgen receptor trinucleotide repeat polymorphism and personality traits. *Psychiatric Genetics, 11*, 19–23.

Kendler, K. S., Kuo, P., Webb, B. T., Kalsi, G., Neale, M. C., Sullivan, P. F., et al. (2006). A joint genomewide linkage analysis of symptoms of alcohol dependence and conduct disorder. *Alcoholism: Clinical and Experimental Research, 30*, 1972–1977.

Kim, C. H., Hahn, M. K., Joung, Y., Anderson, S. L., Steele, A. H., Mazei-Robinson, M. S., et al. (2006). A polymorphism in the norepinephrine transporter gene alters promoter activity and is associated with attention-deficit hyperactivity disorder. *Proceedings of the National Academy of Sciences of the USA, 103*, 19164–19169.

Kim, J. J., Shih, J. C., Chen, K., Chen, L., Bao, S., Maren, S., et al. (1997). Selective enhancement of emotional, but not motor, learning in monoamine oxidase A-deficient mice. *Proceedings of the National Academy of Sciences of the USA, 94*, 5929–5933.

Kim-Cohen, J., Caspi, A., Moffitt, T. E., Harrington, H., Milne, B. J., & Poulton, R. (2003). Prior juvenile diagnoses in adults with mental disorder: Developmental follow-back of a prospective longitudinal cohort. *Archives of General Psychiatry, 60*, 709–717.

Kim-Cohen, J., Caspi, A., Taylor, A., Williams, B., Newcombe, R., Craig, I. W., et al. (2006). MAOA, maltreatment, and gene–environment interaction predicting children's mental health: New evidence and a meta-analysis. *Molecular Psychiatry, 11*, 1–11.

Kirsch, P., Esslinger, C., Chen, Q., Mier, D., Lis, S., Siddhanti, S., et al. (2005). Oxytocin modulates neural circuitry for social cognition and fear in humans. *Journal of Neuroscience, 25*, 11489–11493.

Knafo, A., & Israel, S. (2008). Genetic and environmental influences on prosocial behavior. Retrieved from https://portal.idc.ac.il/en/Symposium/HerzliyaSymposium/Documents/dcKnafo.pdf . Kosfeld, M., Heinrichs, M., Zak, P. J., Fischbacher, U., & Fehr, E. (2005). Oxytocin increases trust in humans. *Nature, 435*, 673–676.

Krakowski, M. (2003). Violence and serotonin: Influence of impulse control, affect regulation, and social functioning. *Journal of Neuropsychiatry and Clinical Neurosciences, 15*(3), 294–305.

Kriegsfeld, L. J., Dawson, T. M., Dawson, V. L., Nelson, R. J., & Snyder, S. H. (1997). Aggressive behavior in male mice lacking the gene for neuronal nitric oxide synthase requires testosterone. *Brain Research, 769*, 66–70.

Kruesi, M. J., Hibbs, E. D., Zahn, T. P., Keysor, C. S., Hamburger, S. D., Bartko, J. J., et al. (1992). A 2-year prospective follow-up study of children and adolescents with disruptive behavior disorders: Prediction by cerebrospinal fluid 5-hydroxyindoleacetic acid, homovanillic acid, and autonomic measures? *Archives of Genetic Psychiatry, 49*, 507–514.

Kulikov, A. V., Osipova, D. V., Naumenko, V. S., & Popova, N. K. (2005). Association between Tph2 gene polymorphism, brain tryptophan hydroxylase activity and aggressiveness in mouse strains. *Genes, Brain and Behavior, 4*, 482–485.

Kumar, A., Choi, K., Renthal, W., Tsankova, N. M., Theobald, D. E. H., Truong, H., et al. (2005). Chromatic remodeling is a key mechanism underlying cocaine-induced plasticity in striatum. *Neuron, 48*, 303–314.

Lesch, K. P., Bengel, D., Heils, A., Sabol, S. Z., Greenberg, B. D., Petri, S., et al. (1996). Association of anxiety-related traits with a polymorphism in the serotonin transporter gene regulatory region. *Science, 274*, 1527–1531.

Liao, D. L., Hong, C. J., Shih, H. L., & Tsai, S. J. (2004). Possible association between serotonin transporter promoter region polymorphism and extremely violent crime in Chinese males. *Neuropsychobiology 50*, 284–287.

Limosin, F., Romo, L., Batel, P., Ades, J., Boni, C., & Gorwood, P. (2005). Association between dopamine receptor D3 gene BalI polymorphism and cognitive impulsiveness in alcohol-dependent men. *European Psychiatry, 20*, 304–306.

Linnoila, M., Virkkunen, M., Scheinin, M., Nuutila, A., Rimon, R., & Goodwin, F. K. (1983). Low cerebrospinal fluid 5-hydroxyindoleacetic acid concentration differentiates impulsive from nonimpulsive violent behavior. *Life Sciences, 33*, 2609–2614.

Liu, D., Diorio, J., Tannenbaum, B., Caldji, C., Francis, D., Freedman, A., et al. (1997). Maternal care, hippocampal glucocorticoid receptors, and hypothalamic-pituitary-adrenal responses to stress. *Science, 277*, 1659–1662.

Lotta, T., Vidgren, J., Tilgmann, C., Ulmanen, I., Melen, K., Julkunen, I., et al. (1995). Kinetics of human soluble and membrane-bound catechol O-methyltransferase: A revised mechanism and description of the thermolabile variant of the enzyme. *Biochemistry, 34*, 4202–4210.

Lyons, W. E., Mamounas, L. A., Ricaurte, G. A., Coppola, V., Reid, S. W., Bora, S. H., et al. (1999) Brain-derived neurotrophic factor-deficient mice develop aggressiveness and hyperphagia in conjunction with brain serotonergic abnormalities. *Proceedings of the National Academy of Sciences of the USA, 96*, 15239–15244.

Manor, I., Tyano, S., Mel, E., Eisenberg, J., Bachner-Melman, R., Kotler, M. et al. (2002). Family-based and association studies of monoamine oxidase A and attention deficit hyperactivity disorder (ADHD): Preferential transmission of the long promoter-region repeat and its association with impaired performance on a continuous performance test (TOVA). *Molecular Psychiatry, 7*, 626–632.

Manuck, S. B., Flory, J. D., Ferrell, R. E., Dent, K. M., Mann, J. J., & Muldoon, M. F. (1999). Aggression and anger-related traits associated with a polymorphism of the tryptophan hydroxylase gene. *Biological Psychiatry 45*, 603–614.

Marino, M. D., Bourdelat-Parks, B. N., Cameron Liles, L., & Weinshenker, D. (2005) Genetic reduction of noradrenergic function alters social memory and reduces aggression in mice. *Behavioral Brain Research, 161*, 197–203.

Mednick, S. A., Gabrielli, W. F., & Hutchings, B. (1984). Genetic influence in criminal convictions: Evidence from an adoption cohort. *Science, 224*, 891–894.

Mill, J., Dempster, E., Caspi, A., Williams, B., Moffitt, T., & Craig, I. (2006). Evidence for monozygotic twin (MZ) discordance in methylation level at two CpG sites in the promoter region of the catechol-O-methyltransferase (COMT) gene. *American Journal of Medical Genetics: Part B. Neuropsychiatric Genetics, 141B*, 421–425.

Monuteaux, M. C., Biederman, J., Doyle, A. E., Mick, E., & Faraone, S. V. (2009). Genetic risk for conduct disorder symptom subtypes in an ADHD sample: Specificity to aggressive symptoms. *Journal of the American Academy for Child and Adolescent Psychiatry, 48*, 757–764.

Moss, H. B., Yao, J. K., & Panzak, G. L. (1990). Serotonergic responsivity and behavioral dimensions in antisocial personality disorder with substance abuse. *Biological Psychiatry, 15*, 325–338.

Nelson, R. J., Demas, G. E., Huang, P. L., Fishman, M. C., Dawson, V. L., Dawson, T. M., et al. (1995). Behavioral abnormalities in male mice lacking neuronal nitric-oxide synthase. *Nature, 378,* 383–386.

Newman, T. K., Syagailo, Y. V., Barr, C. S., Wendland, J. R., Champoux, M., Graessle, M., et al. (2005). Monoamine oxidase A gene promoter variation and rearing experience influences aggressive behavior in rhesus monkeys. *Biological Psychiatry, 57,* 167–172.

Nielsen, D. A., Goldman, D., Virkkunen, M., Tokola, R., Rawlings, R., & Linnoila, M. (1994). Suicidality and 5-hydroxyindoleacetic acid concentration associated with a tryptophan hydroxylase polymorphism. *Archives of General Psychiatry, 51,* 34–38.

Nilsson, K. W., Sjoberg, R. L., Damberg, M., Leppert, J., Ohrvik, J., Alm, P. O., et al. (2006). Role of monoamine oxidase A genotype and psychosocial factors in male adolescent criminal activity. *Biological Psychiatry, 59,* 121–127.

Nilsson, K. W., Sjoberg, R. L., Wargelius, H. L., Leppert, J., Lindstrom, L., & Oreland, L. (2007). The monoamine oxidase A (MAO-A) gene, family function and maltreatment as predictors of destructive behaviour during male adolescent alcohol consumption. *Addiction, 102,* 389–398.

Nobile, M., Giorda, R., Marino, C., Carlet, O., Pastore, V., Vanzin, L., et al. (2007). Socioeconomic status mediates the genetic contribution of the dopamine receptor D4 and serotonin transporter linked promoter region repeat polymorphisms to externalization in preadolescence. *Developmental Psychopathology, 19,* 1147–1160.

Noble, E. P., Blum, K., Khalsa, M. E., Ritchie, T., Montgomery, A., Wood, R. C., et al. (1993). Allelic association of the D2 dopamine receptor gene with cocaine dependence. *Drug and Alcohol Dependence, 33,* 271–285.

Oades, R. D., Lasky-Su, J., Christiansen, H., Faraone, S. V., Sonuga-Barke, E. J. S., Banaschewski, T., et al. (2008). The influence of serotonin and other genes and impulsive behavioral aggression and cognitive impulsivity in children with attention-deficit/hyperactivity disorder (ADHD): Finding from a family-based association test (FBAT) analysis. *Behavioral and Brain Functions, 48,* 4–48.

Ogawa, S., Lubahn, D. B., Korach, K. S., & Pfaff, D. W. (1997). Behavioral effects of estrogen receptor gene disruption in male mice. *Proceedings of the National Academy of Sciences of the USA, 94,* 1476–1481.

Oreland, L., Nilsson, K., Damberg, M., & Hallman, J. (2007). Monoamine oxidases: Activities, genotypes and the shaping of behavior. *Journal of Neural Transmission, 114,* 817–822.

Passamonti, L., Fera, F., Magariello, A., Cerasa, A., Gioia, M. C., Muglia, M., et al. (2006). Monoamine oxidase-A genetic variations influence brain activity associated with inhibitory control: New insight into the neural correlates of impulsivity. *Biological Psychiatry, 59,* 334–340.

Petronis, A., Gottesman, I. I., Kan, P., Kennedy, J. L., Basile, V. S., Paterson, A. D., et al. (2003). Monozygotic twins exhibit numerous epigenetic differences: Clues to twin discordance? *Schizophrenia Bulletin, 21,* 169–178.

Popova, N. K. (2006). From genes to aggressive behavior: The role of the serotonergic system. *Bioessays, 28,* 495–503.

Preuss, U. W., Koller, G., Bondy, B., Bahlmann, M., & Sokya, M. (2001). Impulsive traits and 5-HT2A receptor promoter polymorphism in alcohol dependents: Possible association but no influence of personality disorders. *Neuropsychobiology, 43,* 186–191.

Prichard, Z. M., Jorm, A. F., Mackinnon, A., & Easteal, S. (2007). Association analysis of 15 polymorphisms within 10 candidate genes for antisocial behavioral traits. *Psychiatric Genetics, 17,* 299–303.

Prom-Wormley, E. C., Eaves, L. J., Foley, D. L., Gardner, C. O., Archer, K. J., Wormley, B. K., et al. (2009). Monamine oxidase A and childhood adversity as risk factors for conduct disorder in females. *Psychological Medicine, 39,* 579–590.Ragnauth, A. K., Devidze, N., Moy, V., Finley, K., Googwillie, A., Kow, L. M., et al. (2005). Female oxytocin gene-knockout mice, in a semi-natural environment, display exaggerated aggressive behavior. *Genes, Brain and Behavior, 4,* 229–239.

Rajender, S., Pandu, G., Sharma, J. D., Gandhi, K. P. C., Singh, L., & Thangaraj, K. (2008). Reduced CAG repeats length in androgen receptor gene is associated with violent criminal behavior. *International Journal of Legal Medicine, 122,* 367–372.

Reif, A., Herterich, S., Strobel, A., Ehlis, A. C., Saur, D., Jacob, C. P., et al. (2006). A neuronal nitric oxide synthase (NOS-I) haplotype associated with schizophrenia modifies prefrontal cortex function. *Molecular Psychiatry, 11,* 286–300.

Reif, A., Jacob, C. P., Rujescu, D., Herterich, S., Lang, S., Gutknecht, L., et al. (2009). Influence of functional variant of neuronal nitric oxide synthase on impulsive behaviors in humans. *Archives of General Psychiatry, 66,* 41–50.

Reif, A., Rosler, M., Freitag, C. M., Schneider, M., Eujen, A., Kissling, C., et al. (2007). Nature and nurture predispose to violent behavior: Serotonergic genes and adverse childhood environment. *Neuropsychopharmacology, 32,* 2375–2383.

Ren-Patterson, R. F., Cochran, L. W., Holmes, A., Sherrill, S., Huang, S.-J., Tolliver ,T., et al. (2005). Loss of brain-derived neurotrophic factor gene allele exacerbates brain monoamine deficiencies and increases stress abnormalities of serotonin transporter knockout mice. *Journal of Neuroscience Research, 79,* 756–771.

Retz, W., Freitag, C. M., Retz-Junginger, P., Wenzler, D., Schneider, M., Kissling, C., et al., (2008). A functional serotonin transporter promoter gene polymorphism increases ADHD symptoms in delinquents: Interaction with adverse childhood environment. *Psychiatry Research, 158,* 123–131.

Retz, W., Retz-Junginger, P., Supprian, T., Thome, J., & Rosler, M. (2004). Association of serotonin transporter promoter gene polymorphism with violence: Relation with personality disorders, impulsivity, and childhood ADHD psychopathology. *Behavioral Science and Law, 22,* 415–425.

Retz, W., Rosler, M., Supprian, T., Retz-Junginger, P., & Thome, J. (2003). Dopamine D3 receptor gene polymorphism and violent behavior: Relation to impulsiveness and ADHD-related psychopathology. *Journal of Neural Transmission, 110,* 561–572.

Rhee, S. H., & Waldman, I. D. (2002). Genetic and environmental influences on antisocial behavior: A meta-analysis of twin and adoption studies. *Psychological Bulletin, 128,* 490–529.

Robins, L. N. (1966). *Deviant children grown up.* Baltimore, MD: Williams & Wilkins.

Rocha, B. A., Scearce-Levie, K., Lucas, J. J., Hiroi, N., Castanon, N., Crabbe, J. C., et al.(1998). Increased vulnerability to cocaine in mice lacking the serotonin-1B receptor. *Nature, 393,* 175–178.

Rodriguez-Jimenez, R., Avila, C., Ponce, G., Ibanez, M. I., Rubio, G., Jimenez-Arriero, M. A., et al. (2006). The TaqIA polymorphism linked to the DRD2 gene is related to lower attention and less inhibitory control in alcoholic patients. *European Psychiatry, 21,* 66–69.

Rogeness, G. A., Hernandez, J. M., Macedo, C. A., & Mitchell, E. L. (1982). Biochemical differences in children with conduct disorder socialized and undersocialized. *American Journal of Psychiatry, 139,* 307–311.

Roman, T., Schmitz, M., Polanczyk, G., Eizirik, M., Rohde, L. A., & Hutz, M. H. (2001). Attention-deficit hyperactivity disorder: A study of association with both the dopamine transporter gene and the dopamine D4 receptor gene. *American Journal of Medical Genetics: Part B. Neuropsychiatric Genetics, 105,* 471–478.

Roy, A., Adinoff, B., & Linnoila, M. (1988). Acting out hostility in normal volunteers: Negative correlation with levels of 5HIAA in cerebrospinal fluid. *Psychiatry Research, 24,* 187–194.

Sabol, S. Z., Hu, S., & Hamer, D. (1998). A functional polymorphism in the monoamine oxidase A gene promoter. *Human Genetics, 103,* 273–279.

Sacchetti, P., Mitchell, T. R., Granneman, J. G., & Bannon, M. J. (2001). Nurr1 enhances transcription of the human dopamine transporter gene through a novel mechanism. *Journal of Neurochemistry, 76,* 1565–1572.

Saha, S., Manchanda, S. K., Bhatia, S. C., & Nayar, U. (1993). Midbrain adrenergic mechanism modulating predatory attack behaviour induced by hypothalamic stimulation. *Indian Journal of Physiological Pharmacology, 93,* 121–126.

Sakai, J. T., Young, S. E., Stallings, M. C., Timberlake, D., Smolen, A., Stetler, G. L., et al. (2006). Case-control and within-family tests for an association between conduct disorder and 5HTTLPR. *American Journal of Medical Genetics, 141B,* 825–832.

Saudou, F., Amara, D. A., Dierich, A., LeMeur, M., Ramboz, S., Segu, L, et al. (1994). Enhanced aggressive behavior in mice lacking 5-HT1B receptor. *Science, 265,* 1875–1878.

Savitz, J. B., & Ramesar, R. S. (2004). Genetic variants implicated in personality: A review of the more promising candidates. *American Journal of Medical Genetics: Part B. Neuropsychiatric Genetics, 131,* 20–32.

Schimmelmann, B. G., Friedel, S., Dempfle, A., Warnke, A., Lesch, K. P., Walitza, S., et al. (2007). No evidence for preferential transmission of common valine allele of the Val66Met polymorphism of the brain-derived neurotrophic factor gene (BDNF) in ADHD. *Journal of Neural Transmission, 114,* 523–526.

Schinka, J. A., Letsch, E. A., & Crawford, F. C. (2002). DRD4 and novelty seeking: Results of meta-analyses. *American Journal of Medical Genetics: Part B. Neuropsychiatric Genetics, 114,* 643–648.

Schmidt, L. A., Fox, N. A., & Hamer, D. H. (2007). Evidence for a gene–gene interaction in predicting children's behavior problems: Association of serotonin transporter short and dopamine receptor D4 long genotypes with internalizing and externalizing behaviors in typically developing 7-year-olds. *Developmental Psychopathology, 19,* 1105–1116.

Sengupta, S. M., Grizenko, N., Schmitz, N., Schwartz, G., Ben Amor, L., Bellingham, J., et al. (2006). *COMT* Val [108/158]Met gene variant, birth weight, and conduct disorder in children with ADHD. *Journal of the American Academy of Child and Adolescent Psychiatry, 45,* 1363–1369.

Shih, J. C., Chen, K., & Ridd, M. J. (1999). Monoamine oxidase: From genes to behavior. *Annual Review of Neuroscience, 22,* 197–217.

Shih, J. C., & Thompson, R. F. (1999). Monoamine oxidase in neuropsychiatry and behavior. *American Journal of Human Genetics, 65,* 593–598.

Sjoberg, R., Ducci, F., Barr, C. S., Newman, T. K., Dell-Osso, L., Virkkunen, M., et al. (2008). A non-additive interaction of a functional *MAO-S* VNTR and testosterone predicts antisocial behavior. *Neuropsychopharmacology, 33,* 425–430.

Skowronek, M. H., Laucht, M., Hohm, E., Becker, K., & Schmidt, M. H. (2006). Interaction between the dopamine D4 receptor and the serotonin transporter promoter polymorphisms in alcohol and tobacco use among 15-year-olds. *Neurogenetics, 7,* 239–246.

Stallings, M. C., Corley, R. P., Dennehey, B., Hewitt, J. K., Krauter, K. S., Lessem, J. M., et al. (2005). A genome-wide search for quantitative trait loci that influence antisocial drug dependence in adolescence. *Archives of General Psychiatry, 62,* 1042–1051.

Stallings, M. C., Corley, R. P., Hewitt, J. K., Krauter, K. S., Lessem, J. M., Mikulich, S. K., et al. (2003). A genome-wide search for quantitative trait loci influencing substance dependence vulnerability in adolescence. *Drug Alcohol Dependence, 70,* 295–307.

Summers, C. H., & Greenberg, N. (1994). Somatic correlates of adrenergic activity during aggression in the lizard *Anolis carolinensis. Hormonal Behavior, 28,* 29–40.

Sweet, R. A., Nimgaonkar, V. L., Kamboh, M. I., Lopez, O. L., Zhang, F., & DeKosky, S. T. (1998). Dopamine receptor genetic variation, psychosis, and aggression in Alzheimer disease. *Archives of Neurology, 55,* 1335–1340.

Takeuchi, S., Imafuku, I., Waragai, M., Roth, C., Kanazawa, I., Buettner, R., et al. (1999). AP-2beta represses D(1A) dopamine receptor gene transcription in neuro2a cells. *Brain Research and Molecular Brain Research, 74,* 208–216.

Thapar, A., Langley, K., Fowler, T., Rice, F., Turic, D., Whittinger, N., et al. (2005). Catechol O-methyltransferase gene variant and birth weight predict early-onset antisocial behavior in children with attention-deficit/hyperactivity disorder. *Archives of General Psychiatry, 62,* 1275–1278.

Thome, J., Weijers, H. G., Wiesbeck, G. A., Sian, J., Nara, K., Boning, J., et al. (1999). Dopamine D3 receptor gene polymorphism and alcohol dependence: Relation to personality rating. *Psychiatric Genetics, 9,* 17–21.

Torgersen, S., Skre, I., Onstad, S., Edvardsen, J., & Kringlen, E. (1993). The psychometric–genetic structure of DSM–III–R personality disorder criteria. *Journal of Personality Disorders, 7,* 196–213.

Tuvblad, C., Raine, A., Zheng, M., & Baker, L. A. (2009). Genetic and environmental stability differs in reactive and proactive aggression. *Aggressive Behavior, 35,* 437–452.

Vage, J., Wade, C., Biagi, T., Fatjo, J., Amat, M., Lindblad-Toh, K., et al. (2010). Association of dopamine- and serotonin-related genes with canine aggression. *Genes, Brain and Behavior, 9,* 372–378.

Verdejo-Garcia, A., Lawrence, A. J., & Clark, L. (2008). Impulsivity as a vulnerability marker for substance-use disorders: Review of findings from high-risk research, problem gamblers and genetic association studies. *Neuroscience and Biobehavioral Reviews, 32,* 777–810.

Virkkunen, M., De Jong, J., Bartko, J., Goodwin, F. K., & Linnoila, M. (1989). Relationship of psychobiological variables to recidivism in violent offenders and impulsive fire setters: A follow-up study. *Archives of General Psychiatry, 46,* 600–603.

Waldman, I. D., Rowe, D. C., Abramowitz, A., Kozel, S. T., Mohr, J. H., Sherman, S. L., et al. (1998). Association and linkage of the dopamine transporter gene and

attention-deficit hyperactivity disorder in children: Heterogeneity owing to diagnostic subtype and severity. *American Journal of Human Genetics, 63,* 1767–1776.

Wang, J. C., Hinrichs, A. L., Stock, H., Budde, J., Allen, R., Bertelsen, S., et al. (2004).
Evidence of common and specific genetic effects: Association of the muscarinic acetylcholine receptor M2 (CHRM2) gene with alcohol dependence and major depressive syndrome. *Human Molecular Genetics, 13,* 1903–1911.

Wang, T., Huang, S. Y., Lin, W. W., Lo, H. Y., Wu, P. L., Wang, Y. S., et al. (2007). Possible
interaction between *MAO-A* and *DRD2* genes associated with antisocial alcoholism
among Han Chinese men in Taiwan. *Progress in Neuro-Psychopharmacology and
Biological Psychiatry, 31,* 108–114.

Weaver, I. C., Cervoni, N., Champagne, F. A., D'Alessio, A. C., Sharma, S., Seckl, J. R.,
et al. (2004). Epigenetic programming by maternal behavior. *Nature Neuroscience,
7,* 847–854.

Weaver, I. C. G., Champagne, F. A., Brown, S. E., Dymov, S., Sharma, S., Meaney, M. J.,
et al. (2005). Reversal of maternal programming of stress response in adult offspring
through methyl supplementation: Altering epigenetic marking later in life. *Journal
of Neuroscience, 25,* 11045–11054.

Widom, C. S., & Brzustowicz, L. M. (2006). MAOA and the "cycle of violence":
Childhood abuse and neglect, MAOA genotype, and risk for violent and antisocial
behavior. *Biological Psychiatry, 60,* 684–689.

Xu, K., Lichtermann, D., Lipsky, R. H., Franke, P., Liu, X., Hu, Y., et al. (2004).
Association of specific haplotypes of D2 dopamine receptor gene with vulnerability
to heroin dependence in 2 distinct populations. *Archives of General Psychiatry, 61,*
597–606.

Young, S. E., Corley, R. P., Stallings, M. C., Rhee, S. H., Crowley, T. J., & Hewitt, J. K.
(2002). Substance use, abuse and dependence in adolescence: Prevalence, symptom
profiles and correlates. *Drug and Alcohol Dependence, 68,* 309–322.

Young, S. E., Smolen, A., Hewitt, J. K., Haberstick, B. C., Stallings, M. C., Corley, R. P.,
et al. (2006). Interaction between MAO-A genotype and maltreatment in the risk
for conduct disorder: Failure to confirm in adolescent patients. *American Journal of
Psychiatry, 163,* 1019–1025.

Zaboli, G., Gizatullin, R., Nilsonne, A., Wilczek, A., Jonsson, E. G., Ahnemark, E., et
al. (2006). Tryptophan hydroxylase-1 gene variants associate with a group of suicidal borderline women. *Neuropsychopharmacology, 31,* 1982–1990.

Zak, P. J., Stanton, A. A., & Ahmadi, S. (2007). Oxytocin increases generosity in
humans. *PLoS ONE, 2,* e1128.

Zhang, H. B., Wang, Y. F., Li, J., Wang, B., & Yang, L. (2005). Association between
dopamine beta hydroxylase gene and attention deficit hyperactivity disorder complicated with disruptive behavior disorder [in Chinese]. *Zhonghua Er Ke Za Zhi, 43,*
26–30.

Zimmermann, P., Mohr, C., & Spangler, G. (2009). Genetic and attachment influences on adolescents' regulation of autonomy and aggressiveness. *Journal of Child
Psychology and Psychiatry, 50,* 1339–1347.

Zouk, H., McGirr, A., Lebel, V., Benkelfat, C., Rouleau, G., & Turecki, G. (2007). The
effect of genetic variation of the serotonin 1B receptor gene on impulsive aggressive
behavior and suicide. *American Journal of Medical Genetics: Part B. Neuropsychiatric
Genetics, 155,* 996–1002.

2

Genetic and Environmental Influences on Aggressive and Deviant Behavior

ANA V. KUNY-SLOCK AND JAMES J. HUDZIAK ■

INTRODUCTION

Over the past three decades, and especially in the past 5 years, a great deal of effort has been dedicated to discovering genetic effects on a wide range of human disorders, diseases, and behaviors. In the field of behavioral genetics, there have been a tremendous number of studies examining genetic and environmental contributions to deviant behavior. Improvements in the methodology of twin and adoption studies have demonstrated the influence of genetics on mental disorders throughout the lifespan. This chapter describes different ways in which aggression, rule breaking, and deviant behaviors are defined and then discusses the many approaches to identifying genetic influences on these definitions. Following a brief introduction and literature review, the chapter defines common quantitative measures of deviant behavior, describes the development and subtypes of deviant behavior, and examines behavioral genetic studies of deviant behavior. Specifically, aggression and deviant behavior are examined from a perspective of twin and adoption studies (including gene by environment), as well as of familial variable studies (e.g., assortative mating). Finally, a brief review of future approaches and promising areas of research concludes this chapter.

There are many ways to conceptualize and study deviant behavior in children. According to the research literature, conduct disorder (CD), oppositional defiant disorder (ODD), and attention-deficit/hyperactivity disorder (ADHD) are the most common reasons for which children are referred for mental health services (for a review, see Loeber, Burke, Lahey, Winters, & Zera, 2000), ODD and CD most often being associated with aggression. ODD has often been conceptualized as the milder version and prodrome of CD because it includes symptoms that are close to "normal" behavior (e.g., losing one's temper, arguing with adults). However, as researchers have begun to separate the two disorders, it has become clear that ODD may not be as harmless as previously thought. Instead of serving as a prodrome for CD, ODD exists on its own and may play a role in the development of a wide range of child psychopathology, including anxiety, depression, CD, and, later, antisocial personality disorder (Loeber, Burke, & Pardini, 2009). Furthermore, ODD remains a long-term predictor of many other disorders in childhood and adolescence even when controlling for other disorders (Copeland, Shanahan, Costello, & Angold, 2009). Is it possible, then, to tease apart the relation between genetic and environmental contributions and deviant behavior and their influence on resulting aggression? Using population-based genetics can help researchers to understand the development of deviant and antisocial behavior by allowing the study of genetic and environmental influences on developmental psychopathology, as well as whether disorders occur more often alone or in concert with other disorders.

Several research groups have demonstrated the contributions of both genetic and environmental factors to ODD, to CD, and to direct and relational aggression. This chapter goes into some detail on these findings later; however, suffice it to say that the literature is full of great examples from excellent research that aggression, no matter what name it goes by, is influenced by the complex interplay of genetic and environmental factors. Contrary to the previously held notion that one day science might discover the "gene" that causes a specific disorder, modern researchers have found that, in fact, many disorders are influenced by several risk and genetic factors (Rutter, Moffitt, & Caspi, 2006). Furthermore, the idea that a person's environment can influence and in fact change genetic mechanisms has placed the field of epigenetics at the cutting edge of this research area.

LITERATURE REVIEW

Although aggression is a normative part of human development and is present throughout the lifespan at varying levels, the research literature examining abnormal aggression encompasses several well-studied areas. One of the most consistent findings has been the distinct developmental trajectories found between individuals with childhood-onset conduct problems and those with adolescence-onset conduct problems (for a review, see Moffitt, 2006). These studies suggest that adolescents in the childhood-onset group show a much more aggressive, severe, and chronic pattern of antisocial behavior when compared with the adolescents in the adolescence-onset group (Frick & Loney, 1999; Moffitt, 2003; Woodward, Fergusson, & Horwood, 2002). These two distinct developmental pathways may be differentially related to risk factors for psychopathology throughout the lifespan. Research examining antisocial behaviors specifically has found four antisocial behavior trajectory groups: life-course persistent (LCP), adolescence-onset, childhood-limited, and low-trajectory groups for both sexes (Odgers et al., 2008). Odgers and colleagues (2008) report that social, familial, and neurodevelopmental risk factors frequently typify the childhoods of LCP individuals, but not the childhoods of those individuals on the adolescence-onset pathway. In addition, researchers found that, at age 32, individuals on the LCP pathway were experiencing mental and physical health and economic problems *and* engaging in violence. Individuals on the adolescence-onset pathway were also experiencing difficulties at age 32, but to a much less degree, clearly demonstrating the influence of age of onset on deviant behavior.

The influence of parenting on aggression is another important area of research. Forehand and colleagues, in their development of parenting protocols for noncompliant children, have done significant research on the link between parenting behaviors and the development of externalizing behavior in children. In the development of programs that aim to help parents address aggression, noncompliance, and oppositional behaviors in children (e.g., *Helping the Noncompliant Child*, McMahon & Forehand, 2003), researchers have identified specific parenting behaviors that predict the development and maintenance of externalizing behaviors in children. One such example is parenting behavior that is characterized by parent and child interactions with a high degree of coercion (for a review, see Granic & Patterson, 2006). The coercion hypothesis posits that infants innately use aversive behaviors (e.g., crying) to gain maternal attention and shape behaviors related to the infants' care and well-being (e.g., nourishment). As development progresses, young children develop skills that allow them to communicate more effectively in a less aversive fashion. According to the coercion hypothesis, certain conditions (e.g., ineffective parenting) increase children's reliance on aversive behaviors, and this situation over time leads to increasing levels of noncompliance (McKee, Colletti, Rakow, Jones, & Forehand 2008). For example, the coercive process occurs when a parent withdraws his or her command or fails to follow through in response to noncompliant behavior. This action negatively reinforces the child's behavior and may result in the parent seeking increasingly severe strategies by which to enforce rules or commands. In response, the child may increase his or her resistance (e.g., becoming more aggressive), resulting in a cycle that reinforces parent and child coercive responses.

In a related study operationalizing parent-directed aggression specifically, Nock and Kazdin (2002) examined the characteristics of children who engaged in this type of aggression and compared aggressive and nonaggressive individuals across several domains of functioning. This study found that aggressive individuals had lower frustration tolerance, were less able to adapt to stressful situations, and were more demanding of their parents. The families of these children showed increased levels of parental stress and poorer interpersonal relationships than the less aggressive families. Even after controlling for demographic differences and overall level of oppositional and aggressive behavior, lower frustration tolerance and less adaptability significantly predicted parent-directed aggression. This study suggests that it may be important to examine whether early physical aggression toward a parent is a precursor for other, more violent acts.

The relation between parenting and age of onset specifically was researched by Dandreaux and Frick (2009) in a study that examined theoretical differences between groups of adolescents with childhood-onset versus adolescence-onset conduct problems in a group of preadjudicated boys (ages 11 to 18). Consistent with the findings of other research groups, this study found that the childhood-onset group was characterized by higher rates of callous–unemotional traits, greater levels of dysfunctional parenting, and greater affiliation with delinquent peers in comparison with the adolescence-onset group.The importance of age of onset in differentiating between aggression trajectories has been well studied and is well developed in the research literature. Many research studies have found that there is significant variability in the severity and type of behavior demonstrated by children and adolescents who exhibit antisocial behavior related specifically to age of onset of the child's *first* antisocial behavior (e.g., Dandreaux & Frick, 2009; Lahey et al., 1999; Loeber, 1982; Loeber, Stouthamer-Loeber, & Green, 1991). In the National Institute of Mental Health's Methodology for Epidemiology of Mental Disorders in Children and Adolescents Study, Lahey and colleagues (1999) examined a large cross-sectional sample of individuals and found that 12-month prevalence significantly declined with later age of onset for behaviors such as bullying, starting fights, vandalism, theft, mugging, and use of a weapon. In addition, with the exception of truancy, as age of onset increased, overall aggressive behaviors decreased.

Although many studies have examined boys exclusively, more recent studies have taken a more gender-informed approach. Cullerton-Sen and colleagues (2008) examined the influence of gender on the relation between maltreatment and aggression. In this multi-informant study examining maltreated and non-maltreated children at an inner-city day camp, maltreatment was associated with aggressive conduct but varied based on factors such as gender, maltreatment subtype, and the form of aggression being examined. Overall, maltreatment was associated with physical aggression for boys and relational aggression for girls. Although physical abuse was associated with physical aggression in boys *and* girls, sexual abuse predicted relational aggression only for girls. These findings suggest that it is important to consider the moderating role of gender when examining the associations between maltreatment subtypes and aggression.

Many, if not most, studies tend to research aggressive behaviors by examining children who are at the high end of the distribution of aggression. In other words, to learn about aggression scientists study severe aggression. There may be some problems with such an approach. We know that aggression is continuously distributed across a continuum. All children show at least some symptoms of aggression; some show very few; others show mild, moderate, high, and even severe aggression. To learn about continuously distributed traits such as aggression by studying only the most aggressive is a bit like studying the function of the pancreas by studying only severe diabetes. Thus some scientists, including most who do research in the field of behavioral genetics, choose to study aggression across the continuum from low to high. There is a precedent for this approach. By now even the most critical of thinkers will agree that all behavior is brain based. Thus, if aggression is brain based and is continuously distributed, then regions of interest for aggression in the brain should be able to be identified in children who do not have severe problems with aggression but rather are "normally aggressive." Such work has already been done. In a study by Ducharme and colleagues (2011) that examines neuroanatomical correlates of aggression in healthy children, researchers found that differences in orbitofrontal cortex (OFC) and anterior cingulate cortex (ACC) cortical thickness/surface area and basal ganglia volumes were correlated with increased aggression traits, measured using the Aggression (AGG) scale of the Child Behavior Checklist (CBCL; Achenbach, 1991). Specifically, a positive correlation was found between bilateral striatum volume and AGG scores (right: $r = .187$, $p = .001$; left: $r = 0135$, $p = .015$). A negative correlation was found in males for the right OFC and right ACC ($n = 90$, $p < .005$) for cortical thickness. For females, no association between AGG and cortical thickness was found, although the authors note an unexpected positive correlation with the right temporal lobe. Additionally, females showed a negative correlation with the left OFC surface area ($n = 90$, $p < .005$), whereas males did not. This study suggests that the striatum, the bilateral OFC, and the right ACC play an important role in aggression regulation in children and that important sex differences may exist. Moreover, as the largest neuroanatomical study of aggression in healthy children, in the future this study may lead to the examination of neuroanatomical correlates and specific psychiatric diagnoses.

DEFINITION OF QUANTITATIVE MEASURES OF DEVIANT BEHAVIOR

Although aggression itself can be defined in several ways, for the purpose of this chapter aggressive behavior will be conceptualized as defined by the Aggression syndrome scale (AGG) of the Child Behavior Checklist (CBCL; Achenbach, 1991). This scale has been associated with negative behavioral outcomes and has been shown to be a good predictor of DSM ODD in young children and CD in older children (Hudziak et al., 2003). Furthermore, along with the AGG scale, some research studies have also included the Rule-Breaking Behavior syndrome scale (RB), which is associated with more deviant types of behavior, in order to understand genetic and environmental influences on a variety of aggressive behaviors. RB syndrome behaviors are as they sound; these are kids who break rules. RB behavior has been shown to be most predictive of adolescent substance use (Stanger, Dumenci, Kamon, & Burstein, 2004). The co-occurrence of AGG and RB has been well established in the research literature, as both syndromes are represented by items that point to the same direction of problem behavior. However, factor analyses of the CBCL items clearly results in two distinct syndromes (Achenbach, Verhulst, Baron, & Althaus, 1987; Cole, 1987; De Groot, Koot, & Verhulst, 1994; Verhulst, Achenbach, Althaus, & Akkerhuis, 1988), suggesting that AGG and RB are independent but highly correlated syndromes on the child-, teacher-, and self-report scales of the Achenbach System of Empirically Based Assessment (ASEBA; Achenbach & Rescorla, 2000).

Numerous studies use the Child Behavior Checklist (CBCL), completed by the parents; the Teacher Report Form (TRF), completed by the teacher; and the

Youth Self- Report (YSR) to obtain information on problem behavior throughout childhood (Achenbach & Rescorla, 2000). These data collection measures allow longitudinal multiple-informant assessment. At age 3, seven syndrome scales are obtained (Emotionally Reactive, Anxious/Depressed, Somatic Complaints, Withdrawn, Overactive Behavior, Aggressive Behavior, and Sleep Problems). At ages 7, 10, and 12, eight syndrome scales are obtained (Anxious/Depressed, Withdrawn, Somatic Complaints, Social Problems, Thought Problems, Attention Problems, Rule-Breaking Behavior, and Aggressive Behavior). At all ages, two broadband scales, Internalizing and Externalizing Problems (INT and EXT), are also obtained.

Other measures frequently used to assess aggressive behavior in children are the Conners' Rating Scales—Parent (CPRS-R:S; Conners, 2001) and Teacher Scales (CTRS-R:S; Conners, 2001). These measures summarize items on four scales: Oppositional, Cognitive Problems/Inattention, Hyperactivity, and the ADHD Index. The Oppositional subscale, which consists of the six items that loaded the highest in a factor analysis of all eight items of the DSM-IV ODD criteria (American Psychiatric Association, 2000), is frequently used in the assessment of aggressive behavior.

To assess parent contribution, adults are often assessed using the Adult Self-Report (ASR; Achenbach & Rescorla, 2003). The ASR is an empirically derived self-assessment of psychological problems for adults ages 18–59 that yields a quantitative score for eight empirically based symptom clusters (syndromes/problems) produced by factor analyses of the correlations among items. The eight syndromes are Anxious/Depressed, Withdrawn, Somatic Complaints, Thought Problems, Attention Problems, Aggressive Behavior, Rule-Breaking Behavior, and Intrusive Behavior. The assessment items can also be scored along six DSM-IV disorders relating to depression, anxiety, somatic, avoidant personality, attention-deficit/hyperactivity, and antisocial personality problems.

DEVELOPMENT AND SUBTYPES OF DEVIANT BEHAVIOR

Studies have shown that not only is some aggression normative but also that, in fact, certain aspects of aggression may be protective. In an accelerated longitudinal study, Stanger, Achenbach, and Verhulst (1997) found that although all individuals are at least somewhat aggressive, there are distinct differences across development and between sexes. Researchers in this study found that boys were generally more aggressive than girls. In fact, parent reports showed that parents reported one more AGG symptom for boys than for girls at all ages. Teacher reports were similar to parent reports for boys; however, for girls, teachers tended to report less than parents (by about one-half symptom), suggesting that teachers report differently for males versus females, whereas parents often do not. Furthermore, younger individuals were more aggressive overall than older children. In very young children (3-year-olds), socioeconomic status was found to play a major role in level of deviant behavior, whereas other factors (e.g., day care) did not. In general, these findings suggest that levels of aggression reduce over time and are slightly lower for girls.

Relational aggression has been defined as covert behaviors that are intended to damage a person's social standing or his or her social relationships (Archer & Coyne, 2005; Crick & Grotpeter, 1995). Although some researchers posit that relational aggression is more common in females, often suggesting that this is due to socialization and the high social costs sometimes associated with female physical aggression, a review by Archer and Coyne (2005) found that this changes throughout development. This review found that sex differences in indirect aggression among children are small at younger ages but increase from ages 8 to 11 years, reaching their peak during adolescence. Studies examining differences using self-reports of indirect aggression in adults have not found significant differences between men and women (Björkqvist, 2001; Forrest, Eatough, & Shevlin, 2005; Loudin, Loukas, & Robinson, 2003). In sum, gender differences in overall relational levels are not as large as previously suggested and vary throughout the lifespan. Furthermore, gender-sensitive approaches to measuring deviant behavior have shown that females, as well as males, may exhibit all types of aggressive behavior.

BEHAVIORAL GENETIC STUDIES OF DEVIANT BEHAVIOR

Molecular genetics references are not presented in this chapter because they have been reviewed in the first chapter of this book. Behavioral genetics studies employ a variety of designs, first to determine the degree to which traits are heritable, then to study developmental, sex, and other moderating variables on these traits. These studies have moved far beyond the dated debate of genes versus environments (Hudziak & Faraone, 2010) into gene–environment correlation, interaction, and ultimately epigenetic approaches.

TWIN AND ADOPTION STUDIES (INCLUDING GXE INTERACTIONS)

The development of child delinquent behavior disorders is influenced by genetic and environmental factors and their interaction; thus population-based and genetic studies can help to answer questions regarding whether disorders occur more often alone or co-occur with other disorders. Using population-based genetics can aid researchers in better understanding the development of deviant and antisocial behavior by allowing the study of genetic and environmental influences on developmental psychopathology throughout childhood and adolescence. This is especially important because influences can have different effects at different stages of development. The rationale, then, is for a family-based approach that examines genetic and environmental influences on developmental psychopathology. Because research has shown that all syndromes of child psychopathology are influenced by genetic and environmental factors and that these syndromes run in families (i.e., are often present in some form in one or both parents), a clinical approach should assess the emotional/behavioral functioning and wellness of the *entire* family prior to making health promotion, illness prevention, and intervention recommendations. In fact, child psychopathologies are probably influenced as much by the interaction of genetic and environmental influences as by their unique contributions. Additionally, as psychopathology runs in families (i.e., parents of children with emotional behavioral illnesses are more likely to have emotional behavioral illnesses themselves), parental psychopathology can affect the environment that a child grows up in.

Genetic analyses have suggested that there is a significant contribution from genetic factors to ODD in both boys and girls, in addition to common shared and nonshared environmental effects (Hudziak, Derks, Althoff, Copeland, & Boomsma, 2005). Whether distinct genetic factors can be identified for ODD and CD remains unclear, although some evidence from genetic studies suggests a common underlying condition (Eaves et al., 2000). Hudziak, Copeland, Stanger, and Wadsworth (2004), in a study using the CBCL measure of aggression (AGG), found that AGG was correlated with a diagnosis of ODD, whereas AGG and RB were correlated with a diagnosis of CD.

In a related study using multiple raters to examine genetic and environmental influences on AGG and RB, Bartels and colleagues (2003) found that genetic influences accounted for 79 and 69%, respectively, of the individual differences in RB and AGG behavior (defined as RB and AGG items on which *both* parents agreed) in boys and 56 and 72%, respectively, of the variance in RB and AGG in girls. Shared environmental influences were significant for RB only in girls, explaining 23% of the total variance. Furthermore, genetic influence explained 80% of the covariance between AGG and RB, similarly assessed using items endorsed by both parents. As the co-occurrence of AGG and RB is mainly caused by a common set of genes, children who suffer either AGG or RB in the clinical range are at equal risk to have the comorbid disorder as well. In this sample 50.0–63.9% of the children who were deviant on AGG were also deviant on RB, and vice versa. In sum, AGG and RB are independent but highly heritable behaviors that can co-occur, with genes and environment contributing to the co-occurrence.

In another study examining the ability of the CBCL to distinguish subtypes of aggressive behavior in 7-year-old twins within the AGG scale and exploring to what extent these subtypes are influenced by genetic and environmental factors for both sexes, Ligthart and colleagues (Ligthart, Bartels, Hoekstra, Hudziak, & Boomsma, 2005) identified two aggression subtypes, relational aggression and direct aggression, with a correlation between these subtypes of .58 for boys and .47 for girls. This study suggests that direct and relational aggression are both influenced by shared environmental factors but are influenced less by a shared genetic component (the genetic correlation was .54 for boys and .43 for girls). Researchers in this study found that for relational aggression, additive genetic influences accounted for 66% of the variance, whereas shared environment and nonshared environment accounted for 16 and 18% of the variance, respectively. Moreover, these findings suggest that although boys may have higher mean scores for both direct and relational subtypes of aggression, overall sex differences are largest for direct aggression. Specifically, additive genetic influences accounted for 53% of the variance in males and 60% in females; shared environment accounted for 23% of the variance in males and 13% in females; and nonshared environmental effects explained 24% of the variance in males and 27% in females. Covariance between relational and direct-aggression subtypes was primarily accounted for by additive genetics (55% for boys, 58% for girls) and shared environmental influences (33% for boys, 30% for girls). It is important to note that the aggression subtypes described in this study are not identical to the definitions used by other researchers (e.g., the definitions used by Crick, Casas, and Mosher, 1997, for relational aggression and by Björkqvist, 1994, for direct aggression).

In a review, Slutske and colleagues (2003) examined three behavioral-genetic investigations of ODD with a combined sample size of 4,056 twin pairs. The weighted mean heritability estimate was 60%, and the weighted mean shared family environmental factors estimate was 7% across the three studies (Burt, Krueger, McGue, & Iacono, 2001; Cronk et al., 2002; Eaves et al., 1997). Assuming that the ODD diagnosis had a reliability of approximately .80, Slutske, Cronk, and Nabors-Oberg (2003) estimated that approximately 13% of the variation in the risk for ODD symptoms could be explained by nonshared individual-specific environmental factors. This review suggests that shared familial and genetic factors accounted for approximately 67% of the variation in ODD risk. It is important to note that these results are similar to previous findings for CD.

The findings of the Burt et al. study (2001) examining whether the same genetic and environmental risk factors are involved in the development of both CD and ODD suggest that ODD and CD have some overlapping genetic factors but also specific genetic and unique environmental risk factors. Moreover, this study suggests that CD and ODD do share substantial overlap in shared family environmental risk factors. Within-twin correlations of .50 and .36 were demonstrated for boys and girls with cross-twin correlations of .35 and .28. Together, these findings suggest that ODD and CD may have distinct etiologies at the genetic and nonshared individual-specific environmental levels but may have the same shared familial risk factors.

In reviewing the current research literature examining environmental and genetic influences on child psychopathology, it is clear that behavioral genetic methods are at the cutting edge. New techniques are being applied to detect the most likely environmental causes among many risk factors for child psychopathology by examining the interaction between genes and environments. Recent studies have shown that it is not nature versus nurture, not genes versus environment, but rather genes *and* environment that influence childhood development and the development of mental disorders.

O'Connor, Deater-Deckard, Fulker, Rutter, and Plomin (1998), in a study examining antisocial behavioral problems and coercive parenting using genotype–environment correlations in late childhood and early adolescence, found that the direction of effects in socialization is critical to understanding the influence of nature and nurture. In this study, children who had been adopted were classified as being genetically "at risk" for antisocial behavior based on self-report measures of antisocial behavior completed by their biological mothers. To assess environmental factors, adoptive parents completed self-report measures on parenting styles (e.g., positive or inconsistent parenting) and parenting techniques most often used to manage their children's behavior between the ages of 7 and 12. Results showed that children who were at a "genetic risk" for antisocial behavior received more negative parenting from their adoptive parents than did the children who were in the "nongenetic risk" group.

A more recent study examined the genetic and environmental processes through which conduct problems in parents are transmitted to their children (D'Onofrio et al., 2007) by examining a high-risk sample of twins, their spouses, and their young adult offspring (n = 2,554) from 889 twin families in the Australian Twin Registry. Researchers used the number of CD symptoms in the sample to assess intergenerational transmission of conduct problems and found that intergenerational transmission was dependent on child gender. More specifically, although the magnitude of the intergenerational transmission was significant for all offspring, it was stronger for males (effect size [Cohen's d] = 0.21; 95% confidence interval, 0.15–0.17) than for females (d = 0.09; 95% confidence interval, 0.05–0.14). Moreover, conduct problems were mediated by environmental variables specifically related to parental CD in male but not in female children.

In addition to parenting effects, studies have examined the moderating effects of genetic factors on victimization in childhood (e.g., being bullied by peers). Previous research on the psychological effects of bullying has found that children's reactions to this type of victimization vary. Diathesis-stress models of psychopathology suggest the possibility that genetic differences may result in children having an underlying vulnerability to the effects of victimization in general. In a 2010 study, researchers tested the hypothesis that the relationship between bullying victimization and emotional problems was moderated by variation in the serotonin transporter (5HTT) gene by examining a group of 2,232 British children who made up the Environmental Risk (E-Risk) Study cohort (Sugden et al., 2010). Previous findings suggest that genetic variation in the serotonin transporter gene (5HTT) moderates whether children who have been victimized by stressful life events go on to develop emotional problems (Caspi et al., 2003). In particular, the length of the serotonin transporter linked polymorphic region (5HTTLPR) within the gene's promoter region contains two common alleles, the short (S) allele being associated with lower transcriptional efficiency than the long (L) allele. It has been suggested that this genetic variation of 5HTTLPR contributes to dysregulation of serotonergic neurotransmission (Hariri & Holmes, 2006; Holmes & Hariri, 2003) and that this variation is associated with differences in cortisol response to psychosocial challenges (Gotlib, Joormann, Minor, & Hallmayer, 2008). The Sugden et al. study (2010) found that children who have been frequently victimized by bullying and who have the SS genotype (i.e., two short alleles and thus lower transcription efficiency) were at increased risk for later developing emotional problems when compared with children with either the SL or LL genotype. This study illustrates that GxE studies are in fact observable and relevant when examining psychopathology in childhood. In a review of this area of work, Moffitt (2005) examined behavioral genetic research to examine questions of causation in developmental psychopathology. She has developed a menu of 11 recommendations for investigating the relations between genes and environment and negative outcomes. This list suggests ways in which today's researchers can integrate cutting-edge studies with the wider research literature.

1. "Main effects of G and E are small, but effects in GxE interactions are bigger" (p. 547). Genetically "at risk" populations may be affected more strongly by environmental risk factors.
2. "Gene–environment interplay has real-world authenticity" (p. 547). The research in several areas (e.g., assortative mating) has shown that psychopathology is sometimes clustered in families. Advances in our understanding of GxE interactions are applicable to real-world individuals and families.
3. "Longitudinal gene–environment research could solve the riddle of continuity" (p. 547). More studies combining longitudinal and behavioral genetic approaches are needed to help understand how psychopathology is maintained.
4. "Gene–environment studies should address the most potent risk factors for pathological behavior" (p. 548). Studies need to focus on capturing the full range of the items that are measured, from normal to the most severe. Developing studies that retain and examine families on the most severe end of the spectrum is critical if researchers are to understand which risk factors predict recurrent and persistent psychopathology.
5. "Gene–environment interplay research is valuable outside the family crucible at every point in the life course" (p. 548). Although the focus of this chapter is on the development of aggression and deviant behaviors in childhood and adolescence, the research literature would benefit from examining variables that affect an individual throughout the lifespan.
6. "Gene–environment interplay and endophenotypes for antisocial behavior" (p. 548). Endophenotypes are phenotypic traits or markers that are believed to represent biological factors that are under greater genetic influence than the specific disorder that they underlie (Gottesman & Gould, 2003). These traits may be easier to study because they are more normally distributed than specific disorders and because they can be examined in people without the disorder.

7. "Epigenetic processes as outcome variables in gene–environment interplay" (p. 548). Epigenetic research suggests that environments influence genes just as genes influence environments and provides promising new areas of study.

8. "Quantitative twin and adoption studies will play an important role in the study of gene–environment interplay" (p. 548). These types of studies will continue to be used to help researchers understand which phenotypes are the best candidates for more in-depth molecular studies and to evaluate whether factors such as allele differences are related to behavioral differences. Moreover, the use of twin and adoption data allows researchers to examine variations in genetic expression using matched pairs.

9. "Mouse and other animal models should become more important in the study of gene–environment interplay" (p. 548). The use of animal models may provide an easier avenue for researchers to examine the influence of environmental risk factors on genetic expression.

10. "Gene–environment interplay research requires social and behavioral scientists as well as geneticists" (p. 549). This line of research will promote increased interdisciplinary research.

11. "Gene intervention interplay?" (p. 549). According to Moffitt (2005), interventions are environments that are disentangled from genetic influence, and thus they provide the opportunity for researchers to examine whether specific genetic factors influence intervention success.

FAMILY STUDIES AND ASSORTATIVE MATING

Overall, the area of behavioral genetics is quickly advancing, but how does intergenerational transmission occur? Do humans who engage in increased rule-breaking behavior find other rule-breaking individuals more often than they find individuals with less or average rule-breaking behavior? Substance use disorders and antisocial behavior tend to cluster within families and are highly comorbid. Moreover, familial concentration of crime exists in the general population (Farrington, Jolliffe, Loeber, Stouthamer-Loeber, & Kalb, 2001; Rowe & Farrington, 1997). In fact, fewer than 10% of the families in any community may account for more than 50% of that community's criminal offenses (Moffitt, 2005). This family concentration of antisocial behavior may be explainable by genetic–environmental interplay between genetic risk factors (e.g., assortative mating) and by nongenetic social transmission of criminal behavior within families.

Assortative mating is important in understanding the distribution of genetic and environmental influences on disorders. It occurs when partners select each other from the population based in part on the presence or absence of particular traits shared by the partners (as opposed to random mating). For example, adults who are drug abusers may be more likely to partner and mate with other drug abusers, thus increasing the odds that "high risk" genes will be passed on to their offspring. Marital resemblance refers to mated pairs who are more similar for a phenotypic trait than would be expected by chance. This may result from phenotypic assortment, which refers to partner selection based on phenotype, and/or social homogamy, which refers to assortment due to shared environment. Marital resemblance may also increase over time due to marital interaction (i.e., interaction between partners living together leading to resemblance). Genetic consequences depend on the causes of assortment, but research has shown that under phenotypic assortment, the genetic variance increases, as does the genetic resemblance in first-degree relatives. This may lead to an underestimation of heritability in twin and family studies.

Sakai and colleagues (2004) found significant differences between samples of parents who had children in psychiatric care versus parents of children in a control group. In this study, differences were found in terms of antisocial behavior and substance dependence symptoms, supporting a homogamy hypothesis. For retrospective CD symptoms, significant associations were found between parents with children receiving psychiatric care but not between parents of children in the control group. Furthermore, mates of spouses who had substance dependence disorders displayed higher rates of substance dependence disorders than would be expected given the base rates for these disorders. This finding was supported across samples and regardless of the gender of the spouse with the substance dependence disorder. This study also found that assortment likely occurs for LCP antisocial behavior but not for adolescent-limited CD (Moffitt, 1993). The researchers in this study did not find support for cross-variable assortment for substance abuse or antisocial personality disorder. Overall, findings suggest that phenotypic assortment contributes to the genetic similarities between mates, resulting in offspring with increased genetic risk for CD symptoms. Moreover, it is likely that the home rearing environment of children is less adverse in families in which only one (or neither) parent exhibits antisocial characteristics than is the home environment of families in which both parents exhibit these characteristics.

FUTURE APPROACHES

Perhaps the most promising approach to understanding the variable expression of aggression in individuals is via the emerging field of epigenetics. Epigenetics is defined as postgenomic modification (either through histone acetylation or methylation). Histone acetylation is a common and reversible event that occurs daily, and under chronobiologic control, at a number of locations in the human genome. Methylation is thought to be more permanent and perhaps provides a biological basis for the understanding of how the environment may affect the function of the genome. Hudziak and Faraone (2010) have proposed a new model for the consideration of the classic GxE interaction paradigm. They propose that the model should be considered as GxEe, in which the little "e" represents epigenomic modification. In this model, environmental factors can lead to methylation events that can result in gene function being modified (e.g., being turned on or off). The E effect thus changes G via "e" with the resulting gene sequence unchanged but the function of the genome dramatically different (Bagot & Meaney, 2010). As Weaver and colleagues (2004) demonstrated in mice, the environment can directly influence the number of methyl marks on the NGFI-A promoter region of a gene, which in turn affects the mouse's ability to deal with stress. In a study of human suicides, this same approach has led to the provocative finding that individuals with a history of sustained abuse in their lives who ultimately commit suicide have significantly greater numbers of methylation marks on the promoter region of this same gene when compared with subjects who died in accidents (McGowan et al., 2009).

Using this same approach may benefit the study of genetic influences on aggression. The literature, taken together, indicates that concentrated poverty and the stressors associated with poverty (low educational attainment, parental substance abuse and psychopathology, and housing environment) all are associated with higher rates of CD, antisocial personality disorder, and all measured forms of aggression. It will be important for the field to answer the simple question: What is the biology of the relations between concentrated poverty and maladaptive aggressive outcomes? In other words, how does concentrated poverty affect the genome? How does concentrated poverty affect brain structure and function? One possible explanation is that the environmental factors associated with concentrated poverty directly lead to epigenetic modification of the genes that drive brain development and stress reactivity. This altered genetic function thus can lead to a change in the structure and function of the brain and ultimately to altered and maladaptive behavior.

Our current formulary of research tools will make it possible to test these ideas. By combining large population birth cohorts using genetic (epigenetic) and neuroimaging approaches and taking a developmental longitudinal approach, it may be possible to identify specific environmental contributors to altered epigenetic and ultimately brain–behavior relations of aggression.

REFERENCES

Achenbach, T. M. (1991). *Integrative guide for the 1991 CBCL/4–18, YSR, and TRF profiles*. Burlington, VT: University of Vermont, Department of Psychiatry.

Achenbach, T. M., & Rescorla, L. A. (2000). *Manual for ASEBA school-age forms and profiles*. Burlington, VT: University of Vermont, Department of Psychiatry.

Achenbach, T. M., & Rescorla, L. A. (2003). *Manual for the ASEBA adult forms and profiles*. Burlington, VT: University of Vermont, Research Center for Children, Youth, and Families.

Achenbach, T. M., Verhulst, F. C., Baron, G. D., & Althaus, M. (1987). A comparison of syndromes derived from the Child Behavior Checklist for American and Dutch boys aged 6–11 and 12–16. *Journal of Child Psychology and Psychiatry, 28*, 437–453.

American Psychiatric Association. (2000). *The diagnostic and statistical manual of mental disorders* (4th ed., text revision). Washington, DC: American Psychiatric Association.

Archer, J., & Coyne, S. M. (2005). An integrated review of indirect, relational, and social aggression. *Personality and Social Psychology Review, 9,* 212–230.

Bagot, R. C., & Meaney, M. J. (2010). Epigenetics and the biological basis of gene X environment interactions. *Journal of the American Academy of Child and Adolescent Psychiatry, 49,* 752–771.

Bartels, M., Hudziak, J. J., van den Oord, E. J., van Beijsterveldt, C. E., Rietveld, M. J., & Boomsma, D. I. (2003). Co-occurrence of aggressive behavior and rule-breaking behavior at age 12: Multi-rater analyses. *Behavior Genetics, 33,* 607–621.

Björkqvist, K. (1994). Sex differences in physical, verbal, and indirect aggression: A review of recent research. *Sex Roles, 30,* 177–188.

Björkqvist, K. (2001). Different names, same issue. *Social Development, 10,* 272–275.

Burt, S. A., Krueger, R. F., McGue, M., & Iacono, W. G. (2001). Sources of covariation among attention-deficit/hyperactivity disorder, oppositional defiant disorder, and conduct disorder: The importance of shared environment. *Journal of Abnormal Psychology, 110,* 516–525.

Caspi, A., Sugden, K., Moffitt, T.E., Taylor, A., Craig, I.W., Harrington, H., ... Poulton, R. (2003). Influence of life stress on depression: moderation by a polymorphism in the *5-HTT* gene. *Science, 301,* 386–389.

Cole, D. A. (1987). Utility of confirmatory factor analysis in test validation research. *Journal of Consulting and Clinical Psychology, 55,* 584–594.

Conners, C. K. (2001). *Conners Rating Scales—Revised.* New York/Toronto: Multi-Health Systems.

Copeland, W. E., Shanahan, L., Costello, E. J., & Angold, A. (2009). Childhood and adolescent psychiatric disorders as predictors of young adult disorders. *Archives of General Psychiatry, 66,* 764–772.

Crick, N. R., Casas, J. F., & Mosher, M. (1997). Relational and overt aggression in preschool. *Developmental Psychology, 33,* 579–588.

Crick, N. R., & Grotpeter, J. (1995). Relational aggression, gender, and social psychological adjustment. *Child Development, 66,* 710–722.

Cronk, N. J., Slutske, W. S., Madden, P. A. F., Bucholz, K. K., Reich, W., & Heath, A. C. (2002). Emotional and behavioral problems among female twins: An evaluation of the equal environments assumption. *Journal of the American Academy of Child and Adolescent Psychiatry, 41,* 827–837.

Cullerton-Sen, C., Cassidy, A. R., Murray-Close, D., Cicchetti, D., Crick, N. R., & Rogosch, F. A. (2008). Childhood maltreatment and the development of relational and physical aggression: The importance of a gender-informed approach. *Child Development, 79,* 1736–1751.

Dandreaux, D. M., & Frick, P. J. (2009). Developmental pathways to conduct problems: A further test of the childhood and adolescent-onset distinction. *Journal of Abnormal Child Psychology, 37,* 375–385.

De Groot, A., Koot, H. M., & Verhulst, F. C. (1994). Cross-cultural generalizability of the CBCL cross-informant syndromes. *Psychological Assessment, 6,* 225–230.

D'Onofrio, B. M., Slutske, W. S., Turkheimer, E., Emery, R. E., Harden, K. P., Heath, A. C., ... Martin, N. G. (2007). Intergenerational transmission of childhood conduct problems: A Children of Twins study. *Archives of General Psychiatry, 64,* 820–829.

Ducharme, S., Hudziak, J. J., Botteron, K. N., Ganjavi, H., Lepage, C., Collins, D. L., . . . Karama, S. (2011). Right anterior cingulate cortical thickness and bilateral striatal volume correlate with Child Behavior Checklist aggressive behavior scores in healthy children. *Biological Psychiatry, 70*(3), 283–290.

Eaves, L., Rutter, M., Silberg, J., Shillady, L., Maes, H. H., & Pickles, A. (2000). Genetic and environmental causes of covariation in interview assessments of disruptive behavior in adolescent twins. *Behavior Genetics, 30,* 321–334.

Eaves, L. J., Silberg, J. L., Meyer, J. M., Maes, H. H., Simonoff, E., Pickles, A., . . . Hewitt, J. K. (1997). Genetics and developmental psychopathology: 2. The main effects of genes and environment on behavioral problems in the Virginia twin study of adolescent behavioral development. *Journal of Child Psychology and Psychiatry, 38,* 965–980.

Farrington, D. P., Jolliffe, D., Loeber, R., Stouthamer-Loeber, M., & Kalb, L. (2001). The concentration of offenders in families, and family criminality in the prediction of boys' delinquency. *Journal of Adolescence, 24,* 579–596.

Forrest, S., Eatough, V., & Shevlin, M. (2005). Measuring adult indirect aggression: The development and psychometric assessment of the Indirect Aggression Scales. *Aggressive Behavior, 31,* 84–97.

Frick, P. J., & Loney, B. R. (1999). Outcomes of children and adolescents with oppositional defiant disorder and conduct disorder. In H. C. Quay & A. E. Hogan (Eds.), *Handbook of disruptive behavior disorders* (pp. 507–524). New York, NY: Plenum.

Gotlib, I. H., Joormann, J., Minor, K. L., & Hallmayer, J. (2008). HPA axis reactivity: A mechanism underlying the associations among 5-HTTLPR, stress, and depression. *Biological Psychiatry, 63,* 847–851.

Gottesman, I. I., & Gould, T. D. (2003). The endophenotype concept in psychiatry: Etymology and strategic intentions. *American Journal of Psychiatry, 160,* 636–645.

Granic, I., & Patterson, G. R. (2006). Toward a comprehensive model of antisocial development: A dynamic systems approach. *Psychological Review, 113,* 101–131.

Hariri, A. R., & Holmes, A. (2006). Genetics of emotional regulation: The role of the serotonin transporter in neural function. *Trends in Cognitive Sciences, 10,* 182–191.

Holmes, A., & Hariri, A. R. (2003). The serotonin transporter gene-linked polymorphism and negative emotionality: Placing single gene effects in the context of genetic background and environment. *Genes, Brain and Behavior, 2,* 332–335.

Hudziak, J. J., Copeland, W., Stanger, C., & Wadsworth, M. (2004). Screening for DSM-IV externalizing disorders with the Child Behavior Checklist: A receiver-operating characteristic analysis. *Journal of Child Psychology and Psychiatry, 45,* 1299–1307.

Hudziak, J. J., Derks, E. M., Althoff, R. R., Copeland, W., & Boomsma, D. I. (2005). The genetic and environmental contributions to oppositional defiant behavior: A multi-informant twin study. *Journal of the American Academy of Child and Adolescent Psychiatry, 44,* 907–914.

Hudziak, J. J., & Faraone, S. V. (2010). The new genetics in child psychiatry. *Journal of the American Academy of Child and Adolescent Psychiatry, 49,* 729–735.

Hudziak, J. J., van Beijsterveldt, C. E. M., Bartels, M., Rietveld, M. J. H., Rettew, D. C., Derks, E. M., & Boomsma, D. I. (2003). Individual differences in aggression: Genetic analyses by age, gender, and informant in 3-, 7-, and 10-year-old Dutch twins. *Behavior Genetics, 33,* 575–589.

Lahey, B. B., Goodman, S. H., Waldman, I. D., Bird, H., Canino, G., Jensen, P., . . . Applegate, B. (1999). Relation of age of onset to the type and severity of child and adolescent conduct problems. *Journal of Abnormal Child Psychology, 27,* 247–260.

Ligthart, L., Bartels, M., Hoekstra, R. A., Hudziak, J. J., & Boomsma, D. I. (2005). Genetic contributions to subtypes of aggression. *Twin Research and Human Genetics, 8,* 483–491.

Loeber, R. (1982). The stability of antisocial and delinquent behavior: A review. *Child Development, 53,* 1431–1446.

Loeber, R., Burke, J. D., Lahey, B. B., Winters, A., & Zera, M. (2000). Oppositional defiant and conduct disorder: A review of the past 10 years: Part I. *Journal of the American Academy of Child and Adolescent Psychiatry, 39,* 1468–1484.

Loeber, R., Burke, J., & Pardini, D. (2009). Perspectives on oppositional defiant disorder, conduct disorder, and psychopathic features. *Journal of Child Psychology and Psychiatry, 50,* 133–142.

Loeber, R., Stouthamer-Loeber, M., & Green, S. (1991). Age at onset of problem behavior in boys, and later disruptive and delinquent behaviors. *Criminal Behavior and Mental Health, 1,* 229–246.

Loudin, J. L., Loukas, A., & Robinson, S. (2003). Relational aggression in college students: Examining the roles of social anxiety and empathy. *Aggressive Behavior, 29,* 430–439.

McGowan, P. O., Sasaki, A., D'Alessio, A. C., Dymov, S., Labonté, B., Szyf, M., . . . Meaney, M. J. (2009). Epigenetic regulation of the glucocorticoid receptor in human brain associates with childhood abuse. *Nature Neuroscience, 12*(3), 342–348.

McKee, L., Colletti, C., Rakow, A., Jones, D. J., & Forehand, R. (2008). Parenting and child externalizing behaviors: Are the associations specific or diffuse? *Aggression and Violent Behavior: A Review Journal, 13,* 201–215.

McMahon, R. J., & Forehand, R. (2003). *Helping the noncompliant child: Family-based treatment for oppositional behavior*(2nd ed.). New York, NY: Guilford Press.

Moffitt, T. E. (1993). Adolescence-limited and life-course-persistent antisocial behavior: A developmental taxonomy. *Psychological Review, 100,* 674–701.

Moffitt, T. E. (2003). Life-course-persistent and adolescence-limited antisocial behavior: A 10-year research review and a research agenda. In B. Lahey, T. Moffitt, & A. Caspi (Eds.), *Causes of conduct disorder and juvenile delinquency* (pp. 49–75). New York, NY: Guilford Press.

Moffitt, T. E. (2005). The new look of behavioral genetics in developmental psychopathology: Gene–environment interplay in antisocial behaviors. *Psychological Bulletin, 131,* 533–554.

Moffitt, T. E. (2006). Life-course-persistent versus adolescence-limited antisocial behavior. In D. Cicchetti & D. J. Cohen (Eds.), *Developmental psychopathology: Vol. 3. Risk, disorder, and adaptation* (2nd ed., pp. 570–598). New York, NY: Wiley.

Nock, M., & Kazdin, A. E. (2002). Parent-directed physical aggression by clinic-referred youths. *Journal of Clinical Child and Adolescent Psychology, 31,* 193–205.

O'Connor, T. G., Deater-Deckard, K., Fulker, D., Rutter, M., & Plomin, R. (1998). Genotype–environment correlations in late childhood and early adolescence: Antisocial behavioral problems in coercive parenting. *Developmental Psychology, 34,* 970–981.

Odgers, C. L., Moffitt, T. E., Broadbent, J. M., Dickson, N. P., Hancox, R., Harrington, H., . . . Caspi, A. (2008). Female and male antisocial trajectories: From childhood origins to adult outcomes. *Development and Psychopathology, 20,* 673–716.

Rowe, D. C., & Farrington, D. P. (1997). The familial transmission of criminal convictions. *Criminology, 35,* 177–201.

Rutter, M., Moffitt, T. E., & Caspi, A. (2006). Gene-environment interplay and psychopathology: Multiple varieties but real effects. *Journal of Child Psychology and Psychiatry, 47,* 226–261.

Sakai, J. T., Stallings, M. C., Mikulich-Gilbertson, S. K., Corley, R. P., Young, S. E., Hopfer, C. J., & Crowley, T. J. (2004). Mate similarity for substance dependence and antisocial personality disorder symptoms among parents of patients and controls. *Drug and Alcohol Dependence, 75,* 165–175.

Slutske, W. S., Cronk, N. J., & Nabors-Oberg, R. E. (2003). Familial and genetic factors. In C. A. Essau (Ed.), *Conduct and oppositional defiant disorders: Epidemiology, risk factors, and treatment* (pp. 137–162). Mahwah, NJ: Erlbaum.

Stanger, C., Achenbach, T. M., & Verhulst, F. C. (1997). Accelerated longitudinal comparisons of aggressive versus delinquent syndromes. *Developmental Psychopathology, 9,* 43–58.

Stanger, C., Dumenci, L., Kamon, J., & Burstein, M. (2004). Parenting and children's externalizing problems in substance-abusing families. *Journal of Clinical Child and Adolescent Psychology, 33,* 590–600.

Sugden, K., Arseneault, L., Harrington, H. L., Moffitt, T. E., Williams, B., & Caspi, A. (2010).The serotonin transporter gene moderates the development of emotional problems among children following bullying victimization. *Journal of the American Academy of Child and Adolescent Psychiatry, 49,* 830–840.

Verhulst, F. C., Achenbach, T. M., Althaus, M., & Akkerhuis, G. W. (1988). A comparison of syndromes derived from the Child Behavior Checklist for American and Dutch girls aged 6–11 and 12–16. *Journal of Child Psychology and Psychiatry, 29,* 879–895.

Weaver, I. C., Cervoni, N., Champagne, F. A., D'Alessio, A. C., Sharma, S., Secki, J. R., . . . Meaney, M. J. (2004). Epigenetic programming by maternal behavior. *Nature Neuroscience, 7,* 847–854.

Woodward, L. J., Fergusson, D. M., & Horwood, L. J. (2002). Romantic relationships of young people with childhood and adolescent onset antisocial behavior problems. *Journal of Abnormal Child Psychology, 30,* 231–243.

3

Neuroanatomic Maturation and Aggression during Adolescence

JAY N. GIEDD, ELIZABETH ADEYEMI,
MICHAEL STOCKMAN, AARON ALEXANDER-BLOCK,
NANCY RAITANO LEE, ARMIN RAZNAHAN,
RHOSHEL K. LENROOT, AND MARKUS J. P. KRUESI ■

On the morning of August 1, 1966, Charles Whitman, a 25-year-old student at the University of Texas at Austin, went to the top tier balcony of a the 27-story campus Tower building and opened fire on the people below. By the time he was shot and killed by police, the former Marine, equipped with an arsenal of four high-powered rifles and several handguns, had killed 16 people and wounded 32. An autopsy performed on Whitman revealed a brain tumor affecting his amygdala—an area of the brain involved in anger and fear reactions. The case of the Texas Tower Sniper, as it came to be called, renewed debate about the relationship between violent criminal acts and overt pathology of the brain. It led some to conclude that heinous violence and aggression can often be accounted for by damage to certain parts of the brain. However, in the vast majority of violent aggressive criminal acts, there is no tumor, lesion, or gross "pathology" of the brain in the usual sense of the word. Human behavior is a prototypical example of a multiply determined phenomenon—many factors both biological and environmental contribute to even the simplest of decisions and actions.

From a developmental psychology perspective, factors related to the perpetration of violent criminal acts include aggression, the ability to control impulses, susceptibility to peer pressure, and decision making in highly emotive contexts. Key observations to account for, both supported by a vast amount of international data, are (1) an increase in the amount of violent criminal acts between the ages of 18 and 24 and (2) a much higher percentage of perpetrators and/or victims among males (see Figure 3.1).

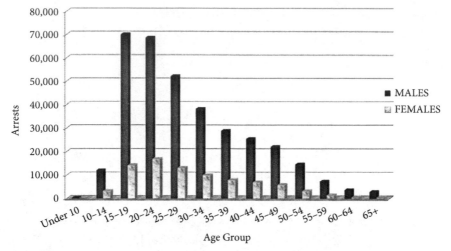

Figure 3.1 Number of arrests made for violent crimes in the United States during 2010 by age group and gender.

SOURCE: Federal Bureau of Investigation Uniform Crime Reports—Crime in the United States—Arrests. http://www.fbi.gov/about-us/cjis/ucr/crime-in-the-u.s.-2010/persons-arrested.

In this chapter we discuss adolescent changes in brain anatomy, as assessed by magnetic resonance imaging (MRI), that may be related to these observations. MRI combines a powerful magnet, radio waves, and sophisticated computer software to produce exquisitely accurate pictures of brain anatomy (i.e., anatomic MRI) and physiology (i.e., functional MRI [fMRI]) without the use of ionizing radiation. The safety of MRI allows not only the scanning of healthy children and adolescents but also repeated scanning throughout the course of development. These features and the widespread availability of MRI technology have led to thousands of studies of brain development in health and illness, launching a new era of pediatric neuroscience.

In anatomic MRI brain tissue is usually classified as gray matter or white matter. The constituents of gray matter vary by age and region (e.g., cortical vs. subcortical) but in general consist of cell bodies, dendrites, and dendritic processes, including synapses—the junctions between communicating brain cells (Braitenberg, 2001). White matter is comprised mainly of axons wrapped in myelin, as elaborated in a later section. Although gray matter and white matter are bound by lifelong reciprocal relationships, they have different developmental trajectories. Whereas gray matter developmental trajectories follow an inverted-U-shaped curve, with peak sizes occurring at different times in different regions, white matter increases throughout childhood and adolescence.

BEHAVIOR ARISES FROM DISTRIBUTED NEURAL NETWORKS

Before examining anatomical maturational trajectories of individual brain components of interest in relation to risk for criminal violence, it is important to emphasize that cognition and behavior are not localized to single brain regions but emanate from complex and dynamic interactions among disparate parts of the brain. With that caveat in mind, we review data regarding key nodes of the relevant circuitry.

Amygdala

We begin with the amygdala because it is the structure most often implicated in the literature on violent behavior. The amygdala (from the Latin word for "almond," denoting its size and shape) is a gray-matter structure located in the medial temporal lobe of the brain. It is not a homogenous structure, being composed of at least 13 distinct nuclei, each with different incoming and outgoing connections. The amygdala is highly connected to the hypothalamus, orbitofrontal region, and ventral striatum as part of a brain network related to the regulation of emotion, reward, decision making, and assessment of the importance of environmental stimuli.

Early understanding of the amygdala's role in processing emotions and salience came from observations of the effects of damage to the area in rhesus monkeys. In the 1930s Heinrich Kluver and Paul Bucy studied the effects of lesions to the amygdala and described a syndrome that now bears their name, characterized by a lack of fear and general dampening of emotional response, hypersexuality, hyperorality (compulsive tendency to examine objects by mouth), and two dietary changes: overeating and eating items not usually in the monkeys' diet. The insights provided by Kluver and Bucy have been extended and refined by subsequent animal lesion studies and human neuroimaging.

Amygdala dysfunction is sometimes described as being related to "rage," although its function seems to be more related to fear than aggression per se. Electrical stimulation of the amygdala causes anxiety, not aggression. Studies with fMRI of anxious or depressed teenagers show an abnormal amygdala response to social stimuli. For instance, when shown pictures of fearful faces, anxious youths show an exaggerated amygdala response, whereas depressed youths show a blunted amygdala response. Anatomic neuroimaging studies of children with conduct disorder (CD) report smaller amygdala volumes (Huebner et al., 2008; Sterzer, Stadler, Poustka, & Kleinschmidt, 2007) or reduced size of the temporal cortex (which encompasses the amygdala; Kruesi, Casanova, Mannheim, & Johnson-Bilder, 2004).

During the second decade of life the size of the amygdala increases slightly, more so in males than in females (see upper panels, Figure 3.2). This male–female

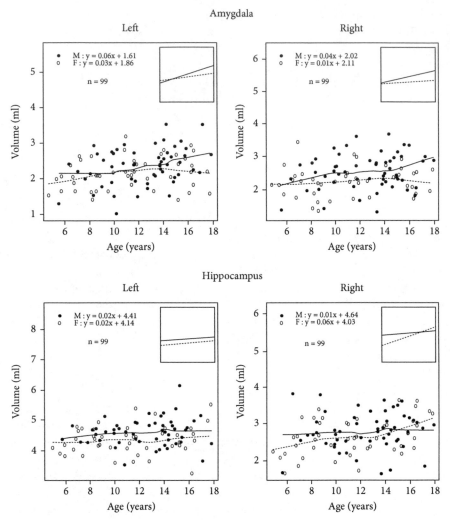

Figure 3.2 Scatterplots by age and gender of left and right amygdala and hippocampal volume for children and adolescents (ages 4–18 years; $n = 99$). Nonlinear, local regression curve fitting is displayed. The boxes in each upper right corner show linear regression models for males (solid lines) and females (dashed lines).

difference is consistent with an abundance of androgenic hormone receptors in the amygdala. However, the relationship between testosterone, amygdala size, amygdala physiology, and behavior has not yet been well characterized.

Hippocampus

A structure closely related to the amygdala is the hippocampus (from the Latin word for "sea horse," describing its shape). The hippocampus lies adjacent to the amygdala in the medial temporal part of the brain. The hippocampus is a node for many neurobehavioral circuits, but it is most known for its role in memory storage and retrieval.

The more-than-50-year contribution of Henry Molaison (HM), one of the most famous case studies in the history of neuroscience, provided an enormous amount of insight into the function of the hippocampus. Due to severe intractable seizures, HM had surgery when he was 27 years old that removed the hippocampi and surrounding tissue on both sides of his brain. The operation was successful in abating the seizures but left HM with a profound anterograde amnesia in which he could not encode new information into long-term memory. Interestingly, his short-term memory was intact, and he could learn new motor skills (i.e., procedural memories) but was not able to remember how he learned them. This indicated that short-term memory, long-term memory, and procedural memory had distinct neural circuitry and paved the way for generations of future studies. HM died on December 2, 2008, and donated his brain for scientific investigation. Efforts are under way at the University of California in San Diego to conduct the most thorough investigation of its kind to catalogue HM's brain at cellular resolution.

Relationships between memory function and hippocampal size have also been noted in several species. Food-storing species of birds have larger hippocampi than related non-food-storing species (Krebs, Sherry, Healy, Perry, & Vaccarino, 1989; Sherry, Vaccarino, Buckenham, & Herz, 1989), and in mammals a similar example can be found in voles. Male voles of the polygamous species travel far and wide in search of mates. They perform better than their female counterparts on laboratory measures of spatial ability and have significantly larger hippocampi (Sherry, Jacobs, & Gaulin, 1992). Conversely, in the monogamous vole species, which do not show male–female differences in spatial ability, no sexual dimorphism of hippocampal size is seen (Jacobs, Gaulin, Sherry, & Hoffman, 1990). In humans, correlations between memory for stories and left hippocampal volume have also been noted (Goldberg, Torrey, Berman, & Weinberger, 1994; Lencz et al., 1992). A study of taxi drivers in London found that they had larger hippocampi than controls, thought to be related to the extensive amount of navigational memory required for their work (Maguire et al., 2000).

Like that of the amygdala, the size of the hippocampus (see lower panels, Figure 3.2) increases slightly after puberty, and the behavioral implications remain to be well characterized. However, in contrast to the amygdala, it has a preponderance of estrogenic receptors and increases more in adolescent females than males. There is less direct evidence for the role of the hippocampus in the manifestation of inappropriate aggression than for the amygdala; however, one might speculate that anomalies of conditioned learning or failing to learn from consequences of previous transgressions may play a part.

Basal ganglia

The basal ganglia are a collection of subcortical nuclei that are involved in circuits mediating decision making, reward, movement, higher cognitive functions, attention, and affective states. Anomalous volumes of basal ganglia structures have been reported for almost all neuropsychiatric disorders that have been investigated by neuroimaging (Giedd, Shaw, Wallace, Gogtay, & Lenroot, 2006). The basal ganglia are composed of the caudate, putamen, globus pallidus, sub-thalamic nucleus, and substantia nigra. Because of the small size and ambiguity of magnetic resonance signal contrast of the borders defining the structures, only the first three are readily quantifiable by MRI, and automated techniques have been established as reliable only for measurement of the caudate. Like the cortical gray matter structures, the caudate nucleus follows an inverted-U-shaped developmental trajectory. Caudate size peaks at age 10.5 years in girls and 14.0 years in boys. The shape of the caudate developmental trajectory is similar to that of frontal gray matter, with which it shares extensive connections.

Interestingly, several scientists have targeted the caudate when examining aggression in both animal and human models. In the 1970s, one such scientist, Jose Manuel Rodriguez Delgado, a professor of physiology at Yale University, became renowned for his "mind-controlling" work. His most famous experiment took place in 1963 in Cordoba, Spain, when Delgado tamed the aggressive instincts of a fighting bull with the push of a button. At the bull-breeding ranch, Delgado implanted radio-equipped electrode arrays, called stimoceivers, into the caudate nucleus of several fighting bulls. He stood in the bullring with one bull at a time, and, by pressing a button on a handheld transmitter, Delgado forced a charging bull to skid to a halt a few feet away from him.

Delgado focused on neural regions (such as the caudate nucleus) that elicit and inhibit aggression and that also have a very high concentration of dopaminergic terminals. Dopamine (DA) is the dominant neurochemical currency of basal ganglia communication. The dopamine system is part of a behavioral activation network that alters incentive-motivated acts (Siever, 2008; Wahlstrom, White, & Luciana, 2010). The dopaminergic system undergoes dramatic changes during adolescence, including a sharp increase in the number of DA receptors. This is consistent with functional MRI studies demonstrating larger activation in the nucleus accumbens, orbitofrontal cortex, and anterior cingulate cortex in response to rewarding stimuli (Wahlstrom et al., 2010).

The serotonin system also undergoes substantial changes during adolescence and, in addition to its involvement in basal ganglia structures, also modulates the expression of aggression via actions in the orbital frontal cortex and anterior cingulate cortex. Selective serotonin reuptake inhibitors may reduce impulsive aggression, and serotonin reduction correlates with decreased learning of cooperation and a lowered perception of trustworthiness (Siever, 2008).

Cerebellum

The cerebellum, although traditionally associated with motor control functions, also plays a prominent role in higher cognitive functions and emotional control. Reports by Aaron Berman on rhesus monkeys that were part of Harry Harlow's maternal deprivation studies showed that lesions of the central part of the cerebellum made highly aggressive rhesus monkeys more docile (Berman, Berman, & Prescott, 1978). This finding led to intervention studies in humans indicating that electrodes implanted in the cerebellum to reduce seizures also had profound effects on reduction of aggression and improvements in anxiety and depression (Riklan, Marisak, & Cooper, 1974). Heath, Cox, and Lustick (1974) noted that neuronal firing patterns in the fastigial nucleus of the cerebellum correlated with subjective reports of fear and anger.

As seen in Figure 3.3, the cerebellum has a different developmental course than the cerebrum and overall a maturational profile unique among brain components. It is late maturing, not reaching peak size until age 15.6 years for males and 11.8 years for females (Tiemeier et al., 2010). The protracted maturation is particularly evident for the neocerebellum, which is evolutionarily the most recent. This pattern of more evolutionarily recent structures taking the longest to mature holds for parts of the frontal lobe as well and seems to be a general pattern of brain development.

Another feature evident from Figure 3.3 is that cerebellum maturation is different for males and females. The cerebellum is among the most sexually dimorphic of brain structures, being 10–13% larger in males depending on the age of comparison. The function and development of the cerebellum are modulated by its many estrogen and progesterone receptors (Ikeda & Nagai, 2006; Perez, Chen, & Mufson, 2003), and the Purkinje cells of the cerebellum are a major site for neurosteroid formation (Tsutsui, 2006).

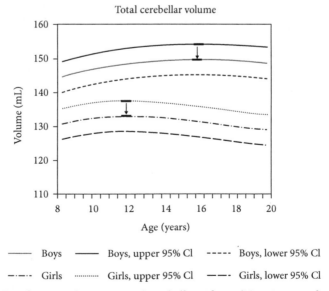

Figure 3.3 Developmental trajectory of cerebellar volume ($N = 181$ scans from 25 males and 25 females ages 4–24 years each scanned at least three times).

The cerebellum is also the least heritable of brain structures examined by our group (Giedd, Schmitt, & Neale, 2007; Wallace et al., 2006). By comparing similarities between monozygotic (MZ) twins, who share approximately 100% of the same genes, and dizygotic (DZ) twins, who share approximately 50% of the same genes, structural equation modeling (SEM) can be used to assess the relative contributions of genetic and nongenetic influences on trajectories of brain development. SEM describes the interacting effects as (A) additive genetic, (C) shared environmental, or (E) unique environmental factors (Neale, Cardon, & North Atlantic Treaty Organization Scientific Affairs Division., 1992). Additive genetic effects (i.e., "heritability") for total cerebral and lobar volumes (including gray matter and white matter subcompartments) range from 0.77 to 0.88 (Wallace et al., 2006). For the cerebellum the additive genetic effects are by far the lowest at 0.49. Low heritability suggests that the cerebellum is especially sensitive to environmental influences, and this, along with its protracted maturation, makes the cerebellum particularly vulnerable to effects of hypoxia, toxins, or other environmental factors (Ciesielski & Knight, 1994; Lesnik, Ciesielski, Hart, Benzel, & Sanders, 1998).

Prolonged maturation, large male–female differences, high influence from the environment, and lesion/electrode studies indicating its role in aggression make the cerebellum a strong target for investigations of the neurobiology of aggression.

PREFRONTAL CORTEX

The prefrontal cortex (PFC) plays a prominent role in the neural circuitry involved in judgment and impulse control. It is a "high association" area integrating input from throughout the brain as it weighs past memories, current environmental circumstances, and future goals to guide decision making.

The relationship between the PFC and decision making was famously demonstrated in the case of Phineas Gage. In 1848 Gage was a 25-year-old, hardworking, responsible railway foreman working on the Rutland and Burlington line near Cavendish, Vermont, when he suffered a horrific accident. While using a 3½-foot tapered iron rod to pack blasting powder, he triggered a spark and an explosion. The iron rod was rocketed into his left cheek, through his prefrontal cortex, and out the top of his skull. He did not lose consciousness and was taken about a mile by oxcart to receive medical attention. He was seen by two doctors, Edward Williams and John Harlow. Dr. Harlow's subsequent reports included the now epic assessment (based on changes in impulse control, personality, and demeanor noted by friends and family) that "Gage was no longer Gage." Although the severity of his impairments in the decade between the accident and his death has recently been challenged, the case has had an undeniable impact on neuroscience and localization of cerebral function.

The role of the PFC in higher cognitive functions and emotional control and the fact that it is one of the brain areas most different from our nearest genetic species, the chimpanzee, has made the prefrontal cortex the focus of many neu-roimaging and psychological investigations. Its maturation is notable as being particularly prolonged, not reaching adult levels of cortical thickness until approximately age 25 (see Figure 3.4).

The relatively late maturation of the PFC has prominently entered discourse affecting social, legislative, judicial, parenting, and educational realms. It is also consistent with a growing body of literature indicating a changing bal-ance between earlier maturing limbic system networks (which are the seat of emotion) and later maturing frontal systems. The frontal–limbic relationship is highly dynamic. Appreciating the interplay between limbic and cognitive systems is imperative for understanding decision making during adolescence. Psychological tests are usually conducted under conditions of "cold cognition"—hypothetical, low-emotion situations. However, real-world decision making often occurs under conditions of "hot cognition"—high arousal, with peer pressure and real consequences. Neuroimaging investigations continue to discern the dif-ferent biological circuitry involved in hot and cold cognition and are beginning to map how the parts of the brain involved in decision making mature.

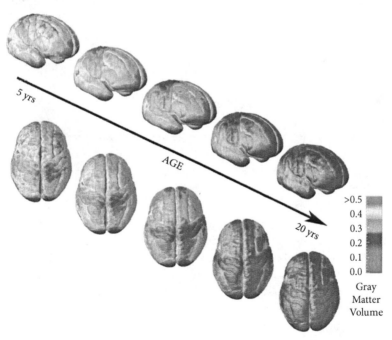

Figure 3.4 Right lateral and top views of the dynamic sequence of gray matter matura-tion over the cortical surface. Red indicates more gray matter, blue less gray matter. As gray matter declines over the course of adolescence "bluing" may be interpreted as maturation in the sense that it is approaching smaller adult values. The prefrontal cortex, an integral part of brain circuitry involved in judgment and impulse control, is among the latest to mature.

WHITE MATTER CHANGES AND "CONNECTIVITY"

The "white" of white matter is from the color of myelin, a fatty insulating sheath from oligodendrocytes that wraps around axons and increases conduction velocity. The electrical insulating properties of myelin allow signals to travel at speeds up to 100 times faster than they do in unmyelinated axons. Also, in myelinated axons the ion pumps need to reset the ion gradients only at nodes between sections of myelin instead of along the entire expanse of the axons. This results in up to a thirtyfold increase in the frequency with which a given neuron can transmit information. The combination of increased speed (100x) and quicker recovery time (30x) can yield a three-thousandfold increase in the amount of information transmitted per second. This nonsubtle impact of myelin on the brain's ability to process information may underlie many of the cognitive abilities associated with our species and provide the substrate for increased "connectivity" during adolescent brain maturation.

"Connectivity" characterizes several neuroscience concepts. In anatomic studies connectivity can mean a physical link between areas of the brain that share common developmental trajectories. In studies of brain function, connectivity describes the relationship between different parts of the brain that activate together during a task. In genetic studies it refers to different regions that are influenced by the same genetic or environmental factors. All of these types of connectivity increase during adolescence. A linguistic metaphor would be to consider the maturational changes not so much as adding new letters to the alphabet as combining existing letters into words, those words into sentences, and the sentences into paragraphs. Characterizing developing neural circuitry and the changing relationships among disparate brain components is one of the most active areas of neuroimaging research.

Studies of maturational changes in brain connectivity increasingly employ a type of mathematics known as graph theory—the analysis of *nodes* (which could represent any entities, including brain components) and *edges* (which model the relationships between nodes). *Modules* are defined as groups of nodes with many links to each other but few links to external groups (Newman & Girvan, 2004). The concept of modularity is fundamental in systems neuroscience and, in fact, is one of the most ubiquitous properties of complex systems in general. Many systems, including the human brain, seem to be organized in a "small world" hierarchy in which groups of highly connected neighboring nodes are connected to other groups of highly connected nodes via a relatively small number of strategically placed long-range connections. The term *small world* comes from the phenomenon of discovering that new people we meet in distant places are often connected socially to people we already know (friends of friends). Small-world topology supports both segregated/specialized and distributed/integrated information processing while minimizing wiring costs and supporting high dynamical complexity (Bassett & Bullmore, 2006).

An emerging line of investigation is to characterize the modular organization of the brain with respect to age, sex, genetics, neurobehavioral measures, and clinical diagnosis. Although research is in the early stages, the use of graph theory approaches to characterize changes in brain connectivity as it relates to the issue of criminal violence is positioned to be a prominent and powerful approach in ongoing and future studies.

DISCUSSION

In summary, the overall pattern of anatomic brain maturation from ages 3 to 30 shows roughly linear increases in white matter and inverted-U-shaped gray matter volume trajectories with latest peaks occurring in high association areas such as the PFC (see Giedd, 2008, for review). PFC thickness continues to undergo dynamic changes throughout the second decade of life, not stabilizing to adult levels on average until the mid-twenties, although there is high individual variation. The extended maturation of the PFC (and related high-association areas) and increased connectivity subserved by white matter growth is consistent with a growing body of literature from multiple imaging modalities and behavioral studies of a changing balance between frontal/executive long-term "top down" influences and subcortical/limbic short-term "bottom up" influences.

The gap between the earlier puberty-related surge in physical strength and testosterone and the maturation of the "let's deal with the immediate pleasure/pain issues" limbic system structures and the later maturing "let's consider the long-term consequences" frontal structures may account for part of the high risk of criminal violence in the 18–24 age range.

It is important not to misinterpret description of frontal and limbic systems as a simple dichotomous contest between reason and emotion. Emotion and reason are not independent opposites vying for control of our actions. They are intimate and inseparable partners interacting in nearly every aspect of our decision making. Our emotions stem from the brain's reward systems that evolved to facilitate our survival and promote the propagation of our genes. Most decisions involve comparing the relative value of different options, and our emotions are imperative in the assignment of those values.

Strong drives for oxygen, food, shelter, and sex have obvious evolutionary utility, reinforcing neurochemical surges for actions that lead to improved chances of survival or reproduction and neurochemically triggered unpleasant feelings toward actions that lessen our chances. The ability to accurately assess opportunities or threats in our environment—when to be calm, when to be afraid, and sometimes when to be aggressive—are critical for our survival. Just as imperfections in our danger assessment networks can lead to maladaptive anxiety disorders, imperfections in our anger/aggression systems may lead to maladaptive aggression. It is not aggression or violence per se that are pathologic; it is their inappropriate application.

In this chapter we have reviewed some of the adolescent changes in brain anatomy that may relate to the issue of violent criminality that so strikingly announces itself during this period. The teen brain is not a defective or broken adult brain. It has been patiently molded by the forces of our evolutionary history and is superbly adapted for the challenges it is likely to face. Its attributes display a double-edged sword of promise and peril. The dynamic changeability and high plasticity of the brain create the most likely conditions for the emergence of neuropsychiatric illness (Paus, Keshavan, & Giedd, 2008) but also allow it to adapt to the specific environmental challenges necessary to achieve independent survivability. Changes in dopaminergic and other neurochemical systems that increase risk taking and sensation seeking also promote separation from our natal families of origin, decreasing the risk of inbreeding and increasing genetic variability. Greater physical strength and aggression increase the risk of violence but may be highly useful attributes for victory in intra- and interspecies competition.

The adolescent brain is inherently neither violence prone nor defective. However, its evolutionarily forged propensities, including greater risk taking and sensation seeking, often interact with the environment to lead to risk for maladaptive aggression. Greater understanding of its age-specific neurobiology, especially in terms of what sorts of environmental conditions may lead to the tragedies of criminal violence, may elucidate the path toward more effective interventions.

REFERENCES

Bassett, D. S., & Bullmore, E. (2006). Small-world brain networks. *Neuroscientist, 12*(6), 512–523.

Berman, A. J., Berman, D., & Prescott, J. W. (1978). The effect of cerebellar lesions on emotional behavior in the rhesus monkey. In I. S. Cooper, M. Riklan, & R. S. Snider (Eds.), *The cerebellum, epilepsy, and behavior* (pp. 277–284). New York: Plenum Press.

Braitenberg, V. (2001). Brain size and number of neurons: An exercise in synthetic neuroanatomy. *Journal of Computational Neuroscience, 10*(1), 71–77.

Ciesielski, K. T., & Knight, J. E. (1994). Cerebellar abnormality in autism: A nonspecific effect of early brain damage? *Acta Neurobiologiae Experimentalis, (Wars), 54*(2), 151–154.

Giedd, J. N. (2008). The teen brain: Insights from neuroimaging. *Journal of Adolescent Health, 42*(4), 335–343.

Giedd, J. N., Schmitt, J. E., & Neale, M. C. (2007). Structural brain magnetic resonance imaging of pediatric twins. *Human Brain Mapping, 28*(6), 474–481.

Giedd, J. N., Shaw, P., Wallace, G., Gogtay, N., & Lenroot, R. K. (2006). Anatomic brain imaging studies of normal and abnormal brain development in children and adolescents. In D. Cicchetti & D. J. Cohen (Eds.), *Developmental psychopathology* (2nd ed., Vol. 2, pp. 127–194). Hoboken, NJ: Wiley.

Goldberg, T. E., Torrey, E. F., Berman, K. F., & Weinberger, D. R. (1994). Relations between neuropsychological performance and brain morphological and physiological measures in monozygotic twins discordant for schizophrenia. *Psychiatry Research, 55*, 51–61.

Heath, R. G., Cox, A. W., & Lustick, L. S. (1974). Brain activity during emotional states. *American Journal of Psychiatry, 131*(8), 858–862.

Huebner, T., Vloet, T. D., Marx, I., Konrad, K., Fink, G. R., Herpertz, S. C., & Herpertz-Dahlmann, B. (2008). Morphometric brain abnormalities in boys with conduct disorder. *Journal of the American Academy of Child and Adolescent Psychiatry, 47*(5), 540–547.

Ikeda, Y., & Nagai, A. (2006). Differential expression of the estrogen receptors alpha and beta during postnatal development of the rat cerebellum. *Brain Research, 1083*(1), 39–49.

Jacobs, L. F., Gaulin, S. J., Sherry, D. F., & Hoffman, G. E. (1990). Evolution of spatial cognition: Sex-specific patterns of spatial behavior predict hippocampal size. *Proceedings of the National Academy of Sciences of the USA, 87,* 6349–6352.

Krebs, J. R., Sherry, D. F., Healy, S. D., Perry, V. H., & Vaccarino, A. L. (1989). Hippocampal specialization of food-storing birds. *Proceedings of the National Academy of Sciences of the USA, 86,* 1388–1392.

Kruesi, M. J., Casanova, M. F., Mannheim, G., & Johnson-Bilder, A. (2004). Reduced temporal lobe volume in early onset conduct disorder. *Psychiatry Research, 132*(1), 1–11.

Lencz, T., McCarthy, G., Bronen, R. A., Scott, T. M., Inserni, J. A., Sass, K. J., . . . Spencer, D. D. (1992). Quantitative magnetic resonance imaging in temporal lobe epilepsy: Relationship to neuropathology and neuropsychological function. *Annals of Neurology, 31,* 629–637.

Lesnik, P. G., Ciesielski, K. T., Hart, B. L., Benzel, E. C., & Sanders, J. A. (1998). Evidence for cerebellar-frontal subsystem changes in children treated with intrathecal chemotherapy for leukemia: Enhanced data analysis using an effect size model. *Archives of Neurology, 55*(12), 1561–1568.

Maguire, E. A., Gadian, D. G., Johnsrude, I. S., Good, C. D., Ashburner, J., Frackowiak, R. S., & Frith, C. D. (2000). Navigation-related structural change in the hippocampi of taxi drivers. *Proceedings of the National Academy of Sciences of the USA, 97*(8), 4398–4403.

Neale, M. C., Cardon, L. R., & North Atlantic Treaty Organization. Scientific Affairs Division. (1992). *Methodology for genetic studies of twins and families.* Dordrecht, The Netherlands: Kluwer Academic.

Newman, M. E., & Girvan, M. (2004). Finding and evaluating community structure in networks. *Physical Review E: Statistical, Nonlinear, and Soft Matter Physics, 69*(2, Pt. 2), 26113.

Paus, T., Keshavan, M., & Giedd, J. N. (2008). Why do many psychiatric disorders emerge during adolescence? *Nature Reviews Neuroscience, 9*(12), 947–957.

Perez, S. E., Chen, E. Y., & Mufson, E. J. (2003). Distribution of estrogen receptor alpha and beta immunoreactive profiles in the postnatal rat brain. *Brain Resarch: Developmental Brain Research, 145*(1), 117–139.

Riklan, M., Marisak, I., & Cooper, I. S. (1974). Psychological studies of chronic cerebellar stimulation in man. In I. S. Cooper, M. Riklan & R. S. Snider (Eds.), *The cerebellum, epilepsy, and behavior* (pp. 285–342). New York, NY: Plenum Press.

Sherry, D. F., Jacobs, L. F., & Gaulin, S. J. (1992). Spatial memory and adaptive specialization of the hippocampus. *Trends in Neurosciences, 15,* 298–303.

Sherry, D. F., Vaccarino, A. L., Buckenham, K., & Herz, R. S. (1989). The hippocampal complex of food-storing birds. *Brain, Behavior and Evolution, 34,* 308–317.

Siever, L. J. (2008). Neurobiology of aggression and violence. *American Journal of Psychiatry, 165*(4), 429–442.

Sterzer, P., Stadler, C., Poustka, F., & Kleinschmidt, A. (2007). A structural neural deficit in adolescents with conduct disorder and its association with lack of empathy. *Neuroimage, 37*(1), 335–342.

Tiemeier, H., Lenroot, R. K., Greenstein, D. K., Tran, L., Pierson, R., & Giedd, J. N. (2010). Cerebellum development during childhood and adolescence: A longitudinal morphometric MRI study. *Neuroimage, 49*(1), 63–70.

Tsutsui, K. (2006). Biosynthesis, mode of action and functional significance of neurosteroids in the developing Purkinje cell. *Journal of Steroid Biochemistry and Molecular Biology, 102*(1–5), 187–194.

Wahlstrom, D., White, T., & Luciana, M. (2010). Neurobehavioral evidence for changes in dopamine system activity during adolescence. *Neuroscience and Biobehavioral Reviews, 34*(5), 631–648.

Wallace, G., Schmitt, J. E., Lenroot, R., Viding, E., Ordaz, S., Rosenthal, M., . . . Giedd, J. N. (2006). A pediatric twin study of brain morphometry. *Journal of Child Psychology and Psychiatry and Allied Disciplines, 47*(10), 987–993.

4

The Use of fMRI Technology in Understanding the Neurobiological Basis of Conduct Disorder and Psychopathy in Children and Adolescents

KAYLA POPE AND JAMES BLAIR ■

Our understanding and conceptualization of pathological aggression in children has evolved over time. The development of noninvasive technologies, including functional magnetic resonance imaging (fMRI), allows us the opportunity to examine the differences in brain function that may underlie the behavioral problems observed in this population. The use of fMRI to evaluate the pathology associated with conduct disorder (CD) and psychopathy is still in its infancy. Most studies to date have looked at brain functioning in adult participants, and only a few have examined the pathology in a developmentally sensitive way. Despite the limited number of studies, differences in brain functioning are emerging, and this knowledge deepens our understanding of the behavior observed within this clinical population. The remainder of this chapter reviews the research to date, the impact of this body of work on our current understanding of antisocial behavior, and future directions for research with this population.

FMRI TECHNOLOGY

To appreciate the strengths and weaknesses of the research that utilizes fMRI analysis, it is helpful to have a basic understanding of the technology. Unlike structural MRI, functional MRI allows us to determine which regions of the brain show a response to specific stimuli. The technique capitalizes on the fact that neurons require more energy when they are activated (Laureys, Boly, & Tononi, 2009). This increase in energy corresponds to an increase in oxygen consumption. Oxygenated hemoglobin is diamagnetic, and deoxygenated hemoglobin is paramagnetic. By applying a magnetic field, this difference in magnetism can be used to measure the amount of oxygenated hemoglobin in a region, producing a BOLD (blood-oxygen-level-dependence) signal. As the amount of oxygenated hemoglobin increases, there is an increase in the BOLD signal, which then correlates to increased activity in the area (Laureys et al., 2009).

There are advantages and disadvantages to using fMRI (Weiller et al., 2006). Advantages include that it is noninvasive and that there is minimal risk associated with its use. Thus it has allowed research to progress with different populations, including children. fMRI also has good spatial resolution; thus it is possible to distinguish areas of activation. It also has the ability to record activity across the brain, which provides us with information regarding how the brain responds to external events. The most significant limitation of fMRI is temporal resolution, which limits the ability to establish temporal sequencing between areas that are activated (Weiller et al., 2006). Thus it is not possible to definitively establish whether one region is influencing the activation of another region.

DEFINING ANTISOCIAL BEHAVIOR AND IDENTIFYING MEANINGFUL SUBTYPES

There have been many different approaches to defining CD and subtyping aggressive behavior. Early efforts to subtype antisocial behavior focused on whether the behavior was aggressive and whether it was more likely to be engaged in individually or as a group (Jenkins & Boyer, 1967–1968; Quay, 1964). Current thinking on subtyping antisocial behavior, specifically the diagnosis of CD, has focused on time of onset, distinguishing childhood onset from adolescence onset (Lahey et al., 1998; Moffitt, 1993). Childhood-onset aggression was thought to result from poor parenting, family dysfunction, and a child at risk due to temperamental factors, whereas adolescence onset was thought to be influenced by peer associations (Broidy et al, 2003; Frick, 2006). Indeed, childhood onset has been associated with more severe and persistent aggression (Moffitt, Caspi, Harrington, & Milne, 2002); greater neuropsychological deficits (Raine, Reynolds, Venables, & Mednick, 2002); greater impulsivity (McCabe, Hough, Wood, & Yeh, 2001); and greater problems with emotion regulation (Caspi, Moffitt, Newman, & Silva, 1996). Childhood onset has also been associated with greater family dysfunction and less effective parenting (Aguilar, Sroufe, Egeland, & Carlson, 2000; Keown & Woodward, 2002; McCabe et al., 2001). In contrast, adolescence-onset aggression was thought to result from misguided efforts by the adolescent to attain adult status and autonomy (Moffitt, 2002) and has been associated with greater involvement with antisocial peers (McCabe et al., 2001; Moffitt, 1993, 2003). However, these group differences have not been consistently found, and a recent large-scale study by Dandreaux and Frick (2009) found the childhood-onset group to have greater association with deviant peers. Although they did find that family dysfunction and more severe aggression were associated with the childhood-onset group, the only association that was significant for the adolescence-onset group was a lower score on traditionalism. The failure to consistently find differences between these groups brings into question whether they are causally distinct (Dandreaux & Frick, 2009). Research has not consistently supported neurobiological differences between these groups when measured by fear conditioning and startle reflex (Fairchild et al., 2008), cortisol response to stress (Fairchild et al., 2008), or amygdala response to facial expressions (Passamonti et al., 2010).

A second approach has been to distinguish whether aggressive behavior is reactive or instrumental in nature (Crick & Dodge, 1996). Reactive aggression occurs in response to frustration or threat and results in an unplanned, enraged attack on the source of the threat. In contrast, instrumental aggression is purposeful and goal directed and need not be accompanied by an emotional state. Indeed, it is has been described as "cold" aggression (Steiner et al., 1999). Data suggest that it is possible to identify individuals who are at increased risk for reactive aggression specifically and others who are at increased risk for *both* reactive and instrumental aggression (Crick & Dodge, 1996). In addition, it is clear that certain psychiatric conditions have a selective impact on increasing the risk for reactive aggression, including posttraumatic stress disorder (PTSD; Silva, Derecho, Leong, Weinstock, & Ferrari, 2001), intermittent explosive disorder (Coccaro, McCloskey, Fitzgerald, & Phan, 2007), borderline personality disorder (New et al., 2009), and childhood bipolar disorder. Currently, only one psychiatric condition is thought to increase the risk for instrumental aggression: psychopathy (Cornell et al., 1996).

A third characteristic, and related to the reactive–instrumental distinction, is whether the individual exhibits callous and unemotional traits (Frick, O'Brien, Wootton, & McBurnett, 1994). Individuals with elevated callous and unemotional traits are thought to lack the ability to feel empathy for their victims. Further, these individuals fail to respond to others who are in distress and do not express remorse for the damage caused by their antisocial acts. Callous and unemotional traits are thought to lie at the core of psychopathy and are predictive of a more severe and aggressive pattern of conduct problems (Frick & Dickens, 2006). Psychopathy was first identified by Cleckley (1941) and was then further refined by Robert Hare, who developed the Psychopathy Checklist (PCL; Hare, 1991) from his work with adult prison populations. Both Paul Frick and Hare have extended this approach to the subtyping of children and adolescents and have developed several commonly used assessment tools, such as the Antisocial Process Screening Device (Frick & Hare, 2001) and the Psychopathy Checklist—Youth Version (Forth, Kosson, & Hare, 2003). More recently, Frick has developed the Inventory of Callous Unemotional Traits (ICU) to specifically assess the emotional core of the disorder, callous–unemotional traits (Essau, Sasagawa, & Frick, 2006; Kimonis et al., 2008).

As with the earlier attempts to subtype antisocial behavior, the question becomes whether there is any biological evidence to support these approaches to subtyping. That is, are there biological differences, either structurally or functionally, between reactive and instrumental aggression, or the presence of callous–unemotional traits? The next section explores imaging research that has examined the neurocircuitry of these subtypes of aggression.

NEUROCIRCUITRY OF REACTIVE AGGRESSION

Reactive aggression results from an emotional response to an environmental event that is perceived as either frustrating or threatening. All mammalian species studied have been shown to behaviorally respond to threatening events in a relatively automatic fashion. Animal work indicates that there is a gradated response to threat: distant threats induce freezing, more proximal threats result in flight, and threats that are so close that escape is not possible result in an aggressive response (Blanchard, Bassett, & Koshland, 1977).

The areas of the brain involved in this response to threat have been extensively studied in animal models and more recently in humans (Mobbs, Lau, Jones, & Frith, 2007; Mobbs et al., 2009). The immediate response to threat begins with activation of the amygdala. From the amygdala, the stimulus travels downward to the hypothalamus and the periaqueductal gray area (PAG; Gregg & Siegel, 2001). This threat response system (amygdala–hypothalmus–PAG) is necessary for processing an environmental threat and allows the individual to mount the physical response to the threat. The threat response system is thought to be regulated by the frontal cortex or, more specifically, the medial, orbital, and inferior frontal cortices. This regulatory activity can involve attending to nonemotional events in the environment (Blair et al., 2007; Ochsner & Gross, 2005) or suppression of the emotional response by the orbitofrontal cortex (Urry et al., 2006).

Thus reactive aggression is an adaptive response to a highly threatening event mediated by a series of neural systems across mammalian species. However, reactive aggression can be maladaptive. Such maladaption can result from one or more deficits in the neurocircuitry involved in generating a response: (1) heightened reactivity of the threat response system and/or (2) an impaired ability to regulate the threat response system (Blair, 2007). Both of these deficits would lead to an increased emotional response to the threatening event and therefore to an increased chance of initiating reactive aggression rather than freezing or flight.

Currently, no fMRI work has specifically examined youths with CD who are at selectively increased risk for reactive aggression (as opposed to being at increased risk for both reactive and instrumental aggression). However, two studies have examined adult offenders who show a selective risk for reactive aggression. These studies examined a population of spouse abusers (Lee, Chan, & Raine, 2008, 2009). Importantly, they found them to be at risk for reactive aggression but not instrumental aggression. In both studies, the spouse abusers showed increased amygdala responses to threatening stimuli relative to healthy individuals.

Considerably more work has examined individuals with psychiatric disorders who are at selectively increased risk for reactive aggression, including PTSD (Silva et al., 2001; Zoccolillo, 1992), intermittent explosive disorder (Coccaro et al., 2007), borderline personality disorder (Herpertz et al., 2001; New et al., 2009), and childhood bipolar disorder (Leibenluft et al., 2003). Unfortunately, very little of this work, with the exception of that on childhood bipolar disorder, has examined youth samples. However, it is notable that all of these conditions are associated with increased amygdala responsiveness to threat in comparison with controls. The research is less clear with respect to decreased regulation of emotional reactivity. It is generally accepted that patients with PTSD show reduced frontal regulation (Lanius et al., 2001; Shin et al., 2004), though a number of findings do not support this claim (Bryant et al., 2005; Shin et al., 1997). Similarly, studies with youths with bipolar disorder have reported increased activity in the amygdala (Pavuluri, O'Connor, Harral, & Sweeney, 2007), as well as decreased activity in areas of the frontal cortex, including the orbitofrontal cortex (Pavuluri et al., 2007). However, these results have not been consistent.

NEUROCIRCUITRY OF INSTRUMENTAL AGGRESSION AND PSYCHOPATHY

Instrumental aggression differs from reactive aggression in that the behavior is goal directed and is not prompted by an emotional response to an environmental event. Individuals who engage in instrumental aggression are making a calculated choice to engage in antisocial behavior, after weighing the risks and benefits of their actions. As such, instrumental aggression is like any other form of instrumental (planned) action. It involves the recruitment of regions implicated in planned motor movement and, indeed, does not differ from other planned motor responses (Blair, 2007). Moreover, it occurs as a result of a risk–benefit-based decision-making process whereby actions are evaluated with respect to whether they will accomplish goals. As such, instrumental aggression can be adaptive for the individual (even if socially undesirable) if the benefits of the antisocial behavior outweigh the negative consequences. However, it can be maladaptive if the individual lacks the capacity to either appropriately learn the value of these benefits–negative consequences and/or cannot appropriately represent the value of these benefits–negative consequences during the decision-making process. These difficulties in learning and decision making are thought to be the core difficulties faced by individuals with psychopathy (Blair, 2007).

To explain the neurobiology that underlies the faulty decision making associated with this group of antisocial individuals, Blair (2004) proposed the integrated emotion system (IES) model. In this model, faulty decision making is linked to dysfunction in two areas of the brain, the amygdala and areas of the prefrontal cortex. It is likely that the caudate is also implicated in the disorder (Finger et al., 2011), as well as other regions (Kiehl, 2006).

The amygdala plays a critical role in responding to the environment by helping to encode the value of objects and experiences (Everitt, Cardinal, Parkinson, & Robbins, 2003; Ledoux, 1996). One of the most important ways humans learn about how to evaluate these experiences is through watching the emotional reactions of others, and the amygdala plays an important role in recognizing and responding to these emotional expressions. This appears to be particularly true of fearfulness (Adolphs, 2002; Blair, 2003). Once stimulated, the amygdala relays this information to the orbitofrontal cortex, which will play a role in evaluating the information and generating a response (Schoenbaum, Chiba, & Gallagher, 1999; Schoenbaum, Setlow, & Ramus, 2003).

Given the role that the amygdala and orbitofrontal cortex play in responding to threatening events, it is thought that deficits in these areas play a significant role in the development of callous–unemotional traits. Dysfunction in these areas would interfere with the ability to properly evaluate risks and rewards, resulting in poor decision making and destructive behavior. The following two sections consider the degree to which these processes are disrupted in youths with CD with and without callous–unemotional traits.

AMYGDALA DYSFUNCTION IN CONDUCT DISORDER AND PSYCHOPATHY

One of the ways that we study the ability of an individual to develop a fear response and thus avoid a harmful situation is an aversive conditioning paradigm. In this paradigm, participants are presented with a neutral object, which is then paired with a noxious experience (noise, shock). Normal participants will learn to fear the neutral object due to the expectation that the noxious experience will follow. Aversive conditioning relies on the amygdala, and damage to this area of the brain has been shown to disrupt the individual's ability to learn to avoid aversive situations (Ledoux, 2000). Impairment in aversive conditioning was one of the first deficits identified in individuals with psychopathy (Hare, 1970; Lykken, 1996), and recent fMRI work has shown that adults with psychopathy show reduced activity within the amygdala during aversive condition paradigms (Birbaumer et al., 2005). Moreover, an individual's ability to show aversive conditioning at age 3 is predictive of his or her probability of engaging in aggressive behavior at age 8 (Gao & Raine, 2010). Thus the more capable an individual is of learning to fear, the less likely he or she is to offend across the lifespan (Gao & Raine, 2010).

One of the most important ways humans learn about the value of things in their environment is through watching the emotional reactions of others to these experiences (Klinnert, Emde, Butterfield, & Campos, 1986). Youths with CD and callous–unemotional traits (CD + CU) and adults with psychopathy show impairment in the recognition of emotional expressions, particularly fearful expressions (Adolphs, 2002; Blair, 2003). A series of studies has examined the response to emotional expressions of youths with CD + CU (Jones, Laurens, Herba, Barker, & Viding, 2009; Marsh et al., 2008), adults with psychopathic tendencies (Deeley et al., 2006; Gordon, Baird, & End, 2004; Pardini & Phillips, 2010) or youths with general CD undifferentiated by CU traits (Passamonti et al. 2010; Stadler et al., 2007; Sterzer, Stadler, Krebs, Kleinschmidt, & Poustka, 2005). Some of this work has supported the suggestion of a disrupted amygdala response to emotional expressions, particularly fearful expressions in these populations. Thus both studies with youths with CD + CU reported reduced amygdala responses to fearful expressions (Jones et al., 2009; Marsh et al., 2008), as did the study by Gordon et al. (2004) in adults with psychopathic tendencies and the study by Passamonti et al. (2010) in youths with early-onset CD (though in this study, the responses were to sad rather than fearful expressions, which were not investigated). Interestingly, all of these studies also reported reduced activity in regions of the temporal cortex that show considerable interaction with the amygdala (e.g., fusiform and superior temporal cortex).

Not all studies to date have found reduced amygdala responses to emotional expressions. One study by Deeley et al. (2006; $N = 6$) did not fund reduced amygdala activation but did find a reduced response within the fusiform cortex, an area that is highly correlated with activity in the amygdala. Also interesting was a study by Sterzer et al. (2005), who found reduced responses in the anterior cingulate cortex but not the amygdala in youths with CD undifferentiated by CU traits. Pardini and Phillips (2010) found increased activation of the amygdala to neutral facial expressions.

Two further studies that examined amygdala responsiveness in antisocial youths are worth noting (Decety, Michalska, Akitsuki, & Lahey, 2009; Herpertz et al., 2008). Both of these studies involved youths with CD who were not differentiated by level of CU traits. In the first, Herpertz and colleagues examined the response to pictures of faces with positive, negative, or neutral expressions. Unlike the studies discussed earlier, this study reported *increased* responsiveness in the amygdala to negative emotional images in the youths with CD. One possible explanation for this finding was the higher levels of anxiety and depressive symptoms in the group with CD. Using a somewhat different approach, Decety (2009) explored whether there was a difference in how children with CD differed in their response to viewing others in pain. The study used animated pictures of people being subjected to and experiencing pain. The pain scenarios were varied as to whether they were intentional or unintentional. Participants in the study included 8 adolescents with aggressive CD and 8 healthy controls. The researchers found that youths with CD showed *greater* activation than the comparison youths to the pain of others in both the amygdala and striatum. They speculated that this activation might indicate a positive affective response to viewing others in pain, an observation that correlated with parent's ratings of daring behavior and sadism.

In summary, studies with youths with CD + CU and adults with psychopathy have for the most part supported the suggestion of amygdala dysfunction. In all cases, there is evidence of reduced amygdala responses (or of reduced responses in connected regions, as seen in the Deeley et al., 2006, study) to emotional expressions. The literature is far more confused with respect to CD more generally, with one study (Passamonti et al., 2010) finding reduced amygdala responses to sad expressions, two studies (Sterzer et al., 2005; Stadler et al., 2007) finding no differences in amygdala response, and two studies (Decety 2009; Herpertz et al., 2008) finding increased amygdala responses to emotional provocation. This inconsistency between the callous–unemotional traits/psychopathy literature and the conduct disorder literature may reflect diagnostic problems and heterogeneity of the participants in their samples.

THE ROLE OF THE ORBITOFRONTAL CORTEX AND DEFICITS IN DECISION MAKING

There are a variety of tasks that index an individual's ability to make decisions. For example, in the passive avoidance task, the individual's goal is to learn which stimuli will result in rewards and which will result in punishments. The goal is similar with a card-playing task called the Iowa Gambling Test (Bechara, Damasio, Tranel, & Damasio, 2005). In extinction and reversal learning tasks the individual's goal is slightly different. In these tasks, a response that the individual has learned to be "good" (i.e., reliably associated with reward) becomes "bad" and starts to give rise to punishment. The individual must learn to stop responding (in extinction tasks) or to change his or her response to reflect the new circumstances. These tasks have been used extensively in work with animals and humans using fMRI and neuropsychological studies. This research has demonstrated the critical role that the orbital frontal cortex plays in the performance of these tasks.

Considerable neuropsychological work with youths with CD + CU and adults with psychopathy shows that individuals with heightened levels of CU traits show impairment on these tasks. Recently, two studies have used fMRI to examine the neural correlates of these deficits in decision making in youths with CD + CU (Finger et al., 2008; Finger et al., 2011). These studies investigated the neural correlates of performance on both the passive avoidance (Finger et al., 2011) and the reversal learning paradigms (Finger et al., 2008). Both studies reported deficits in use of the orbital frontal cortex in processing information in youths with CD + CU. In the Finger et al. (2008) study, the youths with CD + CU failed to show the reduction in orbital frontal cortex activity associated with an unexpected absence of reward (see Kosson et al., 2006). In the Finger et al. (2011) study, the youths with CD + CU showed deficient representation of reward information in the context of the passive avoidance task.

These two studies with youths with CD + CU are worth comparing with two recent studies of decision making, one involving youths with CD who did not differentiate according to CU level (Rubia et al., 2009) and one of youths with antisocial substance disorder who might be expected to show significant

CD symptomatology (Crowley et al., 2010). In the study by Rubia and colleagues (2009), youths were selected who presented either with CD (but did not meet diagnosis for attention-deficit/hyperactivity disorder [ADHD]) or with ADHD (but did not meet criteria for CD). The youths were asked to perform a continuous performance task. In continuous performance tasks, the individual is asked to respond whenever a particular stimulus is present (an X) and not to respond when shown a Y. In the continuous performance task, the X's are presented much less often than Y's so that the individual must pay attention to identify their occurrences. Interestingly, Rubia and colleagues added a reward component to this task. That is, the participant received a monetary reward after three correct responses. Similar to the findings with the youths with CD + CU (Finger et al, 2011), the youths with CD in this study also showed reduced orbital frontal cortex responses to reward. The study by Crowley and colleagues (2010) was similar. This involved youths with antisocial substance disorder and typically developing comparison youths. It too reported reduced orbital frontal cortex responses in the youths with antisocial substance disorder to the receipt of reward relative to the comparison youths.

It is worth making one final note with reference to the studies of Finger and colleagues (2008) and Rubia and colleagues (2009). These studies involved three groups of youths: youths with CD, typically developing comparison youths, and youths with ADHD. The latter is important to note, as approximately 30% of youths with CD also meet criteria for a diagnosis of ADHD (Maughan, Rowe, Messer, Goodman, & Meltzer, 2004). Similarly, approximately 25% of youths with ADHD also meet criteria for a diagnosis of CD (Connor & Doerfler, 2008). Importantly, these studies showed that the deficits seen in the youths with CD with respect to the representation of reinforcement information within orbital frontal cortex were *not* seen in youths with ADHD; that is, they are specific to CD. Moreover, Rubia and colleagues (2009) have done a series of studies investigating the neural correlates of various paradigms in youths with ADHD, and they show significant impairment in the representation of reinforcement information in the orbital frontal cortex. Such paradigms include the card-playing task mentioned earlier, as well as tasks of inhibitory control and cognitive switching. In all cases, the youths with ADHD showed reduced activity in inferior prefrontal cortex during the performance of these tasks. This region is a region previously implicated in the pathophysiology of ADHD. Importantly, none of these tasks identified dysfunctional activity in this region in the youths with CD.

LIMITATIONS OF CURRENT RESEARCH AND FUTURE DIRECTIONS

The use of fMRI to understand the neuropathology that underlies antisocial behavior is in its infancy. Studies to date have provided evidence to support the idea that specific regions of the brain are functioning in a distinctly different pattern than they do in healthy controls. In the majority of studies, both the amygdala and areas of the prefrontal cortex demonstrate deviations in levels of activation when compared with healthy controls. However, the results are at times conflicting. There are several factors that could help to explain the variation in results. A significant problem in the research is the varying definitions of antisocial behavior and the instruments used to diagnose pathology. The studies cited herein varied both in the criteria used to identify CD and in the presence or absence of psychopathic traits. Further, there is little agreement on which characteristics are useful in subtyping this population. Studies have used early-onset versus late-onset CD, aggressive versus nonaggressive behavior, and the presence or absence of callous–unemotional traits. Thus comparing the results of these studies becomes problematic. Consensus on what characteristics are meaningful in differentiating subtypes would help to advance the field, both with fMRI and with other modes of inquiry.

CONCLUSIONS

Animal literature allows the identification of systems involved in reactive aggression. Adults at higher risk for reactive aggression show increased activity in these regions, as do patients with mood and anxiety conditions, which may place them at increased risk for reactive aggression. However, to date the research is less clear as to whether it is possible to identify a population of youths with CD who will show this pattern of dysfunctional neural activity.

In contrast, in children with CD and CU traits, clear neurophysiological differences are beginning to emerge. As noted earlier, reduced amygdala function is clearly shown in this population. Although less clear, this dysfunction in amygdala activity appears to be present as well in adults with psychopathy. There is also clear evidence of orbital frontal cortex reinforcement signaling impairment in CD + CU and possibly CD more generally. What is not clear is whether this would be seen in an identified group of youths with CD with reactive aggression.

Perhaps one of the most exciting features of this literature, besides the fact that we are beginning to identify a clear pathophysiology associated with at least CD + CU (i.e., reduced amygdala and orbital frontal cortex activation) is that the pathophysiology of this population can be objectively differentiated from that with ADHD. This research may also offer clues as to the nature of aggression associated with other mental illnesses.

REFERENCES

Adolphs, R. (2002). Recognizing emotion from facial expressions: Psychological and neurological mechanisms. *Behavioral and Cognitive Neuroscience Reviews, 1*(1), 21–62.

Aguilar, B., Sroufe, L. A., Egeland, B., & Carlson, E. (2000). Distinguishing the early-onset/persistent and adolescence-onset antisocial behavior types: From birth to 16 years. *Development and Psychopathology, 12*(2), 109–132.

Bechara, A., Damasio, H., Tranel, D., & Damasio, A. R. (2005). The Iowa Gambling Task and the somatic marker hypothesis: Some questions and answers. *Trends in Cognitive Sciences, 9*(4), 159–162.

Birbaumer, N., Veit, R., Lotze, M., Erb, M., Hermann, C., Grodd, W., & Flor, H. (2005). Deficient fear conditioning in psychopathy: A functional magnetic resonance imaging study. *Archives of General Psychiatry, 62*(7), 799–805.

Blair, K. S., Smith, B. W., Mitchell, D. G., Morton, J., Vythilingam, M., Pessoa, L., . . . Blair, R. J. (2007). Modulation of emotion by cognition and cognition by emotion. *NeuroImage, 35*(1), 430–440.

Blair, R. J. (2004). The roles of orbital frontal cortex in the modulation of antisocial behavior . *Brain and Cognition, 55*(1), 198–208.

Blair, R. J. R. (2003). Neurobiological basis of psychopathy. *British Journal of Psychiatry, 182*(1), 5–7.

Blair, R. J. R. (2007). The amygdala and ventromedial prefrontal cortex in morality and psychopathy. *Trends in Cognitive Sciences, 11*, 387–392.

Blanchard, E. B., Bassett, J. E., & Koshland, E. (1977). Psychopathy and delay of gratification. *Criminal Justice and Behavior, 4*(3), 265–271.

Broidy, L. M., Nagin, D. S., Tremblay, R. E., Bates, J. E., Brame, B., Dodge, K. A., . . . Vitaro, F. (2003). Developmental trajectories of childhood disruptive behaviors and adolescent delinquency: A six-site, cross-national study. *Developmental Psychology, 39*(2), 222–245.

Bryant, R. A., Felmingham, K. L., Kemp, A. H., Barton, M., Peduto, A. S., Rennie, C., . . . Williams, L. M. (2005). Neural networks of information processing in posttraumatic stress disorder: A functional magnetic resonance imaging study. *Biological Psychiatry, 58*(2), 111–118.

Caspi, A., Moffitt, T. E., Newman, D. L., & Silva, P. A. (1996). Behavioral observations at age 3 years predict adult psychiatric disorders: Longitudinal evidence from a birth cohort. *Archives of General Psychiatry, 53*(11), 1033–1039.

Cleckley, H. M. (1951). The mask of sanity. *Postgraduate Medicine, 9*(3), 193–197.

Coccaro, E. F., McCloskey, M. S., Fitzgerald, D. A., & Phan, K. L. (2007). Amygdala and orbitofrontal reactivity to social threat in individuals with impulsive aggression. *Biological Psychiatry, 62*(2), 168–178.

Connor, D. F., & Doefler, L. A. (2008). ADHD with comorbid oppositional defiant disorder or conduct disorder: Discrete or nondistinct disruptive behavior disorders? *Journal of Attention Disorders, 12*(2), 126–134.

Cornell, D. G., Warren, J., Hawk, G., Stafford, E., Oram, G., & Pine, D. (1996). Psychopathy in instrumental and reactive violent offenders. *Journal of Consulting and Clinical Psychology, 64*(4), 783–790.

Crick, N. R., & Dodge, K. A. (1996). Social information-processing mechanisms in reactive and proactive aggression. *Child Development,67*(3), 993–1002.

Crowley, T. J., Dalwani, M. S., Mikulich-Gilbertson, S. K., Du, Y. P., Lejuez, C. W., Raymond, K. M., & Banich, M. T. (2010). Risky decisions and their consequences: Neural processing by boys with antisocial substance disorder. *PLoS One, 5*(9), e12835.

Dandreaux, D. M., & Frick, P. J. (2009). Developmental pathways to conduct problems: A further test of the childhood and adolescent-onset distinction. *Journal of Abnormal Child Psychology, 37*(3), 375–385.

Decety, J. (2009). Empathy, sympathy and the perception of pain. *Pain, 145*(3), 365–366.

Decety, J., Michalska, K. J., Akitsuki, Y., & Lahey, B. B. (2009). Atypical empathic responses in adolescents with aggressive conduct disorder: A functional MRI investigation. *Biological Psychology, 80*(2), 203–211.

Deeley, Q., Daly, E., Surguladze, S., Tunstall, N., Mezey, G., Beer, D., . . . Murphy, D. G. (2006). Facial emotion processing in criminal psychopathy: Preliminary functional magnetic resonance imaging study. *British Journal of Psychiatry, 189*(6), 533–539.

Essau, C. A., Sasagawa, S., & Frick, P. J. (2006). Callous–unemotional traits in a community sample of adolescents. *Assessment, 13*(4), 454–469.

Everitt, B. J., Cardinal, R. N., Parkinson, J. A., & Robbins, T. W. (2003). Appetitive behavior: Impact of amygdala-dependent mechanisms of emotional learning. *Annals of the New York Academy of Sciences, 985*, 233–250.

Fairchild, G., van Goozen, S. H., Stollery, S. J., Brown, J., Gardiner, J., Herbert, J., & Goodyer, I. M. (2008). Cortisol diurnal rhythm and stress reactivity in male adolescents with early-onset or adolescence-onset conduct disorder. *Biological Psychiatry, 64*(7), 599–606.

Finger, E. C., Marsh, A. A., Blair, K. S., Reid, M. E., Sims ,C., Ng, P., . . . Blair, R. J. (2011). Disrupted reinforcement signaling in the orbitofrontal cortex and caudate in youths with conduct disorder or oppositional defiant disorder and a high level of psychopathic traits. *American Journal of Psychiatry, 168*(2), 152–162.

Finger, E. C., Marsh, A. A., Mitchell, D. G., Reid, M. E., Sims, C., Budhani, S., . . . Blair, J. R. (2008). Abnormal ventromedial prefrontal cortex function in children with psychopathic traits during reversal learning. *Archives of General Psychiatry, 65*(5), 586–594.

Forth, A. E., Kosson, D., & Hare, R. D. (2003). *The Hare PCL: Youth Version.* Toronto, Ontario, Canada: Multi-Health Systems.

Frick, P. J. (2006). Developmental pathways to conduct disorder. *Child and Adolescent Psychiatric Clinics of North America, 15*(2), 311–331.

Frick, P. J., & Dickens, C. (2006). Current perspectives on conduct disorder. *Current Psychiatry Reports, 8*(1), 59–72.

Frick, P. J., & Hare, R. D. (2001). *The Antisocial Process Screening Device.* Toronto, Ontario, Canada: Multi-Health Systems.

Frick, P. J., O'Brien, B. S., Wootton, J. M., & McBurnett, K. (1994). Psychopathy and conduct problems in children. *Journal of Abnormal Psychology, 103*(4), 700–707.

Gao, Y., & Raine, A. (2010). Successful and unsuccessful psychopaths: A neurobiological model. *Behavioral Sciences and the Law, 28*(2), 194–210.

Gordon, H. L., Baird, A. A., & End, A. (2004). Functional differences among those high and low on a trait measure of psychopathy. *Biological Psychiatry, 56*(7), 516–521.

Gregg, T. R., & Siegel, A. (2001). Brain structures and neurotransmitters regulating aggression in cats: Implications for human aggression. *Progress in Neuropsychopharmacology and Biological Psychiatry, 25*(1), 91–140.

Hare, R. D. (1970). *Psychopathy: Theory and research.* New York, NY: Wiley.

Hare, R. D. (1991). *The Hare Psychopathy Checklist—Revised.* Toronto, Ontario, Canada: Multi-Health Systems.

Herpertz, S. C., Huebner, T., Marx, I., Vloet, T. D., Fink, G. R., Stoecker, T., . . . Herpertz-Dahlmann, B. (2008). Emotional processing in male adolescents with childhood-onset conduct disorder. *Journal of Child Psychology and Psychiatry, 49*(7), 781–791.

Herpertz, S. C., Werth, U., Lukas, G., Qunaibi, M., Schuerkens, A., Kunert, H., . . . Sass, H. (2001). Emotion in criminal offenders with psychopathy and borderline personality disorder. *Archives of General Psychiatry, 58*, 737–745.

Jenkins, R. L., & Boyer, A. (1967–1968). Types of delinquent behavior and background factors. *International Journal of Social Psychiatry, 14*(1), 65–76.

Jones, A. P., Laurens, K. R., Herba, C. M., Barker, G. J., & Viding, E. (2009). Amygdala hypoactivity to fearful faces in boys with conduct problems and callous–unemotional traits. *American Journal of Psychiatry, 166*(1), 95–102.

Keown, L. J., & Woodward, L. J. (2002). Early parent-child relations and family functioning of preschool boys with pervasive hyperactivity. *Journal of Abnormal Child Psychology, 30*(6), 541–553.

Kiehl, K. A. (2006). A cognitive neuroscience perspective on psychopathy: Evidence for paralimbic system dysfunction. *Psychiatry Research, 142*(2–3), 107–128.

Kimonis, E. R., Frick, P. J., Skeem, J. L., Marsee, M. A., Cruise, K., Munoz, L. C., . . . Morris, A. S. (2008). Assessing callous–unemotional traits in adolescent offenders: Validation of the Inventory of Callous–Unemotional Traits. *International Journal of Law and Psychiatry, 31*(3), 241–252.

Klinnert, M. D., Emde, R. N., Butterfield, P., & Campos, J. J. (1986). Social referencing: The infant's use of emotional signals from a friendly adult with mother present. *Developmental Psychology, 22*, 427–432.

Kosson, D. S., Budhani, S,. Nakic, M., Chen, G., Saad, Z. S., Vythilingam, M., . . . Blair, R. J. (2006). The role of the amygdala and rostral anterior cingulate in encoding expected outcomes during learning. *NeuroImage, 29*(4), 1161–1172.

Lahey, B. B., Loeber, R., Quay, H. C., Applegate, B., Shaffer, D., Waldman, I., . . . Bird, H. R. (1998). Validity of DSM-IV subtypes of conduct disorder based on age of onset. *Journal of the American Academy of Child and Adolescent Psychiatry, 37*(4), 435–442.

Lanius, R. A., Williamson, P. C., Densmore, M., Boksman, K., Gupta, M. A., Neufeld, R. W., . . . Menon, R. S. (2001). Neural correlates of traumatic memories in post-traumatic stress disorder: A functional MRI investigation. *American Journal of Psychiatry, 158*(11), 1920–1922.

Laureys, S., Boly, M., & Tononi, G. (2009). Functional neuroimaging. In S. Laureys & G. Tononi (Eds.), *The neurology of consciousness: Cognitive neuroscience and neuropathology* (pp. 31–42). London: Academic Press-Elsevier.

Ledoux, J. (1996). Emotional networks and motor control: A fearful view. *Progress in Brain Research, 107,* 437–446.

Ledoux, J. (2000). Emotion circuits in the brain. *Annual Review of Neuroscience, 23,* 155–184.

Lee, T. M., Chan, S. C., & Raine, A. (2008). Strong limbic and weak frontal activation to aggressive stimuli in spouse abusers. *Molecular Psychiatry, 13*(7), 655–656.

Lee, T. M., Chan, S. C., & Raine, A. (2009). Hyperresponsivity to threat stimuli in domestic violence offenders: A functional magnetic resonance imaging study. *Journal of Clinical Psychiatry, 70*(1), 36–45.

Leibenluft, E., Blair, R. J., Charney, D. S., & Pine, D. S. (2003). Irritability in pediatric mania and other childhood psychopathology. *Annals of the New York Academy of Sciences, 1008*, 201–218.

Lykken, D. T. (1996). Psychopathy, sociopathy, and crime. *Society, 34*(1), 29–38.

Marsh, A. A., Finger, E. C., Mitchell, D. G., Reid, M. E., Sims, C., Kosson, D. S., . . . Blair, R. J. (2008). Reduced amygdala response to fearful expressions in children and adolescents with callous–unemotional traits and disruptive behavior disorders. *American Journal of Psychiatry, 165*(6), 712–720.

Maughan, B., Rowe, R., Messer, J., Goodman, R., & Meltzer, H. (2004). Conduct disorder and oppositional defiant disorder in a national sample: Developmental epidemiology. *Journal of Child Psychology and Psychiatry, 45*(3), 609–621.

McCabe, K. M., Hough, R., Wood, P. A., & Yeh, M. (2001). Childhood and adolescent onset conduct disorder: A test of the developmental taxonomy. *Journal of Abnormal Child Psychology, 29*(4), 305–316.

Mobbs, D., Lau, H. C., Jones, O. D., & Frith, C. D. (2007). Law, responsibility, and the brain. *PLoS Biology, 5*(4), e103.

Mobbs, D., Marchant, J. L., Hassabis, D., Seymour, B., Tan, G., Gray, M., . . . Frith, C. D. (2009). From threat to fear: The neural organization of defensive fear systems in humans. *Journal of Neuroscience, 29*(39), 12236–12243.

Moffitt, T. E. (1993). Adolescence-limited and life-course-persistent antisocial behavior: A developmental taxonomy. *Psychological Review, 100*(4), 674–701.

Moffitt, T. E., Caspi, A., Harrington, H., & Milne, B. J. (2002). Males on the life-course-persistent and adolescence-limited antisocial pathways: Follow-up at age 26 years. *Development and Psychopathology,14*(1), 179–207.

New, A. S., Hazlett, E. A., Newmark, R. E., Zhang, J., Triebwasser, J., Meyerson, D., . . . Buchsbaum, M. S. (2009). Laboratory-induced aggression: A positron emission tomography study of aggressive individuals with borderline personality disorder. *Biological Psychiatry, 66*(12), 1107–1114.

Ochsner, K. N., & Gross, J. J. (2005). The cognitive control of emotion. *Trends in Cognitive Sciences, 9*(5), 242–249.

Pardini, D. A., & Phillips, M. (2010). Neural responses to emotional and neutral facial expressions in chronically violent men. *Journal of Psychiatry and Neuroscience, 35*(6), 390–398.

Passamonti, L., Fairchild, G., Goodyer. I. M., Hurford, G., Hagan, C. C., Rowe, J. B., & Calder, A. J. (2010). Neural abnormalities in early-onset and adolescence-onset conduct disorder. *Archives of General Psychiatry, 67*(7), 729–738.

Pavuluri, M. N., O'Connor, M. M., Harral, E., & Sweeney, J. A. (2007). Affective neural circuitry during facial emotion processing in pediatric bipolar disorder. *Biological Psychiatry, 62*(2), 158–167.

Quay, H. C. (1964). Dimensions of personality in delinquent boys as inferred from the factor analysis of case history data. *Child Development, 35*, 479–484.

Raine, A., Reynolds, C., Venables, P. H., & Mednick, S. A. (2002). Stimulation seeking and intelligence: A prospective longitudinal study. *Journal of Personality and Social Psychology, 82*(4), 663–674.

Rubia, K., Halari, R., Smith, A. B., Mohammad, M., Scott, S., & Brammer, M. J. (2009). Shared and disorder-specific prefrontal abnormalities in boys with pure attention-deficit/hyperactivity disorder compared to boys with pure CD during interference inhibition and attention allocation. *Journal of Child Psychology and Psychiatry, 50*(6), 669–678.

Schoenbaum, G., Chiba, A. A., & Gallagher, M. (1999). Neural encoding in orbitofrontal cortex and basolateral amygdala during olfactory discrimination learning. *Journal of Neuroscience, 19*(5), 1876–1884.

Schoenbaum, G., Setlow, B., & Ramus, S. J. (2003). A systems approach to orbitofrontal cortex function: Recordings in rat orbitofrontal cortex reveal interactions with different learning systems. *Behavioral Brain Research, 146*(1–2), 19–29.

Shin, L. M., McNally, R. J., Kosslyn, S. M., Thompson, W. L., Rauch, S. L., Alpert, N. M., . . . Pitman, R. K. (1997). A positron emission tomographic study of symptom provocation in PTSD. *Annals of the New York Academy of Sciences, 821,* 521–523.

Shin, L. M., Orr, S. P., Carson, M. A., Rauch, S. L., Macklin, M. L., Lasko, N. B., . . . Pitman, R. K. (2004). Regional cerebral blood flow in the amygdala and medial prefrontal cortex during traumatic imagery in male and female Vietnam veterans with PTSD. *Archives of General Psychiatry, 61*(2), 168–176.

Silva, J. A., Derecho, D. V., Leong, G. B., Weinstock, R., & Ferrari, M. M. (2001). A classification of psychological factors leading to violent behavior in posttraumatic stress disorder. *Journal of Forensic Sciences,46*(2), 309–316.

Stadler, C., Sterzer, P., Schmeck, K., Krebs, A., Kleinschmidt, A., & Poustka, F. (2007). Reduced anterior cingulate activation in aggressive children and adolescents during affective stimulation: Association with temperament traits. *Journal of Psychiatric Research, 41*(5), 410–417.

Steiner, H., Cauffman, E., & Duxbury, E. J. (1999). Personality traits in juvenile delinquents: Relation to criminal behavior and recidivism. *Journal of the American Academy of Child and Adolescent Psychiatry, 38*(3), 256–262.

Sterzer, P., Stadler, C., Krebs, A., Kleinschmidt, A., & Poustka, F. (2005). Abnormal neural responses to emotional visual stimuli in adolescents with conduct disorder. *Biological Psychiatry, 57*(1), 7–15.

Urry, H. L., van Reekum, C. M., Johnstone, T., Kalin, N. H., Thurow, M. E., Schaefer, H. S., . . . Davidson, R. J. (2006). Amygdala and ventromedial prefrontal cortex are inversely coupled during regulation of negative affect and predict the diurnal pattern of cortisol secretion among older adults. *Journal of Neuroscience, 26*(16), 4415–4425.

Weiller, C., May, A., Sach, M., Buhmann, C., & Rijntjes, M. (2006). Role of functional imaging in neurological disorders. *Journal of Magnetic Resonance Imaging, 23*(6), 840–850. Review.

Zoccolillo, M. (1992). Co-occurrence of conduct disorder and its adult outcomes with depressive and anxiety disorders: A review. *Journal of the American Academy of Child and Adolescent Psychiatry, 31*(3), 547–556.

PART TWO

Advances in Behavioral and Clinical Research

5

Preschool Behavioral Markers
of Antisocial Behavior

ANIL CHACKO, LINDSAY ANDERSON, AND
ESTRELLA RAJWAN ■

The preschool period offers great promise for providing early intervention to reduce risk for the development of antisocial behavior in youths. There is now considerable evidence that behavioral markers can be reliably identified during the preschool period that distinguish children who are at greatest risk for the development of antisocial behavior from children who have transient perturbations (Wakschlag, Tolan, & Leventhal, 2010). Moreover, the development of typologies that represent distinct interrelations of these markers may prove useful in further improving our understanding of which youths will follow a path that leads to antisocial behavior (Sonuga-Barke & Halperin, 2010; Wakschlag et al., 2010). The goal of this chapter is to review the literature in these areas and the implications of these findings for future research, public policy, and clinical practice.

BEHAVIORAL MARKERS

Identifying behavioral markers during the preschool period for the development of antisocial behavior should be a straightforward endeavor. As the adage goes, the best predictor of future behavior is past behavior. As such, it should be the case that preschoolers who exhibit high levels of antisocial behavior are likely the most at risk for exhibiting high rates of antisocial behavior throughout development. Empirical studies support this intuitive reasoning. For example, Tremblay and colleagues (see Tremblay, 2010, for a review) in their longitudinal studies on the development of aggression have found that preschoolers with high levels of aggressive behavior are the most at risk for stable aggressive behavior throughout development. However, it is increasingly clear that a significant number, if not half, of these preschoolers do not go on to have stable or increasing levels of problematic behavior (Campbell, 2002; Tremblay, 2010). As argued in greater detail elsewhere (Chacko, Wakschlag, Espy, Hill, & Danis, 2009), the mere presence of a pervasive, persistent, and frequent behavioral marker during the preschool period does not invariably result in chronic, stable patterns of antisocial/problematic behavior for many youths. Although considering the presence of additional risk factors (e.g., parental psychopathology, characteristics of the neighborhood/residence) may prove useful in determining incremental risk for the persistence or development of antisocial behavior (Rutter, Giller, & Hagell, 1998), the following two lines of empirical inquiry can substantially advance the field of identification of behavioral markers during preschool that predict the development of antisocial behavior problems: (1) integration of the developmental and clinical literatures regarding key behaviors in context and (2) the continuing study of emerging preschool typologies of behavioral challenges in preschool children. A discussion of each of these research areas follows.

INTEGRATING DEVELOPMENTAL/CLINICAL LITERATURES REGARDING KEY BEHAVIORS IN CONTEXT

Key behaviors during preschool that should be a concern for the development of antisocial behavior are varied and numerous. This chapter focuses on several prominent behaviors, including empathy versus callous–unemotional behaviors, hyperactivity, impulsivity, noncompliance, aggression, and temper tantrums. Arguably, this list can be expanded to include other behaviors (e.g., language). We focus on the preceding behaviors for several reasons. Importantly, these behaviors have been associated with the development of antisocial behavior across numerous studies (see Campbell, 2002; Rutter et al., 1998; Tremblay, Hartup, & Archer, 2005, for exhaustive reviews). Moreover, the prominence of these behaviors in current psychiatric nosology (i.e., attention-deficit/hyperactivity disorder [ADHD], oppositional defiant disorder [ODD], conduct disorder [CD]) also attest to the significance of these behaviors.

Although there is a consensus as to the importance of these behaviors, it is increasingly clear that demarcating problematic expression versus typical or transient expressions of these behaviors during the preschool period is critical and to date not fully appreciated in the clinical field. For instance, the problematic behaviors we noted previously are normative misbehaviors of early childhood (e.g., high levels of activity, aggression; Wakschlag et al., 2007). For instance, Egger, Kondo, and Angold (2006) found that many preschoolers exhibited occasions of often losing their tempers (30%), often interrupting or intruding (47%), and often actively defying (57%). Moreover, Pavuluri, Luk, and McGee (1999) found that parents rated 48% and 65% of preschoolers as "often easily distracted" and "often talking excessively," respectively. Even more serious antisocial behaviors occur with surprising frequency during the preschool period. For example, Keenan et al. (2007) found that a significant number of nonreferred preschool children without behavioral concerns met DSM-IV symptom criteria for "uses object to harm" (14%) and "often lies" (20%).

In order to better identify behaviors during the preschool period that lead to the development of antisocial behavior, an emphasis must be placed on homotypic and heterotypic continuity of antisocial behaviors from preschool (or even earlier) to adulthood (Tremblay, 2010). An integration of the developmental and clinical literatures when considering these key behaviors in context offers much promise in elucidating the boundaries between typical and atypical expressions of these behaviors, thereby maximizing homotypic and heterotypic continuities of key behavioral problems across development. More specifically, understanding not only the frequency but also the *quality* of behavior (e.g., intensity, expectability in context, flexibility, and organization of behavior) may be important for such typical–atypical distinctions during the preschool period (Chacko et al., 2009; Wakschlag et al., 2010). Symptoms that overlap with commonly occurring misbehaviors of young children without specification of how frequently they must occur in order for these behaviors to be of clinical concern *and* without clinically defining features beyond frequency are *developmentally imprecise*. Developmental imprecision is likely to contribute to *overidentification* because normative misbehaviors (such as temper tantrums and defiance) may be mistakenly considered problematic.

In contrast, many problematic behaviors found in school-age youths are often assessed in preschool children that are *developmentally impossible* for young children (e.g., truancy). Others are *developmentally improbable:* although preschoolers may be capable of these behaviors (i.e., stealing with confrontation), they represent extreme forms of behavior that are unlikely to occur and are not likely to be the critical defining features at this young age (Wakschlag et al. 2010).

Collectively, reformulating these behaviors to capture the underlying construct being assessed in a manner that better reflects the preschool-age period is necessary in order to better identify the developmental pathways from problematic behavior in preschool that lead to more serious antisocial behaviors seen in older youths. In the following sections, we highlight recent advances in developmental science that may assist in elucidating the parameters, presentation, meaning, and occurrence of these core behavioral markers during the preschool period that may be essential to understanding the development of antisocial behavior.

Aggression

Physical aggression is a developmentally appropriate and expectable behavior during preschool that follows a predictable course. Research suggests that aggression naturally emerges as a reaction to anger and frustration in the first year of life and becomes increasingly sophisticated and varied throughout the second year (Alink et al., 2006; Hay, Castle, & Davies, 2000; Tremblay, 2003).

In typically developing children, physical aggression steadily increases until sometime between the third and the fourth year (Tremblay et al., 2004). In a population-based birth cohort study that followed children from ages 17 to 60 months, Côté, Vaillancourt, LeBlanc, Nagin, and Tremblay (2007) found three distinct developmental trajectories of physical aggression: low (32.5%; $n = 571$), moderate (50.5%; $n = 888$), and high (17%; $n = 299$). The rate of physical aggression increased for each of the groups, peaked at 42 months, slowly declined until 54 months, and seemed to be leveling off at 60 months. By age 5, children in the low group had physical aggression scores of nearly 0, while children in the moderate group were described as "sometimes" exhibiting physical aggression. The remaining children, one-sixth of the sample, followed a high, stable physical aggression trajectory for the length of the study, from ages 2 to 11. Other studies have produced similar results, suggesting that although common, aggression is not frequent in the preschool years (Hay, 2005). In typically developing children, physical aggression decreases as their verbal and problem-solving abilities allow increased socialization (Côté et al., 2006; Hay, 2005; NICHD Early Childcare Research Network, 2004). As cognitive function becomes more sophisticated, physical aggression is replaced by indirect aggression, or social manipulations (such as rumor spreading, peer group exclusion, or breaking confidences; Côté et al., 2006; Crick & Grotpeter, 1995). In a six-site cross-national study, Broidy et al. (2003) make the important distinction that though physical aggression is normal and even spontaneous in typically developing children, most children learn *not* to physically aggress in the preschool years. There is a qualitative aspect of typically developing aggression. Normative aggression is a response to frustration or threat ("reactive aggression"; Blair, 2006; Dodge, 1991), not a premeditated act intended to injure another ("proactive aggression"; Hay, Castle, & Davies, 2000; Vitaro, Gendreau, Tremblay, & Oligny, 1998). Typical physical aggression in preschool children happens impulsively, in defense of a much-loved toy, out of frustration at not being able to express wants or needs verbally, or anger at a perceived provocation (Hay, 2005; Rubin, Hastings, Chen, Stewart, & McNichol, 1998).

Atypically developing physical aggression is marked by its high incidence and stable trajectory. Although nearly 75% of children have shown some aggression by the age of 2 (Alink et al., 2006; Tremblay et al., 1999), less than 10% of 2- to 3-year-olds are described by their parents as "often" hitting others (Baillargeon et al., 2007; Carter, Briggs-Gowan, Jones, & Little, 2003; NICHD, 2004). Numerous studies suggest that there is a relatively small subset (approximately 5–10%) of children who display high, stable rates of physical aggression (Broidy et al., 2003; Côté et al., 2006; Nagin & Tremblay, 1999; NICHD, 2004) and that this measure predicts subsequent aggression. There are important qualitative markers of problematic physical aggression: early, hostile, intense aggression and aggression toward adults are associated with persistent aggression over time (Hay, 2005; Wakschlag & Danis, 2009; Zahn-Waxler, Iannotti, Cummings, & Denham, 1990). In young children reactive aggression is developmentally expectable, but proactive or hostile aggression can be a sign of clinical concern: the Connecticut Early Developmental Project found that only 1% of children at ages 2 and 3 were reported to "hurt others on purpose" (Carter, Briggs-Gowan, McCarthy, & Wakschlag, 2009). Proactive aggression, as defined by its goal-directed, preplanned nature (e.g., to get back at or dominate someone), has been shown to predict future delinquency and disruptive behaviors whereas reactive aggression does not (Hay, 2005; Rubin et al., 1998). Similarly, children will use instrumental aggression to defend a toy from the wandering hand of a neighbor, but hostile, unprovoked aggression has been shown to be both stable and coherent over time and to predict subsequent aggression (Hay et al., 2000). Because of its relative infrequency, discerning either proactive or hostile aggression may have important clinical utility. Behavior with a proactive flavor is an indicator that physical aggression is problematic. For instance, one should be concerned if a child often starts fights with peers, consistently bullies others, or uses weapons (rocks, bats, scissors, chairs) with the intent to harm others. Physically lashing out at a caregiver upon being redirected or repeatedly trying to choke, scratch, or bite a peer are signs of a problem (Keenan & Wakschlag, 2000). Reactive aggression, common in many preschool children, is often not or should not be typically considered pathognomic.

Noncompliance

Noncompliance reflects the degree to which one fails to adapt one's actions to a rule or to necessity. The most common noncompliant behaviors in children are arguing and not adhering to directives, rules, and social norms (Wakschlag et al., 2007). The noncompliance dimension is linked conceptually with previous research that focused on rule breaking (Nagin & Tremblay, 1999). Current research has focused on distinguishing clinical from normative noncompliance by examining this dimension of behavior through a developmentally appropriate lens (e.g., quantifying and qualifying incidences of sneakiness and a reflexive "no" response; Wakschlag 2007). Qualitative distinctions between normative and atypical noncompliance are detectable as early as the second year of life, and there is evidence that these distinctions have predictive significance (Hay et al., 2000; Kochanska, Aksan, & Koenig, 1995).

The process of learning to self-regulate behavior and emotion are fundamental parts of socialization. Typically developing compliance represents a process by which children internalize outside directives/situational demands that require some modification of behavior. Compliance begins with a caregiver request that is not the child's initial goal (Forman, 2007) and requires that the child comprehend the rule or directive and have the motivation to comply (Kochanska & Aksan, 2006). Research has shown that externally controlled compliance is present by the second year of life (Kochanska, Coy, & Murray, 2001) and follows a developmental progression that culminates in the child's ability to internally self-regulate. According to Kopp (1982), between ages 12 and 18 months, children become capable of control, which means that they are aware of social demands and have the ability to initiate, maintain, and cease behavior to comply with a caregiver's developmentally appropriate request. By 24 months, children begin to have the ability to self-control their own behavior. This emerging skill set includes delaying behaviors even in the absence of external directives, though this phase of development is associated with limited flexibility in adapting behavior to new situational demands. By 36 months children begin to be capable of self-regulation, meaning that self-control processes have matured enough that the child has the ability to respond appropriately to situations that have both explicit and implicit rules and expectations. Self-regulation will continue to develop in tandem with cognitive and executive skills: at age 3 there are still very real limitations to a child's self-control, and compliance is more a product of pleasure than of logic or need (Kopp, 1982).

Normative noncompliance begins in the second year of life and increases from the toddler to the preschool period (Forman, 2007), developing along with the language, behavioral control, and self-evaluation skills that allow children to understand and respond to caregiver requests (Kaler & Kopp, 1990; Kochanska et al., 2001; Kuczynski & Kochanska, 1990; Stipek, Gralinski, & Kopp, 1990). The function of normative noncompliance is less understood, but it is behavior that children engage in for a considerable amount of time; typical noncompliance rates are somewhere between 20 and 40% (Forehand, 1977). Kuczynski, Kochanska, Radke-Yarrow, and Girnius-Brown (1987) suggest that noncompliance serves important social developmental opportunities in providing children with a context in which to (1) assert their autonomy within the parent–child relationship and (2) develop social skills and strategies to express their autonomy in a socially acceptable manner. However, as children develop verbally and cognitively, there are significant shifts in the quality of noncompliant behaviors. The direct defiance of the 2s and 3s is replaced by the child's ability to "assertively" and "skillfully" suggest alternatives as he or she becomes increasingly sophisticated in his or her goal-directed behavior (Kuczynski & Kochanska, 1990). Typically developing children can engage in negotiating behavior with their caregivers and maintain a positive or neutral affect upon redirection (Bates, Petit, Dodge, & Ridge, 1998; Crockenberg & Litman, 1990). For instance, when met with a parental directive to clean up or get ready to go, normally developing children may express their desires by attempting to bargain ("five more minutes?") or generating alternatives ("can we leave the blocks?").

There is a dearth of research on developmental outcomes associated with noncompliance in preschoolers. However, there is a recent population-based longitudinal study that tracked developmental rule-breaking trajectories of 1,492 Canadian children from ages 2.5 to 6 years (Petitclerc, Boivin, Dionne, Zoccolillo, & Tremblay, 2009). The study yielded four distinct, relatively stable groups: very low (9.1%), low (56.9%), moderate (29.7%), and chronic (4.3%). The incidence of noncompliant behavior, like physical aggression, decreased over the preschool years, but the decrease was slight and did not reflect an age associated with "peak" noncompliant behavior. The rate at which children broke the rules over the course of the 3 years was remarkably consistent, implying that the most frequent rule breakers at 2.5 years were still the most frequent rule breakers at 6. These results extend earlier research that documented a small subset of elementary and adolescent children who demonstrate chronic behavior problems specifically related to rule-breaking behavior (Bongers, Koot, van der Ende, & Verhulst, 2004; Nagin & Tremblay, 1999; Shaw et al., 2003). An important distinction between normative and atypical noncompliance is the quality of the noncompliant behavior (Crockenberg & Litman, 1990; Drabick et al., 2001; Kuczynski & Kochanska, 1990). Atypical noncompliance is behavior that is an active resistance to control and is associated with negative affect (Bates, Petit, Dodge, & Ridge, 1998; Crockenberg & Litman, 1990). Problematic noncompliance is characterized by its unskilled and defiant nature and is unnecessarily provocative, inflexible, and stubborn. Atypical noncompliant behaviors include the automatically elicited "reflexive no," "doing the opposite" of what was asked, and noncompliance that is associated with angry outbursts. Developmental studies support the qualitative distinction between goal-directed negotiation and defiance: assertiveness and defiance are negatively associated, and defiance is associated with child disruptive behavior and problematic parenting, whereas assertiveness is associated with developmental competencies and promotive parenting (Crockenberg & Litman, 1990; Dix, Stewart, Gershoff, & Day, 2007; Drabick, Strassberg, & Kees, 2001; Kuczynski & Kochanska, 1990). Problematic noncompliance in preschoolers may present as a child who repeatedly refuses to follow adult rules or requests, a child who doesn't seem to feel guilty about misbehaving, or a child who doesn't modify his or her behavior after being punished (Thibault, Jetté, Desrosiers, & Gingras, 2003).

Temper Tantrums

Current literature most commonly defines temper tantrums as "discrete episodes of excessive temper, frustration, or upset manifested by shouting, crying, stamping and/or violence or attempts at damage directed against self, other, or property" (Egger & Angold, 2004, p. 230). Typical tantrums appear by the end of the infant's 1st year (Tremblay, 2008), occur in an expectable context (i.e., hunger, fatigue, and/or sickness) and rarely escalate to excessive crying, shouting, a destruction of property, or violence (Belden, Thompson, & Luby, 2008). Recovery is easy, and the child is able to establish positive mood independently, although in some cases the child might require some adult support, to which the child is responsive.

Frequency in temper tantrums appears to peak at 18 months. In a sample of 18- to 60-month-old children, Potegal and Davidson (2003) found that tantrum behaviors such as crying and hitting occurred once a day on average, with 75% lasting between 1.5 and 5 minutes. Another study of 3- to 12-year-olds found that 3- to 5-year-olds had the highest incidence of tantrums at 75.8%, with prevalence decreasing steadily with increasing age; 20.8% for 6- to 8-year-olds and 3.9% in

9- to 12-year-olds (Bhatia et al., 1990). Although temper tantrums are normative misbehaviors during some developmental periods, certain qualities of tantrum behavior, such as pacing, duration, and predictability, can indicate an atypical and disruptive behavioral trajectory. Poorly modulated tantrums, characterized by intensity (strength and force) of anger expressions, destructiveness of tantrums, and difficulty recovering, have been linked to clinical problems in young children (Belden et al., 2008; Needleman, Stevenson, & Zuckerman, 1991).

Research investigating differences between two groups of preschoolers (one of healthy controls and one of depressed-disruptive preschoolers) suggests five "high"-risk tantrum styles (Belden et al., 2008). The first describes consistent (i.e., greater than 50% of the time during the last 10–20 tantrum episodes) displays of aggression toward caregivers and/or destructive behavior toward an object. The second describes preschoolers who intentionally engage in self-injurious behavior, such as hitting their heads against a wall, using an object to hurt themselves, holding their breath, and biting themselves. Self-injurious behavior is a matter for concern independent of duration, intensity, or context. Frequency of tantrum episodes makes up the third high-risk style: these are children who display 10–20 episodes at home on separate days within a 30-day period and children who have more than five tantrums a day for multiple days either at school or at home. The fourth style consists of extended duration of tantrum episodes lasting more than 25 minutes. The fifth style is based on the child's ability to recover or self-soothe. A preschooler who frequently requires substantial adult assistance to recover from a tantrum is at greater risk of having a clinically concerning problem.

Impulsivity/Activity

Behavioral impulsivity is broadly defined in clinical research as the inability to delay, inhibit, or control behavior in light of reward or direction. Impulsive children are described by parents and teachers with such phrases as "acts without thinking ahead," "speaks at inappropriate times," and "has a hard time waiting for his or her turn"(Barkley, 2005). Hyperactivity has been defined as "excessive" or "inappropriate" levels of activity (Barkley, 2005) and in young children means unrestrained motor movement or vocal restlessness. Hyperactive children are described by parents and teachers in the following ways: "always on the go," "acts as if driven by a motor," "climbs excessively," "often hums or makes odd noises," and "squirmy" (DuPaul, 1998). Recent research has shown that both highly impulsive and hyperactive behavior appear to be powerful diagnostic tools: in young children they appear to be heritable, stable constructs that emerge early in life and predict future impairment (Campbell, 1985; Huijbregts, Seguin, Zoccolillo, Boivin, & Tremblay, 2007; Leblanc, 2008; Romano, Tremblay, Farhat, & Coté, 2006).

Longitudinal studies beginning at birth suggest that individual differences in rates of impulsive and hyperactive behavior emerge as early as the second year of life (Leblanc, 2008; Palfrey, Levine, Walker, & Sullivan, 1985) and remain relatively stable through entry into elementary school (Petitclerc & Tremblay, 2009). Developmental researchers have shown that the preschool years are associated with the ability to increasingly inhibit behavior, follow rules, manage negative emotions (Kochanska, Murray, & Coy, 1997), and generate cognitive hypothetical alternatives (Reznick, Corley, & Robinson, 1997). The set of processes that develop and eventually regulate behavior have been labeled inhibitory control, part of the broad construct of effortful control (Rothbart, Ahadi, & Hershey, 1994; Rothbart & Bates, 2006). Inhibitory control has been conceptualized as part of executive function and is defined as the capacity to self-regulate behavior in response to expectations or instructions (Gagne, 2010). The mechanism of inhibitory control involves flexible problem solving, presenting in some situations as the ability to suppress a dominant response and in others as the ability to activate a subdominant response (Derryberry & Rothbart, 1997; Rothbart, 1989a; Rothbart & Ahadi, 1994; Rothbart & Bates, 2006).

Normative inhibitory control emerges in infancy and through the second year, becomes a distinct part of a child's behavioral response at age 2, and continues to progress in the toddler and preschool years (Kochanska et al., 1998; Rothbart, 1989a). For example, in the Bear/Dragon task (a simpler version of Simon Says), children are told to perform all actions given by the "nice" bear puppet but are told to ignore all commands from the "naughty" dragon puppet. Young 3-year-olds understand the game but have a difficult time suppressing their response to either puppet, whereas older 3-year-olds and most 4-year-olds can perform the task most of the time (Reed, Pien, & Rothbart,1984). Children typically develop greater inhibitory control rapidly from the ages of 3 to 6, growing in their ability to self-regulate attention and motor responses, wait for a reward, and stay on a directed task (Carlson, Davis, & Leach, 2005; Kochanska, Murray, & Harlan, 2000). Children with higher levels of inhibitory control have been shown to have less behavioral maladjustment (Eisenberg et al., 2001; Eisenberg, Smith, Sadovsky, & Spinrad, 2004).

Two important indicators of problematic hyperactive-impulsive behavior are early onset and high, stable rates of symptoms. Toddlers with the highest levels of behavioral disinhibition continue to have significantly more disruptive behavior symptoms for as long as they have been followed, sometimes until the end of adolescence (Tremblay, 2006). Leblanc's 2008 longitudinal study of hyperactive-impulsive behavior of 1,112 preschool twins found that parental assessments as early as 19 months of age significantly predict later hyperactive-impulsive behaviors as rated by a child's teacher in the first 2 years of school. Parent ratings of hyperactive-impulsive behavior were remarkably stable over the course of the study, with 7.1% of the children in the group rated by mothers as "often" hyperactive-impulsive. Interestingly, the finding coincides with prevalence rates of ADHD as assessed in school settings (7%; Barkley, 2005) and at the upper end of prevalence rates during preschool as assessed in community samples (5%; Dreyer, 2006). Problematic impulsive-hyperactive behaviors are often developmentally expectable (interrupting, fidgeting), but not to the degree at which it impairs cognitive and social functioning, as it does with these children. Typically developing 4- and 5-year-olds can sit and listen to a story or watch a demonstration that precedes a hands-on activity for about 10–15 minutes, follow clear two-part instructions ("clean up the tables and then line up by the door"), and take turns (Seefeldt & Wasik, 2006). In contrast, children with dysregulated impulsive-hyperactive behavior have difficulty sitting for group meetings and waiting their turn, are often wandering the room at inappropriate times, and frequently disrupt the play activities of others. They tend to be excessively demanding in both peer and teacher interactions and are especially noisy and talkative (Barkley et al., 2002; Campbell, Endman, & Bernfield, 1977; Campbell, Schleifer, & Weiss, 1978; Schleifer et al., 1975; Shelton et al., 1998). Preschoolers diagnosed with the hyperactive-impulsive subset of ADHD have also been shown to have higher rates of accidental injury (Byrne, Bawden, Beattie, & De Wolfe, 2003).

Empathy

Developmental literature defines empathy as an "affective reaction that results from the apprehension or comprehension of another's emotional state" (Eisenberg & Fabes, 1998) or "an affective response that is more appropriate to another's situation than one's own" (Hoffman, 2000, p. 4). A lack of empathy, known as callous affect, is marked by an absence of guilt and ranges from showing disregard for others' feelings in times of stress to active disregard, including attempts to cause others distress (Wakschlag et al., 2010). Callous–unemotional (CU) traits designate a group with a particularly severe, aggressive, and stable pattern of antisocial behavior (Frick & White, 2008).

Empirical research confirms that there is a "biological preparedness" for the development of empathy already present in infancy (Zahn-Waxler, Radke-Yarrow, Wagner, & Chapman, 1992). According to Hoffman (2000), empathy emerges and matures in several stages based on sociocognitive development, that is, the toddler's sense of self and others as separate entities. The development of empathy progresses from empathic concern during infancy to instrumental attempts to comfort others in toddlers to representations of how to help another in preschool (Hay & Cook, 2007). Normal development during the preschool period leads to an increasing capacity for perspective taking, and the child's focus shifts from feeling "parallel distress" and seeking to comfort him- or herself to "sympathetic distress," expressing concern for, or trying to comfort, the other (Hoffman, 2007).

Hoffman suggests five stages in the development of empathic distress. The first stage is *global empathic distress*, in which a child is empathizing without knowing that he or she is empathizing. For example, newborns automatically start to cry when they hear the sound of another human cry. "Regardless of the cause, the newborn is responding to a cue of distress in others by becoming distressed him- or herself" (Hoffman, 2007, p. 137). The second stage, typically occurring around 13 months, is *quasi-egocentric empathic distress*, in which a child develops a sense of self versus other. In this stage, a child recognizes another's distress and provides a form of comfort to the other through a hug, holding hands, and so forth. These are all behaviors that the child uses to sooth him- or herself in times of distress. At this time the child can only imagine his or her own needs and assumes that his or her perception of the world is universal, and so he or she does not realize that the other child might prefer other forms of comfort. *Veridical empathy* typically occurs between 2 and 3 years of age, when a child can start to recognize another child's states, thoughts, feelings, and desires in different situations and his or her empathic responses become more effective. Once the child develops a good sense of the self versus other, the motive to comfort him- or herself is transformed into the motive to help the other child in distress. For Hoffman (2007), feelings of sympathetic distress or compassion for another person are the first step toward prosocial behavior (e.g., physical affection, helping behaviors, sharing).

In early childhood, normative misbehaviors may include intermittent insensitivity to others (e.g., refusing to share) and/or contextually expectable expressions (e.g., saying mean things to others during a toy dispute). However, certain qualities such as frequency (i.e., whether they happen more often than not) and expectability (i.e., whether they occur when circumstances don't warrant that particular maladaptive response) of these behaviors might warrant clinical concern. Among these behaviors are CU traits such as lack of empathy, lack of concern for others, compromised guilt, and a severe and pervasive pattern of aggressive behavior such as bullying. Physical cruelty and vindictiveness are not normative misbehaviors during the preschool period; their very presence marks clinical significance (Wakschlag et al., 2010). A preschooler who is not typically developing empathy at the age of 2 or 3 might be unable to assume another's perspective when the other is in distress. For example, this child might refuse to share a toy even after eliciting a crying response from a playmate by not sharing (another behavior typical of this age.) A child with CU traits might not respond to distress cues, for example, continuing to play with the toy or moving on to another game without showing remorse. Ultimately, a child might display active disregard for others' needs and feelings (e.g., "takes pleasure in others' distress," "does not try to behave after being punished," and "'does nasty things to others out of the blue"; Wakschlag et al. 2010).

TYPOLOGIES

Although understanding the topography and quality of behaviors in context likely provides greater sensitivity in identifying problematic behaviors during the preschool period, any individual behavior will not capture the complexity inherent in understanding risk for the development of antisocial behavior. Varying typologies currently exist for aggregating these behaviors in order to identify children who are at highest risk for the development of antisocial behavior. Most notable, here in the United States, is the *Diagnostic and Statistical Manual of*

Mental Disorders (4th edition, text revision; DSM-IV-TR; American Psychiatric Association, 2000), which categories youths, including preschoolers, into ADHD, ODD, and CD nosologies. However, these current typologies suffer from lack of precision owing to the downward extension of symptoms to preschool children that are largely derived for school-age children. This limits the utility of these nosologies in predicting longer term stability or problems for preschoolers.

Stability estimates for DSM-defined ADHD, ODD, and/or CD diagnosed during preschool are about 50% over the course of 1–2 years (Chacko et al., 2009) with continued reductions in stability of diagnoses over more extended periods of time. For example, Lavigne and colleagues (Lavigne, Arend, & Rosenbaum, 1998; Lavigne, Cicchetti, & Gibbons, 2001) reported that the 2-year stability of any behavior disorder (ODD, CD, and/or ADHD) or a combination of the three was moderate. Diagnostic stability of ODD dropped substantially with longer follow-up—with stability of 43%, 27%, and 24% at 3-, 4-, and 5-year follow-ups, respectively. Thus the probability of a diagnosis of ODD during the school-age period was substantial if ODD was present during the preschool years. On the other hand, these data also demonstrate that the majority of preschoolers (nearly half of preschoolers with an ODD diagnosis at baseline) do not persist in meeting clinical criteria at school age. Similar patterns were reported by Kim-Cohen, Arseneault, and Caspi (2005) on the 2-year stability of CD in a community sample of children followed from 4½–5 to 7 years of age. Meeting criteria for CD at age 5 significantly increased the odds of a CD diagnosis at age 7 (odds ratio = 20.6). Again, however, half of these children did not exhibit any CD symptoms at age 7, with 60% of these children failing to exhibit any CD symptoms at the subsequent age-10 follow-up (Kim-Cohen, Arseneault, & Newcombe, 2009). Collectively, although the short-term stability of disruptive behavior disorders (DBDs) appears robust, the longer term (2- to 5-year) stability of DBDs is questionable. This lack of clear stability is a particularly critical issue for those invested in preventing poor long-term outcomes in children. As prevention and early intervention efforts are increasingly recognized as key to altering the often poor trajectories of youths with mental health challenges, identifying children who will have persistent problems is essential.

Given the challenges of the current DSM approach in identifying preschool children who continue to have persistently high levels of problems, including the development of antisocial behavior, alternative perspectives integrating the developmental and clinical literatures, as well as concepts from the more dynamic developmental psychopathology approach to understanding problematic behavior, are now increasingly being considered. In the next section, we discuss several novel lines of research that attempt to "carve nature at its joints," thereby identifying increasingly meaningful typologies for identifying categories of high-risk preschool children. We focus here on research that parses key behaviors into dimensions that may better capture typologies of problematic behavior during the preschool years.

Dimensions That May Lead to More Specified Typologies During Preschool

Current typologies, as reflected in DSM ADHD, ODD, and CD nosologies, may be better parsed to reflect underlying dimensions that may be more precisely related to the development of various outcomes, including antisocial behavior. This line of empirical investigation has recently begun to take root, with emerging evidence suggesting some utility in this approach. For example, Stringaris and Goodman (2009) proposed three dimensions within ODD that were hypothesized to be differentially related to various outcomes. Specifically, they proposed that an "Irritable" dimension, reflected in the DSM-IV items of "often loses temper," "is often angry and resentful," and "is often touchy or easily annoyed by others," would be associated with emotional disorders. They proposed that a "Hurtful" dimension, composed of ODD items of spitefulness and vindictiveness, would be hypothesized to be related to callous, premeditated, and aggressive components of CD/antisocial behavior. Lastly, a "Headstrong" dimension was proposed, composed of the remaining DSM ODD items: "often argues with adults," "often actively defies or refuses to comply with adults' requests or rules," "often deliberately annoys other people," and "often blames others for his or her mistakes or misbehavior."

In a sample of over 14,000 children between the ages of 5 and 16, the authors found that the three dimensions of oppositional behavior differed in association with various outcomes, including more serious antisocial/conduct problems. Most notably, the Headstrong dimension was particularly associated with status violations and to a lesser extent with nonaggressive offenses. The Hurtful dimension was strongly associated with ratings of the child as callous or cold-blooded. As the authors suggest, the link between the Hurtful dimension and both nonaggressive and aggressive offenses may reflect callous and premeditated behavior. The authors also found an association between the Irritable dimension and both aggressive symptoms and status violations, which they contend may reflect reactive behaviors triggered by anger.

Although this study was conducted with older youths, the data suggest that a more refined, theory-driven approach to conceptualizing typologies of behavior may lead to a better understanding of the differential trajectories of these typologies as they relate to various pathways, including the development of serious antisocial behavior. Currently, Wakschlag and colleagues (2010) have proposed a refined nosology of preschool disruptive behavior that has great potential in better understanding which preschool children may be at highest risk for the development of antisocial behavior. We briefly describe next this refined nosology, though empirical data on the utility of this refined nosology is now just beginning to be collected and will require empirical validation.

The four-dimensional approach to preschool DBDs proposed by Wakschlag and colleagues (2010) is theoretically, developmentally, and empirically grounded. As the authors note, this approach is derived from "translation" of the core DSM ODD and CD constructs into developmentally meaningful terms based on review of prior conceptual work, studies of preschool DBDs, developmental studies, and extensive clinical research, as well as the authors' role in proposing revisions for DSM-V. The proposed multidimensional model includes four distinct behavioral dimensions: Temper Loss, Noncompliance, Aggression, and Lack of Concern for Others.

The *Temper Loss* dimension encompasses overt expressions of behavioral regulation, particularly management of anger. It ranges from normative mild to moderate expressions of anger in response to frustration to extreme dysregulated temper. Atypical temper loss for preschool DBDs includes destructive and prolonged tantrums, multiple daily tantrums, trouble calming down when angry, and easily precipitated temper loss.

The *Noncompliance* dimension reflects resistance to, and failure to comply with, directives, rules, and social norms. It ranges from normative assertions of autonomy to pervasive, active, and persistent disregard of rules and norms. Some evidence of clinical indicators at preschool age include intense and insistent noncompliance, a "reflexive no," and sneaky misbehavior.

The *Aggression* dimension reflects the tendency to respond aggressively across a variety of contexts (home, school setting, with familiar or unfamiliar peers or adults), ranging from normative self-protection to severe violence. Manifestations of this dimension during preschool include intense, hostile, and proactive forms of aggression, frequent aggression, and aggression toward adults.

The *Low Concern for Others* dimension reflects active disregard for, lack of responsiveness to, and lack of sensitivity to others' feelings. It ranges normatively from mild insensitivity within contexts of stress or conflict to extreme and persistent callous disregard of others across a range of social interactions and contexts. Wakschlag and colleagues (2010) hypothesize that clinical manifestations may include indifference to punishment or consequences, being undeterred by parental anger, lack of interest in pleasing others, and taking pleasure in others' distress.

The value of these refined nosologies is determined by whether these refinements result in a greater understanding of the development and treatment of psychopathology and problematic behaviors in preschool children. Two particular issues that are pertinent are whether these refined nosologies result in a greater long-term stability compared with existing DSM categories and whether these refined nosologies result in improved sensitivity to treatment. For instance, one seminal effort in the literature is to delineate subtypes based on developmental period of onset (e.g., the distinction between "life-course persistent" and adolescence-limited antisocial behavior; Moffitt, Caspi, Dickson, Silva, & Stanton, 1996). Recently such subtype differentiation has led to identification of partially distinct genetic etiologies (Tackett, Krueger, Iacono, & McGue, 2005). Specific DBD dimensional patterns and subtypes in older youths have been identified, including "overt, covert and authority-conflict patterns of delinquency," "socialized and undersocialized" CD, and callous psychopathy (Blair, 2006; Frick et al., 2003). Collectively, a more nuanced approach to classifying youths with behavioral disorders has resulted in a better understanding of the etiology, correlates, trajectories, and, most important, development of preventive and early intervention approaches for identified youths. A refined nosology/typology for preschool behavioral problems offers similar promise.

ASSESSMENT OF PRESCHOOL BEHAVIOR PROBLEMS

The importance of comprehensive assessment of preschool behavior problems must not be understated. Given the variability of behavior of preschool children, the importance of behavior in context when determining whether and to what extent a particular behavior is problematic, the critical role of key relationships (parent–child) during early childhood, and the rapidly developing social, emotional, cognitive, and behavioral competencies during the preschool period, comprehensive assessment is particularly important during this age period. As such, as detailed by Egger (2009), comprehensive assessment during the preschool period includes six essential components: (1) multiple sessions, (2) multiple informants, (3) a multidisciplinary approach, (4) a multicultural perspective, (5) multiple modes of assessment, and (6) a multiaxial diagnostic perspective. A full discussion of each of these components is well beyond the scope of this chapter; however, we focus our attention on multiple modes of assessment, highlighting recent developments in select, semistructured interviews (the Kiddie-Disruptive Behavior Disorder Schedule [K-DBDS] and the Preschool Age Psychiatric Assessment [PAPA]) and observational methods (Disruptive Behavior Diagnostic Observation Schedule [DB-DOS]) assessing disruptive behavior in preschool children. A more comprehensive review of various measures can be found in DelCarmen-Wiggins and Carter (2004) and Zeanah (2009).

K-DBDS

The K-DBDS (Keenan, Wakschlag,, & Danis, 2001; Keenan et al., 2007; Keenan et al., (2011) is a semistructured caregiver interview that was developed to assess disruptive behavior disorders in young children using developmentally appropriate operational definitions of symptoms of DSM ADHD, ODD and CD. DSM-IV ODD symptoms were unchanged from the way they are described in DSM-IV, with the word *often* appearing before the behavioral description (e.g., *often* loses temper). Of the 15 DSM-IV CD symptoms, four were not assessed because of the lack of face validity: (1) breaking into a house, car, or building; (2) running away from home overnight; (3) often staying out late; and (4) truancy. Some of the CD symptoms were adapted with more developmentally appropriate language. For example, the DSM-IV CD symptom "often initiates physical fights" is worded in the K-DBDS as "is often physically aggressive" because it is difficult for parents or teachers to know who initiated the physical fighting. In addition, to assess "forced sexual behavior," the caregiver is asked about inappropriate sexual behavior that is nonconsensual. "Stealing" was defined as knowingly taking something that did not belong to him or her on repeated occasions and concealing it. The one-week test–retest reliability of the K-DBDS was conducted in an independent sample of 31 referred and nonreferred preschoolers. Test–retest reliability for total number of ODD and CD symptoms was high (ICC > .75). Interrater reliability for the total number of ODD and CD symptoms was high (ICC > .95), as was the interrater reliability for diagnoses (kappa > .90). Reliability was not affected by age or sex of the child. Validity of preschool diagnoses was demonstrated via associations with impairment, such as parental ratings of global impairment and differentiation between referred and nonreferred children (Keenan et al., 2007).

PAPA

The PAPA (Egger & Angold, 2004; Egger, Erkanli, et al., 2006) is a comprehensive semistructured caregiver interview assessing 25 modules covering disruptive behaviors (ADHD, ODD, and CD), internalizing problems (separation anxiety, depression), and other key domains for preschool children (e.g., relationship quality, sleep hygiene, child care). The PAPA was developed through an iterative process including identification of behaviors from various classification systems (DSM) and checklists (e.g., Child Behavior Checklist [CBCL]), as well as the broader literature, developmentally informed modification to DSM criteria, inclusion of assessment in key preschool contexts (e.g., in-home and out-of-home child care), and so forth. In addition, minimization of predetermined cutoffs for diagnoses, as well as assessment of impairment specifically related to the presence of symptoms, has been incorporated into the PAPA (see Egger & Angold, 2004, for an extensive discussion of the development of the PAPA).

Egger, Erkanli, et al. (2006) examined the test–retest reliability of the PAPA for use with parents of preschoolers 2–5 years old. In a sample of over 1,000 parents of children attending a large pediatric clinic, 193 parents who rated their children high on the CBCL and 114 parents who rated their children low on the CBCL were interviewed on two occasions. The authors found similar rates of diagnostic reliability to those obtained from interviews with parents of older children and adults, with a kappa ranging from .36 to .79. Test–retest intraclass correlations for DSM-IV syndrome scale scores ranged from .56 to .89. Additionally, no significant differences in reliability by age, sex, or race (African American vs. non-African American). In terms of ADHD, ODD, and CD, the authors also found kappas greater than .67, as well as test–retest intraclass correlations greater than .62. As such, the PAPA provides a reasonably reliable standardized measure for the assessment of various problems in preschool children, including the disruptive behavior problems that are most likely related to the development of antisocial behavior.

The strengths of the K-DBDS and the PAPA are that both utilize developmentally appropriate definitions of ADHD, ODD, and CD symptoms while taking into consideration more developmentally appropriate duration/frequency, context (home, public, school), pervasiveness, and impairment criteria. For those professionals familiar with semistructured interviews, the format and delivery of K-DBDS and PAPA are similar to other well-established semistructured interviews (e.g., Schedule for Affective Disorders and Schizophrenia for School-Age Children). The reliability and validity of the measures are sound. In our opinion, the K-DBDS and PAPA represent among the best available semistructured interviews for the assessment of key disruptive behavior in preschool children and have immediate clinical utility. The drawback to the K-DBDS, as well as the PAPA, is that it perhaps adheres too closely to the current DSM approach to classifying disruptive behaviors as problematic without greater attention to a developmentally informed approach to understanding the nuanced presentation of these behaviors. Future research on semistructured interviews (as well as self-report measures) should begin to consider integrating the clinical and developmental literatures to identify salient behaviors in context, which may provide greater sensitivity and specificity in identifying preschool children with disruptive behaviors.

DB-DOS

The DB-DOS (Wakschlag et al., 2007; Wakschlag, Briggs-Gowan, et al., 2008; Wakschlag & Danis, 2004; Wakschlag, Hill, et al., 2008; Wakschlag et al., 2005) is an observational, primarily clinical research tool for assessing disruptive behavior in young children. The aim of the DB-DOS is to provide a developmentally informed, examiner-directed assessment of disruptive behavior in young children that yields information essential for characterizing disruptive behavior in preschool children and serves as a companion to parent-interview methods.

The DB-DOS is specific to the assessment of disruptive behavior in preschool children in that it attempts to assess for key manifestations specific to disruptive behavior in this period. Specifically, Wakschlag and colleagues conceptualized two core domains of disruptive behavior across developmental periods, which are assessed in the DB-DOS: (1) problems in behavioral regulation, that is, challenges in regulating behavior in keeping with social rules and norms; and (2) problems in anger modulation, which reflects anger dyscontrol. In addition, competence (social engagement and coping/mastery) is also assessed. Moreover, the DB-DOS includes two examiner modules that allow the assessment of how external structure and support may affect the child's capacity for behavioral regulation and anger modulation via systematic variation in the level of support provided by the examiner ("examiner engaged" vs. "examiner busy"). In contrast to the examiner modules, the parent module occurs with no prescripted behavior for the parent to follow; rather, there are variations in task demands. This format allows the parent's behavior to unfold naturally while determining the extent to which demands influence child behavior. The parent module also provides a relatively standardized context within which to assess key clinically concerning parental behavior.

DB-DOS tasks are activities within the modules that are designed as "presses" to elicit these salient behaviors in behavioral regulation and anger modulation. In developing these tasks, Wakschlag and colleagues drew on a number of widely used developmental paradigms to create a series of presses that would be likely to elicit the full range of clinically relevant behavior. Such tasks included compliance "do" and "don't" tasks, cleanup, withdrawal of attention, social play, and frustration tasks. The uniqueness of the DB-DOS is that it utilizes tasks that press for a broad range of behaviors in a clinically informative manner. Essentially, the DB-DOS coding system was specially designed to distinguish the normative misbehavior of the preschool period from clinically concerning behavior via an emphasis on behavioral quality. DB-DOS codes are global, integrated judgments that parallel typical clinical observation (quality and quantity) rather than just frequency counts of discrete behaviors.

In a series of studies (Wakschlag et al., 2007; Wakschlag, Briggs-Gowan, et al., 2008; Wakschlag, Hill, et al., 2008) the DB-DOS was evaluated for reliability and validity. Data demonstrate that the DB-DOS demonstrated good interrater and test–retest reliability. Confirmatory factor analysis demonstrated an excellent fit of the DB-DOS multidomain model of disruptive behavior (Wakschlag, Briggs-Gowan, et al., 2008). In addition, DB-DOS scores were significantly associated with reported and independently observed behavior. Scores from both DB-DOS domains (behavior regulation and anger modulation) and each of the three DB-DOS contexts (examiner engaged, examiner busy, and parent) contributed uniquely to discrimination of disruptive behavior status, concurrently and predictively. Observed behavior on the DB-DOS also contributed incrementally to prediction of impairment over time, beyond variance explained by meeting DSM-IV disruptive behavior disorder symptom criteria based on parent–teacher report (Wakschlag, Hill, et al., 2008).

The DB-DOS, with its emphasis on assessing behavior in context and coding that relies on the integration of developmental and clinical literatures, is an exemplar observational assessment method. Thus far, data support its reliability and validity, with encouraging data supporting its incremental utility relative to other methods in identifying preschool children who will persist with disruptive behavior problems. Given the challenges in sensitivity and specificity of current methods of classifying preschool children who require intervention for the prevention of long-term antisocial problems, the DBD-DOS, in concert with other psychometrically sound assessment methods for the preschool period, offers much hope in more accurately identifying these young children.

IMPLICATIONS FOR FUTURE RESEARCH, PUBLIC POLICY, AND CLINICAL PRACTICE

The preschool period offers a great opportunity to identify problems and intervene in the lives of children. There has been a growing recognition that the roots of problematic behavior can be identified during early childhood (Chacko et al.,

2009). Therefore, we must focus on prevention and early intervention during this time period. Unfortunately, the majority of prevention efforts target older youths and adolescents (Tremblay, 2010). As Tremblay notes, there continues to be an impression on the part of the public that antisocial behavior is an adolescent problem, and therefore valuable and scarce resources are allocated to intervening during this age period. Although adolescent antisocial behavior is more destructive and costly relative to antisocial behaviors committed by younger youths, intervening during adolescence, a relatively late stage in the trajectory of antisocial behavior, likely has very limited benefits. Shifting public policy in order to allocate these valuable resources toward early childhood in efforts to prevent later antisocial behavior will require a dissemination of knowledge not only to policymakers but also, importantly, to the public.

Clinically, it is clear that there are psychometrically sound and developmentally appropriate assessment measures available to utilize when assessing preschool children who are at high risk for stable behavior problems. However, it is unclear to what extent these evidence-based assessment methods (e.g., PAPA, K-DBDS, DB-DOS) for preschoolers can be implemented within the context of routine community-based care. At the very least, incorporating key components of assessment for preschool children can offer the clinician an opportunity to gather information in such a way that takes into account the complex, rapidly developing, multicontextual issues of the preschool period. As discussed earlier, Egger (2009) articulates that assessment for preschoolers should include: (1) multiple sessions, (2) multiple informants, (3) a multidisciplinary approach, (4) a multicultural perspective, (5) multiple modes of assessment, and (6) a multiaxial diagnostic perspective. Adhering to these critical components of assessment will likely provide a clinician with more comprehensive and developmentally sensitive information that can be utilized to inform decision making regarding nosology and treatment. Additionally, there is a growing literature that attempts to integrate the developmental and clinical literatures regarding preschool behavior problems and its relationship to antisocial behavior in older youths that can be a valuable resource for clinicians as they conduct assessments with preschool children.

The literature in the area of preschool behavioral markers that may predict distinct trajectories that lead to the development of more serious antisocial behavior in older youths is in a nascent state. There are several lines of research that may continue to contribute to this area of research. First, further integration of the developmental and clinical literatures in our conceptualization of typologies is necessary. This is particularly true for ADHD. Despite the evidence that early impulsivity, activity, and inattention are concurrently related to oppositional and conduct problems in preschoolers and that these behaviors predict the severity of problematic behavior over time, there has not been nearly enough attention given to bridging the clinical and developmental literatures in the ADHD area. In addition, although several research groups are beginning to explore the utility of varying typologies of preschool behavior problems, ultimately we will have to wait and see whether the approach of integrating developmental and clinical literatures and taking a refined approach to classifying preschool disruptive behavior typologies will provide incremental benefit over other well-established approaches. This is a high hurdle that must be jumped in order to warrant a shift in practice.

REFERENCES

Alink, L., Mesman, J., van Zeijl, J., Stolk, M., Juffer, F., Koot, H., . . . van IJzendoorn, M. (2006). The early childhood aggression curve: Development of physical aggression in 10–50-month-old children. *Child Development, 77*, 954–966.

American Psychiatric Association. (2000). *Diagnostic and statistical manual for mental disorders* (4th ed., text rev.). Washington, DC: Author.

Baillargeon, R., Normand, C., Seguin, J., Zoccolillo, M., Japel, C., Peruse, D., . . . Tremblay, R. (2007). The evolution of problem and social competence behaviors during toddlerhood: A prospective population based cohort survey. *Infant Mental Health Journal, 28*, 12–38.

Barkley, R. A. (2005). *Attention-deficit hyperactivity disorder* (3rd ed.). New York, NY: Guilford Press.

Barkley, R. A., Shelton, T. L., Crosswait, C., Moorehouse, M., Fletcher, K., Barrett, S., . . . Metevia, L. (2002). Preschool children with disruptive behavior: Three-year outcome as a function of adaptive disability. *Development and Psychopathology, 14*, 45–67.

Bates, J., Petit, G., Dodge, K., & Ridge, B. (1998). Interaction of temperamental resistance to control and restrictive parenting in the development of externalizing behavior. *Developmental Psychology, 34*, 982–995.

Belden, A. C., Thompson, N. R., & Luby, J. L. (2008). Temper tantrums in healthy versus DSM-IV depressed and disruptive preschoolers: Defining tantrum behaviors associated with clinical problems. *Journal of Pediatrics, 152*, 117–122.

Bhatia, M. S., Dhar, N. K., Singhal, P. K., Nigam, V. R., Malik, S. C., & Mullick, D. N. (1990). Temper tantrums: Prevalence and etiology in a non-referral outpatient setting. *Clinical Pediatrics, 29*, 311–315.

Blair, R. J. R. (2006). The emergence of psychopathy: Implications for the neuropsychological approach to developmental disorders. *Cognition, 101*, 414–442.

Bongers, I. L., Koot, H. M., van der Ende, J., & Verhulst, F. C. (2004). Developmental trajectories of externalizing behaviors in childhood and adolescence. *Child Development, 75*, 1523–1537.

Broidy, L., Nagin, D., Tremblay, R., Bates, J., Brame, B., Dodge, K., . . . Vitaro, F. (2003). Developmental trajectories of childhood disruptive behaviors and adolescent delinquency: A six-site, cross-national study. *Developmental Psychology, 39*, 222–245.

Byrne, J. M., Bawden, H. N., Beattie, T., & DeWolfe, N. A. (2003). Risk for injury in preschoolers: Relationship to attention deficit hyperactivity disorder. *Child Neuropsychology, 9*, 142–151.

Campbell, S. B. (1985). Hyperactivity in preschoolers: Correlates and prognostic implications. *Clinical Psychology Review, 5*, 405–428.

Campbell, S. B. (2002) *Behavior problems in preschool children: Clinical and developmental issues.* New York, NY: Guilford Press.

Campbell, S. B., Endman, M., & Bernfeld, G. (1977). A three-year follow-up of hyperactive preschoolers into elementary school. *Journal of Child Psychology and Psychiatry, 18*, 239–242.

Campbell, S. B., Schleifer, M., & Weiss, G. (1978). Continuities in maternal reports and child behaviors over time in hyperactive and comparison groups. *Journal of Abnormal Child Psychology, 6*(1), 33–45.

Carlson, S. M., Davis, A. C., & Leach, J. G. (2005). Less is more: Executive function and symbolic representation in preschool children. *Psychological Science, 16,* 609–616.

Carter, A., Briggs-Gowan, M., Jones, S., & Little, T. (2003). The Infant–Toddler Social and Emotional Assessment (ITSEA): Factor structure, reliability, and validity. *Journal of Abnormal Child Psychology, 31,* 495–514.

Carter, A., Briggs-Gowan, M., McCarthy, K., & Wakschlag, L. (2009, April). Developmental patterns of normative misbehavior in early childhood: Implications for identification of early disruptive behavior. In R. Baillargeon (Chair), *The evolution of disruptive behavior problems in young children.* Symposium conducted at the meeting of the Society for Research in Child Development, Denver, CO.

Chacko, A., Wakschlag, L., Espy, K., Hill, C., & Danis, B. (2009). Viewing preschool disruptive behavior disorders and ADHD through a developmental lens: What we know and what we need to know. *Child and Adolescent Psychiatric Clinics of North America, 18,* 627–643.

Côté, S., Vaillancourt, T., Barker, E. D., Nagin, D., & Tremblay, R. (2007). The joint development of physical and indirect aggression: Predictors of continuity and change during childhood. *Development and Psychopathology, 19,* 37–55.

Côté, S., Vaillancourt, T., LeBlanc, J., Nagin, D., & Tremblay, R. (2006). The development of physical aggression from toddlerhood to pre-adolescence: A nation wide longitudinal study of Canadian children. *Journal of Abnormal Child Psychology, 34,* 71–85.

Crick, N. R., & Grotpeter, J. K. (1995). Relational aggression, sex, and social psychological adjustment. *Child Development, 66,* 710–722.

Crockenberg, S., & Litman, C. (1990). Autonomy as competence in 2-year-olds: Maternal correlates of child defiance, compliance, and self-assertion. *Developmental Psychology, 26,* 961–971.

DelCarmen-Wiggins, R., & Carter, A. (Eds.), *Handbook of infant, toddler, and preschool mental health assessment.* New York, NY: Oxford University Press.

Derryberry, D., & Rothbart, M. K. (1997). Reactive and effortful processes in the organization of temperament. *Developmental Psychopathology, 9,* 633–652.

Dix, T., Stewart, A., Gershoff, E., & Day, W. (2007). Autonomy and children's reactions to being controlled: Evidence that both compliance and defiance may be positive markers in early development. *Child Development, 78,* 1204–1221.

Dodge, K. (1991). The structure and function of reactive and proactive aggression. In D. Pepler & K. Rubin (Eds.), *The development and treatment of childhood aggression* (pp. 201–218). Hillsdale, NJ: Erlbaum.

Drabick, D., Strassberg, Z., & Kees, M. (2001). Measuring qualitative aspects of preschool boys' noncompliance: The Response Style Questionnaire. *Journal of Abnormal Child Psychology, 29,* 129–140.

Dreyer, B. (2006). The diagnosis and management of attention-deficit/hyperactivity disorder in preschool children: The state of our knowledge and practice. *Current Problems in Adolescent Health Care, 36,* 6–30.

DuPaul, G. J., Anastopoulos, A. D., Power, T. J., Reid, R., Ikeda, M. J., & McGoey, K. E. (1998). Parent ratings of attention-deficit/hyperactivity disorder symptoms: Factor structure and normative data. *Journal of Psychopathology and Behavioral Assessment, 20*, 83–102.

Egger, H., Kondo, D., & Angold, A. (2006). The epidemiology and diagnostic issues in preschool attention-deficit/hyperactivity disorder. *Infants and Children, 19*, 109–122.

Egger, H. L. (2009). Psychiatric assessment of young children. *Child and Adolescent Psychiatric Clinics of North America, 18*, 559–580.

Egger, H. L., & Angold, A. (2004). The Preschool Age Psychiatric Assessment (PAPA): A structured parent interview for diagnosing psychiatric disorders in preschool children. In R. DelCarmen-Wiggins & A. Carter (Eds.), *Handbook of infant, toddler, and preschool mental health assessment* (pp. 223–246). New York, NY: Oxford University Press.

Egger, H. L., Erkanli, A., Keeler, G., Potts, E., Walter, B. K., & Angold, A. (2006). Test–retest reliability of the Preschool Age Psychiatric Assessment. *Journal of the American Academy of Child and Adolescent Psychiatry, 45*, 538–549.

Eisenberg, N., Cumberland, A., Spinrad, T. L., Fabes, R. A., Shepard, S. A, Reiser, M., . . . Guthrie, I. K. (2001). The relations of regulation and emotionality to children's externalizing and internalizing problem behavior. *Child Development, 72*, 1112–1134.

Eisenberg, N., & Fabes, R. A. (1998). Prosocial development. In W. Damon (Series Ed.) & N. Eisenberg (Vol. Ed.), *Handbook of child psychology: Vol. 3. Social, emotional, and personality development* (5th ed., pp. 701–778). New York, NY: Wiley.

Eisenberg, N., Smith, C. L., Sadovsky, A., & Spinrad, T. L. (2004). Effortful control: Relations with emotion regulation, adjustment, and socialization in childhood. In R. R. Baumeister & K. D. Vohs (Eds.), *Handbook of self-regulation: Research, theory and applications* (pp. 259–282). New York, NY: Guilford Press.

Forehand, R. (1977). Noncompliant children: Effects of parent training on behavior and attitude change. *Behavior Modification, 1*, 93–108.

Forman, D. (2007). Autonomy, compliance and internalization. In C. Brownell & C. Kopp, (Eds.), *Socioemotional development in the toddler years: Transitions and transformations* (pp. 261–284). New York, NY: Guilford Press.

Frick, P. J., Cornell, A. H., Bodin, S. D., Dane, H. E., Barry, C. T., & Loney, B. R. (2003). Callous–unemotional traits and developmental pathways to severe conduct problems. *Developmental Psychology, 39*, 246–260.

Frick, P. J., & White, S. F. (2008). Research review: The importance of callous–unemotional traits for developmental models of aggressive and antisocial behavior. *Journal of Child Psychology and Psychiatry, 49*, 359–375.

Gagne, J., & Saudino, K. J. (2010). Wait for It! A twin study of inhibitory control in early childhood. *Behavior Genetics, 40*, 327–337.

Hay, D. F. (2005). The beginnings of aggression during infancy. In R. Tremblay, W. Hartup, & J. Archer (Eds.), *Developmental origins of aggression* (pp. 107–132). New York, NY: Guilford Press.

Hay, D. F., Castle, J., & Davies, L. (2000). Toddlers' use of force against familiar peers: A precursor of serious aggression? *Child Development, 71*, 457–467.

Hay, D. F., & Cook, K. V. (2007). The transformation of prosocial behavior from infancy to childhood. In C. A. Brownell & C. B. Kopp (Eds.), *Socioemotional development in the toddler years: Transitions and transformations* (pp. 100–131). New York, NY: Guilford Press.

Hoffman, M. L. (2000). *Empathy and moral development: Implications for caring and justice.* Cambridge, UK: Cambridge University Press.

Hoffman, M. (2007). The origins of empathic morality in toddlerhood. In C. Brownell & C. Kopp (Eds.), *Socioemotional development in the toddler years: Transitions and transformations* (pp. 132–148). New York, NY: Guilford Press.

Huijbregts, S. C. J., Seguin, J. R., Zoccolillo, M., Boivin, M., & Tremblay, R. E. (2007). Associations of maternal prenatal smoking with early childhood physical aggression, hyperactivity-impulsivity, and their co-occurence. *Journal of Abnormal Child Psychology, 35,* 203–215.

Kaler, S. R., & Kopp, C. B. (1990) Compliance and comprehension in very young toddlers. *Child Development, 61,* 1997–2003.

Keenan, K., Boeldt, D., Chen, D., Coyne, C., Donald, R., Duax, J., Hart, K., . . . Humphries, M. (2011). Predictive validity of DSM-IV oppositional defiant and conduct disorders in clinically referred preschoolers. *Journal of Child Psychology and Psychiatry, 52*(1), 47–55.

Keenan, K., & Wakschlag, L. (2000). More than the terrible twos: The nature and severity of behavior problems in clinic-referred preschool children. *Journal of Abnormal Child Psychology, 28,* 33–46.

Keenan, K., Wakschlag, L. S., & Danis, B. (2001). *Kiddie-Disruptive Behavior Disorder Schedule* (version 1.1). Available from kkeenan@yoda.bsd.uchicago.edu.

Keenan, K., Wakschlag, L., Dabis, B., Hill, C., Humphries, M., Daux, J., & Donald, R. (2007). Further evidence of the reliability and validity of DSM-IV ODD and CD in preschool children. *Journal of the American Academy of Child and Adolescent Psychiatry, 46,* 457–468.

Kim-Cohen, J., Arseneault, L., & Caspi, A. (2005). Validity of DSM-IV conduct disorder in 4 1/2–5-year-old children: A longitudinal epidemiological study. *American Journal of Psychiatry, 162,* 1108–1117.

Kim-Cohen, J., Arseneault, L., & Newcombe, R., . . . Moffitt, T. E. (2009). Five-year predictive validity of DSM-IV conduct disorder research diagnosis on 4½–5-year-old children. *European Journal of Child and Adolescent Psychiatry, 18,* 284–291.

Kochanska, G., & Aksan, N. (2006). Children's conscience and self-regulation. *Journal of Personality, 74,* 1587–1618.

Kochanska, G., Aksan, N., & Koenig, A. L. (1995). A longitudinal study of the roots of preschoolers' conscience: Committed compliance and emerging internalization. *Child Development, 66,* 1752–1769.

Kochanska, G., Coy, K., & Murray, K. (2001). The development of self-regulation in the first four years of life. *Child Development, 72,* 1091–1111.

Kochanska, G., Murray, K., & Coy, K. C. (1997). Inhibitory control as a contributor to conscience in childhood: From toddler to early school age. *Child Development, 68,* 263–277.

Kochanska, G., Murray, K. T., & Harlan, E. T. (2000). Effortful control in early childhood: Continuity and change, antecedents, and implications for social development. *Developmental Psychology, 36,* 220–232.

Kochanska, G., Tjebkes, T., & Forman, D. (1998). Children's emerging regulation of conduct: Restraint, compliance, and internalization from infancy to the second year. *Child Development, 69,* 1378–1390.

Kopp, C. B. (1982). Antecedents of self-regulation: A developmental perspective. *Developmental Psychology, 18,* 199–214.

Kuczynski, L., & Kochanska, G. (1990). Development of children's noncompliance strategies from toddlerhood to age five. *Developmental Psychology, 26,* 398–408.

Kuczynski, L., Kochanska, G., Radke-Yarrow, M., & Girnius-Brown, O. (1987). A developmental interpretation of young children's noncompliance. *Developmental Psychology, 23,* 799–806.

Lavigne J., Arend, R., & Rosenbaum, D. (1998). Psychiatric disorders with onset in the preschool years: I. Stability of diagnoses. *Journal of the American Academy of Child and Adolescent Psychiatry, 37,* 1246–1254.

Lavigne, J., Cicchetti, C., & Gibbons, R. (2001). Oppositional defiant disorder with onset in preschool years: Longitudinal stability and pathways to other disorders. *Journal of the American Academy of Child and Adolescent Psychiatry, 40,* 1393–1400.

Leblanc, N., Boivin, M., Dionne, G., Brendgen, M., Vitaro, F., Tremblay, R. E., & Perusse, D. (2008). The development of hyperactive-impulsive behaviors during the preschool years: The predictive validity of parental assessments. *Journal of Abnormal Child Psychology, 36,* 977–987.

Moffitt, T. E., Caspi, A., Dickson, N., Silva, P., & Stanton, W. (1996). Childhood-onset versus adolescent-onset antisocial conduct problems in males: Natural history from ages 3 to 18 years. *Development and Psychopathology, 8,* 399–424.

Nagin, D., & Tremblay, R. E. (1999). Trajectories of boys' physical aggression, opposition, and hyperactivity on the path to physically violent and nonviolent juvenile delinquency. *Child Development, 70,* 1181–1196.

Needleman, R., Stevenson, J., & Zuckerman, B. (1991). Psychosocial correlates of severe temper tantrums. *Journal of Developmental and Behavioral Pediatrics, 12,* 77–83.

NICHD Early Childcare Research Network. (2004). Trajectories of physical aggression from toddlerhood to middle childhood. *Monographs of the Society for Research in Child Development, 69*(4, Serial No. 278).

Palfrey, J. S., Levine, M. D., Walker, D. K., & Sullivan, M. (1985). The emergence of attention deficits in early childhood: A prospective study. *Developmental and Behavioral Pediatrics, 6,* 339–348.

Pavuluri, M., Luk, S., & McGee, R. (1999). Parent-reported preschool attention deficit hyperactivity: Measurement and validity. *European Journal of Child and Adolescent Psychiatry, 8,* 126–133.

Petitclerc, A., Boivin, M., Dionne, G., Zoccolillo, M., & Tremblay, R. E. (2009). Disregard for rules: The early development and predictors of a specific dimension of disruptive behavior disorders. *Journal of Child Psychology and Psychiatry, 50,* 1477–1484.

Petitclerc, A., & Tremblay, R. E. (2009). Childhood disruptive behavior disorders: Review of their origin, development, and prevention. *Canadian Journal of Psychiatry, 54,* 222–231.

Potegal, M., & Davidson, R. J. (2003). Temper tantrums in young children: Behavioral composition. *Journal of Development and Behavioral Pediatrics, 24,* 148–154.

Reed, M. A., Pien, D. L., & Rothbart, M. K. (1984) Inhibitory self-control in preschool children. *Merrill-Palmer Quarterly, 30,* 131–147.

Reznick, J. S., Corley, R., & Robinson, J. (1997). A longitudinal twin study of intelligence in the second year. *Monographs for the Society for Research in Child Development, 62*(Serial No. 249).

Romano, E., Tremblay, R. E., Farhat, A., & Coté, S. (2006). Development and prediction of hyperactive symptoms from 2 to 7 years in a population-based sample. *Pediatrics, 117,* 2101–2110.

Rothbart, M. K. (1989a). Biological processes of temperament. In G. A. Kohnstamm, J. E. Bates, & M. K. Rothbart (Eds.), *Temperament in childhood* (pp. 77–110). Chichester, England: Wiley.

Rothbart, M. K. (1989b). Temperament and development. In G. A. Kohnstamm, J. E. Bates, & M. K. Rothbart (Eds.), *Temperament in childhood* (pp. 187–247). Chichester, England: Wiley.

Rothbart, M. K., & Ahadi, S. A. (1994). Temperament and the development of personality. *Journal of Abnormal Psychology, 103,* 55–66.

Rothbart, M. K., Ahadi, S. A., & Hershey, K. (1994). Temperament and social behavior in childhood. *Merrill-Palmer Quarterly, 40,* 21–39.

Rothbart, M. K., & Bates, J. E. (2006) Temperament. In N. Eisenberg (Ed.), *Handbook of child psychology: Vol. 3. Social, emotional, and personality development* (6th ed., pp. 187–247). Hoboken, NJ: Wiley.

Rubin, K., Hastings, P., Chen, X., Stewart, S., & McNichol, K. (1998). Intrapersonal and maternal correlates of aggression, conflict, and externalizing problems in toddlers. *Child Development, 69,* 1614–1629.

Rutter, M., Giller, H., & Hagell, A. (1998). *Antisocial behavior by young people.* Cambridge, England: Cambridge University Press.

Seefeldt, C., & Wasik, B. A. (2006). *Early education: Three-, four-, and five-year-olds go to school* (3rd ed.). Upper Saddle River, New Jersey: Prentice Hall.

Shaw, D., Gilliom, M., Ingoldsby, E., & Nagin, D. (2003). Trajectories leading to school-age conduct problems. *Developmental Psychology, 39,* 189–200.

Shelton, T. L., Barkley, R. A., Crosswait, C., Moorehouse, M., Fletcher, K., Barrett, S., . . . Metevia, L. (1998). Psychiatric and psychological morbidity as a function of adaptive disability in preschool children with aggressive and hyperactive-impulsive-inattentive behavior. *Journal of Abnormal Child Psychology, 26,* 475–494.

Schleifer, M., Weiss, S., Cohen, N., Elman, M., Cvejic, H. and Kruger, E. (1975), Hyperactivity in preschoolers and the effect of methylphenidate. *American Journal of Orthopsychiatry, 45,* 38–50.

Sonuga-Barke, E. J., & Halperin, J. M. (2010). Developmental phenotypes and causal pathways in attention deficit/hyperactivity disorder: Potential targets for early intervention? *Journal of Child Psychology and Psychiatry, 51,* 368–389.

Stipek, D. J., Gralinski, J. H., & Kopp, C. B. (1990). Self-concept development in the toddler years. *Developmental Psychology, 26,* 972–977.

Stringaris, A., & Goodman, R. (2009). Three dimensions of oppositionality in youth. *Journal of Child Psychology and Psychiatry, 50,* 216–223.

Tackett, J., Krueger, R., Iacono, W., & McGue, M. (2005). Symptom-based subfactors of DSM-defined conduct disorder: Evidence for etiologic distinctions. *Journal of Abnormal Psychology, 114,* 483–487.

Thibault, J., Jetté, M., Desrosiers, H., & Gingras, L. (2003). Concept, definitions and operational aspects: Part I. QLSCD: Overview of the study and the survey instruments for the 1999 and 2000 rounds. In *Québec Longitudinal Study of Child Development (QLSCD 1998–2002): From birth to 29 months* (Vol. 2, No. 12). Québec, Canada: Institut de la statistique du Québec.

Tremblay, R. (2003). Why socialization fails: The case of chronic physical aggression. In B. Lahey, T. Moffitt, & A. Caspi (Eds.), *Cause of conduct disorder and juvenile delinquency* (pp. 182–226). New York, NY: Guilford Press.

Tremblay, R., Hartup, W., & Archer, J. (2005). *Developmental origins of aggression.* New York, NY: Guilford Press.

Tremblay, R. E. (2008). Anger and aggression. In M. M. Haith & J. B. Benson (Eds.), *Encyclopedia of infant and early childhood development* (2nd ed., Vols. 1–3). New York, NY: Academic Press.

Tremblay, R. E. (2010). Developmental origins of disruptive behaviour problems: The "original sin" hypothesis, epigenetics and their consequences for prevention. *Journal of Child Psychology and Psychiatry, 51,* 341–367.

Tremblay, R. E., Japel, C., Perusse, D., McDuff, P., Boivin, M., Zoccolillo, M., & Montplaisir, J. (1999). The search for the age of "onset" of physical aggression: Rousseau and Bandura revisited. *Criminal Behavior and Mental Health, 9,* 8–23.

Tremblay, R. E., Nagin, D. S., Séacute;guin, J. R., Zoccolillo, M., Zelazo, P., Boivin, M., . . . Japal, C. (2004). Physical aggression during early childhood: Trajectories and predictors. *Pediatrics, 114,* 43–50.

Vitaro, F., Gendreau, P., Tremblay, R., & Oligny, P. (1998). Reactive and proactive aggression differentially predict later conduct problems. *Journal of Child Psychology and Psychiatry, 39,* 377–386.

Wakschlag, L., Briggs-Gowan, M., Carter, A., Hill, C., Danis, B., Keenan, K., . . . Leventhal, B. (2007). A developmental framework for distinguishing disruptive behavior from normative misbehavior in preschool children. *Journal of Child Psychology and Psychiatry, 48,* 976–987.

Wakschlag, L., Briggs-Gowan, M., Hill, C., Danis, B., Leventhal., B., Keenan, K., . . . Carter, A. S. (2008). Observational assessment of preschool disruptive behavior: Part II. Validity of the Disruptive Behavior Diagnostic Observation Schedule (DB-DOS). *Journal of the American Academy of Child and Adolescent Psychiatry, 47,* 632–641.

Wakschlag, L., & Danis, B. (2004). Assessment of disruptive behavior in young children: A clinical-developmental framework. In R. DelCarmen-Wiggins & A. Carter (Eds.), *Handbook of infant, toddler, and preschool mental health assessment* (pp. 421–442). New York, NY: Oxford University Press.

Wakschlag, L., & Danis, B. (2009). Characterizing early childhood disruptive behavior: Enhancing developmental sensitivity. In C. Zeanah (Ed.), *Handbook of infant mental health* (3rd ed., pp. 392–408). New York, NY: Guilford Press.

Wakschlag, L., Hill, C., Carter, A., Danis, B., Egger, H. L., Keenan, K., . . . Briggs-Gowan, M. J. (2008). Observational assessment of preschool disruptive behavior: Part I. Reliability of the Disruptive Behavior Diagnostic Observation Schedule (DB-DOS). *Journal of the American Academy of Child and Adolescent Psychiatry, 47,* 622–631.

Wakschlag, L., Leventhal, B., Briggs-Gowan, M., Danis, B., Keenan, K., Hill, C., . . . Carter, A. (2005). Defining the "disruptive" in preschool behavior: What diagnostic observation can teach us. *Clinical Child and Family Psychology Review, 8,* 183–201.

Wakschlag, L. S., Tolan, P. H., & Leventhal, B. L. (2010). Research review: "Ain't misbehavin'": Towards a developmentally-specified nosology for preschool disruptive behavior. *Journal of Child Psychology and Psychiatry, 51,* 3–22.

Zahn-Waxler, C., Iannotti, R., Cummings, E. M., & Denham, S. (1990). Antecedents of problem behaviors in children of depressed mothers. *Development and Psychopathology, 2,* 271–293.

Zahn-Waxler, C., Radke-Yarrow, M., Wagner, E., & Chapman, M. (1992). Development of concern for others. *Developmental Psychology, 28,* 126–136.

Zeanah, C. (2009). *Handbook of infant mental health* (3rd ed.). New York, NY: Guilford Press.

6

The Assessment of Antisocial Behavior in Children and Adolescents

CHRISTOPHER T. BARRY AND MALLORY L. MALKIN ■

The importance of the prevention and treatment of youth antisocial behavior has been evident for decades, as individuals with behavioral problems at an early age are at risk for continued and increasingly severe antisocial behavior over time (e.g., Loeber et al., 1993; Moffitt, Caspi, Harrington, & Milne, 2002). A host of empirically supported treatments ranging from parent training for child noncompliance during the preschool years to coping-skills-based interventions for preadolescent children who are aggressive to multisystemic treatment for adolescent delinquency have been widely disseminated. Each of these treatments is based on a solid theoretical view of how and why youth antisocial behaviors emerge. Implicit in this work is that there are clear ways to identify children and adolescents in need of intervention. However, ironically, guidance on sound, evidence-based assessment approaches for child and adolescent antisocial behavior has lagged far behind research advancements on intervention.

Perhaps the greatest challenge in advancing a clear model of assessment of youth antisocial behavior is the heterogeneous forms that such behaviors may take (McMahon & Frick, 2005). Although most practitioners would likely include symptoms of conduct disorder (CD) and oppositional defiant disorder (ODD) in their evaluations, an exclusive focus on these symptoms would severely limit the practitioner's ability to discern the many manifestations of antisocial behavior. Empirically supported treatments are aligned with such diagnostic categories to advance efficacy research and for ease of communication and portability of intervention packages. However, child and adolescent antisocial behavior can be delineated based on the particular behaviors exhibited (e.g., deceitfulness, bullying, overt aggression, relational aggression), legality (e.g., delinquency, criminality), or the apparent functions or antecedents of the behavior (e.g., proactive vs. reactive aggression), to name a few. Although the prospect of thoroughly assessing the presence of so many forms of antisocial behavior may seem cumbersome, the usefulness of such fine-grained distinctions is evident based on the often disparate correlates of these constructs and the particular avenues to treatment that might be indicated by, for example, one type of aggression versus another (McMahon & Frick, 2005).

Existing and continued research on evidence-based assessment of youth antisocial behavior has the chance to guide mental health practice in a way that gives due attention to the empirical findings on the developmental trajectories, as well as the antecedents and associated outcomes, of antisocial behavior prior to adulthood. Furthermore, to best serve youths, their families, and society, mental health professionals are called on to approach assessment in a construct-driven (rather than a diagnosis- or test-driven) fashion. This approach does not attempt to funnel all assessment information into a disruptive behavior disorder diagnosis, a diagnosis which, based on the current nosology, would be quite limited in scope. It does not consider a single piece of evidence or a single test as an infallible indicator of a construct. Instead, a construct-driven approach considers all sources of evidence, potential maintaining and protective factors, and secondary issues of concern to gain the most complete, individualized description of the child's or adolescent's problems in a way that is grounded in developmental science. Doing so then informs intervention by being based on the most central difficulties for a child, rather than defining a child in terms of a quantitative index of symptoms or test scores.

To date, the primary focus on intervention aimed at antisocial behavior is understandable in light of the potential for such problems to develop into later criminality (Frick & Kimonis, 2008) and the tremendous costs of such behaviors to their victims and to society at large (Loeber & Farrington, 2000). Nevertheless, to most appropriately match interventions to the individual's particular presentation of antisocial behaviors, sound assessment approaches are essential. As noted by McMahon and Frick (2005), "a primary goal of an assessment is to carefully and thoroughly assess the number, types, and severity" (p. 479) of behavioral problems, as well as areas of associated impairment. Obtaining such information is necessary but not sufficient for subsequent recommendations and implementation of treatment. This chapter discusses the basic foundation of evidence-based assessment of youth behavioral problems and provides an overview of the developmental, intrapersonal, contextual, maintaining, and protective factors that should be considered in the assessment of child and adolescent antisocial behavior. Included in this discussion are the many challenges that have emerged concerning evidence-based assessment of youth antisocial behavior and potential future directions for related research.

THE STATE OF THE EVIDENCE BASE

Assessment Tools

The state-of-the-art assessment strategy involves clinical interviews, including some degree of client-specific description of the behavioral problems; norm-referenced information; and, potentially, behavioral observations. However, the relative importance of these tools may vary to some extent based on the type of antisocial behavior. Ideally, this information—regardless of the specific tools selected—would be obtained from multiple informants. Fortunately, the empirical literature has provided an array of tools to assess for the heterogeneous forms of antisocial behavior, as well as considerable evidence of their basic psychometric properties. However, as noted by McMahon and Frick (2005), despite this solid foundation and general consensus about the primary assessment approaches to use, little evidence exists on their clinical utility and incremental validity. In other words, it is unclear how well some measures might translate from research use to everyday clinical use. Moreover, further research is needed to determine how much additional understanding can be gleaned from the inclusion of a particular measure in an assessment battery. Nevertheless, some basic guidelines can be taken from the research literature and put into evidence-based practice.

Assessment batteries should include at least some norm-referenced tools. Behavior rating scales are perhaps the most widely used, well-known, and efficient means of obtaining this information (Frick, Barry, & Kamphaus, 2010). Broadband rating scales such as the Behavior Assessment System for Children (BASC-2; Reynolds & Kamphaus, 2004), the Achenbach System of Empirically Based Assessment (ASEBA; Achenbach & Rescorla, 2001), and the Conners-3 (Conners, 2008) are a reasonable place to start in light of their extensive normative samples, their ability to screen for multiple areas of concern that are not limited to conduct problems, and the availability of forms for different informants.

The extensive use of the broadband rating scales mentioned previously warrants consideration of their strengths and weaknesses. Indeed, each is cost-effective in terms of allowing a clinician to gain a great deal of norm-referenced information quickly. In terms of the assessment of antisocial behavior, the clinician should first be aware of the normative sample used and the behaviors sampled by each rating scale system. The BASC-2 was developed from a large normative sample, and the externalizing scales have demonstrated good psychometric support (see Reynolds & Kamphaus, 2004). Subscales include Conduct Problems and Aggression, and although the content of the Conduct Problems scale (e.g., getting into trouble, deceiving others) aligns well with CD symptoms, the Aggression scale appears to focus more on hostile and oppositional behavior rather than physical or verbal aggression per se. The various informant versions of the ASEBA likewise are easy to administer and score and have separate scales (i.e., Rule-Breaking Behavior,

Aggressive Behavior) to assess different types of behavioral problems. In addition, the ASEBA utilizes scales oriented to the *Diagnostic and Statistical Manual of Mental Disorders* (DSM; American Psychiatric Association, 2000) that are well aligned with diagnostic criteria for CD and ODD. There have been some concerns about the representativeness of some segments of the population in the ASEBA normative samples and the heterogeneity of content within some scales (see Frick et al., 2010). The Conners-3 (Conners, 2008) is the latest revision of a rating scale system that was initially designed to provide an extensive assessment of attention-deficit/hyperactivity disorder (ADHD) symptoms. The Conners-3 was developed on a good representative sample and provides extensive assessment of externalizing problems, although there is minimal assessment of potential areas of comorbidity (e.g., depression, anxiety; see Frick et al., 2010). Like the BASC-2 and ASEBA, the Conners-3 has good correspondence among the different informant rating scales, which can serve to assist the clinician in determining areas of convergence and divergence across settings or informants.

It bears mentioning that because broadband rating scales are designed to sample from an array of behavioral, social, and emotional domains, they may provide limited depth of information on the numerous forms of antisocial behavior. Thus structured diagnostic interviews and unstructured clinical interviews also provide important mechanisms through which to gain client-specific information (Mash & Hunsley, 2005). Clinical interviews are indispensable in terms of gathering a complete picture of the child's or adolescent's developmental and behavioral history. Furthermore, working with adolescent populations has an advantage over working with adult populations in that the evaluator often has access to multiple informants who can give some perspective on the young person's behavioral history, with the adolescent also being able to provide an account (if motivated to do so) of his or her own covert antisocial behavior. No other technique has as much potential to gain comprehensive information about an individual's psychosocial functioning, as well as relevant factors that exacerbate or ameliorate issues of concern. However, this idiosyncrasy limits the ability of unstructured clinical interviews to meet the necessary psychometric properties to be regarded as empirically supported (Mash & Hunsley, 2005). Structured interviews can help overcome this issue but suffer by not allowing the clinician to follow up with client-specific questions based on guidelines for standardized administration, including the specific wording to be used and the order in which questions are to be asked (Frick et al., 2010).

Direct behavioral observation may also prove useful, depending on the nature of behaviors of concern (e.g., overt and likely to be observed vs. covert and unlikely to be observed), the child's developmental level (e.g., observations are less susceptible to reactivity for younger children), the contextual influences on the child's behavior (e.g., disruptive behavior that occurs primarily at school), and the specific antecedents that appear to be influential (e.g., aggression is worse when there is considerable noise in the home; Frick et al., 2010). Each of the tools discussed here may provide unique information on the child's or adolescent's presenting problems, yet each also has a number of limitations that should be kept in mind. Furthermore, the discussion herein represents only a small fraction of the specific tools available for the assessment of antisocial behavior and related factors (see Frick et al., 2010, and McMahon & Frick, 2005, for a more detailed review). In short, the clinician's task is to implement a parsimonious, yet comprehensive, battery that will answer the referral question and translate into meaningful, beneficial recommendations for intervention (Frick et al., 2010).

Informants

Generally speaking, and for fairly obvious reasons, parents will be the primary informants for child and adolescent psychological assessments. However, given the nature of antisocial behavior and the limitations of any particular informant, other sources are also of critical importance (see Frick et al., 2010). For example, and again for obvious reasons, adolescents are able to provide much more information regarding their own delinquent activities. Their willingness to do so, on the other hand, is another issue. Perhaps the best starting point in considering which sources to use to obtain information regarding a young person's behavior is his or her developmental level. Children are not considered reliable reporters of emotional and behavioral symptoms prior to age 8 or 9 (Frick et al., 2010). Indeed, well-known clinical rating scales routinely do not offer norms for child self-reports prior to these ages. On the other hand, in only rare instances would a clinician not want to attempt to gain an adolescent's account of his or her own behavior. A clinician can obtain this information through a clinical interview or through a myriad of self-report scales, such as the broadband measures discussed earlier or narrowband measures that focus on a specific type of antisocial behavior (e.g., Self-Report of Delinquency Scale; Elliott & Ageton, 1980). Teachers will play a valuable role in the assessment of problem behaviors in young children due to their high degree of contact with children of a young age. The importance of teacher informants tends to diminish as children progress through school, because any one teacher likely has relatively limited contact with a student each day (see Frick et al., 2010).

Different informants may also provide insight into processes that serve to maintain (or mitigate) these behaviors. For example, extended family members or teachers may provide some insight into the parents' level of involvement with the child or stress due to external factors. In addition, the reports of children and adolescents on their perceptions of important contextual factors (e.g., whether they feel safe in their neighborhoods; DuRant, Cadenhead, Pendergast, Slavens, & Linder, 1994; their perceptions of their parents' parenting; Barry, Frick, & Grafeman, 2008) may be associated with their expression of conduct problems or other antisocial behaviors. In short, the use of multiple informants, particularly in a manner that is developmentally sensitive, not only has the advantage of providing multiple perspectives on the child's behavioral problems but also can provide unique perspectives on important variables that might inform case conceptualization.

CONCEPTUALIZATION OF PROBLEMS

An accurate conceptualization of the type and severity of problems is also critical for the appropriate design of intervention. For example, knowing that a child's problem behaviors are limited to noncompliance and argumentativeness has different implications than determining that a child acts aggressively toward peers and siblings, is destructive of property, and engages in occasional substance use. The latter scenario may very well include a history of noncompliance and argumentativeness, but it would require a more intensive and broader treatment approach than the former scenario, in which the child may not necessarily go on to exhibit more severe problem behaviors (Frick et al., 2010). For instance, children who meet criteria for CD very likely also meet criteria for ODD; however, children with ODD may or may not go on to develop CD (Lahey, Loeber, Quay, Frick, & Grimm, 1992).

Youth behavioral problems can exhibit situational variability and even day-to-day fluctuations (Wright, Zakriski, & Drinkwater, 1999). Therefore, inherent in the preceding discussion of the tools, informants, and descriptors is the need for the information gathered to be sensitive to changes in behavioral presentations that may occur across settings or when stimuli and/or consequences are altered. Professionals involved in decisions regarding diagnoses and/or intervention planning for a child or adolescent must understand the contexts in which the behaviors of concern occur and the factors that appear to influence the manifestation of those behaviors. These factors will play a critical role in case conceptualization and subsequent recommendations. We first discuss developmental processes as comprising one domain that influences our understanding of a child and our initial impressions of his/her prognosis.

Developmental Factors

It is quite difficult to imagine evaluating a child or adolescent's behavior—or any psychological construct, for that matter—without regard for whether his or her presentation is developmentally appropriate or "normal." It follows, then, that many assessment tools are couched in terms of normative data. In essence, the task for the clinician is to determine whether the behavioral problems represent something that is typical for individuals of the child's developmental or cultural background, is essentially abnormal, or is an exaggeration of a normal developmental process. Therefore, the age at onset (i.e., prior to adolescence or during adolescence) of the young person's problems is critical. We make this claim based on Terrie Moffitt's discussion of the phenomenology and correlates of childhood-onset conduct problems and what are referred to as adolescence-limited conduct problems (Moffitt, 1993; Moffitt, Caspi, Dickson, Silva, & Stanton, 1996). In short, early-onset behavioral problems are associated with more severe and prolonged behavioral difficulties and appear to be at least partly the result of genetic or neurodevelopmental factors (Arseneault et al., 2003; Moffitt, 1993). Many of the intrapersonal etiological factors discussed later are consistent with this developmental subtype. On the other hand, antisocial behavior that begins during adolescence is often much more time-limited and appears to be more directly influenced by social/contextual factors, including those discussed later in this chapter (e.g., delinquent peer affiliations; Moffitt, 1993; Patterson & Yoerger, 1997). The latter developmental course is still of concern, may manifest in particularly severe ways, and may be indicative of a variety of early psychosocial stressors (Roisman et al., 2010). Thus simply ascertaining the age at onset of a child's antisocial behavior can assist a clinician in narrowing down potential causal factors and potential avenues for treatment.

Other parameters that are important for conceptualizing a child's or adolescent's antisocial behavior and for communicating the nature of the problems to other professionals are the severity, frequency, and variety of behaviors exhibited (Bird et al., 2005), with the expectation that a young person would have greater opportunity to demonstrate more severe, frequent, and varied behavioral problems later in development. Such descriptions of the client's behavior might be part of some structured diagnostic interviews, but this information can also be gleaned from rating scales or easily incorporated into unstructured interviews. Bird and colleagues (2005) highlight the importance of these dimensions for further refinement of assessment and diagnosis and for informing intervention. Of course, the more intense (i.e., more severe, frequent, and varied) the behavioral problems, the more intensive and comprehensive the interventions recommended. However, even relatively less severe behavioral problems require attention, as they may develop into more significant issues later (Speltz, McClellan, DeKlyen, & Jones, 1999).

Equally informative for this process is the degree of impairment caused by the problem behaviors. Although impairment is part of diagnostic criteria across categories, little information exists on the best strategy for evaluating a child's degree of impairment. Structured diagnostic interviews, such as the Diagnostic Interview Schedule for Children (DISC; Shaffer, Fisher, Lucas, Dulcan, & Schwab-Stone, 2000), provide a mechanism for evaluating the effects of a child's difficulties on his or her performance in a variety of settings, and some rating scales have attempted to incorporate indicators of impairment by asking an informant, for example, in what specific situations the behaviors of concern cause problems (see Frick et al., 2010). Despite these tools, the assessment of impairment is confounded by the fact that impairment is essentially in the eye of the beholder. This issue might be particularly apparent in work with young children. For instance, a child might exhibit a clinically significant level of conduct problems that are of great concern and non-normative in the classroom but that are viewed as relatively minor in the context of a family whose members all have a history of significant antisocial behavior. In addition, impairment due to behavioral problems might not yet have been experienced in the form of aversive consequences, even though there is the potential for significant legal or social consequences from continued antisocial behavior in adolescence and adulthood. Impairment is a factor that directly informs primary versus secondary targets of intervention, and the clinician's skills and judgment, more than any particular measure of impairment, are necessary for arriving at sound decisions in this regard. In addition, a host of individual factors can provide guidance as to the interventions that provide goodness-of-fit for a child or adolescent.

Intrapersonal Factors

Intrapersonal factors that may play a role in the manifestation and persistence of child and adolescent antisocial behavior include, but are not limited to, gender, for both the degree and type of antisocial behavior (e.g., Crick & Grotpeter, 1995); genetic factors (e.g., Maes, Silberg, Neale, & Eaves, 2007); neurobiological factors (e.g., Blair & Mitchell, 2009; Brower & Price, 2001); early temperamental factors (e.g., irritability; Keenan, Shaw, Delliquadri, Giovannelli, & Walsh, 1998); personality or interpersonal styles (e.g., callous–unemotional traits; see Frick & White, 2008); cognitive functioning (Frick & Loney, 2000); frustration tolerance or adaptability to change (Greene et al., 2004); and the presence of comorbid or co-occurring psychopathology (see McMahon & Frick, 2005). Although biological factors are clearly influential (e.g., Dodge & Pettit, 2003), there is limited direct evidence to date on the link between specific biological factors and specific problem behaviors. Moreover, the methods for assessing these variables are not feasible for most practitioners; thus the emphasis is placed on psychosocial variables. Assessment of psychosocial risk factors may range from the direct (e.g., rating scales of current psychopathy-linked tendencies; observation of behavioral responses to transitions or changes in routine) to the indirect (e.g., family history of psychopathology as a potential indicator of genetic predispositions toward antisocial behavior). However, each of these approaches is confounded by variables such as informant bias in the reporting of a young person's personality, the still-unfolding nature of a young person's coping style, and the potential for shared environment to explain similarities among family members in psychopathology. The present discussion provides an overview of issues pertaining to some of these factors with the recognition that knowledge of the roles of these variables and their implications for assessment is rapidly growing.

Research indicates quite clearly that assessment of any clinical issue with children and adolescents must take into account comorbidity of other emotional and behavioral problems (McMahon & Frick, 2005). The most common comorbid issue for individuals with significant behavioral problems is ADHD (Waschbusch, 2002). Indeed, the presence of comorbid ADHD and CD has been associated with a particularly severe presentation of youth behavioral problems (e.g., Barry et al., 2000; Frick & Loney, 1999; Lynam, 1998). Additional areas of concern as associated features, precipitating factors, or effects of antisocial behavior include substance abuse (e.g., Lynskey & Fergusson, 1995), depression (e.g., Fergusson, Lynskey, & Horwood, 1996; Loeber & Keenan, 1994), and anxiety (Loeber & Keenan, 1994). Broadband rating scales such as those mentioned earlier are useful to assess for comorbidity, not only because they address multiple domains of functioning but also because they might help determine which areas of concern might be primary versus secondary for case conceptualization and subsequent treatment planning. Nevertheless, the clinician must not only gain information on the presence of comorbidity or co-occurring problems but also conceptualize how they relate to the behavioral problems of concern and, further, how the complete clinical picture translates into a particular set of recommended interventions.

Another area worthy of exploration in clinical assessment is the child's social-cognitive or problem-solving strategies. An influential and well-known model of childhood aggression proposes that social-cognitive processes help indicate which children are at risk for aggression, particularly reactive forms of aggression. More specifically, individuals who tend to make hostile attributions for ambiguous social situations (e.g., "He did that to make me mad") tend to react aggressively (e.g., Crick & Dodge, 1996). Although these processes are typically researched through the use of hypothetical vignettes (McMahon & Frick, 2005), a functional analysis, even through clearly constructed interview questions, may provide insight into the triggers of a young person's antisocial behaviors. The effectiveness of interventions that target social cognition and social problem solving to reduce behavioral problems (e.g., Lochman & Wells, 2004), especially aggression, point to the usefulness of evaluating this issue.

Early temperament and interpersonal/personality styles also appear relevant for the expression and continuation of youth antisocial behavior. Temperamental factors identified as early as the preschool years appear relevant for both concurrent and later behavioral problems. Long-standing notions of difficult temperament (see Thomas & Chess, 1977), including poor adaptability to change, negative affectivity, and withdrawal from novel environmental stimuli, have demonstrated a wealth of supporting evidence for their role in child behavioral problems. In addition, specific temperamental dimensions such as poor effortful control (i.e., attention, behavioral persistence) have been associated with stable levels of behavioral problems into middle childhood (Zhou et al., 2007), and other early identifiable individual difference variables such as anger and impulsivity are also, not surprisingly, associated with behavioral problems in children (e.g., Karreman, de Haas, van Tuijl, van Aken, & Deković, 2010). A propensity toward thrill and adventure seeking has also been consistently associated with child behavioral problems, including aggression (Crapanzano, Frick, & Terranova, 2010). Again, research has provided numerous tools to assess any of these dimensions, typically through parent- or self-report rating scales. The potential for false positives in assessing temperamental types or styles cautions professionals not to predict with absolute certainty that a young child with such temperamental features will continue to engage in increasingly severe antisocial behavior if not treated. Instead, such factors may point toward difficulties that a child might have in specific situations in which the demands do not match the child's style of interacting with his or her environment (e.g., an unstructured, unpredictable school environment for a child who has trouble adapting to changes).

A growing body of research has implicated psychopathy-linked, or callous–unemotional, personality traits (e.g., lack of empathy, lack of guilt, callous disregard for others) with persistent, severe, and varied behavioral problems (see Frick & White, 2008). This personality style is thought to be relevant for youths who demonstrate an early onset of conduct problems rather than a later onset (Frick, 2006). Importantly, despite some debate, these characteristics appear to be relatively stable (Obradovic, Pardini, Long, & Loeber, 2007); thus there is the potential for a young person who develops such tendencies to engage in significant antisocial behavior throughout development. There are at least a couple of well-studied approaches to assessing psychopathy-linked characteristics in youths, including the 20-item Antisocial Process Screening Device (APSD; Frick & Hare, 2001) rating scale and the Psychopathy Checklist: Youth Version (PCL:YV; Forth, Kosson, & Hare, 2003) interview protocol. Both have enjoyed considerable research attention and appear to have some clinical utility. For example, scores on the Callous–Unemotional (CU) scale of the APSD appear to differentiate among clinic-referred children in terms of severity and variety of conduct problems (e.g., Barry et al., 2000; Christian, Frick, Hill, Tyler, & Frazer, 1997) and have been predictive of later conduct problems in young children drawn from a community sample (Dadds, Fraser, Frost, & Hawes, 2005). The PCL:YV is probably better suited for use in detention settings given its relatively lengthy format and its development from an interview protocol used with adult criminal populations. In addition, it appears to have better predictive validity for adjudicated males than for females (Schmidt, McKinnon, Chattha, & Brownlee, 2006). Overall, recent research, although only briefly mentioned here, suggests that evaluation of psychopathy-linked tendencies may prove useful for case conceptualization and treatment recommendations (see Frick & White, 2008, for a review).

In practice, clinicians may take from each of the areas of research on early temperament and personality styles a need to evaluate a young client's (1) developmental history in terms of response to others, irritability, adaptability to change, and activity level, among other factors; (2) apparent preference for dangerous and thrilling activities and tendency to impulsively engage in such activities; and (3) responsiveness to the feelings of others, sense of remorse for wrongdoings, and tendency to try to manipulate others. Evidence of any of these factors may speak to ways in which interventions may need to be implemented to maximize their effectiveness (see Greene et al., 2004, for an example); however, as yet, the specific intervention implications for intrapersonal factors as they relate to antisocial behavior have not been extensively studied.

Contextual Factors

The emphasis on familial factors in interventions for child conduct problems makes a comprehensive evaluation of family context essential for case conceptualization and treatment planning. These factors include, but are not limited to, parenting practices, stress tied to the parental role, parental psychopathology, parental beliefs about the child's problems and child development, socioeconomic stressors, and marital conflict (McMahon & Frick, 2005).

Because parenting practices (e.g., use of positive reinforcement for desired behaviors, consistent discipline) are primary targets of parenting interventions for children with externalizing behaviors (e.g., Barkley, 1997; McMahon & Forehand, 2003), a description of parenting strategies is highly important in providing recommendations for further intervention. This information can be gathered from a clinical interview or descriptively through a number of available rating scales (see Arnold, O'Leary, Wolff, & Acker, 1993; Shelton, Frick, & Wootton, 1996). Parental stress is another key variable that can be both an effect of a child's difficult behavior and a factor that exacerbates the child's behaviors. Tools such as the Parenting Stress Index (Abidin, 1986) not only ask questions about the parent's degree of stress surrounding the parenting role, but they also tend to gauge the parent's perception of the child's difficulty and the quality of his or her interactions with the child. As with other contextual factors, assessing parental stress will not help a clinician or evaluator determine whether the child engages in antisocial behavior. Instead, it provides information that can promote further understanding of factors that might exacerbate or ameliorate the young person's risk.

Conventional wisdom would also dictate that peer affiliations are an important influence on antisocial behavior for children and especially for adolescents. That line of thought is well supported based on the amount of time that adolescents spend with peers (Larson, Wilson, Brown, Furstenberg, & Verma, 2002) but also, more importantly, based on the evidence that youths with conduct problems tend to have delinquent peer affiliations (e.g., Moffitt, 1993). Moreover, more frequent contact with deviant peers is associated with greater persistence of antisocial behavior (e.g., Shapiro, Smith, Malone, & Calloro, 2010). Less straightforward is the influence of social status among one's peers on a young person's antisocial behavior, with some evidence suggesting that peer rejection places an individual at risk for acting out (Dodge & Pettit, 2003), whereas other research has noted a correlation between aggressive behavior and child popularity (e.g., Bagwell, Coie, Terry, & Lochman, 2000; Rodkin, Farmer, Pearl, & Van Acker, 2000). Further, having an inflated sense of one's social status relative to peers' views of the individual is associated with greater levels of disruptive behavior and aggression (e.g., Hughes, Cavell, & Grossman, 1997; Owens, Goldfine, Evangelista, Hoza, & Kaiser, 2007). Unfortunately, the development of efficient and ecologically valid approaches for practitioners to use to assess the influence of peers on antisocial behaviors has not matched the long-standing idea that this influence exists (McMahon & Frick, 2005). However, if feasible, sociometric exercises and other forms of peer-referenced assessment may provide unique information about a young person's social functioning that cannot be gleaned from other sources (Frick et al., 2010).

Collecting information on the child's neighborhood and broader community context also informs case conceptualization and plans for intervention. The socioeconomic status of the child's or adolescent's family is a pivotal factor insofar as it may be associated with other variables (e.g., exposure to violence, danger in neighborhood, quality of school) that could influence the development of child behavioral problems (Peeples & Loeber, 1994). The role of neighborhood or community context in youth antisocial behavior is complex, but it appears that broad factors (e.g., poverty, residential instability) influence the behavioral functioning of young people through their influence on the socialization processes to which the child is exposed and the parenting practices that are adopted within the community (Mrug & Windle, 2009). Thus assessments should not only include indicators of socioeconomic status and community safety but also attempt to determine the ways in which those factors have shaped more immediate socialization experiences of the child. To aid in this process, some tools have been developed to determine the parent's perception of the neighborhood/community context and the child's report of his or her exposure to dangerous or illegal activities (see McMahon & Frick, 2005).

The literature clearly suggests that the greater the number of contextual risk factors, the poorer the outcomes (e.g., Flouri & Tzavidis, 2008; Forehand, Bigger, & Kotchick, 1998). Of course, to expect a mere additive effect of these variables would grossly oversimplify their complex interplay. It is not enough, for instance, to know that a child comes from a family with a great deal of conflict and also affiliates with delinquent peers and then to conclude that this child is twice as likely to engage in antisocial behavior as a child with only one of these risk factors. Instead, an assessment of the family's response to the child's peer affiliations (e.g., poor monitoring) and the peers' role in how or to what extent the child interacts with his or her family (e.g., defiance, staying out past curfew) would be more appropriate, albeit more difficult.

Maintaining Factors

Functional analysis is a valuable tool for determining the conditions that precipitate or encourage antisocial behavior and the consequences that might serve to reinforce it. Behavioral observation is one strategy that may be used to determine the antecedents and consequences of a child's behavioral problems; however, developmentally, such observation becomes an increasingly greater challenge (with likely lower payoff) as the child gets older. For adolescents, the contexts in which antisocial or conduct problem behaviors occur are likely off limits to observation, and even if they were accessible, they would be subject to significant reactivity. Still, useful functional analyses can be conducted without behavioral observations if the evaluator asks questions that generate detailed descriptions of the maintaining factors of interest.

Accomplishing this goal of assessment may be as straightforward as collecting information about the intrapersonal and contextual risk factors noted earlier, as well as about the child's developmental history. However, merely collecting this information can deceive a clinician into believing that he or she has a firm grasp of the factors that maintain the child's behavioral problems. The next step involves sound case conceptualization such that the interplay of all relevant variables and issues of concern are included in a comprehensive theory that serves to explain the child's or adolescent's problems and the interventions that are likely to be best suited for him or her. Therefore, it is imperative that professionals engaged in the assessment of children and adolescents have current knowledge not only of evidence-based assessment but also of the research regarding the factors that maintain or exacerbate youth antisocial behavior.

Protective Factors

A starting point in determining potential protective factors against antisocial behavior for a child or adolescent is to collect evidence that the inverse of the aforementioned risk factors is present. That is, if low cognitive functioning or delinquent peer affiliations are risk factors for antisocial behavior, then high cognitive functioning or affiliations with prosocial peers may help prevent problem behaviors for youths who are otherwise at risk (e.g., due to high family conflict, inconsistent discipline). Clinicians may also need to consider developmental context in determining whether the presence of an intrapersonal or contextual variable serves as an effective protective factor. For example, although parental monitoring and supervision would be expected to decrease with the child's age, monitoring and supervision still appear important for the prevention of significant behavioral problems in adolescence (Frick, Christian, & Wootton, 1999). Additional factors that appear to be important for reducing the likelihood, severity, or continuity of youth antisocial behavior include, among many others, the absence of marital conflict (e.g., Erath, Bierman, & Conduct Problems Prevention Research Group, 2006) or parental psychopathology (e.g., Kopp & Beauchaine, 2007), as well as connectedness to school (Loukas, Roalson, & Herrera, 2010), academic achievement (e.g., Gerard & Buehler, 2004), and the presence of prosocial peers (e.g., Vance, Bowen, Fernandez, & Thompson, 2002).

No specific protective factor will completely reduce or prevent conduct problems (Shannon, Beauchaine, Brenner, Neuhaus, & Gatzke-Kopp, 2007). In addition, the role of these factors is complex and may not operate most proximally on the child's behaviors but instead on other factors that more directly influence the child's behavior (e.g., the marital relationship affects parenting practices, which then influence child compliance; McMahon & Frick, 2005). In essence, protective factors may point to strengths on which professionals can build in designing and implementing interventions. Therefore, intrapersonal and contextual strengths for the child deserve attention as a routine part of assessments.

FUTURE DIRECTIONS

The discussion herein has primarily regarded assessment as an activity conducted at the beginning of contact with a child and his or her family that is aimed at gathering sufficient information to inform subsequent interventions. However, assessment should be regarded as an ongoing, dynamic process that continues throughout, and even after, intervention. Achenbach (2005, p. 541) described assessment as an activity that involves "initial broad-spectrum assessment, to identify strengths and problems, narrower spectrum assessment of targets for intervention, ongoing assessment during the course of interventions, and outcome assessment." The success of clinical psychology and allied fields in providing a strong evidence base for the latter two components of Achenbach's description has been quite limited. Far more was known about sound procedures for conducting initial assessments of child conduct problems when the initial article summarizing evidence-based assessment was published in 2005 (McMahon & Frick, 2005). There has since been relatively little increased knowledge about sound approaches for program evaluation and outcome assessments. We are confident that many interventions are efficacious and even effective for youth antisocial behavior, but there is no clear consensus on the appropriate ways to assess progress and outcomes in day-to-day clinical practice. The notion that assessment includes other activities beyond an initial evaluation has been clearly recognized (Mash & Hunsley, 2005); thus the next step is for the evidence base to provide guidance on monitoring symptomatology across contexts during intervention and to provide cost-effective mechanisms for evaluating an intervention's role in a child or adolescent's progress. The vast literature on single-case designs, particularly targeting the reduction of a specific problem behavior or set of behaviors, may provide a valuable framework in this regard.

Another endeavor that should prove useful is to form essentially a menu of empirically supported assessment batteries. To do so will require research not only on individual tools but also on the utility of a battery, including the incremental validity contributed by individual measures. In other words, the research community should be prepared to address what is added by the inclusion of a specific tool or set of tools. By extension, practitioners will become better informed consumers of assessment instruments and will be able to convey the rationale for the inclusion (or exclusion) of each measure in their batteries. Establishing this evidence base has the added benefit of providing cost-effective assessment and intervention services.

CONCLUSIONS

Throughout this discussion, an emphasis has been placed on the need to be familiar with the different forms of youth antisocial behavior, as well as the strengths and limitations of the assessment methods available, and to approach assessment from a construct-driven, developmental science approach. To do so, mental health professionals must continually stay up-to-date on the multiple risk factors that can result in problematic behaviors (i.e., the concept of equifinality), particularly those that provide clear avenues for prevention and intervention. In addition, despite the preponderance of evidence demonstrating that early conduct problems can negatively affect later functioning, the concept of multifinality in developmental psychopathology reminds us that a young person with conduct problems is not necessarily doomed to a prolonged life of psychopathology or criminality. Instead, especially with early recognition and intervention, the outcomes may be quite positive.

In addition, it is imperative to recognize that the many variables that play a role in youth antisocial behavior, such as those discussed herein, do not exert their influence in isolation. Instead, intrapersonal factors such as temperament, for example, clearly appear to interact with contextual factors such as parenting to predict behavioral problems (e.g., Lengua, 2008. Therefore, the clinician must not confine his or her case conceptualization to symptom counts and an investigation of the number of risk factors. Sound case conceptualization considers that all of the child's protective and risk factors (past and present), as well as his or her interactions, should help inform recommendations and intervention.

Based on our current knowledge and the current climate of mental health service provision, clinicians should seek to employ a parsimonious assessment approach that includes tools that go beyond the basic psychometric properties of reliability and validity. That is, the clinical utility of an individual test or strategy and a collective battery is based on its ability to (1) reveal the variety of behavioral problems exhibited by a young person; (2) provide information on the various developmental, intrapersonal, contextual, maintaining, and protective factors that influence the presentation of these problems; and (3) answer the referral question in a manner that informs the next step. As knowledge is gained about what works best for whom and under what conditions, the use of informative, portable, evidence-based assessment approaches will become even more essential for matching a child's or adolescent's presentation to the treatment most likely to curtail his or her antisocial behavior.

REFERENCES

Abidin, R. R. (1986). *Parenting Stress Index: Manual* (2nd ed.). Charlottesville, VA: Pediatric Psychology Press.

Achenbach, T. M. (2005). Advancing assessment of children and adolescents: Commentary on evidence-based assessment of child and adolescent disorders. *Journal of Clinical Child and Adolescent Psychology, 34*, 541–547.

Achenbach, T. M., & Rescorla, L. A. (2001). *Manual for the ASEBA School-Age Forms and Profiles.* Burlington, VT: University of Vermont.

American Psychiatric Association. (2000). *Diagnostic and statistical manual of mental disorders* (4th ed., text rev.). Washington, DC: American Psychiatric Association Press.

Arnold, D. S., O'Leary, S. G., Wolff, L. S., & Acker, M. M. (1993). The Parenting Scale: A measure of dysfunctional parenting in discipline situations. *Psychological Assessment, 5*, 137–144.

Arseneault, L., Moffitt, T. E., Caspi, A., Taylor, A., Rijsdijk, F. V., Jaffee, S. R., ... Measelle, J. R. (2003). Strong genetic effects on cross-situational antisocial behaviour among 5-year-old children according to mothers, teachers, examiner-observers, and twins' self-reports. *Journal of Child Psychology and Psychiatry, 44*, 832–848.

Bagwell, C. L., Coie, J. D., Terry, R. A., & Lochman, J. E. (2000). Peer clique participation and social status in preadolescence. *Merrill-Palmer Quarterly, 46*, 280–305.

Barkley, R. A. (1997). *Defiant children: A clinician's manual for assessment and parent training.* New York, NY: Guilford Press.

Barry, C. T., Frick, P. J., DeShazo, T. M., McCoy, M., Ellis, M., & Loney, B. R. (2000). The importance of callous–unemotional traits for extending the concept of psychopathy to children. *Journal of Abnormal Psychology, 109*, 335–340.

Barry, C. T., Frick, P. J., & Grafeman, S. J. (2008). Child versus parent report of parenting practices: Implications for the conceptualization of child behavior and emotional problems. *Assessment, 15*, 294–303.

Bird, H. R., Davies, M., Canino, G., Loeber, R., Rubio-Stipec, M., & Shen, S. (2005). Classification of antisocial behaviors along severity and frequency parameters. *Journal of Child and Family Studies, 14*, 325–341.

Blair, R. J. R., & Mitchell, D. V. G. (2009) Psychopathy, attention and emotion. *Psychological Medicine, 39*, 543–555.

Brower, M. C., & Price, B. H. (2001). Neuropsychiatry of frontal lobe dysfunction in violent and criminal behaviour: A critical review. *Journal of Neurology, Neurosurgery, and Psychiatry, 71*, 720–726.

Christian, R. E., Frick, P. J., Hill, N. L., Tyler, L., & Frazer, D. (1997). Psychopathy and conduct problems: II. Implications for subtyping children with conduct problems. *Journal of the American Academy of Child and Adolescent Psychiatry, 36*, 233–241.

Conners, C. K. (2008). *Conners* (3rd ed.). Toronto, Ontario, Canada: Multi-Health Systems. Crapanzano, A. M., Frick, P. J., & Terranova, A. M. (2010). Patterns of physical and relational aggression in a school-based sample of boys and girls. *Journal of Abnormal Child Psychology, 38*, 433–445.

Crick, N. R., & Dodge, K. A. (1996). Social information processing mechanisms in reactive and proactive aggression. *Child Development, 67*, 993–1002.

Crick, N. R., & Grotpeter, J. K. (1995). Relational aggression, gender, and social-psychological adjustment. *Child Development, 66*, 710–722.

Dadds, M. R., Fraser, J., Frost, A., & Hawes, D. J. (2005). Disentangling the underlying dimensions of psychopathy and conduct problems in childhood: A community study. *Journal of Consulting and Clinical Psychology, 73*, 400–410.

Dodge, K. A., & Pettit, G. S. (2003). A biopsychosocial model of development of chronic conduct problems in adolescence. *Developmental Psychology, 39,* 349–371.

DuRant, R. H., Cadenhead, C., Pendergast, R. A., Slavens, G. G., & Linder, C. W. (1994). Factors associated with the use of violence among urban black adolescents. *American Journal of Public Health, 84,* 612–617.

Elliott, D. S., & Ageton, S. S. (1980). Reconciling race and class differences in self-reported and official estimates of delinquency. *American Sociological Review, 45,* 95–110.

Erath, S. A., Bierman, K. L., & Conduct Problems Prevention Research Group. (2006). Aggressive marital conflict, maternal harsh punishment, and child aggressive-disruptive behavior: Evidence for direct and mediated relations. *Journal of Family Psychology, 20,* 217–226.

Fergusson, D. M., Lynskey, M. T., & Horwood, L. J. (1996). Origins of comorbidity between conduct and affective disorders. *Journal of the American Academy of Child and Adolescent Psychiatry, 35,* 451–460.

Flouri, E., & Tzavidis, N. (2008). Psychopathology and prosocial behavior in adolescents from socio-economically disadvantaged families: The role of proximal and distal adverse life events. *European Child and Adolescent Psychiatry, 17,* 498–506.

Forehand, R., Biggar, H., & Kotchick, B. A. (1998). Cumulative risk across family stressors: Short- and long-term effects for adolescents. *Journal of Abnormal Child Psychology, 26,* 119–128.

Forth, A. E., Kosson, D. S., & Hare, R. D. (2003). *The Psychopathy Checklist: Youth Version.* Toronto, Ontario, Canada: Multi-Health Systems.

Frick, P. J. (2006). Developmental pathways to conduct disorder. *Child and Adolescent Psychiatric Clinics of North America, 15,* 311–331.

Frick, P. J., Barry, C. T., & Kamphaus, R. W. (2010). *Clinical assessment of child and adolescent personality and behavior* (3rd ed.). New York: Springer.

Frick, P. J., Christian, R. E., & Wootton, J. M. (1999). Age trends in the association between parenting practices and conduct problems. *Behavior Modification, 23,* 106–128.

Frick, P. J., & Hare, R. D. (2001). *The Antisocial Process Screening Device.* Toronto, Ontario, Canada: Multi-Health Systems.

Frick, P. J., & Kimonis, E. R. (2008). Externalizing disorders of childhood. In J. E. Maddux & B. A. Winstead (Eds.), *Psychopathology: Foundations for a contemporary understanding* (2nd ed., pp. 349–374). New York, NY: Routledge, Taylor & Francis.

Frick, P. J., & Loney, B. R. (2000). The use of laboratory and performance-based measures in the assessment of children and adolescents with conduct disorders. *Journal of Clinical Child Psychology, 29,* 540–554.

Frick, P. J., & Loney, B. (1999). Outcomes of children and adolescents with oppositional defiant disorder and conduct disorder. In H. C. Quay & A. E. Hogan (Eds.), *Handbook of disruptive behavior disorders* (pp. 507–524). New York: Plenum Press.

Frick, P. J., & White, S. F. (2008) Research review: The importance of callous–unemotional traits for developmental models of aggressive and antisocial behavior. *Journal of Child Psychology and Psychiatry, 49,* 359–375.

Gerard, J. M., & Buehler, C. (2004). Cumulative environmental risk and youth maladjustment: The role of youth attributes. *Child Development, 75,* 1832–1849.

Greene, R. W., Ablon, J. S., Monuteaux, M. C., Goring, J. C., Henin, A., Raezer-Blakely, L., . . . Rabbitt, S. (2004). Effectiveness of collaborative problem-solving in affectively dysregulated children with oppositional defiant disorder: Initial findings. *Journal of Consulting and Clinical Psychology, 72,* 1157–1164.

Hughes, J. N., Cavell, T. A., & Grossman, P. B. (1997). A positive view of self: Risk or protection for aggressive children? *Development and Psychopathology, 9,* 75–94.

Karreman, A., de Haas, S., van Tuijl, C., van Aken, M., & Deković, M. (2010). Relations among temperament, parenting and problem behavior in young children. *Infant Behavior and Development, 33,* 39–49.

Keenan, K., Shaw, D., Delliquadri, E., Giovannelli, J., & Walsh, B. (1998). Evidence for the continuity of early problem behaviors: Application of a developmental model. *Journal of Abnormal Child Psychology, 26,* 441–452.

Kopp, L. M., & Beauchaine, T. P. (2007). Patterns of psychopathology in the families of children with conduct problems, depression, and both psychiatric conditions. *Journal of Abnormal Child Psychology, 35,* 301–312.

Lahey, B. B., Loeber, R., Quay, H. C., Frick, P. J., & Grimm, J. (1992). Oppositional defiant and conduct disorders: Issues to be resolved for DSM-IV. *Journal of American Academy of Child and Adolescent Psychiatry, 31,* 539–546.

Larson, R. W., Wilson, S., Brown, B. B., Furstenberg, F. F., & Verma, S. (2002). Changes in adolescents' interpersonal experiences: Are they being prepared for adult relationships in the twenty-first century? *Journal of Research on Adolescence, 12,* 31–68.

Lengua, L. J. (2008). Anxiousness, frustration, and effortful control as moderators of the relation between parenting and adjustment in middle childhood. *Social Development, 17,* 554–577.

Lochman, J. E., & Wells, K. C. (2004). The coping power program for preadolescent aggressive boys and their parents: Outcome effects at the 1-year follow-up. *Journal of Consulting and Clinical Psychology, 72,* 571–578.

Loeber, R., & Farrington, D. P. (2000). Young children who commit crime: Epidemiology, development origins, risk factors, early interventions, and policy implications. *Development and Psychopathology, 12,* 737–762.

Loeber, R., & Keenan, K. (1994). Interaction between conduct disorder and its comorbid conditions: Effects of age and gender. *Clinical Psychology Review, 14,* 497–523.

Loeber, R., Wung, P., Kennan, K., Giroux, B., Stouthamer-Loeber, M., Van Kammen, W. B., & Maughan, B. (1993). Developmental pathways in disruptive child behavior. *Development and Psychopathology, 5,* 101–131.

Loukas, A., Roalson, L. A., & Herrera, D. E. (2010). School connectedness buffers the effects of negative family relations and poor effortful control on early adolescent conduct problems. *Journal of Research on Adolescence, 20,* 13–22.

Lynam, D. R. (1998). Early identification of the fledgling psychopath: Locating the psychopathic child in the current nomenclature. *Journal of Abnormal Psychology, 107,* 566–575.

Lynskey, M. T., & Fergusson, D. M. (1995). Childhood conduct problems, attention deficit behaviors, and adolescent alcohol, tobacco, and illicit drug use. *Journal of Abnormal Child Psychology, 23,* 281–302.

Maes, H. H., Silberg, J. L., Neale, M. C., & Eaves, L. J. (2007). Genetic and cultural transmission of antisocial behavior: An extended twin–parent model. *Twin Research and Human Genetics, 10,* 136–150.

Mash, E. J., & Hunsley, J. (2005). Evidence-based assessment of child and adolescent disorders: Issues and challenges. *Journal of Clinical Child and Adolescent Psychology, 34,* 362–379.

McMahon, R. J., & Forehand, R. L. (2003). *Helping the noncomplaint child: Family-based treatment for oppositional behavior* (2nd ed.). New York, NY: Guilford Press.

McMahon, R. J., & Frick, P. J. (2005). Evidence-based assessment of conduct problems in children and adolescents. *Journal of Clinical Child and Adolescent Psychology, 34,* 477–505.

Moffitt, T. E. (1993). Adolescence-limited and life-course-persistent antisocial behavior: A developmental taxonomy. *Psychological Review, 100,* 674–701.

Moffitt, T. E., Caspi, A., Dickson, N., Silva, P. A., & Stanton, W. (1996). Childhood-onset versus adolescent-onset antisocial conduct in males: Natural history from age 3 to 18. *Development and Psychopathology, 8,* 399–424.

Moffitt, T. E., Caspi, A., Harrington, H., & Milne, B. J. (2002). Males on the life-course persistent and adolescence-limited antisocial pathways: Follow-up at age 26. *Development and Psychopathology, 14,* 179–207.

Mrug, S., & Windle, M. (2009). Mediators of neighborhood influences on externalizing behavior in preadolescent children. *Journal of Abnormal Child Psychology, 37,* 265–280.

Obradovic, J., Pardini, D. A., Long, J. D., & Loeber, R. (2007). Measuring interpersonal callousness in boys from childhood to adolescence: An examination of longitudinal invariance and temporal stability. *Journal of Clinical Child and Adolescent Psychology, 36,* 276–292.

Owens, J. S., Goldfine, M. E., Evangelista, N. M., Hoza, B., & Kaiser, N. M. (2007). A critical review of self-perceptions and the positive illusory bias in children with ADHD. *Clinical Child and Family Psychology Review, 10,* 335–351.

Patterson, G. R., & Yoerger, K. (1997). A developmental model for late-onset delinquency. In D. W. Osgood (Ed.), *Nebraska Symposium on Motivation: Vol. 44. Motivation and delinquency* (pp. 119–177). Lincoln: University of Nebraska Press.

Peeples, F., & Loeber, R. (1994). Do individual factors and neighborhood context explain ethnic differences in juvenile delinquency? *Journal of Quantitative Criminology, 10,* 141–158.

Reynolds, C. R., & Kamphaus, R. W. (2004). *Behavior assessment of children* (2nd ed.). Circle Pines, MN: American Guidance Service.

Rodkin, P. C., Farmer, T. W., Pearl, R., & Van Acker, R. (2000). Heterogeneity of popular boys: Antisocial and prosocial configurations. *Developmental Psychology, 36,* 14–24.

Roisman, G. I., Monahan, K. C., Campbell, S. B., Steinberg, L., Cauffman, E., & NICHHD Early Child Care Research Network. (2010). Is adolescence-onset antisocial behavior developmentally normative? *Development and Psychopathology, 22,* 295–311.

Schmidt, F., McKinnon, L., Chattha, H. K., & Brownlee, K. (2006). Concurrent and predictive validity of the Psychopathy Checklist: Youth Version across gender and ethnicity. *Psychological Assessment, 18,* 393–401.

Shaffer, D., Fisher, P., Lucas, C. P., Dulcan, M. K., & Schwab-Stone, M. E. (2000). NIMH Diagnostic Interview Schedule for Children Version IV (NIMH DISC-IV): Description, differences from previous versions, and reliability of some common diagnoses. *Journal of the American Academy of Child and Adolescent Psychiatry, 39,* 28–38.

Shannon, K. E., Beauchaine, T. P., Brenner, S. L., Neuhaus, E., & Gatzke-Kopp, L. (2007). Familial and temperamental predictors of resilience in children at risk for conduct disorder and depression. *Developmental Psychopathology, 3,* 701–727.

Shapiro, C. J., Smith, B. H., Malone, P. S., & Collaro, A. L. (2010). Natural experiment in deviant peer exposure and youth recidivism. *Journal of Clinical Child and Adolescent Psychology, 39,* 242–251.

Shelton, K. K., Frick, P. J., & Wootton, J. (1996). Assessment of parenting practices in families of elementary school-age children. *Journal of Clinical Child Psychology, 25,* 317–329.

Speltz, M., McClellan, J., DeKlyen, M., & Jones, K. (1999). Preschool boys with oppositional defiant disorder: Clinical presentation and diagnostic change. *Journal of the American Academy of Child and Adolescent Psychiatry, 38,* 838–845.

Thomas, A., & Chess, S. (1977). *Temperament and development.* New York, NY: Brunner/Mazel.

Vance, J. E., Bowen, N. K., Fernandez, G., & Thompson, S. (2002). Risk and protective factors as predictors of outcome of adolescents with psychiatric disorder and aggression. *Journal of the American Academy of Child and Adolescent Psychiatry, 41,* 36–43.

Waschbusch, D. A. (2002). A meta-analytic examination of comorbid hyperactive-impulsive-attention problems and conduct problems. *Psychological Bulletin, 128,* 118–150.

Wright, J. C., Zakriski, A. L., & Drinkwater, M. (1999). Developmental psychopathology and reciprocal patterning of behavior and environment: Distinctive situational and behavioral signatures of internalizing, externalizing, and mixed-syndrome children. *Journal of Consulting and Clinical Psychology, 67,* 95–107.

Zhou, Q., Hofer, C., Eisenberg, N., Reiser, N., Spinrad, T. L., & Fabes, R. A. (2007). The developmental trajectories of attention focusing, attentional and behavioral persistence and externalizing problems during school-age years. *Developmental Psychology, 43,* 369–385.

7

Relational and Neurodevelopmental Risk: Nurture Meets Nature

JEAN THOMAS AND BENJAMIN BREGMAN ■

From the vantage point of modern mental health, it is clear that a dynamic matrix of neurobiological and social-contextual factors contribute to the development of antisocial behavior. An integrated approach to understanding these complexities is necessary for effective intervention, ongoing research, and social policy. Today, the literature is burgeoning with studies of functional brain imaging and of the complex interplay between genes and the environment. This chapter focuses on *the importance of relational (caregiving) and neurodevelopmental risks in the development of antisocial behavior.* First, we define the conceptual framework of child development as a base from which to examine the ever-evolving complex origins of antisocial behavior. Second, we focus on current social-contextual research that demonstrates how the environment in which the child is growing mediates the development of antisocial behavior. Third, we discuss human and other primate research that augments our understanding of the neurophysiological underpinnings of socialization, empathy, and antisocial behavior. Fourth, we frame the quest toward a more integrated neurobiological/social-contextual evidence base that informs effective intervention, research, and social policy.

CONCEPTUAL FRAMEWORK: THE TRANSACTIONAL MODEL OF DEVELOPMENT

The transactional model of development (Sameroff & Chandler, 1975) conceptualizes development as the unfolding of biological potential within the ever evolving, specific context of the caregiving environment, including the child–parent relationship, community, and culture. Developmental changes are driven by the gene–environment interaction. The primary caregiver is the central regulatory influence on the child's developmental process (Hofer, 1994). Day-to-day experience, in concert with genetic and other factors, "canalizes" behavioral development (Gottlieb, 1991, p. 4). "Whatever the capabilities provided to the child by individual factors, the environment [acts] to limit or expand additional opportunities for development" (Sameroff, 1998, p. 1289). Similarly, the NICHD Early Child Care Research Network (NICHD & Arsenio, 2004, p. 12), summarizes, "it is obvious that the maintenance of aggressive behavior can only be understood in the wider context of the child's family and social environent."

The transactional process of development unfolds within the context of the family and social environment. The parent and the child–parent relationship mediate the child's developmental trajectory toward adaptation or disorder. For example, Chess and Thomas (1984), following their 30-year New York Longitudinal Study, conclude that neither the child's temperament nor ineffectual parenting alone leads to disruptive behavior. Rather, *disruptive behavior emerges from a lack of "goodness of fit" between the parents' expectations of the child and the temperament and capabilites of the child.* A "goodness of fit" between the child and parent facilitates parental pride and the child's sense of safety, self-esteem, active exploration, and learning. Therapy aimed at increasing the goodness of fit supports parents' increased understanding of the child with respect to age-specific expectations, child-specific neurodevelopment, and context-specific vulnerabilities and protective factors. Increased parent understanding of the child's behavior, emotion, and attention improves "goodness of fit" and, in turn, supports parental internal locus of control, parental mental health, reciprocal child–parent interactions, and the child's developmental trajectory toward improved senses of autonomy, competence, and self-regulation.

The mind-versus-brain and nature-versus-nurture debates play central roles in the historical conceptualization of antisocial behaviors. These dichotomies limit our capacity to understand the etiological factors of this complex set of social behaviors. This chapter explores how the interplay of neurobiology and social context guides understanding of the complex factors that contribute to antisocial behavior. Neurobiology defines the base from which development unfolds, as influenced by the specific and ever evolving caregiving context. Emergent research in functional neuroimaging and gene–environment interactions examine the underlying neurobiological factors contributing to the development of maladaptive behaviors in children and their progression to antisocial behaviors.

SOCIAL-CONTEXTUAL RISK FACTORS

Similar to previous studies of older children (Kazdin, 1985), current studies demonstrate that externalizing problems are the most frequent reason for psychiatric referral of preschool children (Keenan & Wakschlag, 2000; Luby & Morgan, 1997; Thomas & Clark, 1998; Thomas & Guskin, 2001).

Studies of correlates of preschool behavioral difficulties are similar to those in older children across child, parenting, family, environmental, and socio-demographic factors (Campbell, 1995; Loeber & Stouthaemer-Loeber, 1986). In comparing early-childhood-onset disruptive disorders and adolescence-onset disruptive disorders, there are two frequently proposed separate developmental pathways that differ not only in age of onset but also in the types of disruptive behavior manifested, in persistence, and "perhaps in etiology" (Hinshaw, Lahey, & Hart, 1993, p. 31; Moffitt, 1993; National Institute of Mental Health [NIMH], 2001).

Early-Onset Disruptive Disorders: The Most Malignant

Here we focus on early-childhood-onset disruptive disorders, which are most malignant. Although they constitute a small proportion of the youths who commit delinquent acts, children with early onset commit a very large proportion of these delinquent acts, especially those associated with lying, bullying, aggression, and recidivism. Adolescence onset tends to be less aggressive and more likely to resolve with age. It frequently occurs through association with deviant peers (Hinshaw et al., 1993; Moffitt, 1993; NIMH, 2001; Tremblay, 2010). This two-pathway model for disruptive disorders is important because it implies that externalizing behaviors differ with development and changing environmental factors (NIMH, 2001). Further understanding of biological and environmental factors that shape early-onset, more malignant and chronic disruptive patterns is key (Hinshaw et al., 1993; NIMH, 2001).

Preliminary work within the early-onset group has begun to delineate specific neurodevelopmental differences (Thomas & Guskin, 2001). Two early developmental tracks, defined by cluster analysis, were proposed by Taylor, Schachar, Thorley, and Wieselberg (1986). The *first track*, with onset before age 2, demonstrated an increased coexistence of a wide range of neurodevelopmental delays, including language and motor delays. The *second track*, with school-age onset, demonstrated fewer, less severe neurodevelopmental delays but increased specific learning difficulties, most often in reading. A *third track*, seen in boys age 7 years in East London (Taylor, Sandberg, Thorley, & Giles, 1991), was associated with parental critical emotion and ineffectual coping strategies. Hyperactive boys with conduct disorder were compared with healthy controls and nonhyperactive oppositional controls. Parental critical emotion and ineffective coping predicted which boys had conduct disorder at age 17 years (Taylor, 1999). These authors concluded that once behavioral disturbance (hyperactivity or oppositionality) had appeared, parental critical emotion and ineffectual coping contributed to a chain mechanism in the development of antisocial conduct. Furthermore, these authors conclude that *neurodevelopmental and psychosocial factors must be understood as mutually influencing each other and the child's presentation and outcome* (Taylor, 1999).

Three Early-Onset Risk Domains

Three domains—child characteristics, parent characteristics, and child–parent interactional characteristics—all contribute well-known risk for disruptive behaviors in preschool children (Gross, Sambrook & Fogg, 1999; Shaw, Owens, Vondra, Keenan, & Winslow, 1996; Taylor, 1999; Wakschlag & Keenan, 2001).

RISK DOMAIN: CHILD CHARACTERISTICS

Child characteristics, including externalizing and internalizing difficulties, especially when combined, are predictive of later antisocial behavior (Eisenberg et al., 2000; NIMH, 2001). Neurodevelopmental vulnerabilities found in children with disruptive disorders appear associated with difficulties in cognitive, autonomic, neuroendocrine, neurochemical, prenatal, and genetic factors (NIMH, 2001; Taylor, 1999). Additional individual child vulnerabilities/risk factors include speech-language differences and delays, motor differences, temperament/sensory reactivity challenges, and intrinsic vulnerabilites to anxiety and mood dysregulation (Chess & Thomas, 1984; Fox & Polak, 2004; Gartstein & Rothbart, 2003). Childhood adversity also creates significant risk. Adversity and associated anxiety and stress are part of typical development. However, when stress increases significantly, it can be developmentally costly to any child, and especially younger children (Lieberman, Van Horn, & Ippen, 2005).

Speech-language disorders significantly increase risk for behavioral and emotional disorders. The "multidomain" model defines development as an interacting, continuous process that occurs in several distinct but interrelated domains: cognitive, linguistic, and motor. Assessments of young children's cognitive abilities must be framed in the context of these rapidly changing systems that may be in or out of synchrony with each other (Gilliam & Mayes, 2000). It is well understood that speech-language disorders are heterogeneous. In a community sample of 169 5-year-old children, scores on measures of articulation, expressive and receptive language, and tests of auditory comprehension and auditory memory demonstrated at age 12 follow-up that progressively severe speech-language impairment was associated with similar impairment across cognitive, visual motor, and academic measures (Beitchman, Wilson, Brownlie, Walters, & Lancee, 1996). Merriman and Barnett (1995) similarly report that language skills, especially auditory comprehension and verbal ability, are significantly related to gross motor skills. In older children and adults, neurodevelopmental difficulties, including speech-language and learning and reading disabilities, are often missed. In particular, speech-language disorders frequently are missed in children with disruptive behavior disorders (Burger & Lang, 1998).

Language disorders increase risk for behavioral and emotional disorders (August & Garfinkel, 1989; Baker & Cantwell, 1987). Early studies demonstrate that more than 50% of children with speech-language difficulties have psychiatric problems (Baker & Cantwell, 1987). Recent studies reinforce this finding and clarify that language impairment at age 5 is associated with young adult psychiatric disorders, especially anxiety disorders and antisocial personality disorder

(Beitchman et al., 2001). Because reciprocal communication is basic to healthy relationships (Tronick & Gianino, 1986), identifying and treating children with speech-language difficulties helps mitigate and prevent psychiatric morbidity.

Motor differences and delays are often associated with a similar level of language and cognitive delays. Motor differences include motor planning difficulties such as apraxia of speech and dyspraxia of the large limb muscles. Low muscle tone and coordination difficulties are often correlated motor problems. Language differences and delays are more easily identified than motor delays, low tone, and cognitive difficulties; therefore, when language disorders are recognized, one should also look for motor and cognitive difficulties.

Temperament and sensory reactivity are overlapping conceptualizations. Infant and early childhood temperament (Fox & Polak, 2004) describe sensory reactivity differences as central factors in behavioral style and in the risk for antisocial behavior. Temperament was originally understood as a stable, innate behavioral quality. More recent understanding of temperament is that it can be modified by contextual experiences (Stringaris, Maughan, & Goodman, 2010). Chess and Thomas (1984), the founders of infant temperament work, used their observations in the New York Longitudinal Study to derive nine temperamental dimensions. According to Chess and Thomas, infants differ in the amount of stimulation they require to react to various stimuli. Some infants respond best to intense stimulation and others to lower levels of stimulation. It is understood that infant behavioral style influences the way that parents perceive their children and their behavioral responses to their children. To this point, Fox and Polak (2004) promote clinical interventions that focus on helping parents to understand their children's sensory reactivity and to develop strategies that facilitate their child's emotional and behavioral regulation. *Intrinsic vulnerability to anxiety/depression and adverse childhood experiences create additive risk.* Moderate to large stress can reset the body's physiologic priorities and put learning on hold. Within the context of moderate stress and especially traumatic stress, rather than focusing on learning, the child must focus on maintaining support and vigilance to potential danger (Lieberman et al., 2005). Adverse childhood experiences (including neglect; emotional, physical, or sexual abuse; domestic violence; household mental illness; and the absence of one or more parents) predict adult disability and death (Felitti et al. 1998; Lieberman et al., 2005). Furthermore, these chronic and traumatic stress experiences can trigger gene–environment interactions that increase the child's intrinsic vulnerability to psychiatric disorders, including antisocial behavior disorder.

RISK DOMAIN: PARENT CHARACTERISTICS (ANXIETY, DEPRESSION)

Risk associated with the caregiving environment centers around negative and inconsistent parenting and family social adversity (Campbell, 1995; Warren, Emde, & Sroufe, 2000). Parental mental illness is the most widely studied and best understood parent risk factor (Zahn-Waxler, 1995). Maternal depressive symptoms at any time (prenatal, postnatal, and current) and the course of parental depressive symptoms over the child's development are associated with disruptive behavior in young children (Luoma et al., 2001). Parent psycho-pathology influences and is influenced by family contextual factors, including adverse events that increase the risk of psychopathology in offspring (Beardslee, Versade, & Gladstone, 1998; Campbell, Pierce, Moore, Marakovitz, & Newby, 1996; Lieberman et al., 2005; Nomura, Wickramaratne, Warner, Mufson, & Weissman, 2002; Shaw, Keenan, Vondra, Delliquadri, & Giovannelli, 1997; Shaw et al., 1996; Seifer, Dickstein, Sameroff, Magee, & Hayden, 2001; Weisman, Warner, Wickaramaratne, Moreau, & Olfson, 1997). Child characteristics, parent characteristics (including current and long-term psychopathology), and family contextual risks (most importantly child–parent relationships) transactionally contribute to child mental health versus child psychopathology.

Maternal prenatal stress can have a lasting effect on infant and early childhood development. In his extensive review, "Developmental Origins of Disruptive Behaviour Problems," Tremblay (2010) concludes that most early environmental risk factors for disruptive behavior can be identified at the time of pregnancy (including the mother's adolescent behavioral problems, young age of pregnancy, and poverty). Gartstein and Rothbart (2003) demonstrated that at 30–32 weeks' gestation, elevated maternal salivary cortisol was significantly associated with maternal report of infant negative reactivity on the Infant Behavior Questionnaire (Gartstein & Rothbart, 2003). In addition, the effects of prenatal maternal stress on infant temperament correlated with maternal prenatal psychosocial stress in 247 full-term infants (Davis et al., 2007). Other studies suggest that children exposed to maternal stress during pregnancy have an elevated risk of behavior problems. Parent–parent conflict and social adversity were most strongly correlated with increased behavioral risk (Ramchandani, Richter, Norris, & Stein, 2010).

Maternal depression is a recognized major risk factor for children's cognitive, social-emotional, and behavioral outcomes (Beardslee, Bemporad, Keller, & Klerman, 1983; Beardslee et al., 1998; Field, 1992; NICHD Early Child Care Research Network, 1999; Zahn-Waxler, Iannotti, Cummings, & Denham, 1990). Maternal major depressive disorder during a child's first year of life is a significant predictor of later childhood internalizing and total behavior problems on the Child Behavior Checklist 4–18 version (Achenbach, 1991; Bagner, Pettit, Lewinsohn, & Seeley, 2010). After the first year, maternal major depression was significantly related to externalizing as well as internalizing and total problems on the Child Behavior Checklist 2–3 version (Achenbach, 1992). Their findings suggest that a child's first year, as compared with the prenatal and later periods, is the most "sensitive period." That is, during the first year, maternal major depression has its "most potent impact on a child's behavior" (Bagner et al., 2010, p. 705).

However, research shows that it is not the mothers' symptoms but their effect on parenting that contribute to transmission of depression (Solantaus-Simula, Punamaki, & Beardslee, 2002). Cohn and Tronick (1989) demonstrated that mothers with significantly elevated levels of depression display more negative expressions, less positive engagement, and less sensitivity during interactions with their 6- to 7-month-old infants and that these behaviors generalize across relationships. More recently, longitudinal studies demonstrate that significant continuity of a child's disruptive behavior is strongly associated with continuity of maternal depressive symptoms (Luoma et al., 2001; NICHD, 1999; Sameroff & Seifer, 1983; Seifer et al., 2001). These and other recent studies of infant and early childhood mental health rely prominently on observation of parent–child interactions (Carter, Garrity-Rokous, Chazan-Cohen, Little, & Briggs-Gowan, 2001; Chatoor, Ganiban, Harrison, & Hirsch, 2001; Keenan & Wakschlag, 2000; Wakschlag & Keenan, 2001).

Risk Domain: Child–Parent Interactional Characteristics

Relational processes and the "attachment behavior system" (Bowlby, 1969/1982) are major mediators in the development of antisocial behavior. Beginning at birth, relational processes, especially those between the primary caregiver and the infant, are essential mediators of the developmental trajectory. Attachment theory and growing data link key domains of behavior, emotion, and cognition. "Knowledge of relational processes . . . [in] attachment relationships, can contribute to an understanding of etiology, maintenance, and treatment of externalizing disorders" (Guttmann-Steinmetz & Crowell, 2006, p. 440). The investigation of relational processes and the development of antisocial behavior demands searching beyond the presenting problems to a broad range of integrated neurodevelopmental and social-contextual risk and protective factors (Guttmann-Steinmetz & Crowell, 2006).

Child–parent relationship characteristics (child–parent conflict, intrusiveness, difficulties with reciprocity, noncompliance, and coping with noncompliance) are a major risk factor for disruptive behaviors in young children (Campbell et al., 1996; DuPaul, McGoey, Eckert, & VanBrakle, 2001; Gardner, Sonuga-Barke, & Sayal, 1999; Hinshaw et al., 1993; Patterson, 1982; Patterson, DeBaryshe, & Ramsey, 1989; Taylor, 1999). Although child–parent attunement challenges begin at birth, misattunement/conflict between the child and the parent typically manifest clinically at about 18 months, with the toddler's assertion of autonomy. The toddler's expectable push for autonomy evokes increased parental frustration, criticism, and ineffectual coping strategies, leading to coercive cycles of toddler–parent behavior (DuPaul et al., 2001; Gardner et al., 1999; Patterson, 1982; Patterson, 1989; Taylor, 1999). These challenges are augmented in the context of parent anxiety and depressive symptoms.

Conflicted child–parent relationships "are often initiated by disruptive behavior, whether it is the ADHD or oppositional-defiant type" (Taylor, 1999, p. 616). Furthermore, once conflict is established, it appears to have an independent effect in determining the course of child behavioral outcome (Taylor, 1999). Conflict in child–parent relationships is increased in association with maternal prenatal stress and maternal depression, as well as adverse events. Parental discipline and conflict management, especially parental use of negative behavior and coercion as early as ages 18 to 24 months, has been identified as a predictive factor for externalizing difficulties at school entry (Campbell,

1994; Fagot & Leve, 1998; Lieberman et al., 2005; NIMH, 2001). Furthermore, the NICHD Child Care Research Network (NICHD & Arsenio, 2004) demonstrates, in a large multisite study, the central role of parents and parent–child interactions in affect regulation and behavioral competence at 24 and 36 months. They also demonstrate the importance of affect regulation in later cognitive and social competence.

NEUROPHYSIOLOGICAL UNDERPINNINGS OF SOCIAL-CONTEXTUAL RISK FACTORS

Effects of Early Secure Attachment and of Maternal Deprivation on Macaque Monkey Offspring

Suomi and colleagues (Shannon, Champoux, & Suomi, 1998) highlight early neurophysiologic relational similarities between humans and macaque monkeys (who share 95% of the human gene pool). They examined the effects of unusually secure early attachment on the biobehavioral development of these monkeys. Macaque infants, selectively bred for high reactivity, who were cross-fostered to highly nurturant mothers showed less clinging and less behavioral disturbance at weaning in comparison with those cross-fostered to less nurturant mothers. These highly reactive monkey infants, when cross-fostered to highly nurturant mothers, also demonstrated earlier exploration, greater social dominance at maturity, and more nurturant mothering of their firstborn infants.

More recently, Suomi and colleagues (Shannon et al., 2005) demonstrated that early maternal deprivation may lead to increased, ongoing serotonin-mediated psychiatric risk. Macaque monkeys ($N = 256$) were reared over 150 days in three rearing conditions: mother reared, peer reared, and surrogate/peer reared. By 30 days, maternal deprivation in the latter two rearing conditions was associated with less cerebral spinal fluid (CSF) 5-HIAA, that is, less serotonin (5-HIAA is a metabolite of serotonin). Furthermore, they found that decreased CSF 5-HIAA level (less serotonin) became "trait-like" in ongoing development. Then Suomi's group compared risk-taking behavior (jumping more than 5 meters) in macaque infants with higher CSF 5-HIAA (more serotonin) with risk-taking behavior in macaque infants with significantly lower CSF 5-HIAA (less serotonin). Those with more CSF serotonin took a significantly smaller percentage of jumps longer than 5 meters, whereas those with less serotonin took a significantly larger percentage of jumps longer than 5 meters, thereby risking their lives (Shannon et al., 2005).

In the first study, Shannon et al. (1998) demonstrate that highly nurturant parenting can facilitate robustly healthy psychosocial development in selectively bred, highly reactive macaque infants,and, by extrapolation, in human infants. In the later study, Shannon et al. (2005) suggest that low CSF serotonin associated with maternal deprivation is a likely mediator of significant risk for psychiatric disorder beginning in the first years of human life. Looking at these studies together, early relational treatment to facilitate attuned and empathic parenting is recommended for infants and young children with genetic and temperamental risk and those who are neglected or maternally deprived.

Mirror Neurons in the Development of Socialization, Empathy, and Antisocial Behavior

Mirror neuron system (MNS) research establishes another link to the neurophysiological underpinnings of socialization, empathy, and antisocial behavior. Originally discovered in the ventral premotor cortex of macaque monkeys (Fabbri-Destro & Rizzolatti, 2008; Rizzolatti & Craighero, 2004), mirror neurons are activated when an individual either performs or observes another performing a series of motor movements (Iacoboni & Dapretto, 2006; Iacoboni & Mazziotta, 2007; Rizzolatti, Fabbri-Destro, & Cattaneo, 2009). Additional studies demonstrate that observing a goal-specific action such as eating or placing an item in a container activates these neurons beyond what would be expected by observing just the gross motor movements involved in the act (Fogassi et al., 2005). That is, mirror neurons fire when a goal-specific act is witnessed *and* the goal of that action is inferred, as when an individual hears sounds associated with a specific act, such as cracking peanuts (Kohler et al., 2002), or when the meaning of a partially observed act is inferred (Umiltà et al., 2001). These findings have led researchers to hypothesize that mirror neurons serve as a way of mapping an observed primate's actions onto the observer's cortical representation of the action, thereby providing the observer with an internalized understanding of the behaviors of others (theory of mind) (Gallese, Fadiga, Fogassi, & Rizzolatti, 1996; Rizzolatti & Craighero, 2004).

Research into the human MNS provides significant insight into the biological underpinnings of human empathy and mentalization, that is, the capacity to attribute to others mental states such as intentions, beliefs, and desires. In the human brain, there are high concentrations of mirror neurons located in brain regions analogous to those in other primates, including the inferior parietal lobe, the ventral premotor cortex, and the caudal part of the inferior frontal gyrus (Iacoboni & Dapretto, 2006; Iacoboni & Mazziotta, 2007; Rizzolatti et al., 2009). These mirror-neuron-rich areas are thought to play an important role in human social cognition (Ferrari et al., 2009). Interestingly, additional brain regions have been identified that appear to have mirror neuron activity, specifically the anterior cingulate cortex (ACC), the insula, Broca's area, and extensions into the limbic system (Iacoboni & Dapretto, 2006; Iacoboni & Mazziotta, 2007; Rizzolatti et al., 2009). These brain regions have traditionally been thought to play a role in typical emotional expression and communication, potentially indicating that the affective-empathy network includes the MNS (Carr, Iacoboni, Dubeau, Mazziotta, & Lenzi, 2003). Recent functional magnetic resonance imaging (fMRI) and positron emitting tomography (PET) imaging studies have found that the ACC and the insula become activated when an

144 ADVANCES IN BEHAVIORAL AND CLINICAL RESEARCH

individual both experiences emotions directly (pain and disgust) and observes facial expressions or witnesses situations in which others experience these emotions (Avenanti, Bueti, Galati, & Aglioti, 2005; Bufalari. Aprile, Avenanti, Di Russo, & Aglioti, 2005; Cattaneo et al., 2007).

Furthermore, researchers examining the neurobiological basis of the social deficits found in autistic spectrum disorders have identified dysfunction in the MNS of these children (Cattaneo et al., 2007; Dapretto et al., 2006; Iacoboni & Dapretto, 2006; Iacoboni & Mazziotta, 2007; Rizzolatti et al., 2009). In addition, a recent fMRI study of children with autism demonstrated reduced mirror neuron activity in tasks related to observation and imitation of facial emotional expressions, as compared with typically developing children (Dapretto et al., 2006). These researchers also demonstrated a correlation between reduced activity in mirror neuron areas and the severity of the autistic disorder.

The MNS appears to be crucial in facilitating relational learning and the development of socialization. Given this, recent research examines the role that mirror neurons play in early childhood development. In studying the effect of maternal–neonate imitation on development in macaque monkeys, Ferrari et al. (2009) found a connection between early (birth to 2 weeks) imitation behaviors and later social functioning. They found that macaque infants that were consistent in their imitative responses with their mothers were more advanced in their behavioral and cognitive development than were inconsistent imitators. Based on previous research (Ferrari, Visalberghi, Fogassi, Ruggiero, & Suomi, 2006). Ferrari et al. (2009) suggest that the MNS is responsible for early imitation behaviors. They hypothesize that the maturity of the MNS in neonates has a direct impact on future behavioral and social functioning in macaque monkeys, and, by extrapolation, other primates. The authors acknowledge the influence of genetic and temperamental factors on maturational differences in the MNS, while underscoring the fact that MNS maturation relies heavily on infant–environment interactions. Great variability in early primate, and specifically human, caregiver–infant interactions strongly suggests that early environmental stimulation of the neonate's developing MNS may have a dramatic impact on the development of a child's interpersonal competence, empathic capabilities, and prosocial behavior (Pfeifer Iacoboni, Mazziotta, & Dapretto, 2008).

A growing area of research focuses on the MNS and deficits in the development of empathy. Given that a core trait of individuals with antisocial behaviors is a near absence or lack of empathy, dysfunction in the MNS is hypothesized to underlie the development of antisocial behaviors. In a recent study examining the connection between psychopathic personality traits and the MNS, Fecteau, Pascual-Leone, and Théoret (2008) asked participants to watch videos that are known to stimulate the MNS for empathic pain. They found, using the Psychopathic Personality Inventory (PPI) (Benning, Patrick, Hicks, Blonigen, & Krueger, 2003), that individuals who scored highest on coldheartedness, a central trait of individuals with antisocial behavior, showed the greatest suppression of their MNS relating to empathic pain. Based on this, the authors hypothesized that even when the ability to empathize with those in pain is attenuated, the mentalization capabilities, that is, the ability to understand the actions and mental states of others, in these individuals may be intact.

The MNS appears to play a central role in socialization and emotions (empathy) of others. The maturity of the MNS, influenced by both genetic and environmental factors (caregiver interactions), is vital to the development of imitation behaviors in primates and may predict social and cognitive capacities, as well as security of attachment in humans. Furthermore, deficits in the ability to mentalize in children with autistic spectrum disorders and deficits in the ability to empathize in individuals with antisocial behaviors appear to be connected with MNS dysfunction. Future research into the neuropsychologic bases of social-contextual risk factors will likely provide key insights into typical emotional and social cognition and stimulate novel clinical approaches in early intervention and prevention.

DIAGNOSTIC CORMORBIDITY: ANOTHER OPPORTUNITY FOR UNDERSTANDING PSYCHOPATHOLOGY

The frequency of diagnostic comorbidity in child and adolescent psychiatry has raised concerns about boundary problems with the DSM nosological system (Angold & Costello, 1993; Caron & Rutter, 1991; Jensen & Watanabe, 1999; Nottelmann & Jensen, 1995; Seifer et al., 2001; Taylor, 1999). "The current system falls short of informing the process of people interacting and being acted upon by complex environments over time" (Nottelmann & Jensen, 1995, p. 120). Previously considered a defect of classification systems, currently comorbidity is considered an opportunity for understanding the etiology, course, and treatment of disorders, especially of those disorders with poorly established validity (Angold, Costello, & Erkanli, 1999), including disruptive disorders in young children. High-risk toddlers with comorbid behavior and speech-language disorders, for example, provide a frame for understanding how comorbidity facilitates early identification and treatment of children with disruptive behavior disorders.

Comorbid DSM diagnoses

Copious studies of attention-deficit disorder with hyperactivity (ADDH) (American Psychiatric Association [APA], 1980) and ADHD (attention-deficit/hyperactivity disorder; APA, 1987, 1994) in older children and adolescents include one done by Biederman and colleagues (Munir, Biederman, & Knee, 1987), who document that comorbidity of ADDH/ADHD with other disruptive disorders and with affective disorders is the rule, not the exception. Using a structured interview, the Diagnostic Interview for Children and Adolescents—Parent Version (DICA-P), 96% of male outpatients ages 5 to 16 years with attention-deficit disorder without hyperactivity (ADD) (APA, 1980) were diagnosed with more than one Axis I disorder, and 82% were diagnosed with more than two disorders. The authors raised concern that, within the heterogeneous group of children meeting criteria for ADD, the presence of additional disorders may be missed. They concluded that grouping children with ADD into subgroups with similar comorbidities is helpful in identifying more homogeneous groups of patients with common course, family history, biological markers, response to treatment, and outcome. More recently, Durston and colleagues (Durston, Belle, & Zeeuw, 2010) concluded that, as we continue to diagnose ADHD on the basis of symptoms and behavioral assessments alone, we ignore many diverse neurobiological pathways to ADHD, which may be delineated by cognitive profiling and neuroimaging. Lewis (1996) came to a similar conclusion regarding DSM-IV conduct disorder. She proposed the use of comorbidities associated with conduct disorder to identify the multiple underlying neuropsychiatric and psychosocial conditions that may be treatable and preventable. *A central goal is to identify these multiple underlying comorbidities of the heterogeneous group of young children with disruptive disorders who may have treatable and preventable neuropsychiatric and psychosocial conditions* (Stringaris et al., 2010; Thomas & Guskin, 2001).

COMORBID EXTERNALIZING AND INTERNALIZING DISORDERS: THE RULE, NOT THE EXCEPTION

In older children, concerns have been raised about the historic dichotomy of externalizing and internalizing symptoms. However, in multiple studies, the overlap of externalizing and internalizing disorders within individuals has been demonstrated (Carlson & Cantwell, 1980; Chiles, Miller, & Cox, 1980; Conners & Wells, 1986). Similarly, in preschool children, Rescorla (1986) and others (Keenan, Shaw, Walsh, Delliquadri, & Giovannelli, 1997; Lavigne et al., 1998; Lavigne et al., 2001; Luby & Morgan, 1997; Luby et al., 2002; Shaw et al., 1997; Thomas & Guskin, 2001) have demonstrated that the co-occurrence of aggressive/destructive behavior with anxiety/mood symptoms is the rule, not the exception. For example, in preschool children with major depressive symptoms, significant symptoms of ADHD were found in 50% and significant symptoms of generalized anxiety disorder were found in 75% (Luby et al., 2002).

Comorbidity guides recent infant and early childhood diagnostic approaches

Growing concern about prevalence, continuity, and comorbidity of disruptive disorders in toddlers and preschool children increases the need for an age-specific, reliable, and valid categorical classification system (Cicchetti & Richters, 1993; Hinshaw et al., 1993; Lavigne et al., 1998; Seifer et al., 2001; Thomas & Guskin, 2001; Thomas & Tidmarsh, 1997). Three interdisciplinary efforts to develop an evidence-based, more age-specific diagnostic classification system for children ages birth through 5 years have been published. First was the Research Diagnostic Criteria—Preschool Age (RDC-PA) (Scheeringa et al., 2003), supported by the American Academy of Child and Adolescent Psychiatry. Second, the *Diagnostic Classification of Mental Health and Developmental Disorders of Infancy and Early Childhood—Revised (Diagnostic Classification: 0–3R;* DC: 0–3R; Zero to Three, 2005) replaced the first DC: 0–3 (Zero to Three, 1994) to establish more evidence-based diagnoses. Third, the American Psychiatric Association's monograph, *Psychiatric Diagnosis in Infants, Toddlers, and Preschoolers* (Narrow, First, Sirovatka, & Regier, 2007), provided nine white papers that further clarify the rapidly burgeoning evidence base that supports the previously mentioned early mental health diagnostic classification systems. Within the DSM-IV and all of these more age-specific early classification systems, diagnostic comorbidity supports early identification, understanding and treatment.

EARLY RELATIONAL TREATMENT OF CHILDREN WITH BEHAVIORAL DIFFICULTIES MITIGATES BEHAVIORAL IMPAIRMENTS

Denham and colleagues (2000) demonstrate that 4- and 5-year-old children show strong continuity of externalizing behaviors 2 and 4 years later, in association with parent–child interaction and child-rearing styles. Increased early identification and relational treatment of children with behavioral and associated emotional and attentional difficulties reduce long-term continuity of these disorders (Taylor, 2010). Because of the prevalence, comorbidity, chronicity, and severity associated with early disruptive disorders and the costs to the individual, the family, and society (Haapasalo & Tremblay, 1994), it is paramount to understand ways in which characteristics of the young child, the parent, and the child–parent relationship contribute to early pathways to disruptive behavior. Treatment studies of children at high risk for antisocial behavior are equally important. In addition to child–parent relational treatment, identification and treatment of the child's neurodevelopmental differences and the parents' charateristics are key. Similarly, NICHD (NICHD & Arsenio, 2004, p. 12) summarizes: *intervention targeting parental discipline, conflict management, engagement, monitoring, and validation consistently show that improvement in these domains leads to improvement in child and adolescent conduct problems* (NIMH, 2001; Olds et al., 1998; Patterson, 1982; Webster-Stratton & Hammond, 1998). Research with preschool children also shows that diminished parental supervision and attention during these early years predicts increased aggression and delinquency in school-age boys (Haapasalo & Tremblay, 1994).

Three randomized controlled intervention studies highlight the importance of relational focus in the treatment of young children with behavioral and emotional problems. Webster-Stratton and Reid (2004) showed that children ages 5–8 years with high baseline levels of conduct problems markedly improved their behavior in association with reduced maternal critical parenting. In addition, Lieberman and colleagues (2005) demonstrated the efficacy of extended child–parent psychotherapy with emotionally and behaviorally dysregulated preschool children exposed to marital violence. More recently, Bagner and Eyberg (2007) demonstrate that parent–child interaction therapy (PCIT) decreases early childhood difficult behaviors and parental stress related to child behaviors. Furthermore, these child and parent gains are shown to generalize to young children with intellectual delays and comorbid oppositional defiant disorder.

Even children with documented callous–unemotional (CU) traits, who are known to be at high risk of antisocial outcomes (Blair, 2007), have demonstrated patterns of change over time. One study showed change associated with treatment in CU boys with a mean age of 6.29 years. Although the boys in the stable-high CU group changed less than in other trajectory groups, CU scores did decrease for a subset of the stable-high boys (Fontaine, Rijsdijk, McCrory, & Viding, 2010; Hawes & Dadds, 2007). In the unstable-trajectory CU groups, recent consensus is that some children have high malleability that responds to positive feedback rather than negative discipline (Fontaine et al., 2010; Hawes & Dadds, 2007). In a group of 4-year-old children, Fontaine and colleagues (2010) also showed that family issues create an important intervention target. They highlight that even earlier intervention is needed.

SUMMARY: INTEGRATED SOCIAL CONTEXT AND NEUROBIOLOGY GUIDE INTERVENTION, RESEARCH, AND SOCIAL POLICY

This chapter highlights the importance of relational (caregiving) and neurodevelopmental risks in the development of antisocial behavior. The transactional model of development conceptualizes development as the unfolding of biological potential within the ever evolving, specific context of the caregiving environment. Three risk domains include the child characteristics, the parent characteristics, and the child–parent interactional characteristics. Individual child characteristics include language, motor, temperament/sensory reactivity delays and differences, and intrinsic vulnerability to anxiety/depression. In addition, exposure to caregiver neglect/abuse or cultural adversity create significant risk for antisocial behavior. Parental anxiety and depressive disorders, especially chronic disorders, create additive risk. Longitudinal studies demonstrate that a child's behavioral difficulties emerge from the lack of "goodness of fit" between the parents' expectations of their child and the child's specific developmental capacities. Repairing this "goodness of fit" facilitates the child's sense of safety and self-esteem and the parent's self-efficacy and parental pride. An empathically attuned child–caregiver relationship facilitates the child's trajectory toward social, behavioral, emotional, attentional, and cognitive health.

We focus on early-childhood-onset disruptive disorders, which are the most malignant. Although they constitute a small proportion of youths who commit delinquent acts, children with early onset commit a very large proportion of these delinquent acts. Current social-contextual research demonstrates how the environment in which the child is growing mediates the development of antisocial behavior. Critical and inconsistent parenting and family social adversity are documented to be major risk factors for early-onset behavioral disorders. The child's intrinsic characteristics, including the normative behavioral transitions around age 2 years, trigger child–parent relational challenges. Child neurodevelopmental difficulties and parental affective vulnerability exacerbate these challenges.

In addition, we focus on diagnostic comorbidity as an opportunity for understanding psychopathology. For example, copious studies of ADHD (DSM-IV) demonstrate that within the heterogeneous group of children meeting criteria for ADHD, the presence of additional disorders may be missed. A similar conclusion regarding conduct disorder (DSM-IV) proposes the use of comorbidities associated with conduct disorder to identify the multiple underlying conditions that may be treatable and preventable. A central goal is to identify the multiple, less salient comorbidies of the heterogenous group of young children with disruptive disorders who may have treatable and preventable psychosocial and neuropsychiatric conditions.

Finally, we frame the quest toward a more integrated social-contextual/neurobiological evidence base that informs intervention, research, and social policy. First, we clarify the point that disruptive behavior, like a "fever of unknown origin," is the most salient manifestation of childhood distress and social/developmental impairment. Underlying these salient behaviors are complex, heterogeneous neurodevelopmental and relational patterns that inform specific intervention and prevention strategies. Second, we focus on human and other primate research that augments understanding of the neurophysiological underpinnings of socialization, empathy, and antisocial behavior. Integrated evidence of social-cultural and neurobiological factors that shape early onset, more malignant and chronic disruptive patterns, is key. Third, early relational treatment, known to mitigate behavioral difficulties and associated emotional and learning impairments, is crucial, especially given the prevalence, comorbidity, chronicity, and severity associated with early disruptive disorders and the long-term costs to the child, the family, and society. The urgency of early, integrated, relational and neurodevelopmental intervention and associated research and social policy is clear.

REFERENCES

Achenbach, T. M. (1991). *Manual for the Child Behavior Checklist/4–18 and 1991 Profile.* Burlington,VT: University of Vermont, Department of Psychiatry.

Achenbach, T. M. (1992). *Manual for the Child Behavior Checklist/2–3 and 1992 Profile.* Burlington,VT: University of Vermont, Department of Psychiatry.

American Psychiatric Association. (1980). *Diagnostic and statistical manual of mental disorders* (3rd ed.). Washington, DC: Author.

American Psychiatric Association. (1987). *Diagnostic and statistical manual of mental disorders* (3rd ed., rev). Washington, DC: Author.

American Psychiatric Association. (1994). *Diagnostic and statistical manual of mental disorders* (4th ed.). Washington, DC: Author.

Angold, A., & Costello, E. J. (1993). Depressive comorbidity in children and adolescents: Empirical, theoretical, and methodological issues. *American Journal of Psychiatry, 150*(12), 1779–1791.

Angold, A., Costello, E. J., & Erkanli, A. (1999). Comorbidity. *Journal of Child Psychology and Psychiatry, 40*(1), 57–87.

August, G. J., & Garfinkel, B. D. (1989). Behavioral and cognitive subtypes of ADHD. *Journal of the American Academy of Child and Adolescent Psychiatry, 28*(5), 739–748.

Avenanti, A., Bueti, D., Galati, G., & Aglioti, S. M. (2005) Transcranial magnetic stimulation highlights the sensorimotor side of empathy for pain. *Nature Neuroscience, 8,* 955–960.

Bagner, D. M., & Eyberg, S. M. (2007). Parent–child interaction therapy for disruptive behavior in children with mental retardation: A randomized controlled trial. *Journal of Clinical Child and Adolescent Psychology, 36*(3), 418–429.

Bagner, D. M., Pettit, J. W., Lewinsohn, P. M., & Seeley, J. R. (2010). Effect of maternal depression on child behavior: A sensitive period. *Journal of American Academy of Child and Adolescent Psychiatry, 49*(7), 699–706.

Baker, I., & Cantwell, D. P. (1987). Comparison of well, emotionally disordered, and behaviorally disordered children with linguistic problems. *Journal of the American Academy of Child and Adolescent Psychiatry, 26*(2), 193–196.

Beardslee, W. R., Bemporad, J., Keller, M. D., & Klerman, G. L. (1983). Children of parents with major affective disorder: A review. *American Journal of Psychiatry, 140,* 825–832.

Beardslee, W. R., Versade, E. M., & Gladstone, T. R. (1998). Children of affectively ill parents: A review of the past 10 years. *Journal of the American Academy of Child and Adolescent Psychiatry, 37,* 1134–1141.

Beitchman, J. H., Wilson, B., Brownlie, E. B., Walters, H., & Lancee, W. (1996). Long-term consistency in speech/language profiles: I. Developmental and academic outcomes. *Journal of the American Academy of Child and Adolescent Psychiatry, 35*(6), 804–814.

Beitchman, J. H., Wilson, B., Johnson, C. J., Atkinson, L., Young, A., Adlaf, E, . . . Douglas, L. (2001). Fourteen-year follow-up for speech/language-impaired and control children: Psychiatric outcome. *Journal of American Academy of Child and Adolescent Psychiatry, 40*(1), 75–82.

Benning, S. D., Patrick, C. J., Hicks, B. M., Blonigen, D. M., & Krueger, R. F. (2003). Factor structure of the psychopathic personality inventory: Validity and implications for clinical assessment. *Psychological Assessment, 15,* 340–350.

Blair, R. J. R. (2007). The amydala and ventromedial prefrontal cortex in morality and psychopathy. *Trends in Cognitive Science, 11,* 387–392.

Bowlby, J. (1982). *Attachment and loss: Vol. I. Attachment*. New York: Basic Books. (Original work published 1969)

Bufalari, I., Aprile, T., Avenanti, A., Di Russo, F., & Aglioti, S. M. (2005). Empathy for pain and touch in the human somatosensory cortex. *Cerebral Cortex, 17,* 2553–2561.

Burger, F. L., & Lang, C. M. (1998). Diagnoses commonly missed in childhood: Long-term outcome and implications for treatment. *Psychiatric Clinics of North America, 21*(4), 927–940.

Campbell, S. B. (1994). Hard-to-manage preschool boys: Externalizing behavior, social competence, and family context at two-year follow-up. *Journal of Abnormal Child Psychology, 22,* 147–166.

Campbell, S. B. (1995). Behavior problems in preschool children: A review of recent research. *Journal of Child Psychology Psychiatry, 36,* 113–149.

Campbell, S. B., Pierce, E. W., Moore, G., Marakovitz, S., & Newby, K. (1996). Boys' externalizing problems at elementary school age: Pathways from early behavior problems, maternal control, and family stress. *Development and Psychopathology, 8,* 701–719.

Carlson, G. A., & Cantwell, D. P. (1980). Unmasking masked depression in children and adolescents. *American Journal of Psychiatry, 137,* 445–449.

Caron, C., & Rutter, M. (1991). Comorbidity in child psychopathology: Concepts, issues and research strategies. *Journal of Child Psychology Psychiatry, 32,* 1063–1080.

Carr, L., Iacoboni, M., Dubeau, M. C., Mazziotta, J. C., & Lenzi, G. L. (2003). Neural mechanisms of empathy in humans: A relay from neural systems for imitation to limbic areas. *Proceedings of the National Academy of Sciences of the USA, 100,* 5497–5502.

Carter, A. S., Garrity-Rokous, F. E., Chazan-Cohen, R., Little, C., & Briggs Gowan, M. J. (2001). Maternal depression and comorbidity: Predicting early parenting, attachment security, and toddler social-emotional problems and competencies. *Journal of the American Academy of Child and Adolescent Psychiatry, 40*(1), 18–26.

Cattaneo, L., Fabbri-Destro, M., Boria, S., Pieraccini, C., Monti, A., Cossu, G., & Rizzolatti, G. (2007). Impairment of actions chains in autism and its possible role in intention understanding. *Proceedings of the National Academy of Sciences of the USA, 104,* 17825–17830.

Chatoor, I., Ganiban, J., Harrison, J., & Hirsch, R. (2001). Observation of feeding in the diagnosis of posttraumatic feeding disorder of infancy. *Journal of the American Academy of Child and Adolescent Psychiatry, 40*(5), 595–602.

Chess, S., & Thomas, A. (1984). *Origins and evolution of behavior disorders: From infancy to early adult life*. New York, NY: Brunner/Mazel.

Chiles, J., Miller, M., & Cox, G. (1980). Depression in an adolescent delinquent population. *Archives of General Psychiatry, 37,* 179–183.

Cicchetti, D., & Richters, J. E. (1993). Developmental considerations in the investigation of conduct disorder. *Development and Psychopathology, 5,* 331–344.

Cohn, J. F., & Tronick, E. (1989). Specificity of infants' response to mothers' affective behavior. *Journal of the American Academy of Child and Adolescent Psychiatry, 28*(2), 242–248.

Conners, C. K., & Wells, K. C. (1986). *Hyperkinetic children: A neuropsychosocial approach*. Beverly Hills, CA: Sage.

Dapretto, M., Davies, M. S., Pfeifer, J. H., Scott, A. A., Sigman, M., Bookheimer, S. Y., & Iacoboni, M. (2006). Understanding emotions in others: Mirror neuron dysfunction in children with autism spectrum disorders. *Nature Neuroscience, 9*(1), 28–30.

Davis, E. P., Glynn, L. M., Schetter, C. D., Hobel, C., Chicz-Demet, A., & Sandman, C. A. (2007). Prenatal exposure to maternal depression and cortisol influences infant temperament. *Journal of the American Academy of Child Adolescent Psychiatry, 46*(6), 737–746.

Denham, S. A., Workman, E., Cole, P., Weissbrod, C., Kendziora, K., Zahn-Waxler, C. (2000). Prediction of externalizing behavior problems from early middle childhood: The role of parental socialization and emotion expression. *Development and Psychopathology, 12,* 23–45.

DuPaul, G. J., McGoey, K. E., Eckert, T. I., & VanBrakle, J. (2001). Preschool children with attention-deficit/hyperactivity disorder: Impairments in behavioral, social, and school functioning. *Journal of the American Academy of Child and Adolescent Psychiatry, 40*(5), 508–515.

Durston, S., Belle, J. V., & Zeeuw, P. D. (2010). Differentiating frontostiatal and fronto-cerebellar circuits in attention-deficit/hyperactivity disorder. *Biological Psychiatry, 69*(12), 1178–1184.

Eisenberg, N., Guthrie, I. K., Fabes, R. A., Shepard, S., Losoya, S., Murphy, B. C., . . . Reiser, M. (2000). Prediction of elementary school children's externalizing problem behaviors from attentional and behavioral regulation and negative emotionality. *Child Development, 71*(5), 1367–1382.

Fabbri-Destro, M., & Rizzolatti, G. (2008). The mirror system in monkeys and humans. *Physiology, 23,* 171–179.

Fagot, B. I., & Leve, L. D. (1998). Teacher ratings of externalizing behavior at school entry for boys and girls: Similar early predictors and different correlates. *Journal of Child Psychology and Psychiatry, 39,* 555–566.

Fecteau, S., Pascual-Leone, A., & Théoret, H. (2008). Psychopathy and the mirror neuron system: Preliminary findings from a non-psychiatric sample. *Psychiatry Research, 160*(2), 137–144.

Felitti, V. J., Anda, R. F., Nordenberg, D., Williamson, D. F., Spitz, A. M., Edwards, V., . . . Marks, J. S. (1998). Relationship of childhood abuse and household dysfunction to many of the leading causes of death in adults: The Adverse Childhood Experiences (ACE) Study. *American Journal of Preventive Medicine, 14*(4), 245–258.

Ferrari, P. F., Paukner, A., Ruggiero, A., Darcey, L., Unbehagen, S., & Suomi, S. J. (2009). Individual differences in neonatal imitation and the development of action chains in rhesus macaques. *Child Development, 80*(4), 1057–1068.

Ferrari, P. F., Visalberghi, E., Fogassi, L., Ruggiero, A., & Suomi, S. J. (2006). Neonatal imitation in rhesus macaques. *PLoS Biology, 4,* 1501–1508.

Field, T. (1992). Infants of depressed mothers. *Developmental Psychopathology, 4,* 49–66.

Fogassi, L., Ferrari, P. F., Gesierich, B., Rozzi, S., Chersi, F., & Rizzolatti, G. (2005). Parietal lobe: From action organization to intention understanding. *Science, 308*(5722), 662–667.

Fontaine, N. M., Rijsdijk, F. V., McCrory, E. J., & Viding, E. (2010). Etiology of different developmental trajectories of callous–unemotional traits. *Journal of the American Academy of Child and Adolescent Psychiatry, 49*(7), 656–664.

Fox, N. A., & Polak, C. D. (2004). Reactivity in understanding infant temperament. In R. DelCarmen-Wiggins & A. Carter (Eds.), *Handbook of infant, toddler, and preschool mental health assessment*. New York, NY: Oxford University Press.

Gallese, V., Fadiga, L., Fogassi, L., & Rizzolatti, G. (1996). Action recognition in the premotor cortex. *Brain, 119*(2), 593–609.

Gardner, F. E. M., Sonuga-Barke, E. J. S., & Sayal, K. (1999). Parents anticipating misbehaviour: An observational study of strategies parents use to prevent conflict with behaviour problem children. *Journal of Child Psychology and Psychiatry, 40*(8), 1185–1196.

Gartstein, M. A., & Rothbart, M. K. (2003). Studying infant temperament via the Revised Infant Behavior Questionnaire. *Infant Behavior and Development, 26*(1), 64–86.

Gilliam, W. S., & Mayes, L. C. (2000). Developmental assessment of infants and toddlers. In C. H. Zeanah (Ed.), *Handbook of infant mental health* (2nd ed., pp. 236–248). New York, NY: Guilford Press.

Gottlieb, G. (1991). Experiential canalization of behavioral development: Theory. *Developmental Psychology, 27*(1), 4–13.

Gross, D., Sambrook, A., & Fogg, L. (1999). Behavior problems among young children in low income urban day care centers. *Research in Nursing and Health, 22*, 15–25.

Guttmann-Steinmetz, S., & Crowell, J. A. (2006). Attachment and externalizing disorders: A developmental psychopathology perspective. *Journal of the American Academy of Child and Adolescent Psychiatry, 45*(4), 440–451.

Haapasalo, J., & Tremblay, R. E. (1994). Physically aggressive boys from ages 6 to 12: Family background, parenting behavior, and prediction of delinqency. *Journal of Consulting and Clinical Psychology, 62*(5), 1044–1052.

Hawes, D. J., & Dadds, M. R. (2007) Stability and malleability of callous–unemotional traits during treatment for childhood conduct problems. *Journal of Clinical Child and Adolescent Psychology, 36*, 347–355.

Hinshaw, S. P., Lahey, B. B., & Hart, E. L. (1993). Issues of taxonomy and comorbidity in the development of conduct disorder. *Development and Psychopathology, 5*, 31–49.

Hofer, M. A. (1994). Hidden regulators in attachment, separation and loss. In N. A. Fox (Ed.), *The development of emotion regulation: Biological and behavioral considerations* (pp. 192–207). Chicago, IL: University of Chicago Press.

Iacoboni, M., & Dapretto, M. (2006). The mirror neuron system and the consequences of its dysfunction. *Nature Reviews Neuroscience, 7*, 942–951.

Iacoboni, M., & Mazziotta, J. C. (2007). Mirror neuron system: Basic findings and clinical applications. *Annals of Neurology, 62*(3), 213–218.

Jensen, P. S., & Watanabe, H. (1999). Sherlock Holmes and child psychopathology assessment approaches: The case of the false-positive. *Journal of the American Academy of Child and Adolescent Psychiatry, 38*, 138–146.

Kazdin, A. E. (1985). *Treatment of antisocial behavior in childhood and adolescence*. Homewood, IL: Dorsey Press.

Keenan, K., Shaw, D., Walsh, B., Delliquadri, E., & Giovannelli, J. (1997). DSM-III-R disorders in preschool children from low-income families. *Journal of American Academy of Child and Adolescent Psychiatry, 36*, 620–627.

Keenan, K., & Wakschlag, L. S. (2000). More than the terrible twos: The nature and severity of behavior problems in clinic-referred preschool children. *Journal of Abnormal Child Psychology, 28,* 33–46.

Kohler, E., Keysers, C., Umiltà, M. A., Fogassi, L., Gallese, V., & Rizzolatti, G. (2002). Hearing sounds, understanding actions: Action representation in mirror neurons. *Science, 297*(5582), 846–848.

Lavigne, J. V., Arend, R., Rosenbaum, D., Binns, H. J., Christoffel, K. K., & Gibbons, R. D. (1998). Psychiatric disorders with onset in the preschool years: I. Stability of diagnoses. *Journal of American Academy of Child and Adolescent Psychiatry, 37,* 1246–1254.

Lavigne, J. V., Cicchetti, C., Gibbons, R. D., Binns, H. J., Larsen, L., & DeVito, C. (2001). Oppositional defiant disorder with onset in preschool years: Longitudinal stability and pathways to other disorders. *Journal of American Academy of Child and Adolescent Psychiatry, 40*(12), 1393–1400.

Lewis, D. O. (1996). Conduct disorder. In M. Lewis (Ed.), *Child and adolescent psychiatry: A comprehensive textbook* (2nd ed., pp. 564–577). Baltimore, MD: Williams & Wilkins.

Lieberman, A. F., Van Horn, P. V., & Ippen, C. G. (2005). Towards evidence-based treatment: Child–parent psychotherapy with preschoolers exposed to marital violence. *Journal of the American Academy of Child and Adolescent Psychiatry, 44*(12), 1241–1248.

Loeber, R., & Stouthaemer-Loeber, M. (1986). Family factors as correlates and predictors of juvenile conduct problems and delinquency. In M. Tonry & N. Morris (Eds.), *Crime and justice: An annual review of research* (Vol. 7, pp. 29–149). Chicago, IL: University of Chicago Press.

Luby, J. L., Heffelfinger, A., Measelle, J. R., Ablow, J. C., Essex, M. J., Dierker, L., . . . Kupfer, D. J. (2002). Differential performance of the MacArthur HBQ and DISC-IV in identifying DSM-IV internalizing psychopathology in young children. *Journal of the American Academy of Child and Adolescent Psychiatry, 41*(4), 458–466.

Luby, J., & Morgan, K. (1997). Characteristics of an infant/preschool psychiatric clinic sample: Implications for clinical assessment and nosology. *Infant Mental Health Journal, 18,* 209–220.

Luoma, I., Tamminen, T., Kaukonen, P., Laippala, P., Puura, K., Salmelin, R., & Almqvist, F. (2001). Longitudinal study of maternal depressive symptoms and child well-being. *Journal of American Academy of Child and Adolescent Psychiatry, 40*(12), 1367–1374.

Merriman, W. J., & Barnett, B. E. (1995). A preliminary investigation of the relationship between language and gross motor skills in preschool children. *Perceptual and Motor Skills, 81*(3), 1211–1216.

Moffitt, T. E. (1993). "Life-course-persistent" and "adolescent-limited" antisocial behavior: A developmental taxonomy. *Psychological Review, 100*(4), 674–701.

Munir, K., Biederman, J., & Knee, D. (1987). Psychiatric comorbidity in patients with attention deficit disorder: A controlled study. *Journal of the American Academy of Child and Adolescent Psychiatry, 26*(6), 844–848.

Narrow, W. N., First, M. B., Sirovatka, P., & Regier, D. A. (Eds.). (2007). *Age and gender considerations in psychiatric diagnosis: A research agenda for DSM-V.* Arlington, VA: American Psychiatric Association.

NICHD Early Child Care Research Network. (1999). Chronicity of maternal depressive symptoms, maternal sensitivity, and child functioning at 36 months. *Developmental Psychology, 35*(5), 1297–1310.

NICHD Early Child Care Research Network & Arsenio, W. F. (2004). Trajectories of physical aggression from toddlerhood to middle childhood: Predictors, correlates, and outcomes. *Monographs of the Society for Research in Child Development, 69*(4), 1–143.

National Institute of Mental Health. (2001). *Taking stock of risk factors for externalizing behavior problems.* Washington, DC: Author.

Nomura, Y., Wickramaratne, P. J., Warner, V., Mufson, L., & Weissman, M. M. (2002). Family discord, parental depression, and psychopathology in offspring: Ten-year follow-up. *Journal of the American Academy of Child and Adolescent Psychiatry, 41*(4), 402–409.

Nottelmann, E. D., & Jensen, P. S. (1995). Comorbidity of disorders in children and adolescents. In T. H. Ollendick & R. J. Prinz (Eds.), *Advances in clinical child psychology* (Vol. 17, pp. 109–155). New York: Plenum Press.

Olds, D., Henderson, C. R., Cole, R., Eckenrode, J., Kitzman, H., Luckey, D., . . . Powers, J. (1998). Long-term effects of nurse home visitation on children's criminal and antisocial behavior: 15-year follow-up of a randomized controlled trial. *Journal of the American Medical Association, 280*(14),1238–1244.

Patterson, G. R. (1982). *A social learning approach: Vol. 3. Coercive family process.* Eugene, OR: Castalia.

Patterson, G. R., DeBaryshe, B. D., & Ramsey, E. (1989). A developmental perspective on antisocial behavior. *American Psychologist, 44,* 329–335.

Pfeifer, J. H., Iacoboni, M., Mazziotta, J. C., & Dapretto, M. (2008). Mirroring others' emotions relates to empathy and interpersonal competence in children. *NeuroImage, 39*(4), 2076–2085.

Ramchandani, P. G., Richter, L. M., Norris, S. A., & Stein, A. (2010). Maternal prenatal stress and later child behavioral problems in an urban South African setting. *Journal of the American Academy of Child and Adolescent Psychiatry, 49*(3), 239–247.

Rescorla, L. A. (1986). Preschool psychiatric disorders: Diagnostic classification and symptom patterns. *Journal of American Academy of Child Psychiatry, 25,* 162–169.

Rizzolatti, G., & Craighero, L. (2004). The mirror-neuron system. *Annual Review of Neuroscience, 27,* 169–192.

Rizzolatti, G., Fabbri-Destro, M., & Cattaneo, L. (2009). Mirror neurons and their clinical relevance. *Nature Clinical Practice Neurology, 5*(1), 24–34.

Sameroff, A. J. (1998). Environmental risk factors in infancy. *Pediatrics, 102,* 1287–1292.

Sameroff, A. J., & Chandler, M. J. (1975). Reproductive risk and the continuum of caretaking casualty. In F. D. Horowitz (Ed.), *A review of child development research* (Vol. 4, pp. 187–241). Chicago: University of Chicago Press.

Sameroff, A. J., & Seifer, R. (1983). Sources of continuity in parent–child relationships. Paper presented at the meeting of the Society for Research in Child Development, Detroit, MI.

Scheeringa, M., Anders, T., Boris, N., Carter, A., Chatoor, I., Egger, H., . . . Weider, S. (2003). *Research Diagnostic Criteria—Preschool Age (RDC-PA).* Durham, NC: Duke University Medical Center.

Seifer, R., Dickstein, S., Sameroff, A. J., Magee, K. D., & Hayden, L. C. (2001). Infant mental health and variability of parental depression symptoms. *Journal of American Academy of Child and Adolescent Psychiatry, 40*(12), 1375–1382.

Shannon, C., Champoux, M., & Suomi, S. J. (1998). Rearing condition and plasma cortisol in rhesus monkey infants. *American Journal of Primatology, 46,* 311–321.

Shannon, C., Schwardt, M. L., Campoux, M., Shoaf, S. E., Suomi, S. J., Linnoila, M., & Higley, J. D. (2005). Maternal absence and stability of individual differences in CSF 5-HIAA concentrations in Rhesus monkey infants. *American Journal of Psychiatry, 162*(9), 1658–1664.

Shaw, D., Owens, E., Vondra, J., Keenan, K., & Winslow, E. (1996). Early risk factors and pathways in the development of early disruptive behavior problems. *Development and Psychopathology, 8,* 679–700.

Shaw, D. S., Keenan, K., Vondra, J. I., Delliquadri, E., & Giovannelli, J. (1997). Antecedents of preschool children's internalizing problems: A longitudinal study of low-income families. *Journal of American Academy of Child and Adolescent Psychiatry, 36,* 1760–1767.

Solantaus-Simula, T., Punamaki, R. E., & Beardslee, W. R. (2002). Children's responses to low parental mood: 2. Associations with family perceptions of parenting styles and child distress. *Journal of the American Academy of Child and Adolescent Psychiatry, 41*(3), 287–295.

Stringaris, A., Maughan, B., & Goodman, R. (2010). What's in a disruptive disorder? Temperamental antecedents of oppositional defiant disorder: Findings from the Avon longitudinal study. *Journal of the American Academy of Child and Adolescent Psychiatry, 49*(5), 474–483.

Taylor, E. (1999). Developmental neuro-psychopathology of attention deficit and impulsiveness. *Development and Psychopathology, 11,* 607–628.

Taylor, E. (2010). From children at risk to adults in need. *Journal of the American Academy of Child and Adolescent Psychiatry, 49*(11), 1089–1090.

Taylor, E., Sandberg, S., Thorley, G., & Giles, S. (1991). *The epidemiology of childhood hyperactivity* (Maudsley Monograph No. 33). Oxford, UK: Oxford University Press.

Taylor, E., Schachar, R., Thorley, G., & Wieselberg, M. (1986). Conduct disorder and hyperactivity: 1. Separation of hyperactivity and antisocial conduct in British child psychiatric patients. *British Journal of Psychiatry, 149,* 760–767.

Thomas, J. M., & Clark, R. (1998). Disruptive behavior in the very young child: Diagnostic classification: 0–3 guides identification of risk factors and relational interventions. *Infant Mental Health Journal, 19,* 229–244.

Thomas, J. M., & Guskin, K. A. (2001). Disruptive behavior in young children: What does it mean? *Journal of the American Academy of Child and Adolescent Psychiatry, 40*(1), 44–51.

Thomas, J. M., & Tidmarsh, L. (1997) Hyperactive and disruptive behaviors in very young children: Diagnosis and Intervention. *Infants and Young Children, 9*(3), 46–56.

Tremblay, R. E. (2010). Developmental origins of disruptive behaviour problems: The "original sin" hypothesis, epigenetics and their consequences for prevention. *Journal of Child Psychology and Psychiatry, 51*(4), 341–367.

Tronick, E. Z., & Gianino, A. (1986). Interactive mismatch and repair: Challenges to the coping infant. *Zero to Three Bulletin National Clinical Infant Program, 6*(3), 1–6.

Umiltà, M. A., Kohler, E., Gallese, V., Fogassi, L., Fadiga, L., Keysers, C., & Rizzolatti, G. (2001). I know what you are doing: A neurophysiological study. *Neuron, 31*(1), 155–165.

Wakschlag, L. S., & Keenan, K. (2001). Clinical significance and correlates of disruptive behavior in environmentally at-risk preschoolers. *Journal of Clinical Child Psychology, 30*(1), 262–275.

Warren, S. L., Emde, R. N., & Sroufe, L. A. (2000). Internal representations: Predicting anxiety from children's play narratives. *Journal of the American Academy of Child and Adolescent Psychiatry, 39,* 100–107.

Webster-Stratton, C., & Hammond, M. (1998). Conduct problems and level of social competence in Head Start children: Prevalence, pervasiveness, and associated risk factor. *Clinical Child and Family Psychology Review, 1,* 101–124.

Webster-Stratton, C., & Reid, M. J. (2004). Strengthening social and emotional competence in young children: The foundation for early school readiness and success: Incredible Years Classroom Social Skills and Problem-Solving Curriculum. *Infants and Young Children, 17*(2), 96–113.

Weisman, M. M., Warner, V., Wickaramaratne, P., Moreau, D., & Olfson M. (1997). Offsping of depressed parents: 10 years later. *Archives of General Psychiatry, 54,* 932–940.

Zahn-Waxler, C. (1995). Parental depression and distress: Implications for development in infancy, childhood, and adolescence. *Developmental Psychology, 31,* 347–348.

Zahn-Waxler, C., Iannotti, R. J., Cummings, E. M., & Denham, S. (1990). Antecedents of problem behaviors in children of depressed mothers. *Developmental Psychopathology, 2,* 271–291.

Zero to Three. (1994). *Diagnostic classification: 0–3. Diagnostic classification of mental health and developmental disorders of infancy and early childhood.* Washington, DC: Author.

Zero to Three. (2005). *Diagnostic classification: 0–3R. Diagnostic classification of mental health and developmental disorders of infancy and early childhood—revised.* Washington, DC: Author.

8

Bullying and the Development of Antisocial Behavior

SOONJO HWANG, YOUNG SHIN KIM, AND
BENNETT LEVENTHAL ■

Bullying, the most common form of school violence, is an aggressive behavior perpetrated by students who hold and/or try to maintain a dominant position over others. Bullying is a behavior that has the intention of causing mental and/ or physical harm or suffering to another (Morita, 1985). It is noteworthy that bullying involves a repetitive action or behavior and almost always involves imbalance of power between victim and perpetrator in which the victim is usually not able to defend him- or herself (Farrington, 1993; Morita, 1985).

Bullying among schoolchildren is a very old phenomenon. It has been described in literary works for generations, and many adults report having such personal experiences during their own school days (Olweus, 1994b). Because bullying is such a common phenomenon, it has been often considered to be either "normal" or "just a part of growing up." This is a belief shared by many adults, including parents and teachers (Spivak, 2003). However, numerous studies indicate that these conclusions could not be further from the truth. Not only is bullying strongly associated with psychopathology in the students involved, but it also leads to long-term sequalae that last well into adulthood.

Bullying takes various forms, including: (Kim, Koh, & Leventhal, 2004)

Exclusion: forced isolation from a social group, including being left out of games and activities during recess or lunchtime, being ignored in social settings, and/or the refusal of the perpetrators to talk to or answer the victim

Verbal abuse: calling names, speaking ill of victims, threatening the victim verbally

Physical abuse: causing pain, suffering or intimidation, damaging or
  injuring persons or property

Coercion: forcing others to do work for someone else, such as homework or
  carrying bags; taking of items such as school supplies and snacks; forcing students give up money or other possessions

Cyberbullying: bullying behavior among students encompassing a wide
  array of online activities, including using the Internet, cell phones, text
  messages, and other electronic means to spread rumors, support social
  exclusion, share insulting or humiliating data or information, and otherwise cause pain and suffering using electronic media. (Pridgen, 2009)

Bullying may be "direct" or "indirect" with respect to the victim. Direct or
overt bullying includes physical and verbal aggression, such as kicking, hitting,
threatening, name-calling, and insulting. Indirect or covert/relational bullying
includes social exclusion/isolation, such as ignoring, excluding from cliques,
rumor mongering, insulting, and humiliation by spreading embarrassing
information about an individual (van der Wal, de Wit, & Hirasing, 2003).

Students are involved in bullying as victims, perpetrators, victim-perpetrators, or bystanders. Victims may experience many forms of bullying, with considerable variability in the form that it takes. Some students may be involved in
bullying as both victim and perpetrator, that is, being bullied by other students
while at the same time bullying others (Schwartz, 2000). These so-called "victim-
perpetrators" are those who appear to have the most serious psychological problems related to bullying experiences, a matter to be discussed later in more detail
(Kim, Koh, & Leventhal, 2005; Menesini, Modena, & Tani, 2009).

Bystanders, or those who are not the actual perpetrators or targets of the
aggression, also can be adversely affected by witnessing bullying experiences in
schools and other settings. These children and adolescents may develop a sense
of hopelessness in the face of inaction by school officials, perhaps leading to
a deficit in empathy for those who are defenseless in the face of bullying (Kowlaski,
Limber, & Agatson, 2008; Pridgen, 2009). At the same time, bystanders can affect
the dynamics of bullying by either ignoring incidents (a passive form of accepting a perpetrator's behavior), encouraging perpetrators, or intervening for victims (Twemlow, 2010).

With recent advances in information technology cyberspace has been added
to the schoolyard and neighborhood as a site for bullying. Although, on the surface, this appears to be a new form of bullying, in fact it is the same process taking place with new tools in a new format. This new tool for bullying is a reflection
of the time and technology available to our youth. According to the Pew Internet
and American Life Project, 87% of U.S. teenagers use the Internet, with more
than half of them going online on a daily basis. Nearly 45% of American teens
own cell phones, and one-third use them regularly for text messaging (Lenhart,
Madden, & Hitlin, 2005; Pridgen, 2009). The relationship between bullying and
the Internet is similar to other forms of bullying in that it often takes place where
and when students are unsupervised, as is often the case with youth Internet

use. However, Internet- or cyber-bullying has two relatively unique character-istics. Bullying can be delivered anonymously, without overt identification of the perpetrators. Further, children or adolescents may not be safe from bullying even in their homes, as unkind text messages, hateful e-mails, videos, or provoc-atively manipulated messages and materials can reach them 24 hours per day, 7 days a week (Pridgen, 2009).

PREVALENCE OF BULLYING

Some studies suggest that students and adults (including researchers) may not share the same impressions as to what are the specific types of behavior that are regarded as bullying (Boulton, Bucci, & Hawker, 1999; Frisén, Jonsson, & Persson, 2007). This raises the important question of how to gauge bullying experiences among students in their natural environments. To deal with this issue, many studies have used self-reports of bullying. The advantages of this method are that it is easy to apply and that it can capture the subjective appraisal of bullying from the students themselves. However, self-reporting also has significant limitations. First, students may underreport, because victims are often afraid of retaliation or embarrassment and perpetrators may not report their own mischievous beha-vior. Second, there are concerns about validity, due to subjective interpretation of individual experiences (Ladd & Kochenderfer-Ladd, 2002).

The use of peer nomination may compensate for some of the shortcomings of self-report. With peer nomination, students are asked to name those peers who are involved in bullying as victims or perpetrators. This method is now regarded as the most effective method for the identification of bullying because it acquires cumulative data from multiple informants (classmates or peers), thus making it a more objective observation of others. However, as with any research method, peer nomination has its own limitations, which are largely due to the fact that it is very labor-intensive to acquire consistent peer nominations and that peer nominations are dependent on the developmental level of students involved (Ladd & Kochenderfer-Ladd, 2002).

Both teachers and parents can take part in the assessment of bullying. However, this method is also of limited value because adults often do not see many ele-ments of students' lives in schools, including bullying experiences. The reason is that bullying tends to occur in places where adult supervision and surveillance is minimal, such as restrooms, playground, or empty classrooms and during tran-sit to school (Hunter, Boyle, & Warden, 2004).

In an attempt to understand bullying and for the purposes of trying to esti-mate prevalence, Ladd and Kochenderfer-Ladd (2002) examined the measure-ment of bullying in live school situations. They found that the concordance between self- and peer report in young children was low but that it improved sig-nificantly as students grew older, not surprisingly indicating that cognitive and social development improves appreciation of these complex social interactions. In addition to the age of the population sampled, variability in types of reports leads to different prevalence estimates for bullying. Studies indicate that there is disagreement between parent report, teacher report, and self- or peer reports of victimization (Ladd & Kochenderfer-Ladd, 2002). For adolescents, there is a discrepancy between adolescent reports and parent or teacher reports of bullying experience. Peer reports are more likely to identify aggressive behavior than are self-reports. This suggests that other methods may be necessary to identify more subtle and indirect types of bullying, such as exclusion or ignoring. Thus choosing optimal methods to identify bullying experience according to developmental stages, sex, and types of bullying to be identified will yield more reliable and valid estimates of bullying (Achenbach, McConaughy, & Howell, 1987). With this in mind, we examine bullying prevalence with a summary of bullying prevalence research from various countries, using different methods (Table 8.1.)

As illustrated in Table 8.1, it appears that the prevalence of experiencing bullying varies depending on study group, method, and measurement. Taken together, one can estimate that at any point in time, about 15–20% of the students in elementary and secondary/junior high schools are involved in bullying as victims or perpetrators (Analitis et al., 2009; Olweus, 1994b). However, as reported in the Health Behavior in School-aged Children Bullying Analyses Working Group report (Nansel et al., 2004), involving 113,200 students in 25 countries (average ages of 11.5, 13.5, and 15.5 years), in which bullying experiences were assessed by a cross-sectional, self-report survey, bullying prevalence varied across countries, ranging from 9 to 54% of youths. This study also found correlations between bullying involvement and a variety of other outcomes, including poor psychosocial adjustment, health problems, and poor emotional and social adjustment. In addition, victims and victim-perpetrators reported poorer relationships with classmates, and perpetrators and victim-perpetrators reported greater alcohol use and weapon carrying (Nansel et al., 2004). This study strongly suggests that bullying is a universal problem that affects multiple areas of developmental functioning.

The 2005/2006 Health Behavior in School-aged Children (HBSC) study (Roberts et al, 2007) in the United States examined 7,506 adolescents using the modified Olweus Bully/Victim Questionnaire. This study found that for the previous 2 months, 20.8% of adolescents were victimized by physical bullying, 53.6% verbally, 51.4% socially, and 13.6% electronically. Boys were more likely to be involved in physical or verbal bullying and girls in relational bullying. Additionally, boys were more likely to be cyberbullies and girls more likely to be cybervictims (Wang, Iannotti, & Nansel, 2009).

More recently, in a nationally representative study of U.S. students ages 12–18 (U.S. Department of Education, 2010), 32% reported victimization at school. Of those victims, 21% reported being made fun of consistently, 18% said they were the subject of rumors, and 11% indicated they had been pushed, shoved, tripped, or spat upon; an additional 6% were threatened with harm, while 5% were excluded from activities on purpose and 4% were made to do things they did not want to or had their property purposefully destroyed (U.S. Department of Education, 2010). Additionally, 4% of the students reported experiences with

(continued)

TABLE 8.1 PREVALENCE OF BULLYING WORLDWIDE

Authors (Year)	Study Subjects	Bullying Measure (items)	Prevalence/Result
Olweus (1994b)	More than 130,000 Norwegian Students	Self-Report: Bully/Victim Questionnaire	Victims: 9% Perpetrators: 7% Victim-Perpetrators: 1.6%
Salmon et al. (1998)	904 8th–11th Graders in U.K.	Self-Report: Olweus Bully/Victim Questionnaire	Victim: 4.2% Perpetrator: 3.4% Victim-Perpetrator: 9.0%
Kaltiala-Heino, et al. (1999)	16,410 8th–9th Graders in Finla nd	Self-Report: WHO Questionnaire	5% girls 6% boys: Weekly victim 2% girls, 9% boys: Weekly perpetrator
Cleary (2000)	1727 9th–12th Graders in N.Y.	Self-Report: YRBS	Victim: 35%
Juvonen et al. (2003)	1985 6th Graders in Los Angeles	Peer Nomination	Victim: 9% Perpetrator: 7% Victim-Perpetrator: 6% Borderline: 22%
Hunter et al. (2004)	830 9- to 14-year-old students in Scotland	Self-Report	Victim: 21%

TABLE 8.1 (CONTINUED)

Authors (Year)	Study Subjects	Bullying Measure (items)	Prevalence/Result
Kim et al. (2005)	1718 7th–8th Graders in South Korea	Peer Nomination: Korean Peer Nomination Inventory	Victim: 14.1% Perpetrator: 16.9% Victim-Perpetrator: 9.0%
Frisén et al. (2007)	119 Adolescents 15–20 years old in Sweden	Self-Report	Victim: 39% Perpetrators: 28%
Campbell et al. (2007)	373 10th–11th Graders in U.K.	Self-Report: Olweus Bully/Victim Questionnaire	Victim: 25% (once—twice during whole school days) Victim: 6.6% (Several times a week)
Ttofi et al. (2008)	182 6th Graders in N.Y.	Self-Report	Victim: Boys: 22.1% Girls: 18.1%
Shojaeie al. (2009)	1,274 children 6–11 years old in France	Self-Report	Victim: 21.0%
National Center for Education Statistics (2010)	Students ages 12–18 in U.S.	Self report: Questionnaire (National Crime Victimization Survey)	Victimization: 32%

cyberbullying, of whom 2% experienced having hurtful information posted on the Internet and 2% were threatened or insulted (U.S. Department of Education, 2010). This study demonstrates that bullying is clearly a complex and nearly universal phenomenon for U.S. students.

The number of both victims and perpetrators tends to decrease among students in older grades (Borg, 1999; Olweus 1994b; Rivers & Smith, 1994; van der Wal et al., 2003; Whitney & Smith, 1993). When bullying is classified as direct or indirect, direct bullying is reported to be more frequent in boys, whereas indirect bullying is more common in girls (Borg, 1999; Rivers, 1994; van der Wal et al., 2003; Whitney & Smith, 1993).

No matter how one looks at it, being a participant in bullying is a common experience for many children and adolescents—far more common than many have expected. So, if bullying is so common, is it a normative life event? Or is it problematic and the cause of other adverse events? If problematic, it is a significant public health issue that demands attention.

ASSOCIATION OF BULLYING AND MENTAL AND PHYSICAL HEALTH

Psychopathology

There is cumulating evidence for the association between bullying and psychopathology. However, this relationship has been the focus of substantial debate, yielding two hypotheses: (1) antecedent psychopathology is a cause of subsequent bullying; (2) bullying can lead to future psychopathology. The first hypothesis is supported by previous findings showing that students with internalizing or externalizing problems, when compared with students without these characteristics, had a higher risk of involvement with bullying (Boulton & Smith, 1994; Hodges & Perry, 1999). The second hypothesis is supported by previous reports of deteriorating behavioral, emotional, and psychosocial functioning in children who experienced peer victimization (Hanish & Guerra, 2002; Ladd & Troop-Gordon, 2003; Olweus, 1994c).

This debate is largely unresolved, because cross-sectional designs have made it impossible to establish causality in either direction. Also, the small subset of prospective studies has suffered from shared method variance, using the same informants to identify both bullying and psychopathology (Bond, Carlin, Thomas, Rubin, & Patton, 2001; Smith, Talamelli, Cowie, Naylor, & Chauhan, 2004). In such studies, self-reports of bullying are based on the individuals' own perceptions of social circumstances, a situation in which the reporters' other psychological characteristics can lead to misinterpretation of otherwise normal social events. Respondent characteristics may also influence the reported psychopathology, resulting in a confounded relationship between psychopathology and bullying. Using peer nomination techniques to identify bullying, coupled with self-reports for assessing psychopathology, can reduce these problems.

Few studies have utilized both a prospective design and different informants to identify bullying and psychopathology. Even with a prospective, multi-informant design, however, it is difficult to make causal inferences due to lack of control of important confounders, such as socioeconomic status (SES) and family structure. In addition, small sample sizes and the lack of representative community samples have limited the generalizability of prior findings.

In this section, we review the research findings from two viewpoints, considering limitations in their methods.

PSYCHOPATHOLOGY AS AN ANTECEDENT OF BULLYING

Children and adolescents may have increased risk of involvement in bullying due to their own psychopathology. Woods, Wolke, Nowichki, and Hall (2009) demonstrated that impairment in social cue recognition, as indicated by difficulties recognizing facial expressions, is associated with an increased rate of victimization in relational bullying, but not in physical bullying. Children and adolescents with attention-deficit/hyperactivity disorder (ADHD), oppositional defiant disorder, and/or conduct disorder are more likely to have increased physical aggression and bullying behavior (Conner, Steeber, & McBurnett, 2010; Olweus, 1992; Olweus 1994a; Olweus 1994b). Children with learning disabilities, autism spectrum disorders (ASD), and ADHD are also at increased risk of bullying victimization (Twyman et al., 2010). Analitis et al. (2009) conducted a comprehensive study of 16,210 children and adolescents, from ages 8 to 18, in 11 European countries, and found that having mental health problems contributed to the risk of being bullied (Analitis et al., 2009).

In addition to psychopathology, the general characteristics of children and adolescents, such as appearance or social status, play roles in increasing the risk for experiencing bullying. Olweus (1994b) observed that boys who are physically weaker are more likely to be victims. When students were asked why individuals were bullied, the most common reason they reported was that victims had a different appearance (Frisén et al., 2007). Often times, victims are characterized as being physically weak or less attractive, wearing glasses or braces, being handicapped (e.g., having hearing problems), short, or obese; they are also described as psychologically fearful, unsure, and nervous (Farrington, 1993). Victims may be worse at sports than perpetrators, and perpetrators are seen as students who are physically bigger and desirous of power (Bender & Losel, 1997; Hawkins, Catalano, Kosterman, Abbott, & Hill, 1999). In the Korean bullying study, taller students were at increased risk for perpetration, whereas shorter or heavier students were at greater risk for victimization (Kim, Boyce, Koh, & Leventhal, 2009). In a recent Finnish cohort study, Luukkonen and colleagues reported that having chronic somatic disease significantly increased the risk of being bullied among the boys (Luukkonen, Rasanen, Hakko, Riala, & the STUDY-70 Workgroup, 2010). In another study, students with cancer also reported high levels of bullying experience compared with controls (31.7% vs. 10.9%), almost always related to their illness or change of appearance due to illness and treatment (Lahteenmaki, Huostila, Hinkka, & Salmi, 2002).

Other studies have demonstrated that children with special education needs are substantially more at risk of being involved in bullying situations (Martlew & Hodson, 1991; Nabuzoka & Smith, 1993; Whitney & Smith, 1993). The National Survey of Children's Health also suggested that children with special health care needs are at higher risk to be both victims and perpetrators, when compared with children without special health care needs, and they are twice as likely to be considered victim-perpetrators (Van Cleave & Davis, 2006).

Olweus (1980) reported little association between levels of aggression in boys and SES and also no (or weak) association between child factors in the development of an aggressive reaction pattern and SES. However, several subsequent studies have reported otherwise. Bowes et al. (2009) reported that when psychosocial factors, including school, neighborhood, and family, were evaluated, a meaningful increase in risk of bullying was associated with larger school size, having problems with neighbors, and negative family factors such as child maltreatment and domestic violence. A different prevalence of school bullying was observed in different regions in Italy, and a different distribution of resources, especially family life conditions and educational levels, and criminal organizations in the community were associated with differences in bullying prevalence (Fonzi, 1999). Also, in a Korean study, low SES was a risk factor for victimization, and paternal lower education or maternal higher education, along with being from a nonintact family, increased risks for victim-perpetrations (Kim et al., 2009).

These studies suggest that there may be a specific group of vulnerable students who need careful attention from teachers and parents to prevent them from becoming involved in bullying as victims, as perpetrators, or as victim-perpetrators.

Psychopathology as a consequence of bullying

The development of psychopathology as a consequence of experiencing bullying has been reported in numerous studies. For example, it is well established that being a victim of bullying is related to increased levels of anxiety and depression, a fear of going to school, feelings of being unsafe and unhappiness at school, as well as low self-esteem (Salmon, James, & Smith, 1998). Victims are also reported to have decreased educational outcomes, including increased rates of school refusal and receiving disciplinary suspensions (U.S. Department of Education, 2010). Studies have also reported that peer victimization is antecedent to the development of eating problems (Eisenberg & Neumark-Sztainer, 2008). Perpetrators and victim-perpetrators are at the highest risk for the future development of mid-adolescent delinquency (Barker, Arseneault, Brendgen, Fontaine, & Maughan, 2008). Children or adolescents who are involved in bullying as victims or perpetrators are at increased risk for the later development of serious and dangerous adverse outcomes, including daily smoking, alcohol abuse, carrying and using weapons, eating disorders, and runaway episodes (Srabstein, 2008). Menesini et al. (2009) revealed that chronic victims or perpetrators of bullying may have more psychological problems than those briefly involved in bullying.

When longitudinal methods are used, most recent U.S. studies of students support the relation between experiencing bullying and the later development of psychopathology (Carbone-Lopez, Esbensen, & Brick, 2010).

Being a perpetrator is associated with increased delinquent conduct or impulsive/violent behavior. Interestingly, one study conducted in the Netherlands reported that students involved as perpetrators in direct bullying reported a meaningful increase in delinquent behavior, and the association between victims of bullying and depression/suicidal ideation is stronger in the cases of indirect bullying compared with direct bullying (van der Wal, 2003). In general, bullying impacts a child's experience of school on numerous levels, including creating problems with school adjustment and attachment, affecting the victim's completion of homework and desire to do well at school (Vreeman & Carroll, 2007).

Bullying is not just associated with the development of psychopathology in children and adolescents; it also appears to be related to adult psychopathology. Olweus (Olweus, 1992, 1994a, 1994b; Spivak, 2003) followed boys who were involved in bullying as perpetrators into adulthood; there was a reported fourfold increase in criminal behavior by the time the former students reached their mid-twenties, with a majority having at least one criminal conviction and more than one-third having multiple convictions. He also reported higher rates of depression and poor self-esteem in adults with a history of being bullied. Gladstone, Parker, and Malhi (2006) reported that a childhood experience of bullying is associated with greater levels of state anxiety and a higher prevalence of social phobia and agoraphobia in adults. Additionally, in a study of patients in a Norwegian outpatient clinic, adults with histories of being bullied as children were more often found to be single and to have lower levels of educational attainment and lower occupational status (Klensmeden Fosse & Holen, 2004). Although some studies demonstrate minimal problems in perpetrators, they still show that involvement in bullying can be a potential cause of relational problems (Juvonen, Graham, & Schuster, 2003). Many other studies indicate that perpetrators also suffer from significant psychological consequences of bullying (Olweus, 1994b; Salmon et al., 1998; van der Wal et al., 2003).

Some studies have specifically tried to disentangle the causal relationship between psychopathology and bullying. In one study, when adolescents were asked, they responded that victims of bullying are chosen because of the "differences" they have, especially physical ones (Frisén et al., 2007). In another study from several European countries, students reported that being bullied was strongly associated with younger age, having probable mental health problems, having problems with mood and emotion, and having poor social support (Analitis et al., 2009). Other studies indicate that victims are also more anxious and insecure than noninvolved students, whereas perpetrators are more likely to be aggressive toward other people and to have a more positive attitude toward violence (Olweus, 1994b).

In a prospective follow-up study of students involved in bullying, Kim, Leventhal, Koh, Hubbard, and Boyce found an increase in psychopathology and problem behaviors, including social problems, aggression, and externalizing problems. The nature of this study made it possible to determine and support the causal inferences that psychopathology can be a consequence of bullying experiences (Kim et al., 2006). In addition, according to a recent report from the Finnish nationwide birth cohort study, when controlling for baseline psychopathology, "sometimes" and "frequent" involvement in bullying independently predicted violence, as well as property and traffic offenses. The strongest predictive association was observed between frequent involvement in bullying and more than five crimes during a 4-year study period. Also, when different informants were compared, teacher reports of bullying were the strongest predictor of adult criminality (Sourander et al., 2010).

Therefore, the association between psychopathology and bullying can be manifested in various ways, and the one can have a significant impact on the other. The relationship between bullying and psychopathology is bidirectional. Some forms of psychopathology put children and adolescents at increased risk to become victims and/or perpetrators of bullying, whereas experiencing school bullying as a victim and/or perpetrator can increase the risk of future development of psychopathology or worsening of preexisting psychopathology. To determine the importance of this relationship, it will be necessary to conduct more comprehensive, longitudinal studies with multiple informants (children/adolescents themselves, as well as parents and teachers), even though this means a vigorous effort and the use of considerable resources.

Suicidality

In the United States, there were 1,231 suicides of youths ages 5–18 during the 2007 calendar year. Suicide is the third leading cause of deaths among 12- to 19-year-old adolescents (Minino, 2010; U.S. Department of Education, 2010). We conducted a systematic review of 37 studies that examined the association between bullying experiences and suicide; it included children and adolescents from communities, as well as special populations such as individuals with developmental disorders (ASD and learning disorder), drug problems, legal problems, and homosexual or bisexual orientation (for a review, please see Kim & Leventhal, 2008). The findings are summarized here.

SUICIDAL IDEATION
In our review of 15 samples from the general population, 12 reported an increased risk for suicidal ideation in the victims of bullying, with odds ratios (ORs) ranging from 1.4 to 5.6. One study reported a statistically significant interaction with gender; that is, female victims of bullying were at a greater risk of suicidal ideation than were male victims. Another three studies reported a dose–response relationship between bullying and suicidality, with frequent victimization being associated with a higher risk for suicidal

ideation than less frequent victimization. Eight of 10 studies that examined the risk of suicidal ideation in the perpetrators reported increased suicidal risk, with ORs ranging from 1.4 to 9.0. All five studies that examined risk of suicidal ideation in the victim-perpetrators of school bullying reported increased risk for suicidality, with ORs ranging from 1.9 to 10.0. The suicidal risk in victim-perpetrators was highest among all the groups involved with bullying in four studies.

Five studies examined risk of suicidal ideation in victims of bullying in special populations, with four of these studies reporting increased risk in juvenile offenders, persons with learning disorders, and those with lesbian or bisexual orientations, with ORs ranging from 1.7 to 2.1. One study that examined the risk of suicidal ideation in perpetrators of bullying among juvenile offenders reported lower risk when compared with those not involved with bullying.

In our longitudinal study of Korean adolescents, we confirmed that involvement in bullying is associated with an increased risk of suicidal ideation, especially in the group of victim-perpetrators and female students (Kim et al., 2009).

SUICIDE ATTEMPTS AND COMPLETED SUICIDES

In our systematic review of 37 studies, 12 out of 13 studies that examined the risk of suicide attempts, including self-injurious behaviors, in the victims of bullying in the general population reported increased risk, with ORs ranging from 1.5 to 5.4. Seven studies investigated the risk of suicide attempts and self-injurious behaviors in the victims of bullying in special populations, and six reported increased risks, with ORs ranging from 1.4 to 4.6.

In a study of 5,302 Finnish children, Klomek et al. (2009) found an association between bullying and suicide attempts/completed suicides. Among boys, frequent bullying and victimization were associated with later suicide attempts and completed suicides, even after adjusting for baseline depression, with ORs of 9.9 for frequent perpetrators and 7.7 for frequent victims. Also, frequent victimization among girls was associated with later suicide attempts and completed suicides, even after controlling for conduct and depression symptoms (OR 5.3; Klomek et al., 2009). Another study reported that girls with a history of being victim-perpetrators were also at the highest risk of mid-adolescent self-harm (Barker et al., 2008).

Srabstein (2008) searched news reports covering a period of 57 years (1950–2007) for deaths associated with bullying and hazing among young people. At least 250 reported cases of deaths were linked to bullying, hazing, or ragging; in 76% of these cases the victim had an alleged history of being bullied (Srabstein 2008).

Although these studies suffer from some methodological limitations, the consistency of the findings, in various populations and different settings, suggests that suicidal ideation and/or behaviors are associated with bullying experiences in a broad spectrum of youth (Kim & Leventhal, 2008).

Physical Health

Bedwetting, having difficulty sleeping, and having headaches and abdominal pain are also common signs associated with being a victim of bullying (Achenbach et al., 1987). According to Brendgen and Vitaro (2008), peer rejection is associated with the development of new physical health problems in girls, even after controlling for physical problems and depression at baseline (Brendgen & Vitaro, 2008). The study by Gray, Janicke, Ingerski, and Silverstein (2008) found that peer victimization can be a factor that limits physical activity, which may cause increase in risk of overweight in youths. Srabstein, Leventhal, and Piazza pointed out that students involved in bullying are at a significant risk of experiencing a wide spectrum of psychosomatic symptoms; they concluded that those students should be provided with appropriate clinical care, and the intervention of primary health care providers, including pediatricians and school nurses, is essential in such cases (Srabstein & Piazza 2008; Srabstein & Leventhal, 2010).

Physical abuse or coercive bullying can increase the risk of physical harm to the students involved. Laflamme, Möller, Hallqvist, and Engström (2008) reported a significant number of physical injuries in adolescents under circumstances in which there was a clear imbalance of power or when perpetrators had the clear intention of harming the victims. Victims of bullying are inherently at risk of harm and problems with physical health (Cleary 2000). Srabstein and Piazza. (2008) reported that students who were involved in bullying as victims, perpetrators, or victim-perpetrators were at a significantly higher risk of suffering from self-inflicted, accidental, and perpetrated injuries; abuse of over-the counter medications; running away from home; absenteeism; purposefully hurting animals and people; and using weapons that could seriously hurt someone (Srabstein & Piazza, 2008). A significant number of the high-profile school shootings over the past decade have involved individuals with histories of bullying or being bullied (Spivak, 2003).

TRAJECTORIES OF BULLYING BEHAVIORS INCLUDING ADULT AND WORKPLACE BULLYING

Bullying is a dynamic process that may change over the time course. It is worth considering the trajectory of bullying experiences, both to anticipate the course of bullying and to implement effective prevention/early intervention.

Pepler, Jiang, Craig, and Connolly (2008) followed 871 students over 7 years, starting at ages from 10 to 14. They found that 9.9% of the children reported consistently high level of bullying. Another 13.4% reported early, moderate levels of bullying that decreased to almost no bullying by the end of high school. And 35.1% reported consistently moderate levels of bullying, whereas the remaining 41.6% reported "almost never" being involved with bullying (Pepler et al., 2008). After following 3,932 adolescents in Scotland for 5 years (from age 12 to age 17),

Barker et al. (2008) reported that victims of bullying are more likely to become perpetrators than perpetrators are to become victims. In the Korean bullying study, when students were followed up at 1 year, 52–58% of baseline victims and perpetrators and 74% of victim-perpetrators continued to be involved in bullying (Kim et al., 2009). These findings indicate that, without appropriate intervention, bullying can be chronic for many students.

Bullying is common among adults, and workplace bullying has become a serious issue in the United States in recent years (Namie & Namie, 2009; Vaughn et al., 2010). Smith, Singer, Hoel, and Cooper (2003) reported a study of 5,288 adults from various work settings in Great Britain, showing that those who had been victim-perpetrators in school were at the highest risk for workplace victimization. Thus this study not only shows that the experience of bullying may continue into adulthood and into the workplace but also that a particular group, victim-perpetrators, may warrant specific concern for adulthood and workplace bullying. Smith and colleagues (2003) also demonstrated that school pupils who consistently cannot cope with bullying or who try to make fun of the victims are more at risk for later problems in the workplace.

PREVENTION OF AND INTERVENTION FOR BULLYING

How can we help those involved in bullying as victims, perpetrators, or both? Merely labeling perpetrators as troublemakers and punishing them is far from therapeutic, and the no-tolerance polices linked to suspension or expulsion that have been adopted by many schools create even more problems and represent serious, missed opportunities to help children in trouble (Spivak, 2003). The failure of authority figures to intervene appropriately when bullying takes place may lead to feelings of hopelessness in victims of bullying and lack of empathy of bystanders (Kowlaski et al., 2008; Pridgen, 2009). In this regard, it is noteworthy that students tend to seek support when they expect authority to be helpful in achieving solutions and not further increase risk. So it is important to give children a powerful sense that when they seek help, they will actually get it (Hunter et al., 2004).

Studies have demonstrated that younger victims of school bullying turn to others for help in dealing with bullying more than do older victims. Also, girls are more willing to seek help than are boys (Borg, 1998; Glover, Gough, Johnson, & Cartwright, 2000; Hunter et al., 2004; Sharp, 1995). Further, there also appear to be differences regarding to whom the victims of different types of bullying may turn for help: victims of verbal bullying (name calling) are least likely to tell, followed by victims of indirect bullying (who are excluded or have rumors spread about them), with victims of direct bullying (violence, property damage/theft) most likely to tell (Elsea, 2001; Hunter, 2004). Victims also seek help from different people, including their friends, teachers, and parents, depending on their age, gender, and social situation (Borg, 1998; Elsea, 2001; Hunter, 2004). Thus specific interventions must be directed to specific populations involved in bullying.

Olweus (1994b) pioneered school-based intervention programs for bullying in Norwegian schools. He implemented this program in 42 primary and secondary/junior high schools, where he achieved significant reductions in the levels of bullying and victimization. Olweus's anti-bullying program is aimed at creating a warm and positive environment in school (and, ideally, also at home), involving adults and implementing firm limits to unacceptable behavior. In case of violation of limits and rules, nonhostile, nonphysical sanctions are to be consistently applied. The core features of the Olweus school-based program can be implemented at the school, class, individual, and community levels.

At the school level, a first step is to administer a questionnaire survey to examine the extent of the school bullying problem. It serves as a basis for parents, teachers, and students to come together and understand the magnitude of school bullying problems in their communities and as a baseline measure for later use in determining whether their anti-bullying intervention has been effective in reducing bullying in the community. A school conference is held for parents, teachers, and all students to share their concerns, to establish their common goals to defeat bullying problems, and to plan how to intervene with bullying problems in their homes, schools, and community. More organized supervision is provided during recess. A coordinating group—consisting of administrators and teachers from each grade level; guidance counselors, psychologists, and school nurses; parents; and student representatives—is formed to manage the anti-bullying program and evaluate its success.

At the class level, students and teachers work together to establish class rules against bullying. Expectations and consequences are made clear to everybody, as are rules that must be followed. For example, a rule may say that "no one shall be involved in bullying, and if we witness bullying, we will tell the students to stop and go to the grown-ups for help."

At the individual level, serious talks with perpetrators and victims are required when bullying occurs in order to stop bullying right there, to process the incident, and to prevent future occurrences of bullying. Serious talks with parents of involved students should also occur in order to share concern among adults and to implement the same interventions at home to further the effectiveness of the interventions.

Community interventions include cultivation of community partnerships with community leaders, including police, administrative personnel, and local politicians. Together all these individuals share in spreading the anti-bullying sentiment throughout the community. Community involvement, along with active involvement of parents and teachers to provide appropriate authority, guidance, monitoring, and surveillance, is essential for the successful and effective implementation of anti-bullying program (Olweus 1994b; Olweus & Limber, 2010). This program has proven to be effective in reducing general antisocial behaviors and producing marked improvement in social climates as well.

Systematic reviews of anti-bullying intervention methods concluded that the most effective intervention was the whole-school approach, whereas curriculum interventions for classes or behavioral skill group trainings for victims or perpetrators have minimal effect in decreasing bullying in schools. The review concludes that school-based interventions can have better results when they involve multiple disciplines with more intensity (Vreeman & Carroll, 2007). In this regard, it is promising, as well as encouraging, that recent studies have demonstrated gradual decreases in the prevalence of school bullying in many countries (Molcho et al., 2009).

Other, similar anti-bullying programs are also available. There are several websites offering these programs, run by governments or community organizations. Those websites are resourceful in providing evaluation and assessment tools, education materials, and prevention and intervention modules (Carlisle et al., n.d.; Committee for Children, 2010; Hazelden Foundation, 2011; Kalman, n.d.; Operation Respect, 2011; *Utterly Global*, n.d.).

In the United States, many state governments have recently passed legislation focusing on anti-bullying programs at the state level. Most state laws require or encourage school officials (typically school boards) to develop and implement policies and programs to prevent and prohibit bullying (Colorado, New Jersey, and Oklahoma). These programs may include employee training on bullying and bullying prevention (Georgia, New Hampshire, Oklahoma, Washington, and West Virginia) or encourage individuals to report school bullying incidents to authorities (Connecticut, New Hampshire, New Jersey, New York, Washington, and West Virginia). Some laws emphasize the importance of disciplinary actions for children who bully (Georgia, New Jersey, and West Virginia; U.S. Department of Health and Human Services 2002). Anti-bullying legislation has increased public attention to and alertness about bullying issues in children and adolescents and has helped school authorities address and intervene appropriately in school bullying. Recently, Olweus and Limber (2010) reported the successful application of the anti-bullying program in several states in the United States (South Carolina, Pennsylvania, Washington, California), with meaningful decreases in bullying among students in those states (Olweus & Limber, 2010).

Also, early detection of bullying is crucial to effective interventions. Often students who are involved in bullying hesitate to report their experiences; they may present with somatic symptoms instead. Thus it is especially important for primary health care providers, including pediatricians, to be well aware of the possibility that bullying may be associated with common, vague, or unclear somatic symptoms. Pediatricians may wish to require screening of bullying when children or adolescents present with characteristics consistent with having experienced bullying (Spector & Kelly, 2006). Students who have difficulty with school refusal or truancy also require heightened attention for the possibility of involvement in bullying (Arseneault et al., 2006).

Pepler (2006) emphasized that an effective intervention for bullying requires a combination of scaffolding and social architecture, which means provision of tailored and dynamic supports, as well as a focus on the social dynamics that promote positive peer interactions and dissipate negative interactions. In this regard, providing appropriate and prompt access to the school health practitioners, including school nurses, for early detection and prevention of bullying may also play a crucial role (Pepler, 2006). School nurses also can participate in anti-bullying programs, especially aimed at students who require special health care due to their disabilities (Vessey & O'Neill, 2010).

CONCLUSION

School bullying is a common phenomenon in many countries. It is also complex and takes various forms in different situations. Although common, bullying is not a normative behavior or experience for any child. Previous and ongoing research clearly indicates that bullying is strongly associated with physical and psychological suffering for those students involved as victims, perpetrators, or victim-perpetrators. The outcomes, including increased psychopathology, school problems, medical problems, suicidality, and persistence of bullying participation, can extend into adulthood. Despite the potentially ominous outcomes, there is substantial opportunity for prevention and intervention. Using evidence-based treatment programs, children and adolescents can work with adults to reduce bullying and make their communities safer; they can also have better overall emotional, educational, and vocational outcomes. Bullying is a true public health problem that can and must be addressed by clinicians, parents, teachers, and communities.

REFERENCES

Achenbach, T. M., McConaughy, S. H., & Howell, C. T. (1987). Child/adolescent behavioral and emotional problems: Implications of cross-informant correlations for situational specificity. *Psychological Bulletin, 101,* 213–232.

Analitis, F., Velderman, M. K., Ravens-Sieberer, U., Detmar, S., Erhart, M., Herdman, M., . . . the European Kidscreen Group. (2009). Being bullied: Associated factors in children and adolescents 8 to 18 years old in 11 European countries. *Pediatrics, 123,* 569–577.

Arseneault, L., Walsh, E., Trzesniewski, K., Newcombe, R., Caspi, A., & Moffitt, T. E. (2006). Bullying victimization uniquely contributes to adjustment problems in young children: A nationally representative cohort study. *Pediatrics, 118,* 130–138.

Barker, E. D., Arseneault, L., Brendgen, M., Fontaine, N., & Maughan, B. (2008). Joint development of bullying and victimization in adolescence: Relations to delinquency and self-harm. *Journal of the American Academy of Child and Adolescent Psychiatry, 47,* 1030–1038.

Bender, D., & Losel, F. (1997). Protective and risk effects of peer relations and social support on antisocial behaviour in adolescents from multi-problem milieus. *Journal of Adolescence, 20,* 661–678.

Bond, L., Carlin, J. B., Thomas, L., Rubin, K., & Patton, G. (2001). Does bullying cause emotional problems? A prospective study of young teenagers. *BMJ, 323,* 480–484.

Borg, M. G. (1998). The emotional reactions of school bullies and their victims. *Educational Psychology, 18,* 433–444.

Borg, M. G. (1999). The extent and nature of bullying among primary and secondary schoolchildren. *Educational Research, 41,* 137–153.

Boulton, M. J., Bucci, E., Hawker, D. D. S. (1999). Swedish and English secondary school pupils' attitudes towards, and conceptions of, bullying: Concurrent links with bully/victim involvement. *Scandinavian Journal of Psychology, 40,* 277–284.

Boulton, M. J., & Smith, P. K. (1994). Bully/victim problems in middle-school children: Stability, self-percieved competence, peer rejection and peer acceptance. *British Journal of Developmental Psychology, 12,* 315–329.

Bowes, L., Arseneault, L., Maughan, B., Taylor, A., Caspi, A., & Moffitt, T. E. (2009). School, neighborhood, and family factors are associated with children's bullying involvement: A nationally representative longitudinal study. *Journal of the American Academy of Child and Adolescent Psychiatry, 48,* 545–553.

Brendgen, M., & Vitaro, F. (2008). Peer rejection and physical health problems in early adolescence. *Journal of Developmental and Behavioral Pediatrics, 29,* 183–190.

Campbell, M. L., & Morrison, A. P. (2007). The relationship between bullying, psychotic-like experiences and appraisals in 14–16-year olds. *Behaviour Research and Therapy, 45*(7), 1579–1591.

Carbone-Lopez, K., Esbensen, F., & Brick, B. T. (2010). Correlates and consequences of peer victimization: Gender differences in direct and indirect forms of bullying. *Youth Violence and Juvenile Justice, 8,* 332–350.

Carlisle, N., DeNike, M., Grey, K., Junker, K., Murphy, L., O'Rourke, T., et al. (n.d.) *No bully.* Retrieved from http://www.nobully.com.

Cleary, S. D. (2000). Adolescent victimization and associated suicidal and violent behaviors. *Adolescence, 35,* 671–682.

Committee for Children. (2010). Retrieved from http://www.cfchildren.org.

Conner, D. F., Steeber, J., & McBurnett, K. (2010). A review of attention-deficit/hyperactivity disorder complicated by symptoms of oppositional defiant disorder or conduct disorder. *Journal of Developmental and Behavioral Pediatrics, 31,* 427–440.

Eisenberg, M., & Neumark-Sztainer, D. (2008). Peer harassment and disordered eating. *International Journal of Adolescent Medicine and Health, 20,* 155–164.

Elsea, M. (2001). School bullying: Severity, distress and coping. Paper presented at the British Psychological Society Centenary Annual Conference, Glasgow, Scotland, UK.

Farrington, D. P. (1993). Understanding and preventing bullying In *Crime and justice: A review of research* (pp. 381–458). Chicago, IL: University of Chicago Press.

Fonzi, A., Genta, M. L., Menesini, E., Bacchini, D., Bonino, S., & Costabile, A. (1999). *The nature of school bullying: A cross-national perspective.* London and New York: Routledge.

Frisén, A., Jonsson, A., & Persson, C. (2007). Adolescents' perception of bullying: Who is the victim? Who is the bully? What can be done to stop bullying? *Adolescence, 42,* 749–761.

Gladstone, G. L., Parker, G. B., & Malhi, G. S. (2006). Do bullied children become anxious and depressed adults? A cross-sectional investigation of the correlates of bullying and anxious depression. *Journal of Nervous and Mental Disease, 194,* 201–208.

Glover, D., Gough, G., Johnson, M., & Cartwright, N. (2000). Bullying in 25 secondary schools: Incidence, impact and intervention. *Educational Research, 42,* 141–156.

Gray, W. N., Janicke, D. M., Ingerski, L. M., & Silverstein, J. H. (2008). The impact of peer victimization, parent distress and child depression on barrier formation and physical activity in overweight youth. *Journal of Developmental and Behavioral Pediatrics, 29,* 26–33.

Hanish, L. D., & Guerra, N. G. (2002). A longitudinal analysis of patterns of adjustment following peer victimization. *Development and Psychopathology, 14,* 69–89.

Hawkins, J. D., Catalano, R. F., Kosterman, R., Abbott, R., & Hill, K. G. (1999). Preventing adolescent health-risk behaviors by strengthening protection during childhood. *Archives of Pediatrics and Adolescent Medicine, 153,* 226–234.

Hazelden Foundation. (2011). *Violence prevention works.* Retrieved from http://www.violencepreventionworks.org .

Hodges, E. V., & Perry, D. G. (1999). Personal and interpersonal antecedents and consequences of victimization by peers. *Journal of Personality and Social Psychology, 76,* 677–685.

Hunter, S. C., Boyle, J. M. E., & Warden, D. (2004). Help seeking amongst child and adolescent victims of peer-aggression and bullying: The influence of school-stage, gender, victimization, appraisal, and emotion. *British Journal of Educational Psychology, 74,* 375–390.

Juvonen, J., Graham, S., & Schuster, M. A. (2003). Bullying among young adolescents: The strong, the weak, and the troubled. *Pediatrics, 112,* 1231–1237.

Kalman, I. C. (n.d.) *A psychological solution to bullying.* Retrieved from http://www.bullies2buddies.com.

Kaltiala-Heino, R., Rimpelä, M., Marttunen, M., Rimpelä, A., & Rantanen, P. (1999). Bullying, depression, and suicidal ideation in Finnish adolescents: school survey. BMJ, 319:7. 348–351.

Kim, Y. S., Koh, Y., & Leventhal, B. L. (2004). Prevalence of school bullying in Korean middle school students. *Archives of Pediatric and Adolescent Medicine, 158,* 737–741.

Kim, Y. S., Koh, Y., & Leventhal, B. (2005). School bullying and suicidal risk in Korean middle school students. *Pediatrics, 115,* 357–363.

Kim, Y. S., & Leventhal, B. (2008). Bullying and suicide: A review. *International Journal of Adolescent Medicine and Health, 20,* 133–154.

Kim, Y. S., Leventhal, B. L., Koh, Y., Hubbard, A., & Boyce, W. T. (2006). School bullying and youth violence: Causes or consequences of psychopathologic behavior? *Archives of General Psychiatry, 63,* 1035–1041.

Kim, Y. S., Boyce, W. T., Koh, Y., & Leventhal, B. L. (2009). Time trends, trajectories, and demographic predictors of bullying: A prospective study in Korean adolescents. *Journal of Adolescent Health, 45,* 360–367.

Klensmeden Fosse, G., & Holen, A. (2004). Cohabitation, education, and occupation of psychiatric outpatients bullied as children. *Journal of Nervous and Mental Disease, 192,* 385–388.

Klomek, A. B., Sourander, A., Niemelä, S., Kumpulainen, K., Piha, J., Tamminen, T., . . . Gould, M. S. (2009). Childhood bullying behavior as a risk for suicide attempts and completed suicides: A population-based birth cohort study. *Journal of the American Academy of Child and Adolescent Psychiatry, 48,* 254–261.

Kowlaski, R. M., Limber, S. P., & Agatson, P. W. (2008). *Cyberbullying: Bullying in the digital age.* Malden, MA: Blackwell.

Ladd, G. W., & Kochenderfer-Ladd, B. (2002). Identifying victims of peer aggression from early to middle childhood: Analysis of cross-informant data for concordance, estimation of relational adjustment, prevalence of victimization, and characteristics of identified victims. *Psychological Assessment, 14,* 74–96.

Ladd, G. W., & Troop-Gordon, W. (2003). The role of chronic peer difficulties in the development of children's psychological adjustment problems. *Child Development, 74,* 1344–1367.

Laflamme, L., Möller, J., Hallqvist, J., & Engström, K. (2008). Peer victimization and intentional injuries: Quantitative and qualitative accounts of injurious physical interactions between students. *International Journal of Adolescent Medicine and Health, 20,* 201–208.

Lahteenmaki, P. M., Huostila, J., Hinkka, S., & Salmi, T. T. (2002). Childhood cancer patients at school. *European Journal of Cancer, 38,* 1227–1240.

Lenhart, A., Madden, M., & Hitlin, P. (2005). Teens and technology: Youth are leading the transition to a fully wired and mobile nation. *Pew Internet and American Life Project.* Available from http://www.pewinternet.org/~/media/Files/Reports/2005/ PIP_Teens_Tech_July2005web.pdf.pdf.

Luukkonen, A., Rasanen, P., Hakko, H., Riala, K., & the STUDY-70 Workgroup. (2010). Bullying behavior in relation to psychiatric disorders and physical health among adolescents: A clinical cohort of 508 underage inpatient adolescents in Northern Finland. *Psychiatry Research, 178,* 166–170.

Martlew, M., & Hodson, J. (1991). Children with mild learning difficulties in an integrated and in a special school: Comparisons of behaviour, teasing and teachers' attitudes. *British Journal of Educational Psychology, 61,* 355–372.

Menesini, E., Modena, M., & Tani, F. (2009). Bullying and victimization in adolescence: Concurrent and stable roles and psychological health symptoms. *Journal of Genetic Psychology, 170,* 115–133.

Minino, A. (2010). Mortality among teenagers aged 12–19 years: United States, 1999–2006. *NCHS Data Brief, 37,* 1–8. Available from http://www.cdc.gov/nchs/ data/databriefs/db37.htm.

Molcho, M., Craig, W., Due, P., Pickett, W., Harel-Fisch, Y., Overpeck, M., & the HBSC Bullying Writing Group. (2009). Cross-national time trends in bullying behavior 1994–2006: Findings from Europe and North America. *International Journal of Public Health, 54,* 225–234.

Morita, Y. (1985). *Sociological study on the structure of bullying group.* Osaka, Japan: Osaka City University, Department of Sociology.

Nabuzoka, D., & Smith, P. K. (1993). Sociometric status and social behaviour of children with and without learning difficulties. *Journal of Child Psychology and Psychiatry, 34,* 1435–1448.

Namie, G., & Namie, R. (2009). U.S. workplace bullying: Some basic considerations and consultation interventions. *Consulting Psychology Journal: Practice and Research, 61,* 202–219.

Nansel, T. R., Craig, W., Overpeck, M. D., Saluja, G., Ruan, W. J., and the Health Behaviour in School-aged Children Bullying Analyses Working Group. (2004). Cross-national consistency in the relationship between bullying behaviors and psychosocial adjustment. *Archives of Pediatrics and Adolescent Medicine, 158,* 730–736.

Olweus, D. (1980). Familial and temperamental determinants of aggressive behavior in adolescent boys: A causal analysis. *Developmental Psychology, 16,* 644–660.

Olweus, D. (1992). *Aggression and violence throughout the lifespan.* London: Sage.

Olweus, D. (1994a). *Aggressive behavior: Current perspectives.* New York, NY: Plenum Press.

Olweus, D. (1994b). Bullying at school: Basic facts and effects of a school based intervention program. *Journal of Child Psychology and Psychiatry, 35,* 1171–1190.

Olweus, D. (1994c). Bullying at school: Long-term outcomes for the victims and an effective school-based intervention program. In L. R. Huesmann (Ed.), *Aggressive behavior: Current perspectives* (pp. 97–130). Ann Arbor, MI: University of Michigan.

Olweus, D., & Limber, S. P. (2010). Bullying in school: Evaluation and dissemination of the Olweus Bullying Prevention Program. *American Journal of Orthopsychiatry, 80,* 124–134.

Operation Respect. (2011). Retrieved from http://www.operationrespect.org.

Pepler, D., Jiang, D., Craig, W., & Connolly, J. (2008). Developmental trajectories of bullying and associated factors. *Child Development, 79,* 325–338.

Pepler, D. J. (2006). Bullying interventions: A binocular perspective. *Journal of the Canadian Academy of Child and Adolescent Psychiatry, 15,* 16–20.

Pridgen, B. (2009). Book Forum: Cyberbullying: Bullying in the digital age. *Journal of the American Academy of Child and Adolescent Psychiatry, 48*(3), 344–346.

Rivers, I., & Smith, P. K. (1994). Types of bullying behaviour and their correlates. *Aggressive Behavior, 20,* 359–368.

Roberts, C., Currie, C., Samdal, O. et al. (2007). Measureing the health and health behaviours of adolescents through cross-national survey research: Recent developments in the Health Behaviour in School-aged Children (HBSC) study. *Journal of Public Health, 15,* 179–186.

Salmon, G., James, A., & Smith, D. M. (1998). Bullying in schools: Self-reported anxiety, depression, and self-esteem in secondary school children. *BMJ, 317,* 924–925.

Schwartz, D. (2000). Subtypes of victims and aggressors in children's peer groups. *Journal of Abnormal Child Psychology, 28,* 181–192.

Sharp, S. (1995). How much does bullying hurt? The effects of bullying on the personal well-being and educational progress of secondary aged students. *Educational and Child Psychology, 12,* 81–88.

Shojaei, T., Wazana, A., Pitrou, I., Gilbert, F., & Kovess, V. (2009). Self-reported peer victimization and child mental health: Results of a cross-sectional survey among French primary school children. *Journal of Developmental and Behavioral Pediatrics, 30*(4), 300–309.

Smith, P. K., Singer, M., Hoel, H., & Cooper, C. L. (2003). Victimization in the school and the workplace: Are there any links? *British Journal of Psychology, 94,* 175–188.

Smith, P. K., Talamelli, L., Cowie, H., Naylor, P., & Chauhan, P. (2004). Profiles of non-victims, escaped victims, continuing victims and new victims of school bullying. *British Journal of Educational Psychology, 74,* 565–581.

Sourander, A., Brunstein Klomek, A., Kumpulainen, K., Puustjarvi, A., Elonheimo, H., Ristkari, T., . . . Ronning, J. A. (2011). Bullying at age eight and criminality in adulthood: Findings from the Finnish Nationwide 1981 Birth Cohort Study. *Social Psychiatry and Psychiatric Epidemiology, 46*(12), 1211–1219.

Spector, N. D., & Kelly, S. F. (2006). Pediatrician's role in screening and treatment: Bullying, prediabetes, oral health. *Current Opinion in Pediatrics, 18,* 661–670.

Spivak, H. (2003). Bullying: Why all the fuss? *Pediatrics, 112,* 1421–1422.

Srabstein, J. (2008). Deaths linked to bullying and hazing. *International Journal of Adolescent Medicine and Health, 20,* 235–239.

Srabstein, J., Leventhal, B. L., & Merrick, J. (2008). Bullying: A global public health risk [Editorial]. *International Journal of Adolescent Medicine and Health, 20,* 99–100.

Srabstein, J., & Piazza, T. (2008). Public health, safety and educational risks associated with bullying behaviors in American adolescents. *International Journal of Adolescent Medicine and Health, 20,* 223–233.

Srabstein, J. C., & Leventhal, B. L. (2010). Prevention of bullying-related morbidity and mortality: A call for public health policies. *Bulletin of the World Health Organization, 88,* 403–404.

Ttofi, M. M., & Farrington, D. P. (2008). Reintegrative shaming theory, moral emotions and bullying. *Aggressive Behavior, 34(4),* 352–368.

Twemlow, S. W. (2010). *Handbook of bullying in schools: An international perspective.* New York, NY: Routledge/Taylor & Francis.

Twyman, K. A., Saylor, C. F., Saia, D., Macias, M. M., Taylor, L. A., & Spratt, E. (2010). Bullying and ostracism experiences in children with special health care needs. *Journal of Developmental and Behavioral Pediatrics, 31,* 1–8.

Utterly global: Stand up, speak out . . . end bullying. (n.d.) Retrieved from http://www.antibullyingprograms.org.

U.S. Department of Education. (2010). *Indicators of school crime and safety: 2010.* Washington, DC: National Center for Education Statistics, Institute of Education Sciences.

U.S. Department of Health and Human Services. (2002). *Stop bullying now: State laws related to bullying among children and youth.* Washington, DC: Author.

Van Cleave, J., & Davis, M. M. (2006). Bullying and peer victimization among children with special health care needs. *Pediatrics, 118,* e1212–e1219.

van der Wal, M. F., de Wit, C. A. M., & Hirasing, R. A. (2003). Psychosocial health among young victims and offenders of direct and indirect bullying. *Pediatrics, 111,* 1312–1317.

Vaughn, M. G., Qiang, F., Bender, K., DeLisi, M., Beaver, K. M., Perron, B. E., Howard, M. O. (2010). Psychiatric correlates of bullying in the United States: Findings from a national sample. *Psychiatric Quarterly, 81,* 183–195.

Vessey, J. A., & O'Neill, K. M. (2011). Helping students with disabilities better address teasing and bullying situations: A MASNRN study. *Journal of School Nursing, 27(2),* 139–148.

Vreeman, R. C., & Carroll, A. E. (2007). A systematic review of school-based interventions to prevent bullying. *Archives of Pediatrics and Adolescent Medicine, 161,* 78–88.

Wang, J., Iannotti, R. J., & Nansel, T. R. (2009). School bullying among adolescents in the United States: Physical, verbal, relational, and cyber. *Journal of Adolescent Health, 45,* 368–375.

Whitney, I., & Smith, P. K. (1993). A survey of the nature and extent of bullying in junior/middle and secondary schools. *Educational Research, 35,* 3–25.

Woods, S., Wolke, D., Nowichki, S., & Hall, L. (2009). Emotion recognition abilities and empathy of victims of bullying. *Child Abuse and Neglect, 33,* 307–311.

9

Neighborhood Influences on the Development of Aggression and Youth Violence

ANTHONY FABIO, CHUNG-YU CHEN, AND
MICHAEL C. BAZACO ■

YOUTH VIOLENCE

Youth violence is one of the major public health concerns in the United States, and the prevention of violence is one of the major public health initiatives (U.S. Department of Health and Human Services, 2001). According to the Bureau of Justice Statistics, since the mid-1980s, the violence victimization rate in the United States has been steadily higher in younger age groups (12–15 and 16–19) than in older. Although the rates have declined since their peak in the early 1990s (more than 100 crimes per 1,000 population), the numbers are still consistently higher in these younger age groups—most recently 42.2 and 37.0 per 1,000, respectively (Bureau of Justice Statistics 2009b) Homicide victimization rate is especially worrisome. According to the Bureau of Justice Statistics, the homicide victimization rate for the ages of 14–24 is consistently three to four times as high as in all other age groups (Bureau of Justice Statistics, 2009a).

Juvenile offender rates have declined somewhat over the past 10 years, from just under 59,000 violent offenses in 1999 to just under 54,000 offenses in 2008 (U.S. Department of Justice, 2009). Even with this decline, the offense rate is still of concern, and juvenile offenders make up over 15% of all violent crime offenders. One area of particular concern to public health officials is the violence and homicide rate of young Black males. Homicide is the leading cause of mortality in Black males between the ages of 15 and 34 and is the second leading cause of death in Black males between the ages of 10 and 14 in the United States, according to the 2006 National Report on Vital Statistics. Homicide accounted for more than 50% of deaths in Black males between the ages of 15 and 24 (Centers for Disease Control and Prevention, 2010).

Adolescent aggression is a strong, consistent early risk factor for predicting later violence (Hawkins et al., 2000). Recently, research and public health initiatives have begun to quantitatively demonstrate the effects of neighborhood on the development of aggression and violence. This chapter aims to describe recent literature that has examined whether and how neighborhood influences the development of individual aggression and violence through a review of the literature published in various disciplines over the past 10 years. Given that these factors disproportionately affect adolescents, the review focuses on youths. The specific aims are as follows: (1) to describe the initial work in the area; (2) to discuss the practical differences between the effects of neighborhood structure and of neighborhood social processes; (3) to discuss whether neighborhood characteristics influence risk beyond an individual's own risk; and (4) to discuss the research that attempts to describe and understand the theoretical pathways by which neighborhood may influence individual development of aggression and violence. The chapter ends with recommendations for future research and implications for clinical practice and public policy.

IMPORTANCE OF POPULATION-LEVEL RESEARCH

The majority of studies on preventing violence have been limited to identifying individual-level factors by which to identify high-risk individuals. Although a lot has been learned in these studies, the addition of population-level research can add substantially to this understanding. The targeting of high-risk individuals can have a dramatic effect on individual risk; however, given that only a small percentage of individuals are at high risk for violence, this approach may not have a major effect on population-level rates. A renewed focus on the population level provides many advantages and should be seen as an integral part of public health research related to violence. Focusing on exposure to a large number of people may yield results applicable to a more absolute and significant number of people.

Applying the population perspective to a health measure means asking why a population has the existing distribution of a particular risk, in addition to asking why a particular individual "got sick" (Rose, 2001). It has been argued that the greatest improvements in a population's health are likely to derive from interventions based on the first question because the majority of cases of poor public health outcomes arise within the bulk of the population outside the extremes of risk (Rose, 2001). Therefore, prevention strategies must be applicable to a broad base of the population. Major successful public health programs have been at the population level. Seat-belt legislation enacted 31 years ago has been estimated to have saved more than 135,000 lives and prevented more than 3.8 million injuries due to motor vehicle accidents (Blincoe et al., 2002). In addition, water fluoridation has had a tremendous impact on dental health in the United States, and the Centers for Disease Control have proclaimed that fluoridation is one of the 10 great public health achievements of the 20th century (American Dental Association 2005). Accordingly, it is important that youth violence prevention include a focus on population level and understand the influence of neighborhood.

THE KEY INITIAL STUDIES

Across all of the social sciences, there is strong consistent evidence that neighborhood context is related to aggression and violence. One of the first empirical works examining the contextual effects of neighborhood on the development of aggression and violence was reported in 1942 by Shaw and McKay (Shaw & McKay, 1942). The authors concluded that delinquency was not determined by individual-level factors but is a normal response by individuals to abnormal conditions. In general, if a community is not self-policing, some individuals will exercise unrestricted freedom to express their desires, leading to delinquent behavior. However, this work focused on neighborhood rates of delinquency and not on the development of individual risk. Bronfenbrenner (1979) first discussed the importance of the "ecological environment" in human development. In his work, Bronfenbrenner combines aspects of sociology and developmental psychology by theorizing that the relationships between individuals and their environments are "mutually shaping." One level of the "ecological environment" is the neighborhood in which an individual resides. The neighborhood that one lives in is theorized to have a significant effect on an individual's development. Over the past several decades there has been a growing body of literature that supports this association. Initial studies focused on cross-sectional, single-level studies of neighborhood structure and demographics. The results of these studies have provided strong consistent evidence that neighborhood context influences the development of aggression and violence (Bursik & Grasmick, 1993; Loeber & Wikstrom, 1993; Ludwig, Duncan, & Hirschfield, 2001; Sampson & Groves, 1989; Simcha-Fagan & Schwartz, 1986; Stouthamer-Loeber, Drinkwater, & Loeber, 2000; Wikstrom, 1991, 1998).

NEIGHBORHOOD STRUCTURE VERSUS NEIGHBORHOOD SOCIAL PROCESSES

Early work examining the effect of neighborhood on the development of individual aggression and violence focused on neighborhood structure (Brown, 2008). Neighborhood structure measures socioeconomic aspects of neighborhoods. Researchers have focused mainly on structural economic disadvantage and related constructs following the seminal work described in Wilson's book *The Truly Disadvantaged* (Wilson, 1987). Typically, neighborhood structure was measured by aggregating individual-level socioeconomic constructs (e.g., unemployment rate, median annual income) to some geographic level representing the neighborhood. These factors are often combined in an analysis as independent constructs or by using a form of data reduction such as factor analysis (Fabio, Li, Strotmeyer, & Branas, 2004).

Neighborhood structure

In a study examining the National Longitudinal Study of Adolescent Health, Bruce (2004) tested the relationships between neighborhood concentrated deprivation and violence. Concentrated deprivation was composed of the following block-level census variables using principal components analysis: percentage below the poverty line, percentage unemployed, percentage without a high school degree, and percentage of female-headed households. He found that concentrated deprivation was positively related to adolescent violence. However, the relationship became nonsignificant once family and individual factors were adjusted.

Several studies have examined neighborhood structural economic disadvantage using data from the Pittsburgh Youth Study (PYS). The PYS is a 14-year longitudinal study of the development of delinquency in three samples (Loeber, Farrington, Stouthamer-Loeber, & Van Kammen, 1998). Beyers, Loeber, Wikstrom, and Stouthamer-Loeber (2001) employed principal components analysis on census tract data for neighborhoods in Pittsburgh based on the process developed by Wikström and Loeber (Wikstrom & Loeber, 2000). The strongest factor was representative of neighborhood socioeconomic status and consisted of percentage of families with children headed by single parents, median household income, percentage of families below the poverty level, percentage of households on public assistance, percentage of individuals unemployed, and percentage of African Americans. The authors looked at 420 males aged 13–19 years and found that adolescents in neighborhoods with high socioeconomic status (SES) were significantly less likely than their counterparts in low-SES neighborhoods to engage in serious and violent delinquency (Beyers et al., 2001). For those in the high-SES neighborhoods, risk factors that emerge early in adolescence and that are thought to be at least partially biologically based (including physical aggression and hyperactivity-impulsivity-attention) were the strongest predictors of later repeated violence. For those in the low-SES neighborhoods, the strongest predictors were those that were more context dependent, which emerge later in adolescence (such as early intercourse, carrying a weapon, and family processes). This suggests that neighborhood effects may be more important later in adolescence, providing evidence for a contextual effect.

A second study looking at the PYS investigated risk and promotive effects as predictors of persistent serious violence (Stouthamer-Loeber, Loeber, Wei, Farrington, & Wikstrom, 2002). Participants were studied from ages 13 to 19 in the oldest sample and from ages 7 to 13 in the youngest sample. Neighborhood disadvantage was measured using principal components analysis, as described in the Beyers et al. (2001) study. The results showed that individuals who lived in disadvantaged neighborhoods had a higher prevalence of risk factors for violence and a lower prevalence of promotive effects compared with more advantaged neighborhoods. Fite, Wynn, and Pardini (2009) investigated discrepancies in arrest rates between Black and White male adolescents by examining the role of early risk for arrest. A population of 418 Black and White boys was followed from childhood to early adulthood. The authors found that most racial discrepancies in juvenile male arrest rates were explained by exposure to disadvantaged neighborhoods.

Neighborhood social processes

More recently, researchers have been moving beyond the idea of structure (or a compositional effect) and are trying to understand the underlying process in which the neighborhood may affect individual risk for aggression and violence. These studies have looked at proxies for neighborhood social processes as opposed to neighborhood structure. Neighborhood social processes relate to a neighborhood's social organization (Chung & Steinberg, 2006) and form a measure of how communities function. Neighborhood processes represent a whole constellation of social, economic, and political disadvantages. These measures of social processes have been referred to as neighborhood disorder (Sampson & Raudenbush, 1999), social connectedness (Rountree & Warner, 1999), social control (Elliot et al., 1996) and collective efficacy (Sampson, Raudenbush, & Earls, 1997). Though the results are less robust, these studies have validated the findings of neighborhood structural studies that neighborhood can influence the development of aggression and violence.

Data from the survey of 118 sixth-grade students were used to test the association between adolescent neighborhood connection and violence-related behaviors (Widome, Sieving, Harpin, & Hearst, 2008). The measures of neighborhood connection included two factors. The first factor, intention to contribute, indicated whether adolescents value and intend to work to improve their neighborhoods. The second factor, neighborhood social resources, reflected adolescents' familiarity with neighbors and perceptions that their neighbors could provide support. Intention to contribute but not neighborhood connection was significantly related to violent behaviors. A prospective study of 3,738 individuals was used to explore the risk factors for youth violence (Herrenkohl et al., 2000). This study examined a large number of risk factors within several different domains. Community disorganization predicted violence at ages 14 and 16 years, and low neighborhood attachment predicted violence for age 16 but not age 14, providing evidence that neighborhood effects have more influence in the later stages of adolescence, suggesting a contextual effect.

NEIGHBORHOOD EFFECT ABOVE AND
BEYOND INDIVIDUAL RISK

There is a large body of evidence that demonstrates the influence of individual-level factors on individual-level risk of aggression and violence (Hawkins et al., 2000). As demonstrated in the studies reviewed in this chapter, neighborhood is a strong correlate of aggression and violence. A neighborhood effect may be either contextual or compositional. At the simplest level, there is a compositional effect. It is reasonable to expect that socioeconomic patterns that concentrate potential offenders and victims in the same setting will increase observed levels of victimization beyond what would be experienced if potential offenders and victims were dispersed more widely across areas. For example, many studies have shown that SES is related to individual risk of violence (Hawkins et al., 2000). When there is a neighborhood with a large proportion of unemployed, there are then a large proportion of high-risk individuals, leading to higher risks of aggression and violence. From the perspective of routine activities theory, crime requires suitable opportunities: the convergence in time and space of potential victims and motivated offenders, as well as the absence of guardians (Cohen, 1981; Felson, 1987). This convergence is much more likely to occur when individuals with higher personal risks as potential victims and offenders live near one another. Though many studies suggest that neighborhood disadvantage has an effect on individual risk, it is not clear whether that risk is simply due to a high proportion of high-risk individuals living in the same neighborhood (a compositional effect) or whether in fact the neighborhood affects an individual above and beyond his or her own inherent risk (a contextual effect).

Though most of the studies discussed previously have reported a significant, and often large, association between community-level factors and aggression and violence, many of these associations are largely attenuated once other factors are controlled. Also, the correlations among many of the explanatory factors are strong, suggesting that confounding may play a part in these associations.

Results of recent individual-level studies taking into account contextual relationships are mixed but have provided initial results showing that individual risk may be moderated by neighborhood. In a longitudinal study, Schonberg and Shaw (2007) investigated whether boys ages 5–12 from less and more advantaged neighborhoods differed in the degree to which they were exposed to familial risk factors for conduct problems (CP) during early childhood and the extent to which risk factors for CP were generalizable across neighborhood SES level (Schonberg & Shaw, 2007). The results showed that there is a small but positive relationship between the shape of a boy's developmental trajectory for CP and neighborhood SES. Moreover, more child and individual risk factors for CP are found in boys with chronic CP from more advantaged neighborhoods compared with their counterparts from less advantaged neighborhoods. Molnar, Cerda, Roberts, and Buka (2008) examined the longitudinal effects of neighborhood resources on aggressive and delinquent behaviors among 2,226 urban youths from ages 9 to 15 years. They found that a higher concentration of neighborhood organizations or services serving young people and adults decreased the levels of aggression, though the association was nonsignificant. The effects of family, peer, and mentor resources were found to be moderated by neighborhood. Meier, Slutske, Arndt, and Cadoret (2008) examined whether neighborhood context (measured by collective efficacy) influenced the effect of impulsive and callous personality traits on delinquent behavior, studying 85,000 schoolchildren ages 10–19. Results suggested that neighborhood context moderated the relationships between both personality risks and delinquency.

Building on the individual-level studies of social structure are more recent studies utilizing hierarchical modeling to assess neighborhood effects simultaneously with individual-level factors. A hierarchical linear modeling approach simultaneously assesses both the individual- and community-level factors, adjusting for clustering of individuals within the neighborhood. This method isolates distinct effects at each level to allow the determination of whether neighborhood context interacts with an individual's own inherent risk to further increase the individual risk of aggression and violence beyond the individual-level risk. One of the first studies to attempt to evaluate the association of neighborhood social process on aggression and violence was reported in *Science* by Sampson, Raudenbush, and Earls (1997). They assessed a measure of social cohesion, referred to as collective efficacy, to determine the extent of social connectedness within the neighborhood. They found that higher levels of collective efficacy were related to lower levels of violence. Chung and Steinberg (2006) examined the relationships between neighborhood disorder, social cohesion, and delinquency among a group of serious juvenile offenders using hierarchical linear modeling. Participants were 14- to 18-year-old boys, primarily economically disadvantaged, ethnic-minority youths living in urban communities. Using principal components analysis, the authors derived three neighborhood structural indexes from census tract data: concentrated poverty, residential instability, and ethnic diversity. Two neighborhood social processes, neighborhood disorder and social cohesion, were measured by self-report. Neighborhood social organization was indirectly related to delinquency through its associations with parenting behavior and peer deviance. The relationships between neighborhood and delinquency were small. When parenting was added to the model, the relationship between neighborhood disorder and peer delinquency was diminished, and the relationship between social cohesion and peer delinquency became significant. This finding provides some evidence that parenting behavior mediated the relationship between neighborhood disorder and delinquency and played a suppressor role between social cohesion and delinquency. Vazsonyi, Cleveland, and Wiebe (2006) analyzed 20,745 male and female adolescents from the National Longitudinal Study of Adolescent Health to examine whether neighborhood disadvantage modified the relationship between impulsivity and a variety of deviance measures. Results showed that the level of neighborhood disadvantage influenced the levels of impulsivity and deviance. Simons, Simons, Conger, and Brody (2004) assessed the relationship between various community factors and child conduct problems among 867 African American children ages 10–12 years. Collective socialization, a measure of collective efficacy, was inversely associated with conduct problems even after controlling for a variety of individual-level factors related to family, peers, and school. However, there were no significant effects of the prevalence of crime and concentrated disadvantage on conduct problems. Overall, the results suggested that communities significantly decreased the risk for child conduct problems when there were strong social ties among children, parents, and teachers in their neighborhoods.

Several studies have assessed the effects of social structure in relation to SES and race. Krivo, Peterson, and Kuhl (2009) assessed the influence of neighborhood socioeconomic disadvantage on levels of violent crime across all urban neighborhoods. Neighborhood socioeconomic disadvantage was measured by an index of joblessness, occupation level, education, female-headed households, and secondary sector workers. The data were from the National Neighborhood Crime Study for 7,622 neighborhoods in 79 cities throughout the United States. Using a multilevel approach and controlling for both racial composition and segregation, the authors found that structural disadvantage was associated with violent crime. A second study looked at the effect of county- and individual-level factors on intentional-injury hospital admissions (Fabio, Sauber-Schatz, Barbour, & Li, 2009). A principal components analysis found distinct demographic, economic, gender, and racial segregation factors at the neighborhood level. The data showed an increased risk of violent injuries for individuals living in more disadvantaged neighborhoods. The results held after adjusting for racial segregation, composition, and individual-level factors, which suggests that neighborhood effects were associated with increased odds of violent injury not attributable to individual risk.

NEIGHBORHOOD PATHWAYS TO VIOLENCE

Recent studies have begun to look at the potential theoretical pathways of this process (Cantillon, 2006; Tolan, Gorman-Smith, & Henry, 2003). There are two dominant theoretical models: *relationship and ties* and *norms and collective efficacy* (Chung & Steinberg, 2006). The relationship-and-ties model suggests that the effects of neighborhood are mediated by parenting behavior and the home environment. The norms-and-collective-efficacy model theorizes that the relationship is mediated by peer group norms and behavior.

Though the results are promising, the strength of the associations and the exact pathways are still unclear.

To examine a developmental-ecological model of violence, Tolan et al. (2003) used the data from a longitudinal study of 294 African American and Latino adolescent boys and their caregivers living in poor urban communities. The authors evaluated the associations between microsystem effects of parenting and peer deviance (peer violence and gang membership), macrosystem effects of community structural characteristics and neighborhood social organization,

and individual involvement in violent behaviors. The results of structural equation modeling showed that neighborhood structural characteristics significantly
predicted neighborhood social processes. Parenting practices were found to be
a mediator between neighborhood social process and gang membership, and
gang membership mediated the relationship between peer violence and individual violence. However, the overall sets of relations did not always follow media-
tion requirements.

In a survey of 103 tenth-grade males, Cantillon (2006) suggested that perceived
neighborhood structural characteristics (i.e., neighborhood stability, income)
measured at the block level have a direct and indirect influence on delinquent and
prosocial activities. Directly, perceived neighborhood advantage can significantly
decrease neighborhood rates of official delinquency and increase rates of prosocial activity. Indirectly, perceived neighborhood advantage positively affected
outcomes by influencing more proximal constructs such as community social
organization, informal social control, parenting practices, and affiliation with
delinquent peers. Neighborhood stability had an influence on delinquent peer
affiliation, which was strongly associated with self-reported problems. The proposed pathway is that neighborhood stability facilitates parenting style, reducing
the adolescent's association with delinquent peers, leading to fewer self-related
pathways. However, parenting style was not directly related to self-reported problem behaviors. Further, the pathway from neighborhood stability to community
social organization and informal social control were not associated with self-
reported problem behaviors. The pathway from neighborhood stability to parenting style was not associated with self-reported problem behaviors.

These studies have begun to quantitatively test specific pathways to show how
neighborhood effects might affect individual risk for aggression and violence.
The models suggest possible pathways from neighborhood structure through
various mediators; however, the results of these first studies are mixed. Full
mediated pathways were not consistent, and the strengths of the associations
were not large. Nevertheless, these results begin to describe a pathway between
neighborhood structure and individual risk for violence through the effects of
neighborhood social processes and parenting practices.

SCHOOL AS ENVIRONMENT

School environment is in many ways similar to neighborhood environment,
and the theories behind how school environment may affect the development
of youth violence and aggression similarly fall into two categories: structure
and social processes. However, school environment is likely a distinct and independent factor in the development of aggression and youth violence. Given these
considerations, we provide a very brief overview of how the school environment
may affect the development of aggression and youth violence based a comprehensive review article by S. L. Johnson, published in 2009. The review examined
the relationships between the school environment and violent perpetration and

victimization. Of the articles that she reviewed, seven pertained to aggression and youth violence.

When considering the structural characteristics of the school, the results were inconsistent, suggesting that there was no relationship between the characteristics of the school and the rate of aggression or violence of the students. There was consistently no significant relationship found with regard to class size, school location, student attendance, or parental involvement in parent–teacher organizations or school type, although the number of studies involved in some of these factors is small (Brookmeyer, Fanti, & Henrich, 2006; Crooks, Scott, Wolfe, Chiodo, & Killip, 2007; Felson, Liska, South, & McNulty, 1994; Gottfredson, Gottfredson, Payne, & Gottfredson, 2005). Results were similar when looking at overall school size, though one study did show a significant relationship between a larger school size and an increased rate of predicted future violent behavior in students (Brookmeyer et al., 2006). Two other studies showed no relationship (Crooks et al., 2007; Felson et al., 1994). One study did show that an increase in the percentage of males in a school led to an increase in student delinquency (Gottfredson et al., 2005), though other studies not reviewed did not (Wilcox, Augustine, & Clayton, 2006)

However, when looking at the school social processes, the results of the studies that were considered showed mixed results. A feeling of group connectiveness led to a reduction in future violent behavior in one study, but the inverse was found in another study utilizing the same measure (Brookmeyer et al., 2006; Crooks et al., 2007). Mixed results were also seen when looking at peer relationships as potential predictors of violence (Espelage, Bosworth, & Simon, 2001; McNeely & Falci, 2004; Reis, Trockel, & Mulhall, 2007). Similarly inconsistent results were shown in the relationship between student school success, classroom culture, and school culture with respect to aggression and violence (Crooks et al., 2007; Felson et al., 1994; McNeely & Falci, 2004; Reis et al., 2007). Teacher–student relationships did appear to have an effect on later delinquency in two different studies (McNeely & Falci, 2004; Reis et al., 2007). It was shown that the better the relationship was, the less likely the student was to continue into a life of violence or delinquent behavior. Additionally, a better acceptance of school-wide accepted norms concerning violence led to a statistically significant decrease in violent actions and delinquency, and these findings were shown evident in the two studies that looked at this as a potential predictor of violence (Felson et al., 1994; Gottfredson et al., 2005).

IMPLICATIONS FOR PUBLIC POLICY AND CLINICAL PRACTICE

Public policy

Of importance in neighborhood effects is how one can use the data for public policy to prevent or reduce aggression and violence. This review sheds light on the importance of considering neighborhood contextual effects in the design of future prevention programs. Designing programs at the individual level cannot be optimally effective without taking into account the societal-level risk factors and how individuals interact with these factors. Future work should address what the important risk factors are. Once these are better understood, prevention programs can address how to predict these societal factors as precursors to increases in violence rates. We also need to better understand whether or not it is efficacious to alter the social structure of the neighborhood or to provide individuals opportunities to overcome the neighborhood's disadvantageous influence. Recent studies suggest that providing opportunities to individuals may not have a large immediate effect. In the Moving to Opportunities (MTO) program, researchers randomly assigned families below the poverty level living in neighborhoods with high levels of concentrated poverty to one of three groups: experimental, Section 8, or control (Kling, Ludwig, & Katz 2005). The experimental group received a housing voucher to live in a neighborhood with low levels of poverty. The Section 8 group received vouchers with no restrictions imposed on where they could live. The controls were given no treatment. The researchers found that moving to a neighborhood with low levels of poverty reduced the arrest rates for violent crime and increased property crime arrests and problem behaviors. Harden et al. (2009) examined the relationship between population density and delinquency by using the longitudinal data on the offspring of a nationally representative sample of mothers ($N = 4,886$). Population density was not related to delinquency across ages 4–13, but youths living in areas of greater population density exhibited more delinquency across ages 10–17. Interestingly, a temporal analysis using generalized linear mixed modeling and treating population density as a time-varying covariate did not find population density to be a risk factor for delinquency. This suggests that moving to a neighborhood with a different population density did not change the adolescents' risk for delinquency.

Clinical practice

Identifying the key elements of a patient's neighborhood would have important implications for clinical care. Understanding the risks generated from a patient's neighborhood may help clinicians provide better long-term treatment planning and reduce the likelihood of relapse and recidivism. Clinicians should take into account the overall quality of a patient's neighborhood or proximity to certain environmental features that might increase risk of violence and aggression. Until more developed measures of the social process are available, clinicians should focus on assessing an individual's neighborhood's social structure. In particular, one can assess the makeup of the patient's neighborhood, including its economic and educational status. Additionally, the clinician should assess the geographic availability of related mental health services. A more explicit focus on an individual's neighborhood is an important area in clinical practice, which can potentially enhance long-term care and treatment planning for patients.

CONCLUSIONS

The literature provides strong consistent evidence that neighborhood context is strongly associated with individual risk of aggression and violence. The more recent literature assessing whether specific social processes increase the risk of an individual's development of aggression and violence is less clear but promising. In particular, the various measures of social processes are inconsistently associated with individual risk. One possible explanation is that the science of measuring neighborhood processes is relatively young. There have been only a few studies that have attempted to measure neighborhood social processes, and these have been measured in various ways. It is likely that more developed and consistent measures of these neighborhood processes would provide clearer results. Additionally, the studies testing the moderation of neighborhood risk on individual risk are less consistent, and the sizes of the associations are often small. Testing these pathways requires complex theoretical models and complex methodological and statistical approaches. The research in this area is at the beginning stages, and further work is needed.

However, when looked at as a whole, the results of studies reviewed here provide intriguing evidence that the effect of neighborhood increases the risk of aggression and violence above and beyond an individual's own risk. Though the complex associations are less clear than the direct associations, the consistency across all types of studies shows promise. These results provide evidence for studies that further develop the theoretical models and methodological approaches.

FUTURE RESEARCH

Future research should focus on the development of the methodological approaches for testing whether neighborhood association with individual risk of aggression and violence is contextual, adding risk above and beyond an individual's inherent risk. Future research should also explore and quantitatively test the theoretical pathways for this association. Within this work should be the further development of the methodological approaches that can adequately tease out the individual risk between these two levels.

Also of importance in future studies is to determine at what age individuals are at most risk from neighborhood effects. There are data that suggest that as children get older the effects of neighborhood risk change. One theory suggests that neighborhood SES initially operates as a risk factor at younger ages of development and then exerts a more direct influence as individuals age and begin to become more exposed to neighborhood factors (Ingoldsby & Shaw, 2002). The current literature is not consistent in demonstrating which ages are most affected by the neighborhood.

One important specific area of research is to assess whether housing relocation policies and providing educational and economic opportunities to individuals are effective or whether more effort should be put into addressing the aspects of disadvantage in existing neighborhoods. For instance, in the MTO project, the researchers found that many families were reluctant to move out of their own neighborhoods and that many families moved back into neighborhoods with high levels of poverty (Ludwig, Duncan, & Hirschfield, 2001), suggesting that it may be more effective to concentrate efforts on addressing the socioeconomic context of the existing neighborhoods of individuals.

REFERENCES

American Dental Association. (2005). *Fluoridation facts.* Chicago, IL: Author.

Beyers, J. M., Loeber, R., Wikstrom, P. O., & Stouthamer-Loeber, M. (2001). What predicts adolescent violence in better-off neighborhoods? *Journal of Abnormal Child Psychology, 29*(5), 369–381.

Blincoe, L., Seay, A., Zaloshnja, E., Miller, T., Romano, E., Luchter, S., & Spicer, R. (2002). *The economic impact of motor vehicle crashes, 2000.* Washington, DC: U.S. Department of Transportation, National Highway Traffic Safety Administration.

Bronfenbrenner, U. (1979). *The ecology of human development:Experiments by nature and design.* Cambridge, MA: Harvard University Press.

Brookmeyer, K. A., Fanti, K. A., & Henrich, C. C. (2006). Schools, parents, and youth violence: A multilevel, ecological analysis. *Journal of Clinical Child and Adolescent Psychology, 35*(4), 504–514.

Brown, B. V. (Ed.). (2008). *Key indicators of child and youth well-being: Completing the picture.* New York, NY: Erlbaum.

Bruce, M. A. (2004). Inequality and adolescent violence: An exploration of community, family, and individual factors. *Journal of the National Medical Association, 96*(4), 486–495.

Bureau of Justice Statistics. (2009a). *Homicide victimization rate by age.* Available from http://bjs.ojp.usdoj.gov/content/glance/tables/homagetab.cfm.

Bureau of Justice Statistics. (2009b). *Violent victimization rates by age, 1973–2008.* Available from http://bjs.ojp.usdoj.gov/content/glance/tables/vagetab.cfm.

Bursik, R. J., & Grasmick, H. G. (1993). *Neighborhoods and crime.* New York, NY: Lexington Books.

Cantillon, D. (2006). Community social organization, parents, and peers as mediators of perceived neighborhood block characteristics on delinquent and prosocial activities. *American Journal of Community Psychology, 37*(1–2), 111–127.

Centers for Disease Control and Prevention. (2010). *National Vital Statistic System mortality tables: Leading Causes of Death by Age Group, Black Males—United States, 2006.* Available from http://www.cdc.gov/men/lcod/2006/BlackMales2006.pdf .

Chung, H. L., & Steinberg, L. (2006). Relations between neighborhood factors, parenting behaviors, peer deviance, and delinquency among serious juvenile offenders. *Developmental Psychology, 42*(2), 319–331.

Cohen, L. E. (1981). Modeling crime trends: A criminal opportunity perspective. *Journal of Research in Crime and Delinquency, 18*(1), 138–164.

Crooks, C. V., Scott, K. L., Wolfe, D. A., Chiodo, D., & Killip, S. (2007). Understanding the link between childhood maltreatment and violent delinquency: What do schools have to add? *Child Maltreatment, 12*(3), 269–280.

Elliot, D. S., Willson, W. J., Huizinga, D., Sampson, R. J., Elliot, A., & Rankin, B. (1996). The effects of neighborhood disadvantage on adolescent development. *Journal of Research in Crime and Delinquency, 33*(4), 389–426.

Espelage, D. L., Bosworth, K., & Simon, T. R. (2001). Short-term stability and prospective correlates of bullying in middle-school students: An examination of potential demographic, psychosocial, and environmental influences. *Violence and Victims, 16*(4), 411–426.

Fabio, A., Li, W., Strotmeyer, S., & Branas, C. C. (2004). Racial segregation and county level intentional injury in Pennsylvania: Analysis of hospital discharge data for 1997–1999. *Journal of Epidemiology and Community Health, 58*(4), 346–351.

Fabio, A., Sauber-Schatz, E. K., Barbour, K. E., & Li, W. (2009). The association between county-level injury rates and racial segregation revisited: A multilevel analysis. *American Journal of Public Health, 99*(4), 748–753.

Felson, M. (1987). Routine activities and crime prevention in the developing metropolis. *Criminology, 25*(4), 911–931.

Felson, R. B., Liska, A. E., South, S. J., & McNulty, T. L. (1994). The subculture of violence and delinquency: Individual vs. school context effects. *Social Forces, 73*(1), 155–173.

Fite, P. J., Wynn, P., & Pardini, D. A. (2009). Explaining discrepancies in arrest rates between Black and White male juveniles. *Journal of Consulting and Clinical Psychology, 77*(5), 916–927.

Gottfredson, G. D., Gottfredson, D. C., Payne, A. A., & Gottfredson, N. C. (2005). School climate predictors of school disorder: Results from a national study of delinquency prevention in schools. *Journal of Research in Crime and Delinquency, 42*(4), 412–444.

Harden, K. P., D'Onofrio, B. M., Van Hulle, C., Turkheimer, E., Rodgers, J. L., Waldman, I. D., & Lahey, B. B. (2009). Population density and youth antisocial behavior. *Journal of Child Psychology and Psychiatry and Allied Disciplines, 50*(8), 999–1008.

Hawkins, J. D., Herrenkohl, T. I., Farrington, D. P., Brewer, D., Catalano. R. F., Harachi, T. W., & Cothern, L. (2000). *Predictors of youth violence.* Washington, DC: U.S. Department of Justice, Office of Justice Programs, Office of Juvenile Justice and Delinquency Prevention.

Herrenkohl, T. I., Maguin, E., Hill, K. G., Hawkins, J. D., Abbott, R. D., & Catalano, R. F. (2000). Developmental risk factors for youth violence. *Journal of Adolescent Health, 26*(3), 176–186.

Ingoldsby, E. M., & Shaw, D. S. (2002). Neighborhood contextual factors and early-starting antisocial pathways. *Clinical Child and Family Psychology Review, 5*(1), 21–55.

Johnson, S. L. (2009). Improving the school environment to reduce school violence: A review of the literature. *Journal of School Health, 79*(10), 451–465.

Kling, J. R., Ludwig, J., & Katz, L. F. (2005). Neighborhood effects on crime for female and male youth: Evidence from a randomized housing voucher experiment. *Quarterly Journal of Economics, 120*(1), 87–130.

Krivo, L. J., Peterson, R. D., & Kuhl, D. C. (2009). Segregation, racial structure, and neighborhood violent crime. *American Journal of Sociology, 114*(6), 1765–1802.

Loeber, R., Farrington, D. P., Stouthamer-Loeber, M., & Van Kammen, W. B. (Eds.). (1998). *Antisocial behavior and mental health problems: Explanatory factors in childhood and adolescence.* Mahwah, NJ: Erlbaum.

Loeber, R., & Wikstrom, P. O. (1993). Individual pathways to crime in different types of neighborhoods. In D. P. Farrington, R. J. Sampson, & P. O. Wikstrom (Eds.), *Integrating individual and ecologic aspects of crime* (pp. 169–204). Stockholm, Sweden: National Council on Crime Prevention.

Ludwig, J., Duncan, G. J., & Hirschfield, P. (2001). Urban poverty and juvenile crime: Evidence from a randomized housing-mobility experiment. *Quarterly Journal of Economics, 116*(2), 655–679.

McNeely, C., & Falci, C. (2004). School connectedness and the transition into and out of health-risk behavior among adolescents: A comparison of social belonging and teacher support. *Journal of School Health, 74*(7), 284–292.

Meier, M. H., Slutske, W. S., Arndt, S., & Cadoret, R. J. (2008). Impulsive and callous traits are more strongly associated with delinquent behavior in higher risk neighborhoods among boys and girls. *Journal of Abnormal Psychology, 117*(2), 377–385.

Molnar, B. E., Cerda, M., Roberts, A. L., & Buka, S. L. (2008). Effects of neighborhood resources on aggressive and delinquent behaviors among urban youths. *American Journal of Public Health, 98*(6), 1086–1093.

Reis, J. P., Trockel, M., & Mulhall, P. (2007). Individual and school predictors of middle school aggression. *Youth and Society, 38*(3), 322–347.

Rose, G. (2001). Sick individuals and sick populations. *International Journal of Epidemiology, 30*(3), 427–432.

Rountree, P. W., & Warner, B. D. (1999). Social ties and crime: Is the relationship gendered? *Criminology, 37*(4), 789–814.

Sampson, R. J., & Groves, W. B. (1989). Community structure and crime: Testing social-disorganization theory. *American Journal of Sociology, 94*(4), 774–802.

Sampson, R. J., & Raudenbush, S. W. (1999). Systematic social observation of public spaces: A new look at disorder in urban neighborhoods. *American Journal of Sociology, 105*(3), 603–651.

Sampson, R. J., Raudenbush, S. W., & Earls, F. (1997). Neighborhoods and violent crime: A multilevel study of collective efficacy. *Science, 277*(5328), 918–924.

Schonberg, M. A., & Shaw, D. S. (2007). Risk factors for boy's conduct problems in poor and lower-middle-class neighborhoods. *Journal of Abnormal Child Psychology, 35*(5), 759–772.

Shaw, C. R., & McKay, H. D. (1942). *Juvenile delinquency and urban areas: A study of rates of delinquents in relation to differential characteristics of local communities in American cities*. Chicago, IL: University of Chicago Press.

Simcha-Fagan, O. M., & Schwartz, J. E. (1986). Neighborhood and deliquency: An assessment of contextual effects. *Criminology, 24*(4), 667–699.

Simons, L. G., Simons, R. L., Conger, R. D., & Brody, G. H. (2004). Collective socialization and child conduct problems: A multilevel analysis with an African American sample. *Youth Society, 35*, 267–292.

Stouthamer-Loeber, M., Drinkwater, M., & Loeber, R. (2000). Family functioning profiles, early onset of offending and disadvantaged neighborhoods. *International Journal of Child and Family Welfare, 4*(3), 247–256.

Stouthamer-Loeber, M., Loeber, R., Wei, E., Farrington, D. P., & Wikstrom, P. O. (2002). Risk and promotive effects in the explanation of persistent serious delinquency in boys. *Journal of Consulting and Clinical Psychology, 70*(1), 111–123.

Tolan, P. H., Gorman-Smith, D., & Henry, D. B. (2003). The developmental ecology of urban males' youth violence. *Developmental Psychology, 39*(2), 274–291.

U.S. Department of Health and Human Services. (2001). *Youth violence: A report of the Surgeon General.* Available from http://www.surgeongeneral.gov/library/youthviolence.

U.S. Department of Justice, Federal Bureau of Investigation. (2009). *Crime in the United States, 2008.* Available from http://www.fbi.gov/ucr/cius2008/data/table_32.htm.

Vazsonyi, A. T., Cleveland, H. H., & Wiebe, R. P. (2006). Does the effect of impulsivity on delinquency vary by level of neighborhood disadvantage? *Criminal Justice and Behavior, 33*, 511–541.

Widome, R., Sieving, R. E., Harpin, S. A., & Hearst, M. O. (2008). Measuring neighborhood connection and the association with violence in young adolescents. *Journal of Adolescent Health, 43*(5), 482–489.

Wikstrom, P. O. (1991). *Urban crime, criminals, and victims: The Swedish experience in an Anglo-American comparative perspective.* New York, NY: Springer Verlag.

Wikstrom, P. O. (1998). Communities and crime. In M. Tonry (Ed.), *The handbook of crime and punishment* (pp. 269–301). New York, NY: Oxford University Press.

Wikstrom, P. O., & Loeber, R. (2000). Do disadvantaged neighborhoods cause well-adjusted children to become adolescent delinquents? A study of male juvenile serious offending, individual risk and protective factors, and neighborhood context. *Criminology, 38*(4), 1109–1141.

Wilcox, P., Augustine, M. C., & Clayton, R. R. (2006). Physical environment and crime and misconduct in Kentucky schools. *Journal of Primary Prevention, 27*(3), 293–313.

Wilson, W. J. (1987). *The truly disadvantaged: The inner city, the underclass, and public policy.* Chicago, IL: University of Chicago Press.

10

Epidemiology of Psychiatric and Substance Use Disorders Among Young Offenders: Current Research, Implications, and Future Directions

NIRANJAN KARNIK, PANOS VOSTANIS,
JULIA HUEMER, ELLEN KJELSBERG, RIITTAKERTTU
KALTIALA-HEINO, AND HANS STEINER ■

INTRODUCTION

Psychiatric and substance use disorders in juvenile justice populations are a relatively new area of research and scholarly focus. These underserved youths have generally been found to have very high rates of psychiatric and substance use disorders. Despite these findings, differences exist between countries around the globe, and these are likely due in part to different penal codes and mental health systems. The effect of these epidemiological findings can be seen in one meta-analysis (Fazel, Doll, & Langstrom, 2008) and one comprehensive review (Vermeiren, Jespers, & Moffitt, 2006). Fazel and colleagues (2008), in their metaregression of more than 25 studies including 16,750 youths, found elevated rates for psychotic disorders, major depression, attention-deficit/hyperactivity disorder (ADHD), and conduct disorder. Most of the rates found in their analysis far exceed community rates for these disorders. Colins and colleagues, looking exclusively at studies of detained male adolescents, found that nearly 70% met criteria for a psychiatric diagnosis, with conduct disorder, substance use disorder, oppositional defiant disorder (ODD), and ADHD being the most prevalent

(Colins et al. 2010). Anxiety disorder, major depression, and posttraumatic stress disorder (PTSD) were also found in a significant proportion of the aggregate population reviewed in their study.

Vermeiren and colleagues (2006) took a broader view of the experience of psychiatric disorders in juvenile justice settings. They found that young offenders with police contact or in preadjudicated settings had higher rates of psychiatric disorders than age-matched populations and that these rates were even higher among detained youths. They also found a generally high level of comorbidity among young offenders across the studies that they examined. In particular, they focused attention on the comorbid presence of substance use disorders, especially multiple substance use.

This chapter summarizes the current research on the juvenile justice system from an epidemiological perspective and lays the groundwork for future research. The chapter takes a global perspective and selectively highlights recent research studies from different international regions to examine the findings of psychiatric morbidity in juvenile justice populations. Generally, we have tried to focus on studies that use empirical and validated evaluation measures, as well as large sample sizes. When these were unavailable, we selected studies that show important information about the juvenile justice population or examined countries where little research has been conducted.

UNITED STATES AND CANADA

The United States has produced the largest number of research studies on juvenile delinquency of any country or region in the world. This is likely reflective not only of the resources present in the United States to pursue research studies but also of the relatively large penal system present in the United States, which incarcerates a larger proportion of youths than any other country. It is likely a mistake to consider the United States as a single entity, and a small number of broad epidemiological studies have argued that the United States is, functionally, many regions held together under a federal bureaucracy. This argument has some validity given the differential nature of individual state policies that govern the various penal systems of the states and the degree to which these systems adjudicate youths differently. Given these types of stark variations, some public health researchers have begun to advocate for a more nuanced approach to studying health disparities and epidemiological studies that emphasizes racial/ethnic and socioeconomic variance at a county level. This approach has produced a preliminary model that defines "eight Americas" (Murray et al., 2006). Such an approach to studying psychiatric morbidity in the U.S. juvenile justice system may serve future research in this area. For now, the studies of the U.S. population can be best grouped and examined by the research groups from which they emerge and as representative of individual states.

Illinois

The most prolific and productive research group in the United States focused on the juvenile justice system is Linda Teplin's group based at Northwestern University. Teplin and her colleagues have pursued a series of rigorously designed studies based at the Cook County Juvenile Temporary Detention Center (CCJTDC) that have led the way in understanding the psychopathology present in these settings (Abram et al., 2008; Abram et al., 2004; Abram, Teplin, McClelland, & Dulcan, 2003; Abram et al., 2007; McClelland, Elkington, Teplin, & Abram, 2004; Teplin, Abram, McClelland, Dulcan, & Mericle, 2002; Teplin, Elkington, et al., 2005). These studies largely focus on preadjudicated youths—meaning that they were being held on charges but had yet to be seen by a judge and no determination had yet been made about their status.

Teplin and colleagues chose to use the Diagnostic Interview Schedule for Children (DISC) with more than 1800 youths detained at the CCJTDC from 1995 through 1998. The findings of this series of studies showed that more than two-thirds of youths in their sample met criteria for a psychiatric or substance use disorder. The highest prevalence for boys and girls was seen in marijuana use disorder, conduct disorder, ADHD, major depression, dysthymia, and separation anxiety disorder (Teplin et al., 2002). In a later study this group also examined the prevalence of PTSD and found that roughly 10% of youths met criteria for PTSD and that these youths were far more likely than youths without PTSD to have a comorbid diagnosis of another psychiatric disorder.

Further studies from this group have examined this same cohort of youths from the CCJTDC. They have found that delinquent youths, especially those belonging to racial or ethnic minorities, are disproportionately at higher risk for early, violent deaths than youths in the general population (Teplin, McClelland, Abram, & Mileusnic, 2005). They also found that delinquent youths were at greater risk for HIV or sexually transmitted infections, especially if they met criteria for a substance use disorder (Elkington et al., 2008). This group is pursuing related studies as this cohort ages and enters adulthood.

California

Adopting a similar strategy to Teplin's methodology, Hans Steiner and his group[1] pursued a series of studies at the California Department of Juvenile Justice (CDJJ), formerly known as the California Youth Authority (Steiner, Humphreys, Redlich, Silverman, & Campanaro, 2001). Steiner and his group opted to use the Structured Clinical Interview for Diagnosis (SCID), along with components of the Diagnostic Interview for Children and Adolescents (DICA) and the Structured Interview for the Diagnosis of Personality Disorders (SID-P) on

---

[1] In the interest of full disclosure, Dr. Steiner and Dr. Karnik are coauthors of this chapter. Dr. Karnik has been a member of Dr. Steiner's research laboratory since 2002.

a sample of 790 ethnically diverse youths of both genders. These measures created an opportunity to revisit diagnoses in adulthood using the same instrument instead of having to change between structured evaluations.

Steiner and colleagues (Karnik et al., 2009; Karnik et al., 2010) generally found the same or higher prevalence rates of psychiatric and substance use disorders compared with those that Teplin found. This may have been due to the sample chosen for the CDJJ studies, which focused on youths at least 9 months following incarceration and who were therefore postadjudication. It is possible that the youths were more willing to report their symptoms than preadjudication youths, who might want to avoid admitting to use of substances or to major psychiatric symptoms. What was most surprising in this series of studies was that despite 9 months of incarceration and treatment associated with this confinement, these youths continued to show high levels of morbidity. The findings in this smaller sample with structured interviews expanded previous findings by incorporating self-reports of high levels of both externalizing and internalizing psychiatric morbidity in over 3000 incarcerated boys and girls (Steiner & Redlich, 2002).

In a related set of studies at the CDJJ, Steiner and colleagues found high levels of PTSD among delinquent boys (Steiner, Garcia, & Matthews, 1997), and even higher rates among girls (Cauffman, Feldman, Waterman, & Steiner, 1998). All of these studies made consistent recommendations that attention be paid to these disorders in the evaluation and treatment of young offenders. Linking psychiatric diagnosis to excessive negative activation and deficient self-regulation, Steiner and colleagues were also able to show that personality traits are probable mediators of criminological outcomes; adaptive styles within delinquents were influenced by psychiatric diagnoses such as PTSD (Cauffman et al. 1998; Steiner et al., 1997) and dissociative disorders (Carrion & Steiner, 2000). These diagnoses influence emotional activation and self-regulation to produce differential outcomes at 4.5 years prospective follow-up. The most compromised youths had the highest relapse rates (Steiner, Cauffman, & Duxbury 1999).

Smaller Studies

Several smaller studies have been completed that also examined the prevalence or incidence of psychiatric disorders in detained populations. Most of these studies range in sample size from 50 to 300. The generalizability of these studies could be questioned due to the small sample sizes, but their overall findings appear to be in agreement with the larger Illinois and California studies outlined previously. Pliszka, Sherman, Barrow, and Irick (2000)sampled a population in Texas ($N =$ 50) and found high rates of affective disorders (42%), conduct disorder (60%), and strong evidence of substance use disorders.

Rogers, Pumariega, Atkins, and Cuffe (2006) studied 240 youths in a detention facility in South Carolina, half of whom were referred for mental health services, whereas the others were not. Using both the DISC and the Child Behavior Checklist (CBCL), they found evidence of psychiatric disorders in 96% of the referred group and 69% of the nonreferred group. The highest rates (all greater than 30% of the population) were found for affective, anxiety, and disruptive disorders, and a positive psychosis screen was obtaind in over 40% of the population.

Wasserman, McReynolds, Lucas, Fisher, and Santos studied 292 male youths in facilities in New Jersey and Illinois using the Voice DISC, which allowed for more rapid and time-efficient evaluations. This group found the expected high levels of mood, anxiety, disruptive, and substance use disorders, but they also noted that 3% of their sample reported a past-month suicide attempt and nearly 10% indicated suicidal ideation within the same 1-month period. This finding is significant because of the potential for self-harm among incarcerated youths who are held in isolation or in stressed circumstances produced by the process of confinement.

Among the few Canadian studies available is a small sample of 49 adolescent and 49 controls studied using the DICA (Ulzen & Hamilton, 1998). Ulzen and Hamilton found that over 60% of the incarcerated youths, drawn from two facilities in the Toronto area, met criteria for a psychiatric diagnosis, with ODD and alcohol dependence having the highest prevalence rates. These disorders were closely followed by conduct disorder, depression, and separation anxiety disorder (all present in greater than 30% of the incarcerated youths). PTSD was found in nearly 25% of the incarcerated youths. Several studies from Canada look at subpopulations such as sex offenders or examine the etiological roots of delinquency and therefore fall beyond the purview of this epidemiological review.

UNITED KINGDOM

In recent years, a number of cross-government department policies have adopted a preventive, interagency and multifocal intervention focus, with greater integration with mental health services, both in secure settings and in the community (Ministry of Justice, 2008a, 2008b). These policies were largely based on evidence from epidemiological and, to a lesser extent, intervention studies with young offenders during the previous decade (Townsend et al., 2010). Earlier studies included incarcerated young people in secure settings. More recent research predominantly originated from community samples, following policy changes, in particular the establishment of the Youth Offending Services, which consist of interagency teams providing interventions on offending, substance abuse, education, parenting, and physical and mental health (Callaghan, Pace, Young, & Vostanis, 2003).

Some studies were precipitated by high-profile cases and inquiries on suicides of young people while in custody and by the need to develop more effective methods of assessment and detection. In such a detention setting, Morgan and Hawton (2004) found a lifetime prevalence of 15.6% for deliberate self-harm and 26.6% for suicidal ideation. Suicidal risk was associated with history of sexual abuse, relationship difficulties, and higher depression and anger scores. In a national survey of all young prisoners, Lader, Singleton, and Meltzer (2003) found rates of any personality disorder among males of 76% for those in remand and 81% for sentenced young people and rates of 7% for male and 11% for female youths. They also found that 70% of the sample had used at least one of the listed illicit substances during the previous year. When Harrington and colleagues (2005) followed up a sample of young people 2 years after their admission to secure settings, they found that their mental health needs had persisted or deteriorated without intervention, in contrast with other needs (educational, occupational, and offending), which had improved to some degree.

Other studies established rates of mental health problems at different points of the judicial process and in relation to a range of offenses and sentences. Dolan, Holloway, Bailey, and Smith (1999) interviewed young people who appeared before juvenile courts and established rates of 42% for substance abuse, 26% for high-risk behaviors, and 7% for psychiatric disorders, although the latter was not based on a standardized instrument. Anderson, Vostanis, and Spencer (2004) also interviewed young people at the point of attending courts. They established high rates of accidents and injuries, a similar rate of substance abuse to the previous study (42%), high rates of mental health problems that would justify assessment and intervention (44%), and self-harm ideation (14%). Young people's perceptions of mental illness varied and were influenced by their views on stigma and offending behaviors, lack of coping strategies, previous trauma, and physical ill health. Consequently, the vast majorities were averse to contacting mental health services at the time.

Some researchers adopted a broad definition of mental health needs by measuring psychopathology, as well as related educational and psychosocial difficulties. Nicol and colleagues (2000) adopted an interesting operational definition by screening young people on risk behaviors from a range of penal and welfare settings in a health region of 11.6 million population. The selected young people were assessed on a range of needs and psychiatric disorders. As this was a selected sample, the established rates (30% anxiety, 13% depression, 53% substance abuse) could not be generalized to the population; this was nevertheless a key study that informed policy and service planning in the United Kingdom. In a later study that also used a broad definition of mental health needs, Chitsabesan and colleagues (2006) found rates of need of 31% for mental health, 36% for education and occupation, and 48% for social relationship, as well as a 20% prevalence of learning disability (IQ < 70) in secure and community (Youth Offending Teams) settings, with higher rates of needs among the community sample. Carswell, Maughan, Davis, Davenport, and Goddard (2004) interviewed young people under the care of an inner-city Youth Offending Team with similarly high rates of depression (14.9%), deliberate self-harm (15.2%), anxiety (22.2%), and substance abuse (48.9%), as well as histories of head injuries and ongoing health problems. These findings were replicated, using different measures, in a Youth Offending Service census from a semiurban and rural area (Stallard, Thomason, & Churchyard, 2003). Young people reported frequently using cannabis (47%), whereas 11% had been using heroin, methadone, or crack cocaine.

A number of studies in the United Kingdom did not measure prevalence rates per se but rather examined the relationship between different types of psychopathology and a number of risk factors. For example, Biggam and Power (1999a, 1999b) investigated the relationship between psychological distress (depressive and anxiety symptoms, parasuicidal behavior) with a number of correlates in a Scottish custodial setting and found them to be increased for victims of bullying and for younger people early in their prison sentence. Ireland, Boustead, and Ireland (2005) conducted a similar study and found psychological distress to be associated with emotion-based coping and to also decline during imprisonment, as detachment gradually became the predominant coping style. Self-harm ideation and acts were more prevalent earlier on in custody (Ireland, 2000). Nieland, McCluskie, and Tait (2001) also studied the effect of stressors and coping styles on psychopathology in a secure setting. Low sociability was the strongest predictor of depression scores.

In summary, studies with young offenders in the United Kingdom during the past decade had varied in their sampling, across different community and residential settings, and in their measures. The latter included standardized or specifically devised diagnostic interviews, self-report questionnaires, symptom checklists, and needs assessment interviews. Consequently, not all studies established generalizable prevalence rates of psychiatric disorders and substance use. There are, however, several emerging common themes, which are consistent with findings from the United States and other countries: the overall high rates across all types of psychopathology, their association with a multitude of needs, the identification of risk factors, and the high level of unmet needs. These findings consequently influenced U.K. policy and the development of services with interagency ethos and interventions that aim to address young people's complex and interrelated needs.

CONTINENTAL EUROPE

Epidemiological studies assessing psychopathology and/or substance abuse among children and adolescents who have violated legal norms are relatively uncommon in central Europe. The following section aims to provide an overview of epidemiological studies in this field, with a particular focus on the time period between 2005 and 2010, including relevant earlier studies.

A study in Germany addressed the question of whether temperament and character differ between 170 antisocial incarcerated girls (14–17 years) with and without psychopathy and whether this model differentiates between groups with varied psychopathy symptoms (Sevecke, Lehmkuhl, & Krischer, 2010). The results corroborated the existence of the psychopathy construct in female delinquents; the percentage of girls with core psychopathy dimensions, though, was very small in the sample. The differentiating temperament factors assessed in girls with high psychopathy dimensions as opposed to female juvenile delinquents without psychopathy might indicate that psychopathy is a valid construct that can help to identify a particular subgroup of antisocial girls with core psychopathy symptoms.

A study in Belgium examined a 1-year prevalence rate of psychiatric disorders and the association between psychiatric disorders and type of offending in a sample of 245 male detained adolescents ages 12–17 years (Colins, Vermeiren, Schuyten, & Broekaert, 2009). They found that 83% met criteria for any psychiatric disorder, with over two-thirds having a disruptive behavior disorder and almost three-quarters a substance use disorder; 73% displayed at least two psychiatric disorders. A combination of both externalizing and affective or anxiety disorders was found in 19% of the sample. The prevalence rate of "pure" externalizing disorders was 59%. Property offenders reported significantly higher frequencies of depression, disruptive behavior disorders, substance use disorders, and comorbidity compared with violent offenders. Versatile offenders did not differ from violent offenders, with the exception of more marijuana use disorder assessed in violent offenders.

Köhler, Heinzen, Hinrichs, and Huchzermeier (2009) assessed the prevalence of mental disorders among 149 newly incarcerated male juvenile delinquents (mean age = 19 years) in Germany. The most prevalent diagnoses were conduct disorders (81%), Cluster B personality disorders (up to 62%), and substance-related disorders (up to 60%). Additionally, psychopathic features were assessed among 21% of the participants. The most problematic subgroup among the assessed sample consisted of youths with multiple psychopathologies, including antisocial traits, personality pathology, higher scores on the Psychopathy Checklist, and multiple substance abuse.

Sevecke, Lehmkuhl, and Krischer (2009) investigated relations between psychopathology and psychopathy among 91 male and 123 female adolescent detainees ages 14–19 years. Higher scores for externalizing behavior and psychopathic dimensions were assessed in delinquent males, whereas delinquent females displayed higher internalizing problem scores. A positive relationship between suicidal behavior and the psychopathy total score, as well as the affective, lifestyle, and antisocial dimensions, were found only in girls. In terms of anxious-depressive behavior, a negative relation to the psychopathy total score and to the affective psychopathy factor was assessed for the boys.

In Greece, Maniadaki and Kakouros (2008) determined the prevalence of mental disorders among 93 young males ages 13–24 years. Over three-quarters of the youths displayed ratings indicative of significant mental health problems, with 76.3% showing externalizing and 72% internalizing problems. Apart from delinquent behavior (66.7%), over half of the sample exhibited withdrawal behavior; over 40% displayed depressive and anxious behavior; and a quarter had attention problems.

In a Belgian study, the parent–child agreement with regard to disruptive behavior disorders (with or without impairment) and disorder-related symptoms was assessed in 115 detained males (12–17 years) and one parent of each (Colins, Vermeiren, Schuyten, Broekaert, & Soyez, 2008). Results revealed poor parent–child agreement on the disorder and symptoms, which is consistent with previous studies. Parents reported significantly more unique information on ADHD and ODD, whereas the detained males reported significantly more unique conduct-disorder-related information.

In a study by Krischer, Sevecke, Lehmkuhl, and Pukrop (2007), psychopathology and the applicability of a dimensional approach to personality pathology were assessed in a sample of detained adolescents ($n = 146$), who were compared with adolescent students ($n = 98$) and a healthy control group of adults ($n = 82$). Results showed higher scores on personality disorder traits for juveniles compared with adult controls, whereas the highest scores were observed in criminal juveniles. The dimensional approach to personality pathology proved to assess personality disorder traits in delinquent and nondetained juveniles with sufficient group and criterion validity.

In a study by Plattner, Karnik, and colleagues (2007), the structure of emotions and affective dysregulation of 56 juvenile delinquents from a juvenile hall and 169 participants from a local high school were examined. Delinquents displayed significantly higher levels of negative state and trait emotions when compared with high school peers, a result that might be related to childhood experiences of trauma. Furthermore, delinquents appeared to experience a wider range of emotions and were more likely to experience a confluence of state emotions of sadness and anger under stressed conditions when compared with the high school youths. In a related study, Plattner and colleagues (2009) also were able to replicate the finding by Steiner et al. (1999) and Vermeiren, Schwab-Stone, Ruchkin, De Clippele, and Deboutte (2002) regarding the prognostic importance of psychiatric morbidity and relapse rates in an Austrian sample of delinquents.

In a study conducted in Switzerland, the prevalence of affective disorder, a history of traumatic events, and the prevalence of PTSD diagnoses in their relationship to "psychopathy" were assessed in a sample of 102 inmates ages 17–27 years (Moeller & Hell, 2003). Affective disorder was assessed in 28% of the sample, and 29% of youths reported a history of suicide attempts. The Psychopathy Checklist score was significantly correlated with the number of prior threatening events, but PTSD could not be assessed in the "psychopathic" group. In the "nonpsychopathic" group, the prevalence of affective disorder was significantly higher (Moeller & Hell, 2003).

Further studies in continental Europe have looked at particular aspects of psychiatric symptoms among juvenile detainees, such as the nature of psychotic experiences (Colins, Vermeiren, Vreugdenhil, et al., 2009), dissociation (Zimmermann, 2006), psychological stress (Krischer & Sevecke, 2008), linkages between alexithymia and delinquency (Plattner et al., 2003), and the association of early childhood victimization (Stasevic, Ropac, & Lucev, 2005) and that of stress (Obschonka, Warns, Schulte-Markwort, & Barkmann, 2010) with juvenile delinquency.

Overall, research has been conducted among specific cohorts of juvenile delinquents or has compared juvenile delinquents with specific psychiatric cohorts

on the following: prevalence, psychiatric comorbidity, and psychosocial implications of ADHD (Rosler, Retz, Yaqoobi, Burg, & Retz-Junginger, 2009); drug
addiction in young offenders with and without ADHD (Retz et al. 2007); externalizing and internalizing psychopathology in delinquent adolescent girls and
suicide attempters (Ribakoviene, Adomaitiene, Danyte, & Kalkyte, 2008); the
relationship between ADHD, conduct disorder, and psychopathy in adolescent
male and female detainees (Sevecke, Kosson, & Krischer, 2009); ADHD and personality disorders in treated inpatient and incarcerated adolescents (Sevecke,
Lehmkuhl, & Krischer, 2008); an evaluation of to what measure typical traits of
psychopathy in adults are present in severe juvenile offenders (Atarhouch et al.,
2004); an assessment of differences between adolescents meeting the DSM-IV
criteria for conduct disorder and a control population, assessed with a dimensional personality inventory (Atarhouch et al., 2004); and the examination of
suicidality, psychopathology, and gender in incarcerated adolescents (Plattner,
The, et al., 2007). We also wish to draw specific attention to a 30-year follow-up
study on the long-term outcome of delinquent children, with a particular focus
on early-onset and late-onset delinquency as a predictor of adult criminality
(Remschmidt & Walter, 2010).

NORDIC COUNTRIES

The Nordic countries make up a region in Northern Europe and consist of five
countries: Denmark, Finland, Iceland, Norway, and Sweden. The combined population is approximately 25 million. The economic and social systems are similar
in the five countries, with mixed-market economies and generous welfare systems relative to many other developed countries. The emphasis is on maximizing
labor force participation and egalitarian and extensive benefit levels.

In spite of widespread similarities, each of the Nordic countries has its own
crime legislation and judicial procedures, and the correctional systems vary
somewhat from country to country. But similarities outshine differences. Crime
levels and incarceration rates are low in all five Nordic countries. The quality
of most correctional facilities is good, with adequate health services (Salize,
Dressing, & Kief, 2007). All countries have the same age of criminal responsibility, 15 years. There is a broad consensus across countries that the imprisonment of young persons should be avoided, if at all possible. Even so, the countries
differ in their attitudes toward establishing specific prisons for young people.
Denmark has juvenile prisons, whereas the other Nordic countries do not. In
Sweden, young offenders sentenced to imprisonment are usually serving their
sentences in social sector institutions. In Finland, the justice system cannot place
youths in social welfare institutions, but young offenders are often placed in such
institutions under the Child Welfare Act. Norway is in the process of planning
a juvenile prison.

The Nordic countries, with their stable and well-monitored populations,
lend themselves easily to epidemiological studies. Even so, there is a paucity of

scientifically sound studies on mental disorders in young prisoners in the Nordic countries. The following review of epidemiological studies of mental disorders in young prisoners is limited to studies that mainly have used established instruments in their diagnostic assessments. We have found seven studies fulfilling these criteria. No studies were found for Sweden or Iceland that met epidemiological criteria.

Finland

Haapasalo and Hämäläinen (1996) compared childhood abuse and neglect, family adversities, and psychiatric problems among young violent and property offenders. A random sample of offenders ages 15–22 serving their prison sentences was studied. The offenders were classified as either violent offenders or property offenders based on their lifetime crime register information. Psychiatric diagnoses were set according to DSM-IV, after diagnostic interview with the Diagnostic Interview for Children and Adolescents—Adolescent Version (DICA-R-A). A structured interview tailored for this study was used to collect information about childhood abuse and neglect. File information was collected from health and welfare agencies. In addition, the parents of the offenders were interviewed, and sociodemographic and family information was collected. Psychiatric disorders and abuse and neglect history, as well as family adversities such as parental alcoholism, were common. There were no differences between the two offender groups. Of the violent (property) offenders, 23.1% (24.3%) had ODD, 48.1% (51.4%) had ADHD, all had conduct disorder, 84.6% (83.7%) had alcohol dependence, 13.5% (16.2%) had a current depressive episode, 71.2% (59.5%) had a history of depressive episode, 61.5% (48.6%) had cannabis dependence, 71.2% (51.4%) had substance abuse, and 61.5% (43.2%) had substance dependence.

Sailas, Feodoroff, Virkkunen, and Wahlbeck (2005) investigated possible time trends in psychiatric morbidity in young prisoners. The study comprised young (15- to 21-year-old) prisoners serving their sentences in 1984–1985 and 1994–1995. Personal identification numbers were linked with hospital discharge registers. The oldest cohort comprised 656 prisoners and the youngest, 370. Hospital discharge register data were monitored for the period 1980–1989 for the oldest cohort and for 1990–1999 for the youngest. Risk for psychiatric hospitalization was calculated for young prisoners, compared with age, sex, and place of birth for matched population controls. In addition, the two prisoner cohorts were compared. The prisoners had an increased risk for psychiatric hospitalization compared with the population controls for all major mental disorders: psychosis (odds ratio [OR] = 3.03 in the oldest cohort and OR = 12.45 in the youngest), depression (4.34 and 5.81), personality disorder (20.17 and 26.73), and substance dependence (19.91 and 54.60). For any psychiatric diagnosis the ORs were 10.66 and 18.73, respectively. The number of prisoners with at least one psychiatric hospitalization increased from the first cohort to the second (age-adjusted OR = 1.8, 95% confidence interval [CI] = 1.3–2.3), whereas in the general population no increased risk for psychiatric hospitalization was seen over the study period. Age-adjusted OR for psychiatric treatment due to psychosis was 2.7 (95% CI = 1.4–5.1) in the youngest cohort and for substance dependence, 3.0 (95% CI = 2.0–4.6). The study concluded that young prison inmates have a high number of mental disorders compared with young people in the general population. And, most important, the prevalence of mental disorders among young prisoners has increased over time, with no parallel increase observed in the general population.

Another study by Sailas and colleagues (2006) also explored the mortality of young offenders sentenced to prison and the relationship between psychiatric morbidity and early death among young prisoners. All prisoners in the country between the ages of 15 and 21 and sentenced between 1984 and 2000 were identified in the prison court register. Register linkages to the death register and to the Finnish Health Care Register were performed in order to monitor deaths and psychiatric hospitalizations, respectively. Information on psychiatric hospitalization was collected for the years 1971–2001. Age- and sex-matched population controls were followed up in the same registers. The standardized mortality ratio (SMR) for young male offenders sentenced to prison was 7.4 (95% CI = 6.7–8.1), with mortality increasing from older to younger cohorts. The SMR for young prisoners who had been psychiatrically hospitalized was 8.3 (95% CI = 7.3–9.4) and for those without psychiatric hospitalization, 6.3 (95% CI = 5.4–7.3). SMR was increased in all psychiatric diagnostic groups. The authors concluded that young prisoners are at high risk of premature death, particularly those with psychiatric disorders.

Lindberg and colleagues (2009) evaluated psychopathic personality traits among adolescent homicide offenders and compared them with adult homicide offenders. Data were taken from a nationwide register-based evaluation of homicide offenders undergoing forensic psychiatric examinations in order to assess criminal responsibility. All male adolescent homicide offenders (n = 57) and a random sample of adult homicide offenders (n = 57) were included. Psychopathy was retrospectively measured by the Hare Psychopathy Checklist—Revised (PCL-R). No significant differences were found between the adolescent and the adult homicide offenders on PCL-R total scores or on Factor 2 (social deviance). However, the adults scored higher on Factor 1 (interpersonal/affective). The boys with high PCL-R scores (> 26) differed markedly from the boys with low scores, having graver crime history, more use of excessive violence, and more psychiatric and social welfare interventions in the past. In conclusion, adolescent homicide offenders were as antisocial as their adult counterparts. Adults did, however, display more affective/interpersonal features of psychopathy.

Hagelstam and Häkkänen (2006) studied the offender and offense characteristics of young offenders accused of homicide in 1990–2001. The material comprised 57 offenders between the ages of 15 and 21. The data were collected from files created in forensic psychiatric examinations and comprised clinical psychiatric diagnoses, psychological tests, family, school, child welfare, psychiatric treatment, and crime histories, as well as characteristics of the present crime: victim, type of violence, setting, motive, acting alone or in group. Of the young homicide offenders, 39% presented with alcohol dependence and 12% with drug dependence. The prevalence of conduct disorder was 40%. Just over half could be diagnosed with personality disorders, mainly antisocial personality disorder, if one discarded the criterion that an antisocial personality disorder diagnosis cannot be given before the age of 18 (not all offenders had turned 18). A total of 7% had schizophrenia, and 19% were known to have displayed self-destructive or suicidal behaviors. Only 9% had a psychiatric treatment contact at the time of the offense. It is noteworthy that 32% did not receive any psychiatric diagnosis, including substance use. As a whole, family adversities and numerous indicators of poor social adjustment were present in this group of young offenders accused of homicide.

Denmark

Gosden, Kramp, Gabrielsen, and Sestoft (2003) investigated the prevalence of mental disorders among one hundred 15- to 17-year-old males consecutively remanded to prison in East Denmark during a 1-year period. East Denmark contains 44% of the country's population. The Present State Examination (PSE-10), Schedule for Affective Disorders and Schizophrenia for School-Age Children—Present and Lifetime Version (K-SADS-PL), and SCID-II were used in the diagnostic assessments eliciting International Classification of Diseases (ICD-10) diagnoses, in addition to DSM-IV ADHD. The past-year prevalence for any mental disorder, including substance use disorder, was 69%. The most prevalent disorder encountered was substance use disorder, 41%. Paranoid schizophrenia was present in 2% of the sample, and 2% had schizotypal disorder. It was probable that 36% had a personality disorder, keeping in mind that ICD-10 assigns personality disorder diagnoses only after 16 years of age. Conduct disorder was found in 31%, and 11% had ADHD (DSM-IV). Comorbidity was high: 41% had two or more disorders. Screening of the Danish Psychiatric Case Register demonstrated that 10% had been in contact with the psychiatric health care services, and 33% of the boys had been in contact with a psychologist. The boys were socially disadvantaged with low educational attainment and low parental SES, compared with the general population. One-half of the sample were of non-Danish ethnicity.

Norway

Sorland and Kjelsberg (2009) approached 42 consecutively admitted males under 20 years of age who had been remanded to one large prison in Norway, and 40 of them agreed to participate in an epidemiological study. Three out of four had immigrant backgrounds. Their mental health was assessed by a structured diagnostic instrument (K-SADS). Only four participants had no mental disorder. Comorbidity was frequent, with a mean of 2.5 diagnoses among those 36 with mental disorders. Psychoactive substance abuse/dependence ($N = 31$) and serious conduct disorders were most frequently encountered ($N = 30$). Nine of those with conduct disorder fulfilled the ICD-10 criteria for a dissocial personality disorder. Anxiety and/or depressive disorders ($N = 14$) and hyperkinetic disorders ($N = 12$) were also frequent. Therapeutic needs were largely unmet. Social problems were frequent, with disrupted education and unemployment.

AUSTRALIA AND THE PACIFIC RIM

Non-Western countries are often neglected in reviews of juvenile delin-quency. In a sample of 100 young female offenders in Sydney, Australia, Dixon, Howie, and Starling (2004, 2005) used the K-SADS-PL. They found that over 90% of the girls in their sample met criteria for conduct disorder and that 85% had a substance use disorder. They further found high rates of alcohol use disorder (separate from other substances) and depression; 20% of the sample had PTSD. These were noted to be significantly different from 100 age- and socioeconomically matched controls from Sydney-area high schools. Dixon and colleagues proceeded to look more closely at their subsample of PTSD-affected girls and found that over 70% had histories of sexual abuse, with about 30% of these having had instances of repeated abuse. More than 10% of their PTSD sample had witnessed a murder, and the presence of PTSD seemed to increase the odds of suicide attempts in this subpopulation.

A very focused study has been published in Japan looking at the prevalence of PTSD among 318 delinquent youths, including 59 females, drawn from a pre-adjudicated detained sample in Tokyo (Yoshinaga, Kadomoto, Otani, Sasaki, & Kato, 2004). Yoshinaga and colleagues found that 8% of their sample met full criteria for PTSD using the Japanese version of the clinician-administered PTSD scale for DSM-IV. The sources of trauma were varied, but males appeared to be more likely to have encountered some type of physical trauma.

AFRICA, THE MIDDLE EAST, AND SOUTH AMERICA

A very small number of studies appeared from these regions. Much of the litera-ture contained reports that lacked validated assessments or used very small sam-ples, and therefore they could not be included in this epidemiological review.

CONCLUSIONS AND FUTURE DIRECTIONS

The psychiatric epidemiological literature on youths in the juvenile justice system is slowly evolving. The research is moving from a very parochial state (i.e., scattered among different bodies of knowledge—sociology, criminology, psychiatry, basic science) toward building a more integrated database (Blair, Karnik, Coccaro, & Steiner, 2009). The broad findings are clear: that virtually regardless of context, young offenders exhibit very high rates of psychiatric morbidity. A small body of research has linked the diagnosis of psychiatric disorders to recidivism (Steiner et al., 1999; Vermeiren et al. 2002). An open issue is how to account for the influence of diagnosis on recidivism. Several models could potentially be used to examine this question. Diagnostic groups (i.e., trauma-related or others), broad bands of psychopathology (i.e., external-izing, internalizing, or personality), or specific diagnoses could all be used to examine this question more closely. Which approach best predicts recidivism and how these understandings can be used from a treatment perspective to reduce reoffending continue to be open questions in need of research.

This review has taken a global perspective on delinquency in order to sur-vey, in the widest possible manner, the state of the literature. Other reviews have taken different approaches. Vermeiren and colleagues (2006) sought to describe the various findings by diagnostic class, and Fazel and colleagues (2008) com-pleted a metaregression. Both of these studies undertake an important task in synthesizing the literature to date. One major gap that neither of these studies examines is the differential effects of the context of the various studies. Health care and penal systems in the various regions of the world undoubtedly affect which youths are incarcerated. In the United States, the high rate of incarcer-ation leads to a significant number of youths with psychiatric diagnoses being placed in the juvenile justice system. Conversely, many European countries have diversion programs that seek to avoid incarceration when possible. The result in some studies has been a finding that there is a greater psychiatric morbidity among the youths in European studies.

One general finding of this review has been that regardless of context, the juvenile justice system is the *de facto* mental health system for youths and that this situation disproportionately affects underserved and minority youths. Such a finding should give pause to policymakers who are often eager to fund the penal system but apt to cut the health service systems. This review concludes that the penal and health care systems are dynamically linked and that changes to one force changes to the other that may not be fully visible to policymakers.

There is certainly a need for research on service delivery. Diagnostic practices within juvenile justice settings are highly varied and in need of critical study. Second, there is a need to consider the various models of care, for instance, comparing inte-grated treatment in which the provider is embedded within the justice system with a consultation model whereby the provider is outside of the system but provides expert advice and occasional treatment. Both of these models are used in various locations, but their differential effects are not understood at this point. Finally, there is a need to study the adequacy of treatment and its effects on young offenders.

There is a continuing need for larger studies in more varied locations. With the significant differences between penal codes of various countries, as well as the presence or absence of diversion programs, the current research findings would benefit significantly from studies that examine both young offenders in diversion systems and those who are incarcerated. It would be valuable to follow cohorts of high-risk youths over time (as Teplin and colleagues are doing) to see how they benefit from or are harmed by various systems of care. Teplin's approach should ideally be expanded and used as a template for other investigators in other locations so as to allow integration of data and better comparative analyses. In this regard, the use of a consistent set of instruments would be beneficial to the field. Instruments designed exclusively for children or adults create problems for ongoing prospective studies. Finally, there would be significant value, despite the differences in the various countries, in doing cross-national studies of juvenile delinquency. Such studies are likely to highlight important gaps and structural features that limit the success of both penal and mental health care systems across the countries and thereby provide a better means for developing integrated interventions.

To this point, the needs of young offenders have been established. The broad consistency of the various studies despite varied systems should serve as a call for better interventions. Intervention studies in this population would benefit from using diagnostic instruments as a means to track efficacy over longer periods of time rather than relying on short-term symptomatic evaluations.

As the field of psychiatric epidemiology in the juvenile justice system develops, more data should become available to guide policymakers, clinicians, and researchers toward the development of more effective strategies for treating young offenders and reducing their recidivism (Steiner et al., 2001).

REFERENCES

Abram, K. M., Choe, J. Y., Washburn, J. J., Teplin, L. A., King, D. C., & Dulcan, M. K. (2008). Suicidal ideation and behaviors among youths in juvenile detention. *Journal of the American Academy of Child and Adolescent Psychiatry, 47*(3), 291–300.

Abram, K. M., Teplin, L. A., Charles, D. R., Longworth, S. L., McClelland, G. M., & Dulcan, M. K. (2004). Posttraumatic stress disorder and trauma in youth in juvenile detention. *Archives of General Psychiatry, 61*(4), 403–410.

Abram, K. M., Teplin, L. A., McClelland, G. M., & Dulcan, M. K. (2003). Comorbid psychiatric disorders in youth in juvenile detention. *Archives of General Psychiatry, 60*(11), 1097–1108.

Abram, K. M., Washburn, J. J., Teplin, L. A., Emanuel, K. M., Romero, E. G., & McClelland, G. M. (2007). Posttraumatic stress disorder and psychiatric comorbidity among detained youths. *Psychiatric Services, 58*(10), 1311–1316.

Anderson, L., Vostanis, P., & Spencer, N. (2004). Health needs of young offenders. *Journal of Child Health Care, 8*(2), 149–164.

Atarhouch, N., Hoffmann, E., Adam, S., Titeca, J., Stillemans, E., Fossion, P., . . . Servais, L. (2004)). Évaluation des traits caractéristiques de la psychopathie chez les adolescents délinquants. [Evaluation of typical psychopathic traits with juvenile offenders.] *Encephale, 30*(4), 369–375.

Biggam, F. H., & Power, K. G. (1999a). Social problem-solving skills and psychological distress among incarcerated young offenders: The issue of bullying and victimization. *Cognitive Therapy and Research, 23*(3), 307–326.

Biggam, F. H., & Power, K. G. (1999b). Suicidality and the state-trait debate on problem-solving deficits: A re-examination with incarcerated young offenders. *Archives of Suicide Research, 5*(1), 27–42.

Blair, R. J., Karnik, N. S., Coccaro, E. F., & Steiner, H. (2009). Taxonomy and neurobiology of aggression. In P. Ash, E. Benedek, & C. Scott (Eds.), *Principles and practices of child and adolescent forensic mental health* (pp. 267–278). Washington, DC: American Psychiatric Publishing.

Callaghan, J., Pace, F., Young, B., & Vostanis, P. (2003). Primary mental health workers within youth offending teams: A new service model. *Journal of Adolescence, 26*(2), 185–199.

Carrion, V. G., & Steiner, H. (2000). Trauma and dissociation in delinquent adolescents. *Journal of the American Academy of Child and Adolescent Psychiatry, 39*(3), 353–359.

Carswell, K., Maughan, B., Davis, H., Davenport, F., & Goddard, N. (2004). The psychosocial needs of young offenders and adolescents from an inner city area. *Journal of Adolescence, 27*(4), 415–428.

Cauffman, E., Feldman, S. S., Waterman, J., & Steiner, H. (1998). Posttraumatic stress disorder among female juvenile offenders. *Journal of the American Academy of Child and Adolescent Psychiatry, 37*(11), 1209–1216.

Chitsabesan, P., Kroll, L., Bailey, S., Kenning, C., Sneider, S., MacDonald, W., & Theodosiou, L. (2006). Mental health needs of young offenders in custody and in the community. *British Journal of Psychiatry, 188*, 534–540.

Colins, O., Vermeiren, R., Schuyten, G., & Broekaert, E. (2009). Psychiatric disorders in property, violent, and versatile offending detained male adolescents. *American Journal of Orthopsychiatry, 79*(1), 31–38.

Colins, O., Vermeiren, R., Schuyten, G., Broekaert, G., & Soyez, V. (2008). Informant agreement in the assessment of disruptive behavior disorders in detained minors in Belgium: A diagnosis-level and symptom-level examination. *Journal of Clinical Psychiatry, 69*(1), 141–148.

Colins, O., Vermeiren, R., Vreugdenhil, C., Schuyten, G., Broekaert, E., & Krabbendam, A. (2009). Are psychotic experiences among detained juvenile offenders explained by trauma and substance use? *Drug and Alcohol Dependence, 100*(1–2), 39–46.

Colins, O., Vermeiren, R., Vreugdenhil, C., van den Brink, W., Doreleijers, T., & Broekaert, E. (2010). Psychiatric disorders in detained male adolescents: A systematic literature review. *Canadian Journal of Psychiatry, 55*(4), 255–263.

Dixon, A., Howie, P., & Starling, J. (2004). Psychopathology in female juvenile offenders. *Journal of Child Psychology and Psychiatry, 45*(6), 1150–1158.

Dixon, A., Howie, P., & Starling, J. (2005). Trauma exposure, posttraumatic stress, and psychiatric comorbidity in female juvenile offenders. *Journal of the American Academy of Child and Adolescent Psychiatry, 44*(8), 798–806.

Dolan, M., Holloway, J., Bailey, S., & Smith, C. (1999). Health status of juvenile offenders: A survey of young offenders appearing before the juvenile courts. *Journal of Adolescence, 22*(1), 137–144.

Elkington, K. S., Teplin, L. A., Mericle, A. A., Welty, L. J., Romero, E. G., & Abram, K. M. (2008). HIV/sexually transmitted infection risk behaviors in delinquent youth with psychiatric disorders: A longitudinal study. *Journal of the American Academy of Child and Adolescent Psychiatry, 47*(8), 901–911.

Fazel, S., Doll, H., & Langstrom, N. (2008). Mental disorders among adolescents in juvenile detention and correctional facilities: A systematic review and metaregression analysis of 25 surveys. *Journal of the American Academy of Child and Adolescent Psychiatry, 47*(9), 1010–1019.

Gosden, N. P., Kramp, P., Gabrielsen, G., & Sestoft, D. (2003). Prevalence of mental disorders among 15–17-year-old male adolescent remand prisoners in Denmark. *Acta Psychiatrica Scandinavica, 107*(2), 102–110.

Haapasalo, J., & Hämäläinen, T. (1996). Childhood family problems and current psychiatric problems among young violent and property offenders. *Journal of the American Academy of Child and Adolescent Psychiatry, 35*(10), 1394–1401.

Hagelstam, C., & Häkkänen, H. (2006). Adolescent homicides in Finland: Offence and offender characteristics. *Forensic Science International, 164*(2–3), 110–115.

Harrington, R. C., Kroll, L., Rothwell, J., McCarthy, K., Bradley, D., & Bailey, S. (2005). Psychosocial needs of boys in secure care for serious or persistent offending. *Journal of Child Psychology and Psychiatry, 46*(8), 859–866.

Ireland, J. L. (2000). A descriptive analysis of self-harm reports among a sample of incarcerated adolescent males. *Journal of Adolescence, 23*(5), 605–613.

Ireland, J. L., Boustead, R., & Ireland, C. A. (2005). Coping style and psychological health among adolescent prisoners: A study of young and juvenile offenders. *Journal of Adolescence, 28*(3), 411–423.

Karnik, N. S., Soller, M., Redlich, A., Silverman, M., Kraemer, H. C., Haapanen, R., & Steiner, H. (2009). Prevalence of and gender differences in psychiatric disorders among juvenile delinquents incarcerated for nine months. *Psychiatric Services, 60*(6), 838–841.

Karnik, N. S., Soller, M. V., Redlich, A., Silverman, M. A., Kraemer, H. C., Haapanen, R., & Steiner, H. (2010). Prevalence differences of psychiatric disorders among youth after nine months or more of incarceration by race/ethnicity and age. *Journal of Health Care for the Poor and Underserved, 21*(1), 237–250.

Köhler, D., Heinzen, H., Hinrichs, G., & Huchzermeier, C. (2009). The prevalence of mental disorders in a German sample of male incarcerated juvenile offenders. *International Journal of Offender Therapy and Comparative Criminology, 53*(2), 211–227.

Krischer, M. K., & Sevecke, K. (2008). Early traumatization and psychopathy in female and male juvenile offenders. *International Journal of Law and Psychiatry, 31*(3), 253–262.

Krischer, M. K., Sevecke, K., Lehmkuhl, G., & Pukrop, R. (2007). Dimensional assessment of personality pathology in female and male juvenile delinquents. *Journal of Personality Disorders, 21*(6), 675–689.

Lader, D., Singleton, N., & Meltzer, H. (2003). Psychiatric morbidity among young offenders in England and Wales. *International Review of Psychiatry, 15*(1–2), 144–147. (Reprinted from Office for National Statistics, 2000).

Lindberg, N., Laajasalo, T., Holi, M., Putkonen, H., Weizmann-Henelius, G., & Hakkanen-Nyholm, H. (2009). Psychopathic traits and offender characteristics: A nationwide consecutive sample of homicidal male adolescents. *BMC Psychiatry, 9*, 18.

Maniadaki, K., & Kakouros, E. (2008). Social and mental health profiles of young male offenders in detention in Greece. *Criminal Behavior and Mental Health, 18*(4), 207–215.

McClelland, G. M., Elkington, K. S., Teplin, L. A., & Abram, K. M. (2004). Multiple substance use disorders in juvenile detainees. *Journal of the American Academy of Child and Adolescent Psychiatry, 43*(10), 1215–1224.

Ministry of Justice. (2008a). *Reducing re-offending: Supporting families, creating better futures.* London: Author.

Ministry of Justice. (2008b). *Youth crime action plan, 2008.* London: Author.

Moeller, A. A., & Hell, D. (2003). Affective disorder and "psychopathy" in a sample of younger male delinquents. *Acta Psychiatrica Scandinavica, 107*(3), 203–207.

Morgan, J., & Hawton, K. (2004). Self-reported suicidal behavior in juvenile offenders in custody: Prevalence and associated factors. *Crisis: The Journal of Crisis Intervention and Suicide Prevention, 25*(1), 8–11.

Murray, C. J., Kulkarni, S. C., Michaud, C., Tomijima, N., Bulzacchelli, M. T., Iandiorio, T. J., & Ezzati, M. (2006). Eight Americas: Investigating mortality disparities across races, counties, and race-counties in the United States. *PLoS Medicine, 3*(9), e260.

Nicol, R., Stretch, D., Whitney, I., Jones, K., Garfield, P., Turner, K., & Stanion, B. (2000). Mental health needs and services for severely troubled and troubling young people including young offenders in an N.H.S. region. *Journal of Adolescence, 23* (3), 243–261.

Nieland, M., McCluskie, C., & Tait, E. (2001). Prediction of psychological distress in young offenders. *Legal and Criminological Psychology, 6*(1), 29–47.

Obschonka, M., Warns, M., Schulte-Markwort, M., & Barkmann, C. (2010). Psychische Belastung bei deutschsprachigen jugendlichen und heranwachsenden Inhaftierten in der Hafteingangssituation. [Psychological distress among German-speaking young prison inmates after imprisonment]. *Praxis der Kinderpsychologie und Kinderpsychiatrie, 59*(2), 101–118.

Plattner, B., Karnik, N., Jo, B., Hall, R. E., Schallauer, A., Carrion, V., . . . Steiner, H. (2007). State and trait emotions in delinquent adolescents. *Child Psychiatry and Human Development, 38*(2), 155–169.

Plattner, B., Silvermann, M. A., Redlich, A. D., Carrion, V. G., Feucht, M., Friedrich, M. H., & Steiner, H. (2003). Pathways to dissociation: intrafamilial versus extrafamilial trauma in juvenile delinquents. *Journal of Nervous and Mental Disease, 191*(12), 781–788.

Plattner, B., Steiner, H., The, S. S., Kraemer, H. C., Bauer, S. M., Kindler, J., . . . Feucht, M. (2009). Sex-specific predictors of criminal recidivism in a representative sample of incarcerated youth. *Comprehensive Psychiatry, 50*(5), 400–407.

Plattner, B., The, S. S., Kraemer, H. C., Williams, R. P., Bauer, S. M., Kindler, J., . . . Steiner, H. (2007). Suicidality, psychopathology, and gender in incarcerated adolescents in Austria. *Journal of Clinical Psychiatry, 68*(10), 1593–1600.

Pliszka, S. R., Sherman, J. O., Barrow, M. V., & Irick, S. (2000). Affective disorder in juvenile offenders: A preliminary study. *American Journal of Psychiatry, 157*(1), 130–132.

Remschmidt, H., & Walter, R. (2010). The long-term outcome of delinquent children: A 30-year follow-up study. *Journal of Neural Transmission, 117*(5), 663–677.

Retz, W., Retz-Junginger, P., Schneider, M., Scherk, H., Hengesch, G., & Rosler, M. (2007). Suchtmittelgebrauch Bei Jungen Erwachsenen Straftatern Mit Und Ohne Aufmerksamkeitsdefizit-/Hyperaktivitatsstorung (Adhs). [Drug addiction in young prison inmates with and without attention deficit hyperactivity disorder (ADHD)]. *Fortschritte der Neurologie-Psychiatrie, 75*(5), 285–292.

Ribakoviene, V., Adomaitiene, V., Danyte, D., & Kalkyte, R. (2008). Bandžiusių žudytis ir delinkventinio elgesio mergínų psichologiniai veiksniai. [Psychological factors of delinquent adolescent girls and suicide attempters]. *Medicina (Kaunas), 44*(2), 147–155.

Rogers, K. M., Pumariega, A. J., Atkins, D. L., & Cuffe, S. P. (2006). Conditions associated with identification of mentally ill youths in juvenile detention. *Community Mental Health Journal, 42*(1), 25–40.

Rosler, M., Retz, W., Yaqoobi, K., Burg, E., & Retz-Junginger, P. (2009). Attention deficit/hyperactivity disorder in female offenders: Prevalence, psychiatric comorbidity and psychosocial implications. *European Archives of Psychiatry and Clinical Neuroscience, 259*(2), 98–105.

Sailas, E. S., Feodoroff, B., Lindberg, N. C., Virkkunen, M. E., Sund, R., & Wahlbeck, K. (2006). The mortality of young offenders sentenced to prison and its association with psychiatric disorders: a register study. *European Journal of Public Health, 16*(2), 193–197.

Sailas, E. S., Feodoroff, B., Virkkunen, M., & Wahlbeck, K. (2005). Mental disorders in prison populations aged 15–21: National register study of two cohorts in Finland. *BMJ, 330*(7504), 1364–1365.

Salize, H. J., Dressing, H., & Kief, C. (2007). *Mentally disordered persons in European prison systems: Needs, programmes and outcomes (EUPRIS).* Mannheim, Germany: Central Institute of Mental Health.

Sevecke, K., Kosson, D. S., & Krischer, M. K. (2009). The relationship between attention deficit hyperactivity disorder, conduct disorder, and psychopathy in adolescent male and female detainees. *Behavioral Sciences and the Law, 27*(4), 577–598.

Sevecke, K., Lehmkuhl, G., & Krischer, M. K. (2008). Aufmerksamkeitsdefizit-/Hyperaktivitätsstörung und Persönlichkeitsstörungen bei klinisch behandelten und bei inhaftierten Jugendlichen. [Attention-deficit hyperactivity disorder and personality disorders in treated in-patient and incarcerated adolescents]. *Praxis der Kinderpsychologie und Kinderpsychiatrie, 57*(8–9), 641–661.

Sevecke, K., Lehmkuhl, G., Krischer, M. K. (2009). Examining relations between psychopathology and psychopathy dimensions among adolescent female and male offenders. *European Child and Adolescent Psychiatry, 18*(2), 85–95.

Sevecke, K., Lehmkuhl, G., & Krischer, M. K. (2010). Psychopathy-, Temperaments-und Charakterdimensionen bei inhaftierten Mädchen. [Psychopathy, temperament and antisocial behaviour in girls]. *Zeitschrift für Kinder- Jugendpsychiatrie und Psychotherapie, 38*(2), 91–101.

Sørland, T. O., & Kjelsberg, E. (2009). Mental helse hos varetektsfengslede tenårings-gutter. [Mental health among teenage boys remanded to prison]. *Tidsskrift for den Norske legeforening 129*(23), 2472–2475.

Stallard, P., Thomason, J., & Churchyard, S. (2003). The mental health of young people attending a Youth Offending Team: A descriptive study. *Journal of Adolescence, 26*(1), 33–43.

Stasevic, I., Ropac, D., & Lucev, O. (2005). Association of stress and delinquency in children and adolescents. *Collegium Antropologicum, 29*(1), 27–32.

Steiner, H., Cauffman, E., & Duxbury, E. (1999). Personality traits in juvenile delinquents: Relation to criminal behavior and recidivism. *Journal of the American Academy of Child and Adolescent Psychiatry, 38*(3), 256–262.

Steiner, H., Garcia, I. G., & Matthews, Z. (1997). Posttraumatic stress disorder in incarcerated juvenile delinquents. *Journal of the American Academy of Child and Adolescent Psychiatry, 36*(3), 357–365.

Steiner, H., Humphreys, K., Redlich, A., Silverman, M., & Campanaro, A. (2001). *The assessment of the mental health system of the California Youth Authority: Report to Governor Gray Davis.* Sacramento: State of California.

Steiner, H., & Redlich, A. (2002). Child psychiatry and the juvenile court. In M. Lewis (Ed.), *Child psychiatry* (pp. 1417–1425). New York, NY: Williams & Wilkins.

Teplin, L. A., Abram, K. M., McClelland, G. M., Dulcan, M. K., & Mericle, A. A. (2002). Psychiatric disorders in youth in juvenile detention. *Archives of General Psychiatry, 59*(12), 1133–1143.

Teplin, L. A., Elkington, K. S., McClelland, G. M., Abram, K. M., Mericle, A. A., & Washburn, J. J. (2005). Major mental disorders, substance use disorders, comorbidity, and HIV-AIDS risk behaviors in juvenile detainees. *Psychiatric Services, 56*(7), 823–828.

Teplin, L. A., McClelland, G. M., Abram, K. M., & Mileusnic, D. (2005). Early violent death among delinquent youth: A prospective longitudinal study. *Pediatrics, 115*(6), 1586–1593.

Townsend, E., Walker, D. M., Sargeant, S., Vostanis, P., Hawton, K., Stocker, O., & Sithole, J. (2010). Systematic review and meta-analysis of interventions relevant for young offenders with mood disorders, anxiety disorders, or self-harm. *Journal of Adolescence, 33*(1), 9–20.

Ulzen, T. P., & Hamilton, H. (1998). The nature and characteristics of psychiatric comorbidity in incarcerated adolescents. *Canadian Journal of Psychiatry, 43*(1), 57–63.

Vermeiren, R., Jespers, I., & Moffitt, T. (2006). Mental health problems in juvenile justice populations. *Child and Adolescent Psychiatric Clinics of North America, 15*(2), 333–351, vii–viii.

Vermeiren, R., Schwab-Stone, M., Ruchkin, V., De Clippele, A., & Deboutte, D. (2002). Predicting recidivism in delinquent adolescents from psychological and psychiatric assessment. *Comprehensive Psychiatry, 43*(2), 142–149.

Wasserman, G. A., McReynolds, L. S., Lucas, C. P., Fisher, P., & Santos, L. (2002). The voice DISC-IV with incarcerated male youths: Prevalence of disorder. *Journal of the Amrican Academy of Child and Adolescent Psychiatry, 41*(3), 314–321.

Yoshinaga, C., Kadomoto, I., Otani, T., Sasaki, T., & Kato, N. (2004). Prevalence of posttraumatic stress disorder in incarcerated juvenile delinquents in Japan. *Psychiatry and Clinical Neurosciences, 58*(4), 383–388.

Zimmermann, G. (2006). Delinquency in male adolescents: The role of alexithymia and family structure. *Journal of Adolescence, 29*(3), 321–332.

11

Family Integrated Transitions: A Promising Program for Reducing Recidivism in a Cost-Effective Manner

TERRY G. LEE AND
SUZANNE E. U. KERNS ■

CONTEXT: REENTRY

The American juvenile justice system is rooted in providing rehabilitation and treatment (Snyder & Sickmund, 1999), though the range and quality of treatment provided to youths in detention facilities varies widely (Desai, Goulet, Robbins, Chapman, Migdole, & Hoge., 2006; Pajer, Kelleher, Gupta, Rolls, & Gardener, 2007; Sedlak & McPherson, 2010). This rehabilitation system represents a significant financial investment. It is estimated that states spent approximately $5.7 billion in 2007 to commit youths to residential facilities (Petteruti, Walsh, & Velazquez, 2009). Approximately 100,000 juvenile offenders are released annually from custody facilities following adjudication or conviction (Snyder, 2004). Despite the significant investment in rehabilitating these youths, the return on the investment in terms of societal benefits is largely lacking. When positive changes are made in residential detention settings, youths and families may experience difficulties generalizing these positive changes to postrelease settings, and they often encounter additional adversities associated with reentry from juvenile justice residential placements (Chapman, Desai, & Falzer, 2006; Desai et al., 2006; Nellis & Wayman, 2009; Trupin, Turner, Stewart, & Wood, 2004; Underwood & Knight, 2006).

Youths reentering their communities from secure detention are at high risk for recurring involvement with the juvenile justice system. In some states, 12-month rearrest rates are as high as 55% (Snyder & Sickmund, 2006), and within 2–3 years, approximately 50–80% of youths released from juvenile correctional facilities are rearrested (Nelson, 2008). The tragic social and fiscal consequences of recidivism highlight the need for more effective services targeting the root causes of recidivism. Although the transition phase from secure detention back to the community is a time of increased risk for negative behaviors and consequences, it also represents an opportune time for strategic intervention. Strategies such as transition planning for juveniles with mental health disorders (e.g., linking families with community supports, facilitating continuity of psychiatric care, and ensuring smooth transitions back to educational/vocational services) has been shown to decrease recidivism (Trupin et al., 2004). Currently, few programs specifically target this high-risk period (Nellis & Wayman, 2009).

Furthermore, several programs designed to improve outcomes of this high-risk population have had challenges in demonstrating reduced recidivism. For example, the Intensive Aftercare Program (IAP), sponsored by the Office of Juvenile Justice and Delinquency Prevention (OJJDP) to reduce recidivism, was implemented in three sites in three different states from 1995 to 2000. The IAP model emphasized individualized case planning, continuity of case management and treatment throughout program phases, coordination between institution and aftercare staff, formal transition structures and processes for facilitating reentry, small caseloads, intensive supervision with access to a wide range of community services, and graduated sanctions and rewards. Eligible youths were randomly assigned to IAP or traditional services. Implementation challenges and small sample sizes complicate interpretation of the outcome data. However, when multiple types of recidivism were evaluated at the 12-month follow-up period, there were few statistically significant differences between the IAP and control groups. The only statistically significant differences in recidivism were that IAP youths in two of the sites were more likely to be charged with a technical violation—likely due to increased monitoring—and that IAP youths in the third site were more likely to be recommitted or sentenced to a jail/prison term in the adult system (Wiebush, Wagner, McNulty, Wang, & Le, 2005).

The Serious and Violent Offender Reentry Initiative (SVORI) was funded by the National Institute of Justice to develop programs to improve criminal justice, employment, education, health, and housing outcomes for released prisoners. Four of the 16 evaluated programs targeted juvenile males. The SVORI evaluation of the programs working with juvenile males used a matched-control design. The SVORI and non-SVORI groups were similar on many of the several hundred measures (e.g., demographic, education, family, mental health, substance use, victimization, delinquency), but the SVORI group was more likely to be older, to be non-White, and to report that they had family members who had been convicted of crimes and were gang members; the differences represent risk factors that arguably put the SVORI group at higher risk to reoffend. At 3, 9, and 15 months postrelease, there were no differences between the SVORI and non-SVORI groups in self-reported core criminal behavior or recidivism (Hawkins, Dawes, Lattimore, & Visher, 2009).

The high rates of mental health and substance use disorders in juvenile justice populations are well documented (Abram, Teplin, McClelland, & Dulcan, 2003;

Sedlak & McPherson, 2010; Stewart & Trupin, 2003; Teplin, Abram, McClelland, & Dulcan, 2002; Wasserman, McReynolds, Lucas, Fisher, & Santos, 2002) and complicate the transition planning and treatment process. Mental health and substance use disorders are among several known risk factors for juvenile delinquency, arrests, and recidivism (Barnes, Welte, & Hoffman, 2002; Duncan, Alpert, Duncan, & Hops, 1997; Loeber, Farrington, Stouthamer-Loeber, & Van Kamen, 1998; Mallett, Stoddard Dare, & Seck, 2009; Molina et al., 2008; Mulder, Brand, Bullens, & Van Marle, 2010; National Center on Addiction and Substance Abuse at Columbia University, 2004; Newcombe & McGee, 1989; Stewart & Trupin, 2003; Sullivan, Veysey, Hamilton, & Grillo, 2007; Trupin et al., 2004) and present additional challenges for negotiating reentry (e.g., advocating for the most appropriate educational setting, difficulty finding prosocial peer-group activities, ensuring consistency of medication compliance, if applicable). For the large number of youths with co-occurring disorders, multiple biological, psychological, family, and social-ecological factors interact to mediate the likelihood of delinquent behavior (Henggeler, Schoenwald, Borduin, Rowland, & Cunningham, 2009; Loeber et al., 1998). Each of these domains is associated with dynamic risk and protective factors that can be strategically targeted within an integrated, ecological intervention. This chapter describes the Family Integrated Transitions (FIT) program, a novel approach to reducing recidivism through the integrated implementation of existing evidence-based practices within multiple biopsychosocial domains during the period of transition from incarceration to the community.

A CONSTITUENCY

In the 1990s, when the rates of juvenile and adult crime were increasing nationally and in Washington State, the Washington State legislature undertook a series of measures to address the problem. In 1997, the Washington State legislature passed legislation significantly altering the state's juvenile sentencing laws and intervention policies. Part of the 1997 legislation established the Community Juvenile Accountability Act (CJAA), which changed the way some local courts in Washington State are funded—CJAA funds only programs shown to reduce recidivism in a cost-effective manner (Barnoski, 1999). In 2000, the Washington State legislature initiated a pilot rehabilitation program for youths with co-occurring mental health and substance disorders who are transitioning back to their home communities after adjudicated stays in secure detention in Washington State Juvenile Rehabilitation Administration (JRA) facilities (Senate Bill 6853). This pilot set the stage for a research trial of FIT.

FIT CLINICAL UNDERPINNINGS

The FIT program is a manualized, intensive, and time-limited family- and community-based treatment specifically designed to address the multidomain risk and protective factors of adjudicated adolescents diagnosed with co-occurring mental health disorders and substance use problems (Lee & DeRobertis, 2006). Specifically, FIT aims to work with the families of youths generally between the ages of 12 and 17 who have diagnosed mental health disorders beyond conduct disorder or oppositional defiant disorder (e.g., depression, anxiety, ADHD) and problematic substance use, who are transitioning from secure detention back to their home communities. The targeted impacts for FIT include: (1) lower recidivism rates, (2) connection of youths and family with community services, (3) reduction/elimination of substance use, (4) improvement in mental health symptoms, (5) increased prosocial behavior, (6) improved educational and vocational outcomes, and (7) stronger family support for youths.

To address both the systemic and individual needs of the youths and their families, the FIT intervention incorporates three evidence-based programs: multisystemic therapy (MST; Henggeler et al, 2009), which provides the foundation of FIT; dialectical behavior therapy (DBT; Linehan, 1993a); and motivational interviewing (MI; Miller & Rollnik, 1991), discussed later; along with a parent skills training module. FIT also builds on the therapeutic strategies used in JRA facilities—the integrated treatment model (ITM), described later—and promotes generalization of skills acquired in JRA facilities to community settings.

Families in the FIT program receive services when youths are transitioning from JRA back into the community. The delivery of FIT occurs in two phases: *prerelease*, lasting approximately 2 months while youths are still in secure detention, and *postrelease*, lasting approximately 4 months. FIT is an intensive intervention, with families receiving an average of 3 hours of service per week—often more intensive at the beginning and tapering as families are able to maintain their goals more independently. Services are provided primarily in the family's home and community and are individualized to each youth and family's unique needs.

FIT THERAPEUTIC COMPONENTS

MST specifically addresses the multiple determinants of serious antisocial behavior in juvenile offenders within a social-ecological framework and is described extensively in the literature (Henggeler, Mihalic, Rone, Thomas, & Timmons-Mitchell, 1998; Henggeler et al., 2009). Briefly, MST is a manualized, family-and community-based, time-limited program that addresses youth and family treatment goals and individualizes treatment to specific youth and family risk and protective factors within their natural ecology. Readers are referred to Henggeler et al. (2009) and other MST resources for more information on the MST intervention. Examples of MST school interventions include facilitating good family-school collaboration, identifying supportive personnel within the school who can provide youth assistance and advocacy for a youth, role-playing with parents to strategically and assertively request appropriate educational services for their child, and supporting parents to provide structure and reinforcement for good school functioning. Examples of MST peer interventions include parents meeting their child's friends and the parents of their child's friends, supporting association with prosocial peers by providing verbal encouragement and instrumental support such as car rides, and discouraging association with antisocial peers, which in extreme cases may involve the use of restraining orders. Results from multiple studies demonstrate that youths participating in MST experience reduced rates of arrest and recidivism, reduced out-of-home placements, improvements in family functioning, and decreased mental health problems. The Washington Institute of Public Policy calculated the cost savings of MST to be $18,213 per youth when considering the savings to taxpayers and crime victims (Aos, Miller, & Drake, 2006).

Although the ecological interventions of MST address antisocial behaviors particularly prominent for youths involved in the juvenile justice system, juveniles with co-occurring disorders also have persistent problems with emotion regulation, anger, impulse control, and moodiness requiring intensive individualized, youth-focused intervention strategies. These individual-focused strategies are addressed with the ITM in the institution, and generalization of DBT skills is promoted and supported with MI strategies during the postrelease phase.

The JRA ITM emphasizes skills-based training to promote more effective management of emotions and behavior. The residential portion of the ITM is founded on cognitive-behavioral therapy principles, including behavioral analysis, shaping, reinforcement, extinction, and contingency management. The ITM also employs DBT (Linehan, 1993a) and aggression replacement training (ART; Goldstein, Glick, & Gibbs, 1998). Both in JRA facilities and in the FIT treatment model, DBT seeks to replace ineffective maladaptive emotional and behavioral issues with more effective and skillful responses.

Readers are referred to Linehan (1993a, 1993b) and other DBT resources for more information on DBT. Briefly, DBT incorporates acceptance and change skills strategies. DBT emphasizes skills training in the areas of core mindfulness, distress tolerance, emotion regulation, and interpersonal effectiveness (Linehan, 1993b). Core mindfulness skills coach youths to be more intentional in the moment through integrating their "emotion mind"—a state when an individual is influenced mainly by emotions—with "reasonable mind," a thinking, rational state, into what Linehan calls "wise mind." Wise mind represents a balanced state between emotional experiences and rational thoughts. Interpersonal effectiveness skills in DBT are similar to traditional assertiveness and interpersonal problem-solving skills training—effectively asking for what one wants, setting limits, and coping with interpersonal conflict. Emotion regulation skills are complex and may be more difficult to teach. The emotion regulation skills training conceptualizes that an individual's distress often arises from secondary responses to primary emotions. Primary emotions such as anger and hurt are often adaptive and appropriate to a situation, whereas secondary responses, such as shame or embarrassment, to primary responses may cause distress. Extinction of maladaptive, distressing secondary responses requires exposure to the primary emotion in a nonjudgmental setting. The distress tolerance skills in DBT promote tolerating and surviving crises, without making things worse, and accepting the situation in the moment. DBT distress tolerance skills are organized as skills for distracting, self-soothing, improving the moment, and thinking of pros and cons (Linehan, 1993b). During the prerelease phase, and following the traditional DBT model, youths participate in institution-sponsored weekly group and individual therapy to learn and apply DBT skills. DBT skills are modeled by JRA staff, including in their day-to-day interactions. Youths practice, rehearse, and role-play skills with staff, then generalize in the milieu with "on-the-fly" coaching. Skill acquisition is further promoted through multimodal reinforcements for incrementally more skillful behavior. FIT will work with families to help them become familiar with the DBT skills their children have learned in the facility and the manner in which JRA staff support and encourage youths to use specific DBT skills. After release, FIT coaches work with youths and their families to identify opportunities for active skill generalization. Studies of DBT with adolescents indicate that this a promising approach for reducing parasuicidal behavior, disruptive behavior, interpersonal problems, and anger control problems (Miller, Rathus, & Linehan, 2007; Rathus & Miller, 2002; Walsh, 2004). Promising trends have also been recently found with studies of detained youths in Washington State (Drake & Barnoski, 2006).

MI (Miller & Rollnick, 1991) is an engagement approach that is utilized throughout all phases of FIT to promote youth and family engagement, enhance motivation for change, encourage adherence to treatment, and support relapse prevention efforts. The reader is referred to Miller and Rollnick (1991) and other MI resources for more information on MI. During the prerelease phase, FIT coaches identify relapse prevention plans and identify youths' "readiness to change" with regard to their substance use. Studies of MI with adolescents with problematic substance use have found that MI techniques, alone and paired with cognitive-behavioral strategies, are effective in reducing substance use and associated negative consequences (Bailey, Baker, Webster, & Lewin, 2004; Dennis et al., 2004; Monti et al., 1999). MI techniques are also used flexibly throughout the FIT intervention to address issues related to ongoing family engagement and when relapse does occur.

The parent training in FIT is based on behavioral skills training, utilizing components of techniques outlined in Russell Barkley and colleagues' manual for working with defiant teens (Barkley, Edwards, & Robin, 1999), Karen Pryor's *Don't Shoot the Dog* (1999), and Scott Sells's *Parenting Your Out-of-Control Teenager* (2002). Major themes addressed with parents/caregivers during these training components include establishing reasonable expectations, supervision and monitoring, facilitating relationship-enhancing practices, strategies for encouraging desirable behavior, and developing effective and positive disciplinary skills.

FIT QUALITY ASSURANCE

Quality assurance for FIT is made up primarily of the well-researched MST quality assurance measures, which are slightly modified for use in FIT. Specifically, MST uses the Therapist Adherence Measure—Revised (TAM-Rs). TAM-R is a parent report of the coach's use of skills and strategies. Scores on the TAM-R have been associated with therapist adherence and fidelity, as well as client outcomes (Schoenwald, Chapman, Sheidow, & Carter, 2009; Schoenwald, Henggeler, Brondino, & Rowland, 2000). FIT has developed supplementary items to assess DBT implementation. The supplementary items are currently undergoing study.

FIT TREATMENT MODEL

Initial Referral and Prerelease Phase

Once a FIT-eligible youth is identified, the FIT coach initially engages the family and youth while the youth is incarcerated, ideally approximately 2 months before release. Strong engagement and collaboration with the family is critical to the success of FIT and thus is a critical focus of the early family meetings. FIT coaches seek to enhance engagement by meeting at times and places convenient for the family, emphasizing a nonjudgmental strengths-based approach, and demonstrating respect and responsiveness to the family's priorities. FIT coaches engage youths in motivational assessment and enhancement activities designed to help the youth articulate expectations of his or her life after release and to increase his or her sense of urgency and confidence to make positive changes. Similarly, FIT coaches engage families with analogous motivational assessment and enhancement activities to increase the parents' urgency and sense of self-efficacy to make desired changes.

The general framework and foundation for the various components of the FIT intervention are introduced to the youth and family initially, and then in more detail after establishing engagement and a therapeutic alliance. Coaches work in collaboration with the parents/caregivers to come up with a viable plan for postrelease activities and expectations, based on personal goal setting. Coaches work with families to develop individualized intervention plans for the youth. Youth supervision and monitoring by responsible adults is emphasized. Enrolling the youth in school and/or finding employment or volunteer activities are priorities which serve to promote productive activities and minimize unstructured postrelease time. Reenrolling youths in school after juvenile justice placement can be challenging (Nellis & Wayman, 2009) and may require significant effort. Prosocial activities of interest to the youth and family are identified and scheduled. Prosocial peers are identified, and socializing with prosocial peers is encouraged, supported, and reinforced. At the same time, socialization with antisocial and substance-using peers is strongly discouraged, and consequences are applied as appropriate.

If applicable, psychiatric medication management is arranged and appointments are scheduled. Families take an active role in monitoring medication compliance and follow-up. If families have questions or concerns about psychiatric medications, they are supported in articulating these questions with the psychiatric prescriber.

FIT coaches help identify natural supports within the family and community and target the specific individualized needs of the youth and family in their social-ecological context. Parents are taught the DBT skills their son or daughter learned while incarcerated in Washington State JRA facilities, as parents are uniquely situated to reinforce and assist in generalization of these skills at home. A specific relapse prevention plan is developed. Finally, joint sessions between the coach, the youth, and his or her parents begin at the JRA facility. The goals of these sessions are to review the youth's and family's goals, to present the youth with the initial behavior management plan, to explain any preparations that have been made for homecoming, to discuss use of DBT skills at home, and to address any concerns family members may have with postrelease plans.

FIT coaches also engage juvenile parole counselors, who are important partners during the FIT intervention. Parole counselors can help the family access resources and programs and provide additional incentives and consequences. Compliance with the conditions of his or her individualized parole contracts is in the youth's best interest. In Washington State, noncompliance can result in a series of graduated sanctions, including curfew, electronic home monitoring, and return to confinement for up to 30 days. FIT coaches work with parents to interact effectively with the juvenile parole counselor; this can include reporting progress and challenges, advocating for the youth, requesting drug urine analysis if substance use is suspected, and strategic use of graduated sanctions—usually after parent-mediated consequences are exhausted, but more urgently when there are safety concerns.

Transition and Postrelease

During transition and the postrelease period, the MST components of the FIT intervention are individually tailored and are delivered in alignment with MST core values and principles. The focus turns to implementing changes designed to achieve overarching goals, generalizing newly developed skills, shaping behavior, and troubleshooting problem situations and experiences as they arise. The challenge during this period is to transform the plans and ideas into action. Especially during the initial few weeks after the youth is transitioned back home, the coach is in regular, often daily, contact with the family. The coach works in collaboration with the family to assist the family in meeting their goals and needs. Therapeutic activities are designed to achieve the family's goals and may include interventions designed to maintain engagement, promote high levels of motivation, support changes, address barriers to positive change, prevent relapses, deal with any relapses that do occur, support family during periods of crisis, modify the intervention as necessary, promote positive family interactions, assist in maintaining contingencies and monitoring, promote school attendance, manage demands of parole, and/or help the youth to engage in prosocial activities with prosocial peers.

Because of the intensity of work and multiple community contacts, FIT-trained coaches operate in small teams of three to five coaches and carry relatively small caseloads (typically four to six families), and they participate in extensive supervision and quality assurance activities, averaging approximately 2.25 hours per week. Similar to the MST supervision model, each team is supervised by a half-time supervisor; FIT teams have weekly hour-long consultations with two expert consultants, who are versed in the component treatments of FIT: MST, MI, and DBT. Consultants also closely monitor the quality assurance measures and work with supervisors and coaches to maintain sufficient levels of treatment adherence. A psychiatrist consultant versed in the FIT model also consults at least monthly during the regular consultation time and is also available to teams and coaches at other times to address specific youths and situations. FIT training activities also include monthly booster sessions to provide additional training on specific knowledge and skills to coaches and supervisors.

FIT EVALUATIONS

The FIT pilot program was developed and funded by legislation responding to the need for effective reentry services for the juvenile offenders who are at high risk to reoffend. For the pilot study, the FIT eligibility criteria were defined as:

1. Any youth 17½ years or younger, being released from a Washington State Rehabilitation Administration residential commitment to four months or more of parole supervision; **WITH**
2. Any substance use disorder (past or present); **AND**
3. Mental health concerns as evidenced by:
   a. Any Axis I Disorder (except for youth who have only a diagnosis of Conduct Disorder, Oppositional-Defiant Disorder, substance use disorder and/or a Paraphilia; youth with other Axis I disorders in addition to these disorders meet the mental health concern criteria for FIT), **AND/OR**
   b. Currently prescribed psychiatric medication, **AND/OR**
   c. Engaging in self-harm behavior in the last four months; **AND**
4. Residing in one of the four counties served by the FIT Program.

Youths living outside of the service area who did not have caregivers committed to letting the youths reside with them or whose caregivers declined participation in the FIT intervention did not receive the FIT intervention.

The legislation creating the FIT pilot program also required and funded an independent evaluation of the effectiveness of FIT and a cost-benefit analysis by the Washington State Institute for Public Policy (WSIPP). The WSIPP study (Aos, 2004) utilized a matched-control design, in which youths who participated in FIT were compared with youths who met criteria for FIT but lived in counties in which the FIT intervention was not available (treatment $n = 104$; control $n = 169$). The FIT youths were more likely to be African American, less likely to be Latino, and had fewer prior property offense convictions (Aos, 2004; Aos, personal communication, 2007). The FIT youths also had slightly higher scores on JRA's tool for measuring overall risk for reoffending—the Initial Security Classification Assessment (ISCA; Barnoski, 1998). The ethnic difference between groups is consistent with the FIT counties being more urban, with higher percentages of African Americans, whereas the non-FIT counties were more rural and had relatively higher percentages of Latinos. There were no significant differences between groups on gender, age at release, Native American ethnicity, age at first conviction, prior drug convictions, criminal history, or prior violent convictions. Arguably, with higher ISCA scores, the FIT group was more likely to reoffend. Recidivism was defined as subsequent juvenile and adult criminal convictions recorded in Washington State databases maintained by the Administrative Office of the Courts and Department of Corrections. FIT was found to have a statistically significant effect on the 18-month felony recidivism rate ($p = .0472$), with a mean-adjusted 18-month felony recidivism rate of 41% for the non-FIT control group and 27% for the FIT group. There were no significant differences between the FIT and non-FIT groups in rates of total recidivism, the sum of misdemeanor and felony recidivism, and violent felony recidivism, though trends favored the FIT group.

A longer term follow-up analysis of FIT used the same groups of 273 youths from the 18-month FIT follow-up study (Aos, 2004)—youths met clinical eligibility criteria for FIT but were sorted based on whether FIT was available in their home county—and the same Washington State administrative databases were used to ascertain reconviction rates. Recidivism was measured 36 months after release. A nonproportional hazards model using Cox regression was used to evaluate the difference in survival rate—not being reconvicted—between the FIT and non-FIT groups for overall and felony recidivism. Survival analysis was stratified by ethnicity to account for increased risk of recidivism of African American youths, who were overrepresented in the FIT group. The analysis determined that the FIT intervention reduced felony recidivism by approximately 30% compared with the non-FIT group. In this study, FIT was also found to be equally effective at reducing recidivism for African American and non-African American youths and families (Trupin, Kerns, Walker, DeRobertis, & Stewart, 2011). Similar to 18-month outcomes, no significant differences were found between groups on violent felony recidivism and misdemeanor recidivism.

The legislation that provided for the FIT pilot also directed WSIPP to perform a cost-benefit analysis of the FIT program. Based on lower rates of 18-month felony recidivism, WSIPP (Aos et al., 2006) estimated that for each youth and family receiving FIT, the cost benefits to crime victims ($30,708) and taxpayers ($19,502) is $50,210 ($30,708 + $19,502). With an average cost of $9,665 for each youth/family participating in FIT, FIT provides a net gain of $40,545 ($50,210 – $9,665) per FIT participant. Thus, for each $1 spent on FIT, there is a savings to crime victims and taxpayers of $4.20 ($40,545/$9,665), based on lower rates of 18-month felony recidivism. Cost-benefit estimates based on lower 36-month recidivism rates have not been calculated.

CURRENT AND FUTURE DIRECTIONS

The lower 18- and 36-month felony recidivism rates of FIT participants, compared with matched controls, support FIT as a promising treatment for youths with co-occurring disorders transitioning from secure detention back to their home communities. The cost-effective manner (Aos et al., 2006) in which FIT lowers felony recidivism make FIT a fiscally viable option for governments and agencies seeking to improve juvenile justice reentry outcomes. A randomized trial will provide further support for the FIT approach of an intensive, community-based multisystem transition program that builds on individual skills training in residential detention facilities, emphasizes engagement and motivation, and is founded on MST.

Similar to previous findings that African American ethnicity did not moderate outcomes in multiple studies of MST (Huey & Polo, 2008), FIT was found to be as effective for African American youths as for non-African American youths (Trupin et al., 2011. It is important to reaffirm FIT findings for different cultural-ethnic groups and various types of communities. FIT processes and outcomes for Latinos are currently being evaluated, and cultural adaptations are being contemplated (Trupin, personal communication, 2010).

The impact of FIT on other functional psychosocial outcomes beyond recidivism must be better understood and characterized. For example, in various studies of court-involved and at-risk youths, MST has demonstrated not only lower rates of criminal offending but also improved family relations, improved parent–child interactions, reduced substance use, decreased out-of-home placements, increased school attendance, improved peer relations and social functioning, decreased out-of-home placement, decreased youth psychiatric symptoms, and fewer suicide attempts (Henggeler et al., 2009). Although the IAP was associated with few differences in recidivism rates compared with a randomized control group, youths receiving the IAP intervention were less likely to test positive for substance abuse during parole in two of the three sites, and, at all three sites, IAP youths were more likely to be involved in vocational training for at least 2 months during the aftercare period (Wiebush et al., 2005). Using a matched-control design, the multisite evaluation of the SVORI also did not find any differences in the recidivism at the four evaluated sites for juvenile males; however, the youths participating in the SVORI were more likely to be in school 3 months after release and more likely to have a job with benefits 15 months after release (Hawkins et al., 2009). Given FIT's MST foundation and association with lower felony recidivism rates, it is hypothesized that FIT may demonstrate improved functional psychosocial outcomes. At this time, a number of jurisdictions and agencies have procured or allotted resources to implement and evaluate FIT and are in various stages of planning. A randomized controlled trial of FIT in New York State began in 2011, and FIT has been disseminated to Connecticut and Illinois (Trupin, personal communication, 2012). Adapting FIT to address the transition-related needs of youths from residential or other out-of-home mental and child welfare settings is also under consideration.

SUMMARY AND CONCLUSIONS

FIT is a manualized, family-based treatment for youths with co-occurring mental health and substance use disorders who are transitioning from juvenile justice residential placement back to their home communities. FIT is founded on multisystemic treatment to address the multisystemic drivers of delinquent and substance using behavior. FIT incorporates motivational interviewing to encourage and support engagement and enthusiasm for change, cognitive-behavioral and dialectical behavior therapy skills training to promote more effective coping strategies, and parent skills training. The evaluations to date utilize a quasi-experimental, single-matched-control-group design with a cohort of 273 youths. Based on 18- and 36-month follow-up, FIT reduces felony recidivism by approximately 30%. FIT reduces recidivism in a cost-effective manner: based on an 18-month follow-up, for each $1 spent on FIT, there is a savings of $4.20 to taxpayers and crime victims. Randomized controlled trials in other sites that are testing additional functional outcomes with ethnically diverse populations will potentially provide stronger support for the effectiveness of the FIT intervention. FIT is currently undergoing a more rigorous evaluation involving a randomized controlled trial with youth transitioning from New York State's Office of Children and Family Services secure detention facilities back to their home communities in New York City.

REFERENCES

Abram, K. M., Teplin, L. A., McClelland, G. M., & Dulcan, M. K. (2003). Comorbid psychiatric conditions in youth in juvenile detention. *Archives of General Psychiatry, 60*(11), 1097–1108.

Aos, S. (2004). *Washington State's family integrated transitions program for juvenile offenders: Outcome evaluation and benefit-cost analysis.* Olympia, WA: Washington State Institute for Public Policy.

Aos, S., Miller, M., & Drake, E. (2006). *Evidence-based public policy options to reduce future prison construction, criminal justice costs, and crime rates.* Olympia, WA: Washington State Institute for Public Policy.

Bailey, K. A., Baker, A. L., Webster, R. A., & Lewin, T. J. (2004). Pilot randomized controlled trial of a brief alcohol intervention group for adolescents. *Drug and Alcohol Review, 23*(2), 157–166.

Barkley, R. A., Edwards, G. H., & Robin, A. L. (1999). *Defiant teens: A clinician's manual for assessment and family intervention.* New York, NY: Guilford Press.

Barnes, G. M., Welte, J. W., & Hoffman, J. H. (2002). Relationship of alcohol use to delinquency and illicit drug use in adolescents: Gender, age and racial/ethnic differences. *Journal of Drug Issues, 32*(1), 153–178.

Barnoski, R. (1998). *Juvenile Rehabilitation Administration assessments: Validity review and recommendations.* Olympia, WA: Washington Institute for Public Policy.

Barnoski, R. (1999). *The community juvenile accountability act: Research-proven interventions for the juvenile courts.* Olympia, WA: Washington Institute for Public Policy.

Chapman, J. F., Desai, R. A., & Falzer, P. R. (2006). Mental health service provision in juvenile justice facilities: Pre- and postrelease psychiatric care. *Child and Adolescent Psychiatric Clinics of North America, 15*(2), 445–458.

Dennis, M., Godley, S. H., Diamond, G., Tims, F. M., Babor, T., Donaldson, J, . . . Funk, R. (2004). The Cannabis Youth Treatment (CYT) study: Main findings from two randomized trials. *Journal of Substance Abuse Treatment, 27*(3), 197–213.

Desai, R. A., Goulet, J. L., Robbins, J., Chapman, J. F., Migdole, S. J., & Hoge, M. A. (2006). Mental health care in juvenile detention facilities: A review. *Journal of the American Academy of Psychiatry and the Law, 34*(2), 204–214.

Drake, E., & Barnoski, R. (2006). *Recidivism findings for the Juvenile Rehabilitation Administration's Dialectical Behavior Therapy program: Final report* (No. 06-05-1202). Olympia: Washington Institute for Public Policy.

Duncan, S. C., Alpert, A., Duncan, T. E., & Hops, H. (1997). Adolescent alcohol use development and young adult outcomes. *Drug and Alcohol Dependence, 49*(1), 39–48.

Goldstein, A. P., Glick, B., & Gibbs, J. C. (1998). *Aggression Replacement Training: A comprehensive intervention for aggressive youth.* Champaign, IL: Research Press.

Hawkins, S. R., Dawes, D., Lattimore, P. K., & Visher, C. A. (2009). *Reentry experiences of confined juvenile offenders: Characteristics, service receipt, and outcomes of juvenile male participants in the SVORI multi-site evaluation.* Washington, DC: National Institute of Justice.

Henggeler, S. W., Mihalic, S. F., Rone, L., Thomas, C., & Timmons-Mitchell, J. (1998). *Blueprints for violence prevention: Book 6. Multisystemic therapy.* Boulder, CO: Center for the Study and Prevention of Violence.

Henggeler, S. W., Schoenwald, S. K., Borduin, C. M., Rowland, M. D., & Cunningham, P. B. (2009). *Multisystemic therapy for antisocial behavior in children and adolescents.* New York, NY: Guilford Press.

Huey, S. J., & Polo, A. J. (2008). Evidence-based psychosocial treatments for ethnic minority youth. *Journal of Clinical Child and Adolescent Psychology, 37*(1), 262–301.

Lee, T. G., & DeRobertis, M. T. (2006). Overview of the FIT treatment model. *Focal Point, 20,* 17–19.

Linehan, M. M. (1993a). *Cognitive-behavioral treatment of borderline personality disorder.* New York, NY: Guilford Press.

Linehan, M. M. (1993b).*Skills training manual for treating borderline personality disorder*. New York, NY: Guilford Press.

Loeber, R., Farrington, D. P., Stouthamer-Loeber, M., & Van Kamen, W. B. (1998). *Antisocial behavior and mental health problems: Explanatory factors in childhood and adolescence*. Mahwah, NJ: Erlbaum.

Mallett, C. A., Stoddard Dare, P., & Seck, M. M. (2009). Predicting juvenile delinquency: The nexus of childhood maltreatment, depression and bipolar disorder. *Criminal Behaviour and Mental Health, 19*(4), 235–246.

Miller, A. L., Rathus, J. H., & Linehan, M. M. (2007). *Dialectical behavior therapy with suicidal adolescents*. New York, NY: Guilford Press.

Miller, W. R., & Rollnick, S. (1991). *Motivational interviewing: Preparing people to change addictive behavior*. New York, NY: Guilford Press.

Molina, B. S. G., Hinshaw, S. P., Swanson, J. M., Arnold, L. E., Vitiello, B., Jensen, P. S., . . . MTA Cooperative Group. (2008). The MTA at 8 years: Prospective follow-up of children treated for combined type ADHD in a multisite study. *Journal of the American Academy of Child and Adolescent Psychiatry, 48*(5), 484–500.

Monti, P. M., Colby, S. M., Barnett, N. P., Spirito, A., Rohsenow, D. J., Myers, M., . . . Lewander, W. (1999). Brief intervention for harm reduction with alcohol-positive older adolescents in a hospital emergency department. *Journal of Consulting and Clinical Psychology, 67*(6), 989–994.

Mulder, E., Brand, E., Bullens, R., & Van Marle, H. (2010). A classification of risk factors in serious juvenile offenders and the relation between patterns of risk factors and recidivism. *Criminal Behaviour and Mental Health, 20*(1), 23–39.

National Center on Addiction and Substance Abuse at Columbia University. (2004). *Criminal neglect: Substance abuse, juvenile justice, and the children left behind*. New York, NY: Author.

Nellis, A., & Wayman, R. H. (2009). *Back on track: Supporting youth reentry from out-of-home placement to the community*. Washington, DC: Youth Reentry Task Force of the Juvenile Justice and Delinquency Prevention Coalition.

Nelson, D. W. (2008). *KIDS COUNT 2008 Essay: A road map for juvenile justice reform*. Baltimore, MD: Annie E. Casey Foundation.

Newcombe, M. D., & McGee, L. (1989). Adolescent alcohol use and other delinquent behavior: A one-year longitudinal analysis controlling for sensation seeking. *Criminal Justice and Behavior, 16*(3), 345–368.

Pajer, K. A., Kelleher, K., Gupta, R. A., Rolls, J., & Gardener, W. (2007). Psychiatric and medical health care policies in juvenile detention facilities. *Journal of the American Academy of Child and Adolescent Psychiatry, 46*(12), 1660–1667.

Petteruti, A., Walsh, N., & Velazquez, T. (2009, May). *The costs of confinement: Why good juvenile justice policies make good fiscal sense*. Washington, DC: Justice Policy Institute.

Pryor, K. (1999). *Don't shoot the dog: The new art of teaching and training*. New York, NY: Bantam Books.

Rathus, J. H., & Miller, A. L. (2002). Dialectical behavior therapy adapted for suicidal adolescents. *Suicide and Life Threatening Behavior, 37*(2), 146–157.

Sedlak, A. J., & McPherson, K. S. (2010, April). Findings from the survey of youth in residential placement. *OJJDP Juvenile Justice Bulletin*.

Schoenwald, S. K., Chapman, J. E., Sheidow, A. J., & Carter, J. E. (2009). Long-term youth criminal outcomes in MST transport: The impact of therapist adherence and organizational climate and structure. *Journal of Clinical Child and Adolescent Psychiatry, 38*(1), 91–105.

Schoenwald, S. K., Henggeler, S. W., Brondino, M. J., & Rowland, M. D. (2000). Multisystemic therapy: Monitoring treatment fidelity. *Family Process, 39*(1), 83–103.

Sells, S. (2002). *Parenting your out-of-control teenager*. New York, NY: St. Martin's Press.

Senate Bill 6853. (2000). An act relating to a pilot program for supervision of juvenile offenders with mental disorders and chemical abuse disorders, Washington State Senate, 1999–2000 Session.

Snyder, H. N. (2004). An empirical portrait of the youth reentry population. *Youth Violence and Juvenile Justice, 2*(1), 39–55.

Snyder, H. N., & Sickmund, M. (1999). *Juvenile offenders and victims: 1999 national report*. Washington, DC: U.S. Department of Justice, Office of Justice Programs, Office of Juvenile Justice and Delinquency Prevention.

Snyder, H. N., & Sickmund, M. (2006). *Juvenile offenders and victims: 2006 national report*. Washington, DC: U.S. Department of Justice, Office of Justice Programs, Office of Juvenile Justice and Delinquency Prevention.

Stewart, D. G., & Trupin, E. W. (2003). Clinical utility and policy implications of a statewide mental health screening process for juvenile offenders. *Psychiatric Services, 54*(3), 377–382.

Sullivan, C. J., Veysey, B. M., Hamilton, Z. K., & Grillo, M. (2007). Reducing out-of-community placement and recidivism: Diversion of delinquent youth with mental health and substance use problems from the justice system. *International Journal of Offender Therapy and Comparative Criminology, 51*(5), 555–557.

Teplin, L. A., Abram, K. M., McClelland, G. M., & Dulcan, M. K. (2002). Psychiatric disorders in youth in juvenile detention. *Archives of General Psychiatry, 59*(12), 1133–1143.

Trupin, E. W., Kerns, S. E. U., Walker, S. C., DeRobertis, M. T., & Stewart, D. G. (2011). Family integrated transitions: A promising program for soon-to-be released incarcerated juvenile offenders. *Journal of Child and Adolescent Substance Abuse, 20*(5), 421–436.

Trupin, E. W., Turner, A. P., Stewart, D., & Wood, P. (2004). Transition planning and recidivism among mentally ill juvenile offenders. *Behavioral Sciences and the Law, 22*(4), 599–610.

Underwood, L. A., & Knight, P. (2006). Treatment and postrelease rehabilitative programs for juvenile offenders. *Child and Adolescent Clinics of North America, 15*(2), 539–556.

Walsh, B. (2004). Using dialectical behavior therapy to help troubled adolescents return safely to their families and communities. *Psychiatric Services, 55*(10), 1168–1170.

Wasserman, G. A., McReynolds, L. S., Lucas, C., Fisher, P., & Santos, L. (2002). The voice DISC-IV with incarcerated youth: Prevalence of disorder. *Journal of the American Academy of Child and Adolescent Psychiatry, 42*(2), 314–321.

Wiebush, R. G., Wagner, D., McNulty, B., Wang, Y., & Le, T. N. (2005). *Implementation and outcome evaluation of the Intensive Aftercare Program*. Washington DC: Office of Juvenile Justice and Delinquency Prevention.

PART THREE

Legal and Policy Implications

12

Neuroscience and Legal Proceedings

JAMES S. WALKER AND WILLIAM BERNET ∎

This generation is experiencing the early years of a remarkable explosion of research regarding neuroscience and the practical application of this new knowledge in almost every aspect of life. The Decade of the Brain (1990–2000) featured giant steps forward in neurophysiology (research regarding neurotransmitters), human genetics (the Human Genome Project), and neuroimaging (particularly the development of functional magnetic resonance imaging [fMRI] of the brain). These new technologies have prompted much research in both the biological sciences and psychology and have driven discussions regarding consciousness, free will, and the nature of man himself. Although it is hard to know where neuroscience, psychology, and psychiatry will be 20 or 30 years from now, the neuroscience revolution of our time seems comparable to the industrial revolution of the 19th century and the digital revolution of the 20th century.

It is well known that technological innovation leads to new questions and dilemmas that society must address, especially in terms of legal and ethical considerations. For example, new knowledge regarding human reproduction quickly led to practical applications, such as oral contraception, in vitro fertilization, and the prospect of human cloning. These new possibilities quickly led to many hard questions, such as: When divorce occurs, which parent controls the fate of the frozen embryos that they previously created as a couple? Also, advances in medical science have greatly extended human life, which also led to difficult questions, such as: Should limited resources be allocated to prolong the lives of severely damaged, unconscious, unresponsive patients?

This chapter considers the admissibility and use in legal proceedings of some of the techniques developed in the course of the neuroscience revolution. We focus on the legal questions that may arise when neuroscientific data—both basic research and clinical findings—are introduced in legal proceedings. This topic has already been addressed by other writers and study groups. Some authors have addressed broad legal and philosophical issues, such as whether current or future neuroscience research will affect or undermine the basic premises of free will and criminal responsibility (Farahany & Coleman, 2009; Jones, 2009; Onay, 2006). Personnel at the Hastings Center, which addresses bioethics and public policy, have expressed an interest in this topic (Dresser, 2008). The John D. and Catherine T. MacArthur Foundation recently launched the Law and Neuroscience Project, which "investigates the diverse and complex issues that neuroscience raises for the criminal justice system in the United States." For example, Does neuroscience affect our view of criminal punishment? (See www. lawandneuroscienceproject.org.)

In this chapter, we are not discussing broad philosophical issues. Instead, we are addressing the practical predicaments of expert witnesses—typically, psychologists, psychiatrists, and neurologists—who rely on neuroscience research and neuroscience-based evaluations when testifying in civil and criminal legal proceedings. In the first part of this chapter, we discuss various methods of assessing brain structure and function and how they have been viewed by courts. The second part of the chapter addresses a series of legal questions that involve neuroscience. Through short vignettes, we address the issues that arise in these scenarios.

NEUROSCIENCE METHODS AND PROCEDURES

Neuroscientists use numerous tools and techniques in studying the human brain, identifying brain lesions, diagnosing mental disorders, and assessing patients' responses to treatment. Most of these procedures have been introduced in court during criminal or civil proceedings as scientific evidence to support the contentions of a given party or of the state. These neuroscientific tests and procedures are discussed in this section.

The admissibility of such evidence into court is governed by several legal factors, including the Federal Rules of Evidence (FRE) and case law. FRE Rule 702 identifies the precise criteria that govern whether scientific testimony can be admitted into consideration in a federal trial. These criteria include whether the procedure has been validated by peer review, whether an error rate has been established for the procedure, and whether the procedure has gained acceptance in the relevant scientific community. Most states have very similar standards, which are based on *Daubert v. Merrell Dow Pharmaceuticals* (1993). Some states (e.g., California, Florida, Illinois, New Jersey, New York, Pennsylvania) have a rule based on *Frye v. United States* (1923). The *Frye* rule allows evidence to be admitted based on general acceptance in the scientific community alone.

Electroencephalogram and Quantitative Encephalography

These techniques take advantage of the fact that the brain produces constant electrical activity that can be measured and that reflects the type and quantity of the brain's activity in different regions and across time. The electroencephalogram (EEG)—the recording of the brain's electrical activity—has been studied since the 1920s. The quantitative electroencephalogram (QEEG), which originated in the 1960s, is a procedure that utilizes the summation of electrical measurements of the brain and can also demonstrate the presence of brain abnormalities.

The use of EEG is a well-established medical procedure, and EEG results are used thousands of times each day in this country for the diagnosis of abnormal brain states such as seizure disorder and metabolic encephalopathy (Ropper & Samuels, 2009). As such, EEG evidence is regularly admitted into court in cases of alleged seizure disorder and other illnesses.

QEEG is another matter. EEG test results can be digitized and summed by computer, producing a "quantitative EEG" profile. This procedure has been utilized in the assessment and treatment of many disorders, including seizure disorder, Alzheimer's disease, and traumatic brain injury. However, the methodology is very susceptible to manipulation by the operator and has been shown to produce an excessive number of false positives due to random, statistical abnormalities.

The position statement of the American Academy of Neurology (AAN) sums up a widely accepted professional perspective on the use of QEEG in legal proceedings:

> A major disadvantage of these tests in legal disputes is the occurrence of false-positive results, i.e., "abnormal" results in normal subjects and incorrect diagnoses in patients. Results also can be dramatically altered during the subjective process of selecting portions of an EEG for quantitative analysis. There are no objective safeguards to prevent statistical or unintended errors. . . . There is great potential for abuse. . . . The use of these techniques to support one side or the other in court proceedings can readily result in confusion, abuse, and false impressions. . . . On the basis of clinical and scientific evidence, opinions of most experts, and the technical and methodologic shortcomings, QEEG is not recommended for use in civil or criminal judicial proceedings. (Nuwer, 1997).

Although that statement was published several years ago, the usefulness of QEEG in diagnosis in forensic proceedings remains suspect (Grafton, 2010), and this position remains the official one of the AAN (see http://www.aan.com/practice/guideline).

Computed Tomography

Computed tomography (CT) utilizes X-ray technology processed by a computer to create detailed visual images of the brain. When CT was introduced in the 1970s, it led to a revolution in the field of medical engineering.

CT is especially useful for identifying the presence of hemorrhagic strokes and brain lesions that alter the shape and configuration of the brain and its ventricles.

CT technology is well established, and its validity and utility are demonstrated in the thousands of such images taken every day in the course of medical practice (Ropper & Samuels, 2009). The use of CT images to support a diagnosis of brain injury in the course of a forensic consultation should find no barriers to its admissibility in the courtroom.

The most famous use of CT technology in the courtroom occurred in 1982 in the case of John Hinckley, Jr., the man who shot President Ronald Reagan. A defense expert testified that a CT scan of Hinckley's brain showed shrinkage and enlarged ventricles, consistent with the diagnosis of schizophrenia. A prosecution expert testified that the scan appeared normal to him. Hinckley was found not guilty by reason of insanity (Kulynch, 1996).

Magnetic Resonance Imaging and Magnetic Resonance Angiography

Magnetic resonance imaging (MRI) scans of the brain produce the most detailed and highest resolution images of the overall structure of the brain. The technology uses extremely powerful magnets to "line up" the subatomic emissions of particles of matter throughout the brain, thus creating the potential for highly detailed images. Contrast material can also be injected into the vascular system, and highly detailed images made of the brain's arteries and veins, yielding a magnetic resonance angiography (MRA) scan.

MRI and MRA scans also represent well-established, face-valid technology for assessing brain structure. Brain MRI is a routine procedure in assessing many potential brain abnormalities, such as brain infarcts, encephalitis, tumors, contusions, and dementia. Its high resolution makes it particularly valuable for such conditions as multiple sclerosis or suspected small vessel disease. MRI and MRA evidence are routinely admitted as evidence in court proceedings as part of comprehensive neurological workups (Bufkin & Luttrell, 2005).

Positron Emission Tomography

Positron emission tomography (PET) utilizes the electrical signals given off by the molecules of the brain involved in metabolism. It can create an image of the brain's actual activity, and the metabolism of one area of the brain can be compared with the metabolism in another area, thereby identifying sections of relatively decreased activity. These areas of decreased activity, or hypometabolism, are associated with brain lesions and dysfunction. Areas of hyperactivity tend to be associated with seizure events. Thus the PET scan offers a powerful tool in the identification of abnormalities of brain function.

Although PET has valid clinical uses (e.g., identification of a seizure focus in a patient with epilepsy), the validity of its use as a diagnostic tool for other conditions, such as traumatic brain injury, has not been established. Like the QEEG, analysis of the PET scan can be manipulated by the operator, who can visually choose areas of apparent contrast and find significant statistical differences in essentially any subject. This susceptibility toward false positives reduces the value of the PET procedure in courtroom proceedings.

Although PET has been admitted as evidence in some courts, others have found against its admissibility. For instance, in *People v. Protsman* (2001), a murder defendant claimed a history of traumatic brain injury as mitigating evidence in the sentencing phase of his trial. After expert testimony established that PET was not accepted by the scientific community for identifying head trauma, the court ruled against its admission, a decision that was later upheld by the California Court of Appeals.

Conversely, in the same judicial district, the same appeals court permitted testimony based on PET results in another murder case, *People v. Williams* (2004). In that case, Elton Williams shot and killed his uncle during an argument. The defense expert testified that PET results showed decreased activity in the frontal lobes, basal ganglia, and hypothalamus, findings often consistent with poor judgment and difficulty inhibiting aggression. The court allowed this testimony without comment, though they affirmed Williams's guilty verdict.

We recommend that PET evidence be restricted to supporting testimony for which it is clearly suited. For example, PET evidence of a seizure focus in an epileptic patient may well be acceptable and admissible. PET evidence of a mild traumatic brain injury, on the other hand, may not. The use of PET evidence to establish reduced efficiency of frontal cortical functioning in a very impulsive, psychiatrically disturbed patient may well be acceptable if there is other evidence supporting the presence of the mental syndrome and the impulsivity. But to testify de novo that evidence of frontal hypometabolism on a PET scan reflects impulsivity or severe psychiatric disturbance is inappropriate, in our opinion.

Single Photon Emission Computed Tomography

Single photon emission computed tomography (SPECT) scans also create visual images of the brain's activity (Simon, Greenberg, & Arminoff, 2009). This technology produces images at much lower resolution than PET scans. SPECT utilizes CT technology in combination with a radioactive tracer that is injected into the bloodstream. The tracer gives off gamma rays, which are visualized by the scanner. It is a much less expensive technology than either PET or fMRI.

This method has been proffered by some centers as an effective method of detecting the sequelae of mild traumatic brain injury. However, research on this topic has been quite variable in methodology and findings, leading one reviewer to conclude, "Expert testimony regarding SPECT findings should be admissible only as evidence to support clinical history, neuropsychological test results, and structural brain imaging findings and not as stand-alone diagnostic data" (Wortzel, Filley, Anderson, Oster, & Ardnilegas, 2008).

As with PET, courts have varied in their admissibility decisions with regard to SPECT. In *People v. Hix* (2009), a lower court ruled that SPECT scans were inadmissible as evidence of brain injury in a murder case involving an insanity plea, a finding that was upheld by the California Court of Appeals. In contrast, a Michigan appeals court ruled that SPECT evidence was admissible for diagnosing brain injuries under the "general acceptance" standard (*Fini v. General Motors*, 2003). As with PET scans, we suggest that the use of SPECT technology in the courtroom be restricted to a supportive role and used only among evaluees for whom a given diagnosis has been otherwise established.

Functional Magnetic Resonance Imaging

FMRI also creates visual images of the brain's activity and metabolism, though at higher resolution than the PET or SPECT technologies. It relies on the fact that when the activity of a given region of the brain increases, blood flow to that area also increases. The scanner detects the blood-oxygen-level-dependent (BOLD) signal produced by the increased blood flow. FMRI is the choice of researchers who wish to measure the activity of given, discrete areas of the brain during specific functional tasks. Indeed, fMRI represents a technology much hoped for by brain researchers, a technology that allows for correlating specific functional tasks with specified areas of the brain. It is the technique of choice in the current avalanche of functional brain studies that aim to localize specific functions, traits, and behaviors.

A proposed use of fMRI has been to establish whether there are functional brain correlates to antisocial or psychopathic behavior (Kiehl et al, 2001). Such evidence may be appropriate to admit in the sentencing phase of a criminal trial, presumably in order to mitigate the actions of the defendant. If antisocial personality characteristics are at least partially the product of biology, the reasoning goes, then the defendant had limited control of those traits that influenced the criminal behavior. In an unpublished Illinois case (*People v. Dugan*, 2009), a defendant was accused of raping and murdering a 10-year-old girl. Evidence from fMRI—reportedly showing that the defendant had a psychopathic brain organization—was admitted by a trial court. Despite this evidence and expert testimony to support it, Dugan was nevertheless sentenced to death.

Diffusion Tensor Imaging

Diffusion tensor imaging (DTI) utilizes the same technology as the MRI scan but creates highly detailed images of the white matter, or nerve tracts, within the human brain. It can identify the presence of connective lesions within the brain with a high degree of sensitivity.

To our knowledge, DTI has rarely been offered as proof in United States courts. The single case that we identified, *Booth et al. v. KIT et al.* (2009), involved a series of individuals who had been exposed to carbon monoxide and were suing those believed responsible. The plaintiffs' expert in the case had MRIs performed of each of the plaintiffs, as well as a DTI scan performed on one of them. In its decision regarding the admissibility of the expert testimony, the court did not comment on the DTI procedure itself but overall found the expert's methods and testimony admissible according to Daubert criteria.

In our opinion, DTI findings should be admissible as evidence in cases in which DTI has been shown to produce reliable and valid data. If a question at issue in a lawsuit depends on the integrity of the white matter of the brain, then DTI may well be the preferred technology for responding to that question. Again, rarely will the technology itself be dispositive, but rather supportive of the overall diagnosis and opinions of the assessor.

Genotyping

With the completion of the Human Genome Project, all of the areas of the human DNA that give rise to specific developmental and structural changes have been identified. Many of these genetic functions relate, of course, to specific areas of brain development and the processing of neurotransmitters throughout the nervous system. Many genes have been implicated in specific forms of human illness, such as Down syndrome (trisomy 21), Huntington's disease, and Alzheimer's disease. Many psychiatric disorders are known to have heritable components in some populations. Also, genetic variation helps to explain why particular psychotropic medications are effective in some individuals but not in others. The use of genetic testing to identify these individual differences will revolutionize clinical psychiatry.

Violence and psychopathy are presumably influenced by a person's genetic makeup and his or her life experiences, as well the exercise of one's free will. We predict that in the future, genetic testing will be more precise, and gene-by-environment (GxE) interactions will be understood more completely, making it possible to demonstrate causal links between genetic and environment factors, the organization and functioning of the brain, patterns of thought and behavior, and psychiatric syndromes (Rutter, Moffitt, & Caspi, 2006). For example, one line of research indicates that there is a GxE interaction between the *MAOA* gene and a history of severe child abuse, such that individuals with both of these risk factors are more likely to engage in violent behaviors and be arrested (Caspi et al., 2002; Kim-Cohen et al., 2006; Weder et al., 2009). A second line of research indicates that when a person with the short allele of the *SLC6A4* gene experiences a number of adverse life experiences, the person is at an increased risk of becoming depressed and suicidal (Caspi et al., 2003; Caspi, Hariri, Holmes, Uher, & Moffitt, 2010; Xie et al., 2009). In an extensive recent review, Gunter and her colleagues said, "The greatest current evidence seems to point to *MAOA* and *5HTT* as promising sites for additional inquiry for antisocial spectrum disorders and psychopathy" (Gunter, Vaughn, & Philibert, 2010).

In some circumstances, this type of information will be relevant in civil and criminal trials (Bernet & Alkhatib, 2009; Bernet, Vnencak-Jones, Farahany, & Montgomery, 2007). We do not anticipate that individual genes will be found that directly cause specific behaviors or mental disorders. Rather, it is likely that the interaction of multiple genes and multiple life experiences will be highly influential risk factors for maladaptive behavior. Also, these GxE interactions will usually not prove that a person has a particular diagnosis, but they will support and explain the diagnosis that has been made through traditional evaluation methods.

Is it proper to testify regarding this type of GxE interaction in a legal proceeding? We believe that it is if certain conditions are met: (1) the GxE interaction is not assessed in isolation, but is part of a comprehensive biopsychosocial evaluation; (2) the evaluator presents the underlying research in an accurate manner, including research that supports as well as research that contradicts the genomic theory under consideration; (3) the evaluator does not exaggerate or overstate the implications of the findings.

In our experience, testimony regarding behavioral genomics has sometimes been allowed by trial judges and sometimes excluded. We expect that in individual cases testimony regarding behavioral genomics will or will not pass *Daubert* and *Frye* challenges depending on several factors: the thoroughness of the expert witness in explaining the scientific basis for the testimony; the nature of the underlying science regarding the particular test or tests that have been performed; and the relevance of the tests to the issues being addressed at each specific trial.

Neuropsychological Evaluation

Standardized testing to measure cognitive abilities has been available for a long time, but the correlation of identified deficits with specific brain lesions is a relatively recent development. With the advent of standardized neuropsychological testing batteries in the 1950s and 1960s (e.g., the Halstead-Reitan Neuropsychological Test Battery), neurocognitive testing became a powerful tool in the measurement of brain function and dysfunction. Today, comprehensive neuropsychological evaluation is a well-accepted and useful tool in assessing those with known or suspected brain lesions.

Properly credentialed neuropsychologists are able to serve as expert witnesses in most jurisdictions. In some states, such as North Carolina and Georgia, case law has limited neuropsychologists in expressing opinions regarding the medical causation of brain injuries. In Georgia, this issue was remedied with legislation. In most states, however, courts have consistently found that neuropsychologists are qualified to render opinions regarding the causation and pathology of brain insults. The Iowa Supreme Court case decision in *Hutchison v. American Family Mutual Insurance Company* (1994) provides an outline for the use of neuropsychological testimony in court, including the statement that neuropsychologists are qualified to diagnose the general state of the brain and the causation of brain pathology. The American Academy of Neurology (American Academy of Neurology, 1996) has produced official guidelines affirming the value of neuro-psychological assessment in the practice of neurology.

APPLICATIONS OF NEUROSCIENCE IN LEGAL PROCEEDINGS

The relevance of testimony regarding behavioral genomics and neuroimaging to legal proceedings depends on the exact nature of the scientific data and their role in the particular case—for example, whether genotyping is intended to establish a specific diagnosis or to support a diagnosis made on clinical grounds; or whether neuroimaging is used to support a diagnosis or simply to explain a person's behavior or mental condition. Also, the significance of the testimony depends on the legal issue that is being addressed—for example, whether it relates to competency to engage in some aspect of the legal procedures, criminal responsibility, risk assessment, or some other question. We consider several legal questions that might be addressed through neuroscience.

Criminal Responsibility—Insanity

Most states in the United States have some form of the insanity defense, although there are varying definitions of what constitutes insanity. A typical definition is that "at the time of the commission of the acts constituting the offense, the defendant, as a result of a severe mental disease or defect, was unable to appreciate the nature or wrongfulness of such defendant's acts" (Tennessee Code §39-11-501). Some states also include in their definitions that the mental disorder prevented the defendant from controlling his behavior. For example: "A person is not responsible for criminal conduct if at the time of such conduct, as a result of mental illness or retardation, he lacks substantial capacity either to appreciate the criminality of his conduct or to conform his conduct to the requirements of law" (Kentucky Revised Statutes §504.020).

In some instances, genetic testing may help to establish that the defendant has one of the criteria for an insanity defense, that is, "a severe mental disease or defect." For example, genetic testing could be used to show that the defendant has Huntington's disease, a neurological condition that sometimes evolves to a severe mental disease. The exact genetic basis for Huntington's disease has been known for decades. The following unpublished case, *Commonwealth v. Bobby Gene Parker,* illustrates how testimony regarding Huntington's disease may be very helpful in determining the outcome of a criminal proceeding.

> **Case 1.** In 2001, at age 61, Mr. Parker was found to have Huntington's disease. Mr. Parker had uncontrollable movements in his face, legs, and

feet and cognitive impairment in concentration and memory. He manifested psychiatric and behavioral symptoms, including physical violence toward people and property, delusions involving his wife, and reckless spending of money. In 2003, Mr. Parker allegedly solicited another person to burn down the family farm. He reportedly stated various motives at different times, such as wanting to collect the insurance on the farmhouse, thinking his wife was having an affair with the sheriff, and thinking the fire would bring his wife closer to him. The pretrial forensic evaluator thought Mr. Parker met criteria for the insanity defense because he had a severe mental disease that caused him to lack substantial capacity to conform his conduct to the requirements of the law. Ultimately, the charges against Mr. Parker were dismissed.

We believe that such testimony regarding Huntington's disease easily fulfilled both *Frye* and *Daubert* criteria for vetting expert testimony. This type of testimony is admissible because the evaluator based his opinions on established scientific standards for the diagnosis of Huntington's disease and came to conclusions about the effects of that disorder in a way that was consistent with accepted standards of practice.

The diagnosis of a neurological or psychiatric condition does not, however, prove the additional criteria for an insanity defense, that is, the defendant's inability "to appreciate the criminality of his conduct or to conform his conduct to the requirements of law." To determine whether the defendant met one of these additional criteria, a forensic psychiatrist or psychologist must collect information regarding the person's functional abilities, which typically includes interviews and psychological testing of the defendant; interviews of collateral sources, such as family members, who observed the defendant about the time of the alleged offense; and the report of law enforcement personnel regarding their investigation of the circumstances of the crime and the defendant's behavior and statements when he or she was arrested.

Criminal Responsibility—Diminished Capacity

Most criminal offenses are defined by a particular *mens rea* ("guilty mind") and *actus reus* ("guilty act"). For example, the *actus reus* for first-degree murder is the killing of another person. In Tennessee, the *mens rea* for first-degree murder is that the killing of another person was done in a premeditated and intentional manner. Also, the Tennessee Code defines "premeditation" as "an act done after the exercise of reflection and judgment," and it is required that "the mental state of the accused at the time the accused allegedly decided to kill . . . was sufficiently free from excitement and passion as to be capable of premeditation" (Tennessee Code § 39-13-202). "Diminished capacity" refers to a defendant's inability— usually as a result of neurological or psychiatric illness or substance abuse—to achieve the mental state required for a particular crime. For instance, a person who is very intoxicated on cocaine or a person who is extremely depressed might not be able to exercise reflection and judgment and therefore might lack the capacity to commit first-degree murder.

Some jurisdictions allow mental health professionals to testify regarding diminished capacity. In those jurisdictions, the mental health professional might incorporate neuroscientific investigation—such as genetic testing, neuroimaging, or neuropsychological testing—into a comprehensive pretrial assessment of a defendant's mental ability to achieve the mental state required for a particular crime. As in the previous discussion regarding the insanity defense, the diagnosis by itself would not prove diminished capacity, but it would be part of the testimony to show why the person lacked the capacity to form a particular mental state. The following case, *Tennessee v. Jason Clinard*, illustrates how testimony regarding a possible GxE interaction might be appropriate to introduce at a criminal trial. The GxE data did not prove the defendant had a particular diagnosis, but they supported the diagnosis that was made through a traditional forensic psychiatric evaluation.

> **Case 2.** Jason Clinard was a 14-year-old ninth-grade student who experienced an unusual number of psychosocial stressors. He became seriously depressed and suicidal. One morning in 2005, Jason woke up and considered committing suicide that day. Jason obtained a handgun from the family gun cabinet and loaded it. However, when the bus came to take him to school, Jason suddenly shot and killed the bus driver. As part of a comprehensive, pretrial, forensic psychiatric evaluation, Jason had genetic testing. He was homozygous for the short allele of the *SLC6A4* gene. At Jason's trial in criminal court, a forensic psychiatrist explained the significance of the *SLC6A4* genotyping associated with his history of psychosocial stressors—that is, that these two factors together created a vulnerability for Jason to become depressed and suicidal. The genetic testing supported the expert's conclusion that Jason had a serious mental disorder at the time of the alleged offense: major depressive disorder. The defense attorney argued that the jury should consider this information when deciding whether Jason committed first-degree murder (requiring premeditation, i.e., the exercise of reflection and judgment) or second-degree murder. However, this neuroscientific data did not appear to benefit Jason; the jury found him guilty of first-degree murder.

The following case, *Tennessee v. Waldroup* (2011), illustrates how testimony regarding this GxE interaction might help explain the defendant's behavior and also his limited capacity to form the intent to commit first-degree murder.

> **Case 3.** Mr. Bradley Waldroup was a 32-year-old man who was charged with one count of first-degree murder and one count of attempted

first-degree murder. The alleged assaults were quite violent, and the prosecution sought the death penalty. Mr. Waldroup's defense attorneys arranged for a comprehensive, pretrial forensic evaluation, which included a psychiatric assessment, neuropsychological testing, brain scans, an electroencephalogram, and behavioral genetic testing. Mr. Waldroup had a history of child maltreatment and a more recent history of stressful life experiences. The genotyping revealed that Mr. Waldroup had the low-activity allele of the *MAOA* gene (which, together with a history of child maltreatment, put him at increased risk of violent behavior) and had both short and long alleles of the *SLC6A4* gene (which, together with a history of stressful life experiences, put him at increased risk of depression and suicidality). After a *Daubert*-type hearing, the judge ruled that this information could be presented to the jury, along with the rest of the psychiatric and neuropsychological assessments. The jury took the behavioral genomic testimony into consideration and found Mr. Waldroup guilty of voluntary manslaughter rather than first-degree murder.

Although the authors conclude that testimony regarding behavioral genomics in these cases was appropriate, that does not necessarily mean that this type of testimony will always fulfill *Frye* and *Daubert* criteria. For instance, a court may decide that at the time of some future trial, the scientific research for this testimony is inadequate. Or a court may decide that the behavioral genomic research—although quite adequate—is not directly relevant to the legal issue in the current trial.

Criminal Responsibility—Mitigation

In the guilt phase of the trial, the jury or the judge decides whether the defendant committed the crime. If the defendant is found guilty, additional evidence is presented in the penalty phase of the trial, and the jury or the judge decides what the defendant's sentence will be. During the penalty phase, the defense attorney can present a very broad range of information to influence the jury and judge to be lenient toward the defendant. If the defendant was found guilty of a capital crime such as first-degree murder, the jury may forgo the death penalty and sentence the person to life in prison, either with or without the possibility of parole. If the defendant was found guilty of a felony and the range of imprisonment is 15–25 years, the judge may rely on mitigation testimony to impose a sentence at the lower end of that range.

Is neuroscience testimony relevant during the penalty phase of a trial? Many topics may be relevant during the penalty phase of a trial, including: the defendant's youth; the defendant's old age; acting under duress or under the domination of another person; the defendant's mental or physical condition that significantly reduced his culpability; or a mental or physical condition that reduced the defendant's ability to appreciate the wrongfulness of his conduct or to conform his conduct to the requirements of the law. Often, the defense presents testimony about the defendant's difficult childhood, such as experiencing chronic illness, child maltreatment, or poverty.

It may be relevant to present testimony that a person's neuropsychological makeup—along with other factors—predisposed the person to commit a violent, antisocial act. Neurocognitive testing can establish that a given defendant has cognitive deficits or organic personality changes that place him or her at greater risk for impulsive, violent acts. Because these conditions are outside the offender's conscious control, they may be considered as mitigating factors in the penalty phase of a trial. Consider the following unpublished case of *Tennessee v. Jack Brumbalough*.

> **Case 4.** Mr. Jack Brumbalough, 44, was arrested and charged with first-degree murder in connection with the killing of his friend and roommate. Mr. Brumbalough had suffered several serious head injuries over the years, with prolonged episodes of unconsciousness, and brain scans showed evidence of brain injuries. His family reported that following one of these injuries his personality changed. Though previously pleasant and calm, he developed a very short temper and was prone toward aggressive, violent outbursts. These outbursts were particularly frequent when he was under the influence of alcohol. One night, Mr. Brumbalough had been drinking heavily. He got into an argument with his roommate, who pulled a gun on him and fired shots into the floor. Mr. Brumbalough grabbed a crowbar and struck his roommate several times with it. The roommate was found dead the next day. Neuropsychological testing showed that the defendant had an IQ in the mentally retarded range, despite a history of low average performance in school. He also had notable deficits in his memory skills, language ability, attention, and executive functioning skills. At the trial, a neuropsychologist offered testimony that Mr. Brumbalough's cognitive problems and impulsivity should be considered as potentially mitigating factors in his crime. Despite the cognitive testing evidence, the neuroimaging evidence, and the supporting testimony from several family members, Mr. Brumbalough was still sentenced to life in prison.

Criminal Responsibility—Plea Bargain

Plea bargaining means that a defendant is offered a lower penalty in exchange for a guilty plea to a lesser offense. The prosecution avoids the uncertainty that a defendant may be found innocent, and the defendant avoids a potentially much harsher sentence by accepting the deal offered. Most criminal cases are resolved in this way.

Neuroimaging may help establish that the defendant has a psychiatric condition that constitutes "a severe mental disease or defect," which raises the possibility of a successful insanity defense and leads the prosecution to offer a better plea deal to the defendant. Occasionally, a PET scan or an MRI scan clearly proves that a person has a neuropsychiatric disorder that can cause a severe mental disease, for example, a large tumor in a person's temporal lobe. More frequently, the brain scan simply confirms a diagnosis that has been made on clinical grounds. In the following unpublished case, *Tennessee v. Brenda DeBerry,* a woman had cerebral lupus erythematosus, which was visible on the MRI of her brain.

> **Case 5.** Ms. Brenda DeBerry, 38, was charged with first-degree murder, conspiracy to commit first-degree murder, contributing to the delinquency of a minor, and tampering with evidence. The state was seeking the death penalty. Ms. DeBerry had gotten involved in a feud among drug dealers, and she allegedly assisted a group of men when they killed one of the competing drug dealers. She had a long history of mental illness, which had gotten much worse in the weeks prior to the murder. Following the murder of the drug dealer, Ms. DeBerry had visual hallucinations, auditory hallucinations, and bizarre delusions. Ms. DeBerry was admitted to a state hospital, where she was diagnosed with lupus erythematosus. It was later determined that this illness had started several years previously. The diagnosis of lupus erythematosus was supported by laboratory testing: positive antinuclear antibody, positive anti-DNA antibody, and elevated sedimentation rate. The diagnosis of a lupus inflammation of the brain was supported by an MRI, which showed 10 to 15 small foci of increased T2 signal in the white matter of her brain. Although Ms. DeBerry did not meet criteria for insanity, she had a medical condition that caused a serious chronic psychiatric disorder. This psychotic mental disorder impaired—but did not eliminate—her capacity to appreciate the wrongfulness of her conduct, to conform her conduct to the requirements of the law, and to deliberate and premeditate. Instead of risking the death penalty at trial, Ms. DeBerry pled guilty to second-degree murder and was sentenced to 22 years.

The actions of the forensic evaluator in the DeBerry matter were appropriate because the diagnosis of lupus and the interpretation of the brain scan were each based on sound scientific principles. The forensic psychiatrist simply identified clinical information that was relevant to the defendant's actions, assisting both the prosecution and the defense in successfully resolving their case in a way that was acceptable to both sides.

Competency to Waive Miranda Rights

Mental competency is a very important issue in many aspects of the criminal justice system. In an important case, *Miranda v. Arizona* (1966), the Supreme Court established the principle that a person who has been arrested has a right to remain silent and a right to an attorney. The Supreme Court also said that an individual may waive these rights, "provided the waiver is made voluntarily, knowingly and intelligently." Mental health professionals are frequently asked to assess whether a defendant was competent at some time in the past when he or she waived Miranda rights and made a statement to investigators. Consider the following unpublished case.

> **Case 6.** A 54-year-old man who was known to be mentally retarded was charged with seven counts of rape of a child, four counts of aggravated sexual battery, and twelve counts of contributing to the delinquency of a minor. On standardized tests of malingering, there was no evidence that the defendant was trying to make his mental skills appear worse than they really were. On the Wechsler Adult Intelligence Scale—III (WAIS-III), his Verbal IQ was 52, Performance IQ was 64, and Full-Scale IQ was 53. On Grisso's Test of Assessing, Understanding, and Appreciation of Miranda Rights, the defendant scored below the 1st percentile compared with a population of adult offenders. On the Gudjonsson Suggestibility Scales, he was shown to be easily led and profoundly susceptible to suggestion. The forensic psychologist concluded that the defendant was moderately mentally retarded, that he was not competent to waive his Miranda rights, and that he was not competent to stand trial and probably never would be. If this defendant is not competent to go to trial but is considered dangerous to children in the community, he could be committed to a long-term residential facility.

Forensic experts also evaluate competency to stand trial. In another important decision, *Dusky v. United States* (1960), the Supreme Court endorsed the position taken by the solicitor general that the test for competency to stand trial "must be whether [the defendant] has sufficient present ability to consult with his lawyer with a reasonable degree of rational understanding—and whether he has a rational as well as factual understanding of the proceedings against him." Occasionally, forensic experts are asked to evaluate an inmate's competency to waive his or her appeals. For example, an inmate on death row may assert that he wants to waive additional appeals and proceed with his execution. His attorneys, however, may assert that the man is not competent to waive his appeals, so this may lead to evaluations by forensic psychiatrists and psychologists. These forensic evaluations may include neuroimaging, psychological testing, and neuropsychological testing.

Competency to be Executed

In *Ford v. Wainwright* (1986), the Supreme Court established that individuals may not be executed unless they are mentally competent. In this circumstance, the test for competency is whether the individual understands that an execution will take place and that the execution is meant as a penalty for the acts for which the person was found guilty. This is a very low standard for competence and one which presumably all but the most severely impaired individuals would meet.

In evaluating a person's competency to be executed, the mental health professional would ordinarily assume the person is competent unless there is some reason to think otherwise. To conclude that an individual is not competent, the evaluator would have to identify some mental disorder that is causing the impairment in mental functioning. Of course, making the diagnosis of mental illness or mental defect does not in itself mean the person is not competent, and that conclusion would require additional assessment of the person's actual functioning. In an appellate case, *Coe v. Ball, Coe* (2000), the court reviewed the roles of forensic experts who were asked to evaluate whether a convicted murderer and rapist was competent to be executed.

> **Case 7.** Robert Glen Coe was convicted in 1981 of the aggravated kidnapping, rape, and murder of an 8-year-old girl. He was sentenced to death. In January 2000, a hearing was held with regard to his competency to be executed. At the hearing, a forensic psychiatrist offered opinions that Mr. Coe was schizophrenic and not competent to be executed due to his delusional belief that he would be reincarnated after his death. The psychiatrist's opinion was based partially on MRI and PET findings that were reportedly consistent with schizophrenia, reflecting ventricular enlargement and areas of cortical hypometabolism. Other experts testified that Mr. Coe was feigning the presence of mental illness, as established by results on several well-accepted neuropsychological tests of malingering. The U.S. Court of Appeals for the Sixth Circuit affirmed the decision of the judge that Mr. Coe was competent to be executed. Mr. Coe was executed in April 2000.

Dangerousness

The clinical vignettes in this chapter have all involved criminal cases. In most instances, the evaluations based on neuroscience—brain imaging, behavioral genomics, and neuropsychological testing—were requested by the defense attorneys. In fact, forensic psychiatric and psychological evaluations are usually initiated by defense attorneys. However, we consider neuroscience to be neutral with regard to legal issues, and we believe that both defense attorneys and prosecuting attorneys may make use of these techniques.

For example, in the penalty phase of a trial, both the defense and the prosecution have an opportunity to present additional evidence. In some cases, the prosecution may argue that behavioral genomic testimony is not mitigating but is an aggravating factor that should increase the length of a sentence. The prosecution may say, for instance, that because of the defendant's genetic makeup and his or her childhood experiences, he or she has violent tendencies and should have a longer sentence in order to protect society for a longer time.

Whether testimony regarding behavioral genomics favors the prosecution or the defense depends on the circumstances. In a case of aggravated burglary, for instance, the prosecution may logically argue that a person's genotype and bad life experiences constitute a serious risk factor and indicate that he or she should be imprisoned longer in order to protect society. In a case of capital murder, on the other hand, the jury realizes that the defendant is never going to leave prison and threaten society. In that situation, it may be logical for the defense to argue that the person's genotype and bad life experiences mean he should have a life sentence rather than the death penalty.

Deception Detection

Courts have been concerned—probably since the origins of systematic jurisprudence—with whether defendants and witnesses were telling the truth. Investigators and court officers have devised many techniques for the detection of deception, ranging from the outright barbaric to rather sophisticated approaches. Readers are probably familiar with the use of polygraphy and psycholinguistic analysis for lie detection. Two approaches to deception detection based on contemporary neuroscience involve the EEG and the fMRI.

Farwell (Farwell & Smith, 2001) extensively studied the use of a particular feature of the EEG to distinguish truth from deception. His method was based on the observation that a specific EEG response—called a "memory and encoding related multifaceted electroencephalographic response," or MERMER— occurred when the subject saw or heard personally relevant information. The most prominent MERMER was termed the P300 response because it occurred 300 milliseconds after exposure to the stimulus. Farwell thought that the events at a crime scene could be linked to the memories in the mind of the criminal who was present when the events occurred, which he called "brain fingerprinting." Rosenfeld and his colleagues have also studied and refined the P300-based deception detection test (Meixner & Rosenfeld, 2010; Rosenfeld, Angell, Johnson, & Qian, 1991).

In 2000, an Iowa District Court allowed Farwell to testify regarding Terry Harrington, who was appealing his conviction of murdering a man in 1978. Harrington's conviction was ultimately overturned by the Iowa Supreme Court in 2003. However, Harrington's conviction was not overturned because of Farwell's testimony but primarily because it was determined that the prosecution at the

original trial had withheld crime scene information that would have been helpful to Harrington's defense.

Langleben and his colleagues studied the use of fMRI in identifying deception
(Hakun et al., 2008; Langleben et al., 2002). Their premise is that there are neurophysiological differences between deception and truth, which can be detected
by fMRI technology. Two companies, No Lie MRI and Cephos, offer technology
that purports to correctly distinguish truth-tellers and liars with greater than
90% accuracy.

In the apparent first attempt in a U.S. court to introduce fMRI deception
detection evidence (*United States v. Semrau*, 2010), the attempt failed. In its rul-
ing, the court found that the Cephos deception detection technology met two
prongs of FRE Rule 702: whether the method could be tested and whether it had
been subjected to appropriate peer review. However, the court ruled that Cephos
failed to meet the criteria of having an established error rate and having standards that govern its administration, as well as the general acceptance criteria.
Also, the court criticized the expert for violating his own standards by testing
the defendant a second time after an initial test showed him to be deceptive.

Most reviewers have concluded that testimony regarding EEG and fMRI
deception detection is not yet ready for the courts. Moriarty (2008, 2009),
a law professor, said, "How will courts likely respond to neuroimaging 'lie detec-
tors' and 'brain fingerprinting?' With skepticism, one would imagine and hope.
Jurists and legal scholars are discomforted by physiological measurements of
truth, both as a matter of evidentiary reliability and as a policy question impli-
cating privacy and autonomy." Also, in an extensive review of this topic, Wagner
concluded that there has been insufficient research to establish the accuracy of
these procedures in identifying deception at the individual level (Wagner, 2010).
Despite the skepticism of these and other reviewers, these companies have tested
hundreds of potential litigants, and there will doubtless be numerous attempts to
introduce novel lie detection evidence into court proceedings.

Juvenile Court

Juvenile courts are generally based on the principle of rehabilitation, so juvenile
court officers are usually interested in understanding the biological, psychological, and social factors that contributed to a youngster's problematic behaviors.
In order to arrive at appropriate dispositions of their cases, juvenile court judges
take into consideration social histories, psychological testing, and psychiatric
evaluations. Judges consider these data helpful when they design interventions
or corrective actions to reduce the likelihood of more trouble in the future.

With regard to the influence of neuroscience in juvenile court, MRI-based
research has shown that adolescents' brains are typically not fully myelinated
(a developmental process of encoating the nerves of the brain by a substance that
increases efficiency of neural transmission) until their early to mid-20s (Giedd
et al., 1999; Maroney, 2009; Sowell, Thompson, Holmes, Jernigan, & Toga, 1999).

This fact is thought to be related to the relatively lower degree of executive functioning that adolescents demonstrate, for example, functions such as impulse control, delayed gratification, self-awareness, and higher-order reasoning. Some writers concluded that this research supports the proposition that the law should not consider adolescents to be as accountable for their actions as adults, including the imputation of similar legal penalties for similar crimes. For example, should an adolescent who commits an impulsive murder be subject to the same penalties as an adult who commits a similar crime?

In *Roper v. Simmons* (2005), the U.S. Supreme Court decided that adolescents will not be subject to capital punishment. Amicus briefs were submitted to the Court, one from the American Psychological Association and a second from the American Medical Association, the American Psychiatric Association, and other organizations. Those briefs explained how MRI research helped to clarify the process of adolescent brain development. However, the Court chose not to comment on those findings in the course of its opinion. The Court seemed to say that we all know that adolescents are less mature than adults, so we do not need MRI research to prove that point.

It is likely that defense attorneys will introduce research regarding adolescent brain development during the sentencing phase of trials in which adolescents are convicted of serious crimes. For instance, in *Gall v. United States* (2007), the Supreme Court affirmed the finding of a lower court that had granted a shorter sentence to a man whose offense had occurred before he was 21, citing the findings of the relevant research. However, most of the MRI research on adolescent brain development has been based on group data. This type of evidence will be more significant if it can be shown that a particular adolescent appears to have an unusually immature brain, when his or her MRI is compared with group norms.

Also, early research regarding GxE interactions has started to explain why some children manifest oppositional defiant disorder and conduct disorder whereas others do not (Foley et al., 2004; Jaffee et al., 2005; Kim-Cohen et al., 2006; Prom-Wormley et al., 2008). Of course, juvenile court judges are not interested simply in theories and research; they want interventions and rehabilitation that actually works. We predict that in the future, practitioners will develop more specific and more effective treatments that are based on neuroimaging and an understanding the GxE risk factors. For example, perhaps it will be determined that some forms of adolescent violence are treatable with medication, whereas other forms of violence require lengthy residential treatment.

Sex Offenders

We also predict that in the future, neuroscience research will contribute to the classification and disposition of sex offenders. Mental health professionals conduct evaluations of sex offenders with the goals of identifying any psychopathology that may be driving the sexual offending, assessing the person's capacity for

treatment and rehabilitation, and assessing the person's risk for future danger-
ousness as a sex offender. Psychosexual evaluations are typically conducted after
a person has been found guilty of a sexual offense and prior to sentencing, so the
evaluation is intended to help the court decide on the sentence or other disposition of the case. In some states, psychosexual evaluations are performed when an
incarcerated sexual offender is approaching the end of his or her sentence. In that
scenario, the purpose of the evaluation is to determine whether the individual is
a sexually violent predator and whether civil commitment is appropriate.

There are many types of sex offenders. At one extreme, some sex offenders
are compulsive, violent, and sadistic; they are likely to offend again at the earli-
est opportunity. At the other extreme, some sex offenders have simply manifested transitory bad judgment and are unlikely to reoffend. In the future,
assessments based on neuroscience—both neuroimaging and an analysis of GxE
interactions—may help evaluators separate the malignant from the benign sex
offenders. We are not suggesting that an assessment based simply on an fMRI or
behavioral genomics would be used to make conclusions or recommendations.
However, we are predicting that the components of a psychosexual evaluation
that are currently in use—the clinical interview, actuarial methods, deception
detection through polygraphy, and measuring sexual arousal by penile plethys-
mography and visual reaction time—will be supplemented with data from neuroimaging and behavioral genomics.

CONCLUSIONS

As our understanding of the human brain and its links to human behavior continues to grow, so will attempts to utilize the findings of clinical tests of brain
structure and function in legal proceedings. Forensic evaluators have a wide
range of diagnostic tests at their command to assist in the assessment of brain
disorders. The admissibility of these test findings in court is governed by legal
rules of evidence. To a large degree, the admissibility of these techniques into
evidence is governed by the quality of the science underlying them. As techniques become better researched and accepted as well-validated neuroscientific
procedures, the likelihood that courts will admit the results into evidence will
increase. Forensic evaluators have a duty to be aware of the science and research
underlying the procedures they use in the course of their evaluations and to be
prepared to educate courts about their respective validity. They also have a duty
to confine themselves to using procedures that are scientifically defensible.

REFERENCES

American Academy of Neurology. (1996). Assessment: Neuropsychological testing of
    adults. Considerations for neurologists. *Neurology, 47*, 592–599.

Bernet, W., & Alkhatib, A. (2009). Genomics, behavior, and testimony at criminal trials. In N. Farahany (Ed.), *The impact of behavioral sciences on criminal law* (pp. 291–315). New York, NY: Oxford University Press.

Bernet, W., Vnencak-Jones, C., Farahany, N., & Montgomery, S. (2007). Bad nature, bad nurture, and testimony regarding *MAOA* and *SLC6A4* genotyping at criminal trials. *Journal of Forensic Sciences, 52,* 1362–1371.

Booth et al. v. KIT, Inc. et al. (2009). Dist. Court D., New Mexico.

Bufkin, J. L., & Luttrell, V. R. (2005). Neuroimaging studies of aggressive and violent behavior: Current findings and implications for criminology and criminal justice. *Trauma Violence and Abuse, 6,* 176–191.

Caspi, A., Hariri, A. R., Holmes, A., Uher, R., & Moffitt, T. E. (2010). Genetic sensitivity to the environment: The case of the serotonin transporter gene and its implications for studying complex diseases and traits. *American Journal of Psychiatry, 167,* 509–527.

Caspi, A., McClay, J., Moffitt, T. E., Mill, J., Martin, J., Craig, I. W., . . . Poulton, R. (2002). Role of genotype in the cycle of violence in maltreated children. *Science, 297,* 851–854.

Caspi, A., Sugden, K., Moffitt, T. E., Taylor, A., Craig, I. W., Harrington, H., . . . Poulton, R. (2003). Influence of life stress on depression: Moderation by a polymorphism in the 5-HTT gene. *Science, 301,* 386–389.

Daubert v. Merrell Dow Pharmaceuticals, 509 U.S. 579 (1993).

Dresser, R. (2008). Neuroscience's uncertain threat to criminal law. *Hastings Center Report, 38,* 9–10.

Dusky v. United States, 362 U.S. 402 (1960).

Farahany, N., & Coleman, J. E. (2009). Genetics, neuroscience, and criminal responsibility. In N. Farahany (Ed.), *The impact of behavioral sciences on criminal law* (pp. 183–240). New York, NY: Oxford University Press.

Farwell, L. A., & Smith, S. S. (2001). Using brain MERMER testing to detect knowledge despite efforts to conceal. *Journal of Forensic Sciences, 46,* 135–143.

Fini v. General Motors, WL1861925 (Mich. Ct. App. 2003).

Foley, D. L., Eaves, L. J., Wormley, B., Silberg, J. L., Maes, H. H., Kuhn, J., & Riley, B. (2004). Childhood adversity, monoamine oxidase a genotype, and risk for conduct disorder. *Archives of General Psychiatry, 61,* 738–744.

Ford v. Wainwright, 477 U.S. 399 (1986).

Frye v. United States, 293 F. 1013 (D.C. Cir. 1923)

Gall v. United States, 552 U.S. 38 (2007).

Giedd, J. N., Blumenthal, J., Jeffries, N. O., Castellanos, F. X., Liu, H., Zijdenbos, A., . . . Rapoport, J. L. (1999). Brain development during childhood and adolescence: A longitudinal MRI study. *Nature Neuroscience, 2,* 861–863.

Grafton, S. T. (2010). Has science already appeared in the courtroom? In A. S. Mansfield (Ed.), *A judge's guide to neuroscience: A concise introduction* (pp. 54–59). Santa Barbara, CA: University of California.

Gunter, T. D., Vaughn, M. G., & Philibert, R. A. (2010). Behavioral genetics in antisocial spectrum disorders and psychopathy: A review of the recent literature. *Behavioral Sciences and the Law, 28,* 148–173.

Hakun, J. G., Seelig, D., Ruparel, K., Loughead, J. W., Busch, E., Gur, R. C., & Langleben, D. D. (2008). fMRI investigation of the cognitive structure of the Concealed Information Test. *Neurocase, 14,* 59–67.

Hutchison v. American Family Mutual Insurance Company, 514 N.W.2d 882 (Iowa, 1994).

Jaffee, S. R., Caspi, A., Moffitt, T. E., Dodge, K. A., Rutter, M., Taylor, A., & Tully, L. A. (2005). Nature X nurture: Genetic vulnerabilities interact with physical maltreatment to promote conduct problems. *Development and Psychopathology, 17,* 67–84.

Jones, O. (2009). Behavioral genetics and crime, in context. In N. Farahany (Ed.), *The impact of behavioral sciences on criminal law* (pp. 125–146). New York, NY: Oxford University Press.

Kentucky Legislature. (2011). *Kentucky revised statutes.* Retrieved from http://www.lrc.ky.gov/krs/titles.htm.

Kiehl, K.A., Smith, A.M., Hare, R.D., Mendrek, A., Forster, B.B., Brink, J., Biddle, P.F. (2001). Limbic abnormalities in affective processing by criminal psychopaths as revealed by functional magnetic resonance imaging. *Biological Psychiatry, 50,* 677–684.

Kim-Cohen, J., Caspi, A., Taylor, A., Williams, B., Newcombe, R., Craig, I. W., & Moffitt, T. E. (2006). MAOA, maltreatment, and gene-environment interaction predicting children's mental health: New evidence and a meta-analysis. *Molecular Psychiatry, 11,* 903–913.

Kulynch, J. (1996). Brain, mind, and criminal behavior: Neuroimages as scientific evidence. *Jurimetrics, 36,* 235–244.

Langleben, D. D., Schroeder, L., Maldjian, J. A., Gur, R. C., McDonald, S., Ragland, J. D., … Childress, A. R. (2002). Brain activity during simulated deception: An event-related functional magnetic resonance study. *NeuroImage, 15,* 727–732.

Maroney, T. A. (2009). The false promise of adolescent brain science in juvenile justice. *Notre Dame Law Review, 85,* 89–176.

Meixner, J. B., & Rosenfeld, J. P. (2010). Countermeasure mechanisms in a P300-based concealed information test. *Psychophysiology, 47,* 57–65.

Miranda v. Arizona, 384 U.S. 436 (1966).

Moriarty, J. C. (2008). Flickering admissibility: Neuroimaging evidence in the U.S. courts. *Behavioral Sciences and the Law, 26,* 29–49.

Moriarty, J. C. (2009). Visions of deception: Neuroimages and the search for truth. *Akron Law Review, 42,* 739–761.

Nuwer, M. (1997). Assessment of digital EEG, quantitative EEG, and EEG brain mapping: Report of the American Academy of Neurology and the American Clinical Neurophysiology Society. *American Academy of Neurology, 49,* 277–292.

Onay, O. (2006). The true ramifications of genetic criminality research for free will in the criminal justice system. *Genomics, Society and Policy, 2,* 80–91.

People v. Hix (Cal. Ct. App. 2009 2nd Dist., Div. Two).

People v. Protsman, 105 Cal. Rptr.2d 819 (Cal. Ct. App. 4th Dist. 2001).

People v. Williams, WL740049 (Cal. Ct. App. 4th Dist. 2004).

Prom-Wormley, E. C., Eaves, L. J., Foley, D. L., Gardner, C. O., Archer, K. J., Wormley, B. K., … Silberg, J. L. (2008). Monoamine oxidase A and childhood adversity as risk factors for conduct disorder in females. *Psychological Medicine, 39*(4), 1–12.

Robert Glenn Coe v. Ricky Bell. 209 F.3d 815 (2000).

Roper v. Simmons, 543 U.S. 551 (2005).

Ropper, A. H., & Samuels, M. A. (2009). *Adams and Victor's principles of neurology* (9th ed.). New York, NY: McGraw-Hill.

Rosenfeld, J. P., Angell, A., Johnson, M., & Qian, J. H. (1991). An ERP-based, control-question lie detector analog: Algorithms for discriminating effects within individuals' average waveforms. *Psychophysiology, 28,* 319–335.

Rutter, M., Moffitt, T. E., & Caspi, A. (2006). Gene-environment interplay and psychopathology: Multiple varieties but real effects. *Journal of Child Psychology and Psychiatry, 47,* 226–261.

Simon, R. P., Greenberg, D. A., & Arminoff, M. J. (2009). *Clinical neurology* (7th ed.). New York, NY: McGraw-Hill.

State of Tennessee v. Jason Clinard (Tenn. Crim. App. 2008).

State of Tennessee v. Davis Bradley Waldroup, Jr. (Tenn. Crim. App. 2011)

Sowell, E. R., Thompson, P. M., Holmes, C. J., Jernigan, T. L., & Toga, A. W. (1999). In vivo evidence for post-adolescent brain maturation in frontal and striatal regions. *Nature Neuroscience, 2,* 859–861.

Tennessee Code Unannotated. (2012). Retrieved from http://www.lexisnexis.com/hottopics/tncode

United States v. Semrau. No. 2:10-cr-10074 JPM, 2011 WL9258

Wagner, A. (2010). Can neuroscience detect lies? In A. S. Mansfield (Ed.), *A judge's guide to neuroscience: A concise introduction* (pp. 13–25). Santa Barbara, CA: University of California.

Weder, N., Yang, B. Z., Douglas-Palumberi, H., Massey, J., Krystal, J. H., Gelernter, J., & Kaufman, J. (2009). MAOA genotype, maltreatment, and aggressive behavior: The changing impact of genotype at varying levels of trauma. *Biological Psychiatry, 65,* 417–424.

Wortzel, H. S., Filley, C. M., Anderson, C. A., Oster, T., & Ardnilegas, D. B. (2008). Forensic applications of cerebral single photon emission computed tomography in mild traumatic brain injury. *Journal of the American Academy of Psychiatry and the Law, 36,* 310–322.

Xie, P., Kranzler, H. R., Poling, J., Stein, M. B., Anton, R. F., Brady, K., . . . Gelernter, J. (2009). Interactive effect of stressful life events and the serotonin transporter 5-HT-TLPR genotype on posttraumatic stress disorder diagnosis in 2 independent populations. *Archives of General Psychiatry, 66,* 1201–1209.

13

Public Policy Implications of Research on Aggression and Antisocial Behavior

LOUIS KRAUS AND CHRISTOPHER R. THOMAS ∎

In addition to direct use in practical applications, scientific findings and theories have been used as evidence in courts of law and to inform legal statutes and judicial procedures in policy development. This chapter covers the development and current use of scientific testimony and research findings in policy, legislation, and court decisions regarding juvenile justice and implications for the future. Although neuroscience plays a role in policies concerning adult offenders as well, these issues are most sharply brought into focus in juvenile justice, as it confronts the fundamental question of how to handle the developmental transition from lack of criminal culpability in childhood to presumption of competency and responsibility in adulthood. Juvenile justice in the United States originated with the Illinois Juvenile Court Act of 1899, which separated children and adolescents from adults within the justice system and established a juvenile court with the aim to provide rehabilitation rather than punishment. The relationship between juvenile justice and scientific inquiry was established shortly afterward in 1908 when William Healy was appointed to direct clinical intervention and conduct research to better understand and treat juvenile offenders in the same Illinois juvenile court (Healy, 1915).

Since that time, U.S. public policy toward antisocial or delinquent behavior has often reflected public reaction to headlines more than it has actual research. As efforts to provide early intervention seemed to produce little change, questions arose regarding the utility of rehabilitation, even with young offenders. Public reaction to shocking crimes questioned a system that appeared to require no consequences or no punishment for personal behavior. Both the prosecution and the defense used psychiatric and neurologic testimony in the infamous Leopold and Loeb trial in 1924 (Batz, 2008). The contradictory findings of the leading psychiatric experts of the time, including William A. White, William Healy, Bernard Gluek, and Harold Hurbert for the defense and William Krohn and Archibald Church for the prosecution, raised questions in both the public mind and the courts as to the real utility of such evidence in criminal proceedings.

In addition, the presumption that the juvenile court provided rehabilitation rather than punishment resulted in procedures that did not define or protect the juvenile in court hearings, resulting in dispositions sometimes harsher than they would have been if the youth had been tried in adult criminal court. This changed somewhat in 1967 with the U.S. Supreme Court decision *In re: Gault* (1967) that ruled that some constitutional rights afforded to those tried in adult criminal court must also be afforded to those appearing in juvenile court, including the right to be represented by counsel. The constitutional privilege guarding against self-incrimination was deemed applicable to the 15-year-old Gerald Gault, who had pled guilty to making a lewd telephone call. The court determined that Gault's admission of guilt could not be used against him in the absence of clear and unequivocal evidence and that the admission was made with knowledge by the adults interrogating him that he was not obliged to speak and would not be penalized for remaining silent. This decision was followed by a series of subsequent court rulings that have gradually introduced procedures from the adult criminal system into juvenile justice to ensure due process and protection of individual rights of youths (Snyder & Sickmund, 2006).

Similarly, there have been failures in the juvenile justice system following disposition to protect the rights of incarcerated juveniles. Punitive reaction by correctional staff to aggressive and defiant behaviors and outright abuse of vulnerable youths in correctional facilities have resulted in Eighth Amendment violations (cruel and unusual punishment), triggering interventions by the Civil Rights Division of the U.S. Department of Justice. The Civil Rights of Institutionalized Persons Act (CRIPA) has been invoked in numerous states to help youths in detention facilities address system failures to protect and properly treat them (U.S. Department of Justice Civil Rights of Institutionalized Persons, n.d.). The court rulings and federal statutes have resulted in a criminalization of juvenile justice in an effort to protect individual rights. Further changes followed public reaction to the rise in youth violence and crime in the late 1980s and early 1990s as states moved toward more punitive action and away from rehabilitation in their handling of juvenile offenders. The view that "adult crime deserves adult time" and that the juvenile justice system was not adequate in handling violent young offenders resulted in states reforming their transfer procedures to facilitate juveniles being tried in adult criminal courts (Snyder & Sickmund, 2006). Unfortunately, subsequent research found that these efforts actually increased recidivism in youths tried in adult courts compared with keeping them in the juvenile justice system (Mason et al., 2003) and that minority youths were disproportionately transferred (Snyder et al., 2000).

Part of the reluctance to provide treatment to incarcerated and delinquent youths has stemmed, in part, from the erroneous assumption that these youths do not respond to treatment intervention. Only a minority of children with antisocial behavior will not respond to any treatment approaches, and research has shown that even those with the most severe behaviors have much to gain from intervention (Woolfenden, Williams, & Peat, 2002). A variety of treatments are effective, including individual therapies, functional family therapy, multisystemic therapy (MST), and treatment foster care (Thomas, 2007). MST was specifically developed for intervention with serious delinquents as a community-based alternative to residential treatment, and this approach has been adopted as one of the primary treatment paradigms yielding positive outcomes for delinquent youths (Henggler & Sheidow, 2003). Mental health treatment of detained or incarcerated youths is also complicated by the special legal and ethical demands of the juvenile justice system (Zerby & Thomas, 2006). Care providers must pay close attention to the circumstances of evaluation and treatment in order to protect both the legal and patient rights of incarcerated youths. Parallel to the development of new interventions, federal and state agencies have focused on outcomes and evidence-based approaches. Perhaps one of the more innovative policy initiatives is the Washington State Institute for Public Policy, which actively investigates outcomes of interventions with juvenile offenders, conducting cost-benefit analyses of programs (see http://www.wsipp.wa.gov/ and Lee & Kerns, Chapter 11, this volume).

Research on antisocial behavior in youths focused on how youths and adults differ, as well as on how delinquent youths differ from their typical peers, in terms of their psychopathology and treatment needs. Recent findings from the field of neuroscience have contributed enormously to our understanding of these issues, and courts and policymakers have considered this new information in decisions regarding juvenile justice matters. Public opinion and public policy, however, have continued to swing between the *parens patriae* model, in which the juveniles are regarded as needing assistance and treatment, and a criminal model focused on the need to protect the citizens of the state and punish offenders. Recent epidemiological research underscores that many young offenders also suffer with mental disorders apart from their antisocial behavior at rates greater than nonoffending peers and that these disorders are interrelated with their antisocial behavior, such as alcohol and substance use (Kessler & Kraus, 2007; Teplin, Abrams, & McClelland, 1996). These studies also found an increase in early violent death in this population (Teplin, McClelland, Abram, & Mileusnic, 2005). This research highlights the complex pathology in young offenders, as well as their need for treatment (Thomas & Penn, 2002).

The impact of neuroscience research on issues regarding youth competency to understand Miranda and stand trial, waiver to adult court, capital punishment for minors, and juvenile life without parole cannot be underestimated. Prior to the development of radioimaging, such as MRI and CT scans, brain researchers typically used brain slicing and other radiological techniques to study the brain. Early researchers first identified differences in the brains of teenagers and adults (Yakovlev & Lecours, 1967). It was found that the brain did not reach adult weight until the early 20s (Debakan & Sadowsky, 1978). Hettenlocher was the first to describe a process of neuronal elimination over the course of development, which he termed "pruning" (Hettenlocher, 1979; Sowell, Thompson, Holmes, Jernigan, & Toga, 1999). Kruezi and colleagues, in a pivotal National Institute of Mental Health (NIMH) study and 1992 follow-up, found a decrease in 5 HIAA metabolites in the cerebral spinal fluid of children with conduct disorder when compared with controls without conduct disorder. This may be the first biological study to show actual differences in serotonin metabolism, which would represent a decrease in serotonin in children with conduct disorder (Kruezi et al., 1990; Kruezi et al., 1992). In the late 1980s and early 1990s researchers began using MRIs to study the developing brain; however, it was not until the invention of the functional MRI that we truly began to understand the neuroconnections, pruning, and mylenation that occurs over the course of development until adulthood (Giedd et al., 1996; Giedd et al., 1999).

Giedd and colleagues have used functional MRIs to map changes in developing brains. For example, in early work they found a preadolescent increase in cortical gray matter, although questions remain as to the etiology of this increase. Specifically, it is unclear whether it is related to changes in neuropil, neuronal size, or dendritic or axonal arborization. Giedd and colleagues have since continued to perform functional MRI studies on teens (Giedd et al., 1996; Giedd et al., 1999; Gogtay et al., 2004). They have found that frontal lobe maturation progresses in a back-to-front direction, beginning in the primary motor cortex and spreading anteriorly over the superior and inferior frontal gyri, with the prefrontal cortex developing last (Spear, 2000). In other words, the neural connections between the frontal lobe, the executor of the brain, and the midbrain, a far more primitive area responsible for, among other things, the fight-or-flight response, are not as well connected during adolescence as they become later, in adulthood. As a result, children are less likely to show the type of control that their adult counterparts will show. They tend to be more emotional and reactive to situations. They are more impulsive than adults and lack insight into the short- and long-term consequences of their behaviors.

This better understanding of brain development has likely had the most significant impact on current public policy on delinquency (Giedd et al., 1999). Even prior to the brain imaging studies by Giedd and others, there still existed the obvious awareness that juveniles were different from their adult counterparts. Actuaries have known this for years, which is the reason a person must be 25 years old to rent a car. Higher levels of impulsivity in adolescence, together with difficulties thinking through ramifications of behaviors, particularly in stressful situations, make them poor risks. Although we have a much better understanding of the manner in which the brain develops, particularly in regard to pruning, myelination, and the development of white matter, at this point there is no research showing a causal connection between brain development and adolescent behaviors, particularly delinquency. At the same time, even though the current research has shown a temporal correlation rather than causality, it appears evident that one could understand the correlation and explain the correlative relationship without the definitive research yet completed. The difficulty with the current research in terms of policy is that it can be considered valid for groups but lacks sensitivity when applied to single individuals.

In addition to direct study of the development of antisocial and aggressive behavior and associated risks, scientific study provides a basis to understand the legal issues of culpability and competency and the development of those capacities. Prior to the introduction of due process and individual protections in juvenile justice, questions about a youth's competency were irrelevant. The establishment of those procedures necessarily raised issues about juvenile offenders' ability to understand their rights and act accordingly. The MacArthur Foundation initiated studies on this question, assessing juveniles' abilities to waive Miranda rights and regarding competency to stand trial. This research found that juveniles below 15 years of age had a relatively low likelihood of fully understanding Miranda rights or meeting adult competency definitions and were far less likely than their older counterparts to be able to stand trial. Issues of competency to stand trial are quite complex. As time progresses, it has become evident that there are tremendous variations within the same state, sometimes within the same court and county. It is clear, however, that the general level of competency expected for juveniles is less stringent and not as specifically designed as what is expected for adults. As such, one would expect that if a juvenile is transferred to adult court, his or her competency would be reassessed using the more strict standards expected of adults; if they were unable to meet those standards, this would be a reason for reverse waiver (Grisso, 1981, 2005a, 2005b; Scott & Grisso, 2004). Research by Grisso and others provides a scientific basis for forming opinions about a juvenile's ability to understand Miranda and in regard to a youth's competency to stand trial. These abilities are related to developmental factors, as opposed to specific mental health concerns or significant developmental delays such as mental retardation, as is the case with adult competency. The question as to how to handle juvenile competency is evolving, given that existing legal definitions of competency to stand trial are based on mental deficit rather than normal development and that restoration of competency cannot be achieved prior to capacity. Research has clearly contributed in defining the issue, providing the courts and the public a better understanding of the needs of youths in regards to understanding Miranda rights and competency to stand trial.

Issues related to developmental neuroscience have played a prominent role in the question of capital punishment for juvenile offenders. Prior to the U.S. Supreme Court decision abolishing the juvenile death penalty in *Roper v. Simmons* (2005), there were two important Supreme Court cases that addressed with the death penalty for juveniles. The first case, *Thompson v. Oklahoma* (1988), dealt with youths who were under the age of 16 at the time of their crimes. In writing the majority decision, Justice Stevens noted, " there is also broad agreement on the proposition that adolescents as a class are less mature and responsible than adults." The decision did not focus so much on neuroscience or research as on previous court decisions and on the observation that adolescents are different from adults. The issue of culpability under the age of 16 played a major role in the majority decision. The case was won by a relatively narrow margin of 5–4; nonetheless, from that point on, executing children under the age of 16 was deemed unconstitutional. From the age of 16 and up, children could still be executed in the United States.

The following year, a U.S. Supreme Court case, *Stanford v. Kentucky* (1989), determined that it was not cruel and unusual punishment to execute 16- or 17-year-olds. Writing for the majority, Justice Scalia rejected purely scientific evidence regarding reduced culpability, and Justice O'Connor concurred in the results. Justice Scalia stated "The day may come when there is such general legislative rejection of the execution of 16- or 17-year-old capital murderers that a clear national consensus can be said to have developed . . . . I do not believe that day has yet arrived" (Grisso, 1981). The question of culpability was again addressed by the U.S. Supreme Court in 2002, this time pertaining to capital punishment of mentally retarded individuals. In *Atkins v. Virginia* (2002), it was determined that there was diminished capacity within this special population. Specifically, deficits in reasoning, judgment, and impulse control make them less morally culpable than cognitively intact adult criminals.

In 2003, contrary to the *Stanford v. Kentucky* case, the Missouri Supreme Court stated that executing 16- and 17-year-olds should be considered cruel and unusual punishment as a matter of state, not federal, law (Fassler & Harper, 2007). The attorney general of the State of Missouri petitioned the U.S. Supreme Court for consideration of this federal issue. The court agreed to hear the case of *Roper v. Simmons*. An argument was held on October 13, 2004. This case again dealt with the issue of capital punishment of children 16 and 17 years old at the time of their crimes. In this case, in the 5–4 majority decision, the court opined that it was unconstitutional to execute children of this age secondary to the 14th Amendment violations. Although the opinion was primarily based on the changing view of the juvenile death penalty as a majority of states (33 at the time) no longer permitted the execution of individuals for crimes committed as juveniles, Justice Kennedy in his majority opinion also used current studies and research to justify the court's opinion.

Professional societies had filed *amicus curiae* briefs arguing the abolition of the juvenile death penalty in *Roper v. Simmons*. One *amicus curiae* brief was jointly filed by the American Medical Association (AMA), the American Psychiatric Association (APA), the American Society for Adolescent Psychiatry (ASAP), the American Academy of Child and Adolescent Psychiatry (AACAP), the American Academy of Psychiatry and the Law (AAPL), and the National Association of Social Workers (NASW). A separate *amicus curiae* brief was filed by the American Psychological Association. The former *amicus curiae* brief focused on the recent discoveries in neuroscience and their behavioral implications. It stated:

> The adolescent mind works differently from ours. Parents know it. The court has said it, the legislatures have presumed it for decades or more and now, new scientific evidence sheds light on the differences. . . . Behavioral sciences have observed these differences for some time. Only recently,

however, have studies yielded evidence of concrete differences that are anatomically based. Cutting-edge brain imaging technology reveals that regions of the adolescent brain do not reach a full mature state until after the age of 18. These regions are precisely those associated with impulse control, regulation of emotions, risk assessment and moral reasoning. Critical developmental changes in these regions occur only after late adolescence. Science cannot, of course, gauge moral culpability. Science can, however, shed light onto certain measurable attributes that the law has long treated as highly relevant culpability (American Medical Association, 2005; Fassler & Harper, 2007).

It cited research documenting the impulsive and risk-taking behaviors of normal adolescents (Gardner & Herman, 1990; Spear, 2000) and stating that this is in part due to an inability to conduct any cost-benefit analysis (Furby & Beyth-Marom, 1992), discounting any future consequences (Scott, Reppucci, & Woolard, 1995). In support of the behavioral studies, the *amicus curiae* brief went on to describe neuroanatomical research on the differences in the immature adolescent brain (Durston et al., 2001; Gogtay et al., 2004). Studies describing how adolescent brains are more active in regions related to aggressive behaviors and less active in those related to impulse control were also mentioned in support of this argument (Sowell et al., 2003). The *amicus* brief concludes that violent and aggressive youths are more likely to have mental disorders that compound the problems of the relative immaturity of their brains in comparison with those of adults (Mallet, 2003).

The *amicus curiae* brief filed by the American Psychological Association focused on the behavioral science research that has taken place since *Stanford*. Agreeing with the brief filed by the American Medical Association (2005), the American Psychological Association stated that 16- and 17-year-olds as a group are not yet mature in ways that affect their decision making. It went on to argue that delinquent, even criminal, behavior is characteristic of many adolescents, often peaking around age 18, and that this risk taking often represents a tentative expression of adolescent identity rather than an enduring mark of behavior arising from a fully formed personality. In summary, both *amicus curiae* briefs argued that developmentally immature decision making, paralleled by immature neurological development, diminishes an adolescent's ability to deal specifically with issues surrounding management of aggressive behavior. With regard to deterrence, adolescents often lack an adult ability to control impulses and to anticipate the consequences of their action. As previously mentioned, research studies do not support the efficacy of harsher criminal sanctions on juvenile recidivism (Fassler & Harper, 2007; Snyder, Sickmund, & Poe-Yamagata, 2000).

Similar reasoning and research was used in arguments with the subsequent *Graham v. Florida* decision that addressed the issue of juvenile life without parole for noncapital offenses before the U.S. Supreme Court. This case concerned Terrance Graham, who was 16 when he was incarcerated for armed burglary and one other crime. Under a plea agreement, the Florida court sentenced Graham to probation, and he was held to adjudication of guilt. Subsequently, the trial court found that Graham had violated the terms of his probation by committing additional crimes. He was then adjudicated guilty of the earlier charges, his probation was revoked, and he was sentenced to life in prison for the burglary. Because Florida had abolished its parole system, the life sentence left Graham no possibility of release except for executive clemency. As a result, Graham challenged his sentence under the Eighth Amendment's cruel and unusual punishment clause, but the Florida's First District Court of Appeal upheld his sentence (Spear, 2000).

The U.S. Supreme Court heard the case on May 17, 2010, considering Graham's early social and mental health history. Specifically, they noted that Terrance's parents were addicted to crack cocaine and that their drug use persisted into his early years. Terrance himself was diagnosed with attention-deficit/hyperactivity disorder in elementary school. He began drinking alcohol and using tobacco at the age of 9 and smoked marijuana at the age of 13. His initial crime involved Graham and another youth entering a barbeque restaurant to rob it after hours and hitting the manager twice in the head with a steel bar. The prosecutor elected to charge Graham as an adult, with armed burglary and assault or battery, which carries a maximum penalty of life in prison without possibility of parole. On December 18, 2003, Graham pled guilty to both charges of attempted armed robbery and armed robbery. The first 12 months of his probation were to be served in the county jail, but he had received time served while waiting for trial and was released on June 25, 2004. Graham was again arrested 6 months later after participating in a home invasion robbery. At that time he was 34 days short of his 18th birthday. His minimum sentence would have been 5 years and maximum sentence would be life without parole, but for violation of his probation, he received life without parole.

Justice Kennedy wrote for the majority in this case, stating that Graham did not commit murder and therefore cannot be given life without parole, which would constitute an Eighth Amendment violation. Within the majority opinion there was tremendous amount of information regarding current court history and sentencing practices. Justice Kennedy quoted the Roper case, stating "Roper established that because juveniles have less culpability they are less deserving of the most severe punishment . . . . As compared to adults, juveniles have a lack of maturity and an undeveloped sense of responsibility: They are more vulnerable or susceptible to negative influences and outside pressures, including peer pressure . . . ". He also stated "No recent data provided reason to reconsider the court's observation in Roper about the nature of juveniles." The *amicus curiae* brief from professional societies was quoted, stating "juveniles were more capable of change than are adults and their actions are less likely to be evidence of irretrievably depraved character than are the actions of adults." As with the *amicus curiae* brief for *Roper v. Simmons,* research was presented describing the relative immaturity of the adolescent and the correlated deficiencies in decision making and controlling aggressive and impulsive behavior. It argued that the differences in adolescent behavior do not reflect an inability to distinguish right from wrong but rather cognitive ability to control their behavior (Cauffman & Steinberg, 2000). It also included research findings on neuroanatomical differences correlated to these cognitive differences (Sowell et al., 2003).

The *Graham v. Florida* case addressed cases of noncapital crime, which account for 120 youths or adults currently incarcerated nationally on sentences of life without parole for noncapital crimes committed when they were juveniles. In their decision, the Supreme Court did not consider the issue of whether their sentences should be revised following the Supreme Court decision rendering their sentences unconstitutional. If their sentences are to be revised, the question remains of when and how to evaluate these individuals. These are all issues that will need consideration following the *Graham v. Florida* decision (*Graham v. Florida*, 2010). At the same time, there are still upward of 2500 incarcerated individuals who committed murder as juveniles and have been given sentences of life without parole and without the chance to ever be released.

Apart from the broader scientific description of normal adolescent development and factors contributing to aggressive and antisocial behavior, scientific evidence regarding individual defendants continues to play a role in juvenile justice and criminal courts. The new techniques of genetic studies and neuroimaging have already been used to evaluate defendants and introduced as evidence for the court to consider. Both legal and ethical questions arise as to the proper use of new technologies in characterizing individuals both in screening for amenability for rehabilitation and in assessing culpability overall (Carey & Gottesman, 2006; Hoop & Spellecy, 2009). Studies report general findings with prediction of risk that can be difficult to apply to any one individual. In addition, research has shown that it is not one single factor that predicts antisocial or aggressive behavior but the interplay of multiple factors across the lifespan that must be taken into account. The introduction of evidence regarding monoamine oxidase A gene polymorphism in the trial of Stephen Mobley, accused of murder in 1993 (*Mobley v. State*, 1993), is an example of just such an error (Denno, 1996). Although those relationships and interactions are better understood with advances in scientific study, much remains to be done.

SUMMARY

Research continues to shape public policy and judicial rulings. It shows that many delinquents can be treated and can grow to be productive citizens. It also shows us that youths respond to interrogations, and to leading questions in particular, differently than do adults. They are less likely than adults to have the abstract reasoning or cognitive ability to understand their Miranda rights, and younger adolescents are more likely to be considered incompetent to stand trial by adult standards. Research with delinquents finds that they are far more likely to have underlying mental health diagnoses and learning disabilities as compared with nondelinquent peers. Both their short- and long-term needs regarding mental health interventions, education, and ongoing development must be

taken into account if juvenile justice is to fulfill its intended purpose of rehabilitation. Although new scientific findings offer much hope, there still remain
many challenges as to how best to use our new understanding in policy development and our justice system. It is important to remember the mistakes of the
past in applying science in social policy and the courts by too quickly assuming
that our knowledge is complete. There is still more research needed, particularly
in the area of identifying causal connections between brain development and
behavior. As this occurs, public policy regarding delinquency and appropriate
interventions will continue to be more effective and just.

REFERENCES

American Medical Association. (2005). *On Writ of Certiorari to the Supreme Court
of Missouri* [Amicus Brief]. Retrieved from www.ABAnet.org/crimjust/juvjus\sim-
mons\ama.pdf .

Atkins v. Virginia, 122 S.CP. 2242 (2002).

Batz, S. (2008). *For the thrill of it: Leopold and Loeb and the murder that shocked
Chicago.* New York, NY: Harper Collins.

Carey, G., & Gottesman, I. I. (2006). Genes and antisocial behavior: Perceived versus
real threats to jurisprudence. *Journal of Law, Medicine and Ethics, 34*(2), 342–351.

Cauffman, E., & Steinberg, L. (2000). (Im)maturity of judgment in adolescence: Why
adolescents may be less culpable than adults. *Behavioral Sciences and the Law, 18,*
741–760.

Debakan, A. S., & Sadowsky, Y. (1978). Changes in brain weight during the span of
human life. *Annals of Neurology, 4,* 345–356.

Denno, D. W. (1996). Legal implications of genetics and crime research. In G. R. Bock
& J. A. Goode (Eds.), *Ciba Foundation Symposium: 194. Genetics of criminal and
antisocial behaviour* (pp. 248–264). Chichester, UK: Wiley.

Durston, S., Hulshoff Pol, H. E., Casey, B. J., Giedd, J. N., Buitelaar, J. K., & van
Engeland, H. (2001). Anatomical MRI of the developing human brain: What have
we learned? *Journal of the American Academy of Child and Adolescent Psychiatry,
40,* 1012–1020.

Fassler, D., & Harper, S. K. (2007). Science in juvenile death penalty. In C. L. Kessler
& L. J. Kraus (Eds.), *The mental health needs of young offenders: Forging paths
towards reintegration and rehabilitation* (pp. 241–254). Cambridge, UK: Cambridge
University Press.

Furby, L., & Beyth-Marom, R. (1992). Risk taking in adolescence: A decision-making
perspective. *Developmental Review, 12*(1), 9–11.

Gardner, W., & Herman, J. (1990). Adolescents' AIDS risk taking: A rational choice
perspective. *New Directions for Child and Adolescent Development, 50,* 17–34.

Giedd, J. N., Blumenthal, J., Jeffries, N. O., Castellanos, F. X., Liu, H., Zijdenbos, A., . . .
Rapoport, J. L. (1999). Brain development during childhood and adolescence: A longitudinal MRI study. *Nature Neuroscience, 2,* 861–863.

Giedd, J. N., Snell, J. W., Lange, N., Rajapakse, J. C., Casey, B. J., Kozuch, P. L., . . .
Rapoport, J. L. (1996). Quantitative magnetic resonance imaging of human brain
development: Ages 4–18. *Cerebral Cortex, 6*(4), 551–559.

Gogtay, N., Giedd, J. N., Lusk, L., Hayashi, K. M., Greenstein. D., Vaituzis, A. C., . . . Thompson, P. M. (2004). Dynamic mapping of human cortical development during childhood through early adulthood. *Proceedings of the National Academy of Sciences, 101*(21), 8174–8179.

Graham v. Florida, 560 U.S. (2010).

Grisso, T. (1981). *Juveniles' waiver of rights.* New York, NY: Plenum Press.

Grisso, T. (2005a). *Clinical evaluations of juveniles' competence to stand trial: A guide for legal professionals.* Sarasota, FL: Professional Resource Press.

Grisso, T. (2005b). *Evaluating juveniles' adjudicative competence: A guide for clinical practice.* Sarasota, FL: Professional Resource Press.

Healy, W. (1915). *The individual delinquent.* Boston, MA: Little, Brown.

Henggler, W., & Sheidow, A. J. (2003). Conduct disorder and delinquency. *Journal of Marital and Family Therapy, 29*(4), 505–522.

Hettenlocher, P. R. (1979). Synaptic density in human frontal cortex: Developmental changes and effects of age. *Brain Research, 163,* 195–205.

Hoop, J. G., & Spellecy, R. (2009). Philosophical and ethical issues at the forefront of neuroscience and genetics: An overview for psychiatrists. *Psychiatric Clinics of North America, 32*(2), 437–449.

In re: Gault, 387 U.S. 87 S.Ct. 1428 (1967).

Kessler, C. L., & Kraus. L. J. (2007). Mental health needs of young offenders. In L. A. Teplin, A. Abrams, K. M. McClelland, A. A. Mericle, N. A. Dulcan, J. J. Washburn, & S. Butt (Eds.), *Psychiatric disorders of youth in detention* (pp. 7–47). Cambridge, UK: Cambridge University Press.

Kruezi, M. J., Hibbs, E. D., Zahn, T. P., Keysor, C. S., Hamburger, S. D., Bartko, J. J., & Rapoport, J. (1992). A 2-year prospective follow-up study of children and adolescents with disruptive behavior disorders: Prediction by cerebrospinal fluid 5-hydroxyindoleacetic acid, homovanillic acid, and autonomic measures? *Archives of General Psychiatry, 49*(6), 429–435.

Kruezi, M. J., Rapoport, J. L., Hamburger, S., Hibbs, E., Potter, W. Z., Lenane, M., & Brown, G. L. (1990). Cerebrospinal fluid monoamine metabolites, aggression and impulsivity in disruptive behavior disorders in children and adolescents. *Archives of General Psychiatry, 47*(5), 419–426.

Mallet, C. (2003). Socio-historical analysis of juvenile offenders on death row. *Criminal Law Bulletin, 39*(4), 445–468.

Mason, C. A., Chapman, D. A., Chang, S., & Simons, J. (2003). Impacting re-arrest rates among youth sentenced in adult court: An epidemiological examination of the Juvenile Sentencing Advocacy Project. *Journal of Clinical Child and Adolescent Psychology, 32*(2), 205–214.

Mobley v. State, 426 SE and 150, Ga. (1993).

Roper v. Simmons, 125 S.Ct.1183 (2005).

Scott, E. S., Reppucci, D., & Woolard, J. L. (1995). Evaluating adolescent decision making in legal contexts. *Law and Human Behavior, 19,* 221–244.

Scott, E., & Grisso, T. (2004). *Developmental incompetence, due process, and juvenile policy* (Working Paper No. 11). Charlottesville: University of Virginia Law School.

Snyder, H. N., & Sickmund, M. (2006). Juvenile justice system and process. In *Juvenile offenders and victims: 2006 National Report* (pp. 93–119). Washington, DC: U.S. Department of Justice, Office of Justice Programs, Office of Juvenile Justice and Delinquency Prevention.

Snyder, H., Sickmund, M., & Poe-Yamagata, E. (2000). *Juvenile transfers to criminal court in the 1990's: Lessons learned from four studies.* Washington, DC: Office of Juvenile Justice and Delinquency Prevention.

Sowell, E. R., Thompson, P. M., Holmes, C. J., Jernigan, T. L., & Toga, A. W. (1999). In vivo evidence for post-adolescent brain maturation and frontal and striatal regions. *Nature Neuroscience, 2*(10), 859–861.

Sowell, E. R., Peterson, B. S., Thompson, P. M., Welcome, S. E., Henkenius, A. L., & Toga, A. W. (2003). Mapping cortical change across the human life span. *Nature Neuroscience, 6*(3), 309–315.

Spear, L. P. (2000). The adolescent brain and age-related behavioral manifestations. *Neuroscience and Biobehavioral Reviews, 24*(4), 417–463.

Stanford v. Kentucky, 492 U.S. 361 (1989).

Teplin, L. A., Abrams, K. M., & McClelland, G. M. (1996). Prevalence of psychiatric disorders among incarcerated women: Pretrial jail detainees. *Archives of General Psychiatry, 36*(3), 357–365.

Teplin, L. A., McClelland, G. M., Abram, K. M., & Mileusnic, D. (2005). Early violent death among delinquent youth: A prospective longitudinal study. *Pediatrics, 115,* 1586–1583.

Thomas, C. (2007). Community alternatives to incarceration. In C. L. Kessler & L. J. Kraus (Eds.), *The mental health needs of young offenders: Forging paths toward reintegration and rehabilitation* (pp. 368–384). Cambridge, UK: Cambridge University Press.

Thomas, C., & Penn, J. (2002). Juvenile justice mental health services. *Child and Adolescent Psychiatric Clinics of North America, 11*(4), 731–748.

Thompson v. Oklahoma, 487 E.S. 815 (1988).

United States Department of Justice Civil Rights of Institutionalized Persons. (n.d.) Available at http://www.justice.gov/crt/about/spl/cripastat.php.

Woolfenden, S. R., Williams, K., & Peat, J. K. (2002). Family and parenting interventions for conduct disorder and delinquency: A meta-analysis of randomized controlled trials. *Archives of Disease in Childhood, 86*(4), 251–256.

Yakovlev, P. I., & Lecours, A. R. (1967). The myelogenetic cycles of regional maturation of the brain. In A. Minowski (Ed.), *Regional development of the brain in early life* (pp. 3–65). Oxford, UK: Blackwell.

Zerby, S., & Thomas, C. (2006). Legal issues, rights, and ethics for mental health in juvenile justice. *Child and Adolescent Psychiatric Clinics of North America, 15*(2), 373–390.